The Horn

THE HORN

*A Comprehensive Guide to the
Modern Instrument & its Music*

by

ROBIN GREGORY

FREDERICK A. PRAEGER, Publishers
New York · Washington

BOOKS THAT MATTER

Published in the United States of America in 1969
by Frederick A Praeger, Inc., Publishers
111 Fourth Avenue, New York, N.Y, 10003

© 1961, 1969 in London, England by Robin Gregory

Library of Congress Catalog Card Number: 69-20022

First published in the United States of America
in 1961 by Oxford University Press.
This edition has been revised and enlarged

Printed in Great Britain

To
MARGARET
who endured so much
while this book
was being written

Mein Rufen wandelt
In herbstgetönten Hain den Saal,
Das Eben in Verschollnes,
Dich in Gewand und Brauch der Ahnen,
In ihr Verlangen und Empfahn dein Glück.
Gönn teuren Schemen Urständ,
Dir Halbvergessener Gemeinschaft,
Und mir mein tongestaltnes Sehnen.

PAUL HINDEMITH—*Concerto for Horn and Orchestra*

(*Reprinted by permission of Schott & Co. Ltd., London*)

Contents

9

CONTENTS

Part IV

THE INSTRUMENT IN CONSORT

Illustrations

11

ILLUSTRATIONS

DIAGRAMS

ILLUSTRATIONS

Note

The following system of notation is used in the text, where necessary, to identify particular notes:

Unless otherwise stated, references in the text or in musical examples are to notes as written for the horn in the key concerned and not to the actual sounds.

Preface

The purpose of this book is easily explained. There appears to be in existence no single volume giving all the information about that fascinating instrument, the horn, which a prospective player might reasonably be expected to require, and the following pages are an attempt to remedy that deficiency. There are several excellent tutors which provide fingering charts and technical exercises in plenty; works on musical acoustics which explain, though often in somewhat forbidding technical language, the physical basis of its method of sound production; books on orchestration which treat exhaustively, but not always accurately, of its technical possibilities and limitations; occasional articles and manufacturers' catalogues which deal with the mechanical side of the instrument; and there is some literature, though it is not at present very extensive, on the physiology of the player.

All this information, however, is so widely scattered as to require much time and patience in tracking it down, and in this book the attempt has been made to assemble it in a form in which it can be digested without undue difficulty by the reader of modest mathematical and scientific attainments. No apology is made for introducing a certain amount of technical matter, but mathematical and acoustical technicalities have been kept to the minimum necessary for a satisfactory understanding of the horn as a sound-producing mechanism.

There is, however, a wide divergence in some respects between theory and practice in horn playing. I have not hesitated, where such a conflict arises, to place more reliance in the word of the player who tells me what actually happens, than in that of the theorist who tells me what ought to happen. I feel, moreover, that there is something particularly attractive about an instrument which so stubbornly resists being browbeaten into conformity. Though the horn has moved with the times, it has managed to retain an air of mystery which all the resources of modern science have not succeeded in sweeping away. In an age when so much is laid bare, many facets of the behaviour of the horn remain inexplicable. As a consequence, the instrument gives endless scope for experimentation; the choice of mouthpiece or of mute, the exact position of the right hand, the fingering of a particular note — all these are still governed very largely by purely empirical considerations. What suits one player or a particular instrument fails ignominiously with another. It is no great exaggeration to say, 'If it works, it's correct,' however contrary to theory the procedure may be.

Controversy is bound to surround so protean an instrument as the horn. This is all to the good, provided it is realised that there is a great deal about which it is impossible to be dogmatic. Every player has his own ideas about the instrument, and so long as he is careful not to thrust them down the throats of his colleagues as incontrovertible truths, no harm is done. Quite the reverse, in fact, for the more thought that is given to the many problems involved in the construction and playing of the horn the better.

The horn has undergone three major changes during the last two hundred years, each of which has provoked the cry of *sic transit gloria*; yet it still exerts a fascination on those who have studied and played it. The *mystique* of the horn is as strong as ever, and as long as this is so the instrument will continue to flourish.

I have received advice and information from many friends while this book has been in preparation, but particularly from Mark Foster, with whom I have had many stimulating discussions, and from Raymond Bryant, who has given me the benefit of his wide knowledge and experience. Neither they, however, nor any others from whom I have sought help must be held responsible for any of the opinions expressed.

In this second edition part of Chapter 6 has been rewritten in the hope of throwing a little more light on the problem of the embouchure. Two new chapters dealing with the use of the horn in the orchestra and in chamber music have been added, and a number of minor alterations and additions have been made in order to bring the book up to date.

The list of works in Appendix C has been considerably extended and revised. The primary aim has been to make it as useful as possible to the practising horn player, by giving, where practicable, some indication of the availability of the works listed. This may usually be inferred from the data provided about each item, though in some cases complete information has not been accessible. A secondary purpose has been to provide a conspectus of horn music in all the many varied combinations for which works have been written; unpublished works and those long out of print have therefore also been included. Where the locations of manuscripts or early editions are known, enterprising horn players might find it interesting to investigate the possibilities of some of these works.

Hurstpierpoint   ROBIN GREGORY
1968

Part I

THE INSTRUMENT

CHAPTER 1

Introductory

The modern horn may be described as a narrow-tubed brass instrument of approximately conical bore ending in a widely flaring bell. It is fitted with a valve mechanism facilitating the instantaneous alteration of the length of the tubing within comparatively narrow limits. This instrument is sounded by the vibration of the lips in contact with a more or less funnel-shaped mouthpiece fitted into the narrower end of the tubing. The tubing, which is about twelve feet long in the F horn, and about nine feet in the horn in B♭, is coiled so that the instrument can be conveniently held across the body with the right hand in the bell, the valve mechanism being operated by the left hand. The first three fingers are used to depress the three main valves; in some instruments the thumb or the little finger, or occasionally both, are used to operate additional valves. Even if the little finger is required to work a valve, a ring or hook is usually provided for it to ensure more stable support of the instrument. The method of holding the instrument across the body with the bell to the right is now universally adopted, though before the introduction of valves both right- and left-handed horns were in use, and later some manufacturers even produced horns on which a detachable valve cluster could be reversed as required. The exact conformation of the tubing and its coils, and the position of the valve system within this conformation, vary with the maker, and indeed in some cases with the particular model of the maker, and diagrams showing some of the variations in current models are shown in Figs. 4, 14 and 15. The precise shape into which the tubing is bent appears to exercise little or no effect on the tone of the instrument, the main object being to ensure that the horn is well-balanced and comfortable to hold in the playing position, with the valves lying so that they are easily controlled by the fingers.

The name of the instrument obviously derives from the practice followed by primitive man of using the horns of animals as simple

21

instruments which could be made to produce a noise by blowing through them. Of the wide variety of modern instruments which may claim descent from these early horns the term 'horn' *tout court* is reserved for the orchestral instrument; the name 'French horn', whose significance will be explained later, still lingers on in this country, though the instrument itself is practically obsolete, and the horn in common use today, at least in professional circles, would more justifiably be called the 'German' horn. The flügelhorns, alto and tenor horns and saxhorns at present in use in the brass band, though related to the orchestral horn, should be classified in a separate sub-group by reason of their wider bores and differently shaped mouthpieces. The Wagner tubas are, in fact, the nearest in kin to the modern horn, which nevertheless stands alone as the sole surviving representative of its type. Nor does the horn exist, as do most other instrumental families, in a considerable number of different sizes, corresponding to different pitches, ranges and often tone qualities. It is, in fact, an instrument *sui generis*, and at the present time is rarely made in more than two or three sizes: in F and in B♭, and sometimes in high F. Even then it is the aim of the maker to match the tone of these different sizes, particularly when, as is often the case, the F and B♭ horns are combined together in a single duplex instrument whose many advantages more than balance the disadvantages of increased complexity and weight.[1]

For acoustical reasons it is not possible to construct a horn of either true treble or true bass range which possesses the real horn tone quality. Hence the horn may be said, for practical purposes, to cover the tenor and baritone range approximating to that of the 'cello, though it is not capable of reaching the heights attainable by the virtuoso 'cellist. The working compass of the horn is from

chromatically to

sounding on the F horn and

on the horn in B♭. A small downward extension of a few semitones is possible on the B♭ horn owing to the ability of the shorter tube to sound its fundamental. These so-called pedal notes, corresponding to those of the trombone, can on occasion prove valuable. At the beginning of Beethoven's fourth symphony, for example, the second horn has a long-held low *B'♭* (actual sound), a note which

[1] The weight of a horn varies from about four pounds for a single B♭ instrument to six pounds or more for the double horn, depending upon the accessory valves fitted.

theoretically does not exist at all on the F horn, but which can be produced on it with some difficulty by forcing down the low $F'\sharp$ (sounding $B'\natural$) obtained with all three valves depressed. On the B♭ horn, on the other hand, this note is the fundamental and speaks quite readily.

Wide as the range appears on paper, in practice it is not attainable by any but the most outstanding players, owing to the difficulty of forming an embouchure capable of tackling both extremes with equal certainty and comfort. Consequently orchestral players, by developing different embouchures and also by using mouthpieces of slightly different shapes and diameters, have come to specialize either in the upper or lower parts of the range. Composers have acquiesced in this procedure and always divide their four horns into two pairs. The first and third players are given parts lying mainly in the upper part of the compass, and the second and fourth the lower parts. Between them the four players divide the complete range into two overlapping portions as follows:

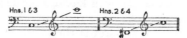

though these limits are not, of course, rigidly applied, especially if, as often happens, all four are required to play in unison. In most of the leading orchestras a fifth player assists the first, either by relieving him in tutti passages, thus enabling him to reserve himself and his lip for important solo parts, or, as often on the continent, there are two equal first horns who share the work, only one of them being on the platform at a time.

Like most instruments, the horn is happiest in the region lying comfortably between the two extremes of its compass — say

from

Below this lower limit the tone can easily become somewhat harsh and coarse, though a really good player is capable of a beautiful velvety quality — a quality of considerable value in the orchestra when the horn can be used as a bass in quiet passages, for sustaining a rich harmonic background, or for delineating a slow-moving melodic part. Such low-lying melodic parts are by no means out of the character of the instrument, though they are usually steadier if played by two or more horns in unison, especially as this can be done with negligible increase in the volume of tone. Owing to the comparative slowness of emission of sound in this register more rapidly-moving parts are not so easy to play, nor are they so effective in performance.

Above the upper limit of the medium register the tone becomes somewhat brighter. In addition, a *pianissimo* at this altitude is very difficult to achieve, though composers often ask for it. Nevertheless, the horn has its uses in this region, for it stands out well, particularly if doubled, above quite heavy orchestration, not with the challenging quality of the trumpet, but with a broader, mellower and less sharp-edged prominence, a crimson rather than a scarlet line.

It is in its medium register, however, that the horn is at its most characteristic. When given time to deploy its sound it can produce a broad, sonorous quality of tone unmatched in the whole orchestra, and many fine solos have been written for it in this range.

As with all instrumental timbres, it is impossible to describe the the tone of the horn adequately in words. 'Rich, poetic, colourful but mellow, profoundly expressive, romantic, exquisitely limpid': these are some of the terms in which the attempt has been made. None of them is incorrect, yet none of them gives the complete picture, perhaps because the horn has so many sides to its character. In the days when crooks were in common use this many-sided character was even more apparent; the low-pitched crooks in B♭, C and D gave an instrument sensibly darker in tone than the modern medium-pitched horn in F, while the higher crooks were more brilliant and approached without ever attaining the incisiveness of the trumpet. At the present time any variation in tone colour as between different instruments is due mainly to the size of the bore. This vexed question, which will be dealt with later on, has now been practically settled in favour of the wide-bore German type, with its rich broad tone, while the narrow-bore French horn, with its brighter, thinner, more open tone, is fast becoming a thing of the past.[1]

Nevertheless, whatever instrument is used, wide- or narrow-bore, F or B♭, there is still a considerable variation in timbre between the various parts of the compass, and even in a particular part of the range various means are available to the player of colouring his tone.

It would be carrying partisanship too far to claim that the horn produces the most beautiful sound of any instrument in the orchestra, though there are times when one is tempted to think so. It can hardly be disputed, however, that it is one of the most versatile of orchestral voices. It blends, with becoming reticence,

[1] It is of interest that Dr. Johnson, on hearing some solemn music played on French horns, remarked 'This is the first time that I have ever been affected by musical sounds.' The impression made upon him, Boswell relates, was of a melancholy kind.

INTRODUCTORY

with all other orchestral groups; indeed it is surprising that so individual a voice can submerge itself so successfully, when required, in a predominantly string or woodwind or brass texture. It acts, too, as a sort of orchestral cement, binding two or more of these groups together surely but unobtrusively. It has no rival as an instrument for giving body to a melodic line in the tenor register, and as a solo instrument it is, within its range, profoundly expressive if allowed to speak with its natural singing voice.

The horn is not, of course, without its limitations, though some modern composers would have us believe so. It is these limitations, however, which help to give the instrument its character. They are largely determined by the acoustical properties of a tube with an expanding bore blown with a conical mouthpiece, the efficiency of the mechanism forming the valve system, and the physiological characteristics of the player who blows the instrument, and it is these topics which will therefore be dealt with in the first two parts of this book. First, however, it may be helpful to trace, very briefly, the steps by which the horn has reached its present state.

CHAPTER 2

Historical: An Outline of the Evolution of the Modern Horn

In many respects the development of a musical instrument closely resembles the evolution of an organic species. Starting from very primitive beginnings, each gradually increases in complexity as variations arise. Some of these variations help it to survive by adapting it more closely to its environment; others, either putting it at a disadvantage with its competitors or serving no useful purpose, lead to varieties which sooner or later become extinct. With the passage of time there eventually develops a species having a fairly stable relationship with its environment. But the environment is also continually changing, sometimes almost imperceptibly, sometimes comparatively rapidly, and if the species is to survive it must maintain its adaptation to its surroundings. It does this by introducing innovations, some of which lead only into blind alleys, while others are of permanent value and are still to be found in the present-day type.

The evolution of the horn has taken just such a course. Much of its early history is only to be deduced from the study of the comparatively rare specimens of the ancestral types which have survived, like fossils, and are now to be found only in museums and collections. The only other source of information is in references, often far from precise, in various written records, though examination of the type of music written for the instrument gives valuable clues. The closer one approaches to the present time, the more complete the picture; the later history of the horn is fairly well documented and more numerous examples of the actual instru-

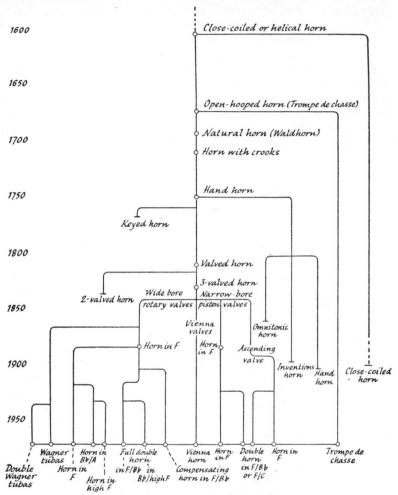

Fig. 1. The pedigree of the horn.

ments remain in being. Fig. 1 gives a partly conjectural view of the pedigree of the modern horn, with approximate dates.

As a musical instrument — that is, as something more than a mere adjunct to the chase — the horn has a comparatively short history. Its entry into the orchestra dates back only to the early eighteenth century, and its story since that time falls into four fairly distinct but overlapping phases:

(*a*) The era of the natural horn.

(*b*) The invention of crooks and the emergence of the hand horn.

27

(c) The addition of valves, and the gradual divergence into German wide-bore and French narrow-bore types.

(d) The development of the double horn, and the increasing use of the short B♭ single horn.

The early close-coiled *Jägertrommet* and helical horns bore little external resemblance to the orchestral horn into which they eventually developed, for their many coils ended in a four- to five-inch bell and they were pitched no lower than eight-foot C and therefore capable of sounding only a few harmonics. As such they would have been of little use in the orchestra except for the purpose of providing local colour in operatic hunting scenes. Gradually, however, the tube length was increased and its taper became more pronounced, until by the second half of the seventeenth century a twelve-foot instrument of narrower bore was in existence. The increased length was accommodated, not by adding to the number of coils of the helical horn, but by widening their diameter to something of the order of twenty inches, so that an open-hooped instrument, the *trompe de chasse*, resulted. This horn, as its name implies, originated in France, and was soon introduced into Germany and Bohemia, where it became known as the *Jagdhorn*. The bell diameter was now about seven inches and showed a continual tendency to increase. Owing to the ability of the longer tube to produce a larger number of harmonics it was now ready to take its place in the orchestra, which it first did at Hamburg just after the turn of the century. According to Mattheson (1713) its tone quality was 'less raucous than the trumpet's. . . . It produces a rounder tone. . . .' It was played with a funnel-shaped mouthpiece, and became known as the *Waldhorn*. Its tone, though more refined than that of the *trompe de chasse* with its cup-shaped mouthpiece, would still appear coarse to modern ears, for as yet the instrument was played in the old style with the bell up.

At first the *Waldhorn* was allowed in the orchestra only on sufferance, for though it had available a wider selection of notes than its immediate ancestor, these were all derived from a fundamental of fixed pitch, limiting the use of any one instrument to a particular key. It was not long, however, before the principle of the crook was evolved, or rather, adapted for use with the horn. This involved the replacement of a fixed mouthpipe by one or more of a series of coils of tubing of various lengths designed to put the horn into any one of a variety of keys — B♭ alto, A, A♭, G, F, E, E♭, D, C and B♭ basso. These coils, known as Vienna crooks, were usually six in number, and could be used, either singly or in combinations of two or even three, to give the required acoustical length of tubing. The disadvantage of this system, first devised in about

1718, was that the mouthpiece was at varying distances from the main body of the instrument, according to the number and size of the crooks in use — a matter of some consequence even while the horn was still played with the bell at shoulder level, but producing an extremely unstable arrangement when later it became the custom to hold the instrument with the right hand in the bell.

About 1760, during the course of experiments on muting which he was carrying out in order to try to modify the still raucous tone of the horn, the Dresden player Hampel discovered that the presence of the hand in the bell went a long way towards achieving his aim. Moreover he found that by changing the position of the hand in the bell it was possible to fill in many of the gaps between the notes of the harmonic series, although these 'stopped' notes were of somewhat inferior tone quality. To Hampel, therefore, is given the credit for founding the great Bohemian school of hand horn virtuosi, whose influence later spread to France, where the hand horn had its heyday in the first half of the nineteenth century.

Once the hand was used in this way, it became essential that the position of the horn relative to the body of the player should be standardized, so that the hand could fulfil its function efficiently. Again at the instance of Hampel, there came into being the *Inventionshorn*, in which the crooks were inserted into sockets in the middle of the hoop while the mouthpipe reverted to the fixed type. This arrangement incidentally led also to the incorporation of a tuning slide as now universally fitted. The *Inventionshorn*, improved by the famous maker Raoux, was used particularly by the great French hand horn soloists such as Dauprat and Gallay.

The horn was now probably at its peak, both in beauty of tone quality and elegance of appearance, and it is not surprising that though it was soon to be rendered obsolete by the invention of the valve in 1815, the hand horn lingered on almost to the end of the century.

The origin of the valve has never been completely cleared up. The first examples were imperfect, both mechanically and acoustically, and the valved horn did not really begin to make much headway, in face of not unreasonable opposition, until towards the middle of the century. The first valves were of the piston type, moving up and down in a vertical plane, but the invention of the rotary valve in which a cylinder moves with a circular motion soon followed, and the mechanism became so popular in Germany that it rapidly became the standard fitting on horns made in that country. France and England, on the other hand, remained faithful to the piston valve.

At about the same time as the introduction of the valve an attempt was made, in the shape of the so-called omnitonic horn, to construct an instrument which would overcome the disadvantages of separate crooks by having them built in, selection of the appropriate crook being by means of a slide or key. This, however, was practically obsolete as soon as it came into being, for the valve system accomplished the same process without the necessity for removing the hand from the bell to adjust the slide or turn the key. Indeed, the valve was originally used as no more than a quick means of changing crook.

As early as 1820 there began to arise the distinction between the wide-bore German type of horn and the narrow-bore French type, a distinction which has persisted to the present day. The Austrians evolved a bore of their own which to some extent partook both of the French and the German types, and used the Vienna valve, a double piston type which originated at about the same time as the rotary valve.

Once the valve system had been taken into common use the need for a wide variety of crooks diminished, and though hand horn enthusiasts deplored the move, players began to discard the longer crooks and eventually settled on those in F, E♭, and E, using the shorter ones for special purposes. Before the end of the century the F horn was the standard instrument for orchestral use.

Horn parts were now becoming much more complex, particularly in the range they covered. The large-bore instrument gave the greater power required in the larger orchestras now employed by composers, but the high tessitura commonly required of first and third players imposed a considerable strain upon them, and they began to search for some means of mitigating it. The obvious solution was to use the shorter B♭ horn, on which the higher parts could be played with less deleterious effects upon the lip, and with much greater surety owing to the wider spacing of the harmonics. Many players, however, were reluctant to dispense entirely with the F horn, and about the turn of the century the firm of Kruspe in Erfurt produced the first double horn in F and B♭. This model was of the compensating type as described in Chapter 4. It was followed in 1909 by a double horn made by Gebr. Alexander of Mainz in which the valve tubes of the two sections were completely independent of each other. These instruments, with minor modifications and additions, and others of the same pattern by other German, British and American makers, are those most commonly used in the great orchestras of Britain and America. Many 'first-chair' men, however, use the single B♭ horn, which is practically always fitted with an extra valve, used variously as an A valve, for stopping, or, with a long extension, for low notes not otherwise available on the B♭ instrument.

In France the ascending third valve was adopted before the end of the last century and became more or less standard, even on the double horns with piston valves which were the chosen instruments of her orchestral players. The ascending valve is still used, but some French players have now changed over to the standard German horn.

This, in brief, is the situation at the present time. It is extremely difficult to forecast what further developments are likely to take place. There is a physical limit to what can be achieved by the human lip, and this limit must by now have been reached. The range has been extended to the utmost possible if horn tone quality is to be retained. Technique has improved, so that a good player is capable of tackling almost anything which is put before him that lies within that range. 'Horn playing of the future', wrote Dennis Brain,[1] 'will, I suppose, follow the trend and get bigger and better, louder and higher.' If this proves to be the case, then the heyday of the horn is past, for at its best and most characteristic it is not a 'big' instrument, nor a 'loud' nor a 'high' one. This pessimistic prophecy, however, is not at present being fulfilled. The modern trend is certainly towards the use of the higher-pitched instruments, not so much in order to extend the range of the horn as to gain greater certainty in the upper reaches of the compass. The present time is, in fact, a period of considerable interest in the history of the instrument. The technique of the double horn has now become more or less standardized, and enquiring minds are at work seeking other and perhaps better solutions to the problems posed by modern horn parts. For example, the potentialities of the fourth valve of the B♭ instrument are still being explored and its technique worked out; the single horn in F alto and the double in F alto and B♭ are coming more into use, and recently a triple horn in F, B♭ and F alto, to combine the best of all worlds, has been introduced. The possibilities, too, of the ascending third valve are being investigated in other countries than France. The more progressive players are constantly trying out their theories, and ideas are freely exchanged when foreign orchestras visit this country. Such a state of affairs cannot but be healthy, for it is a sign that the instrument is being adapted to meet changing conditions; and while it would be foolish to suppose that all change must be good, there is every reason to believe that players will not voluntarily allow the horn to lose the individuality which has been its major asset for the past two hundred years.

[1] *The French Horn.*

31

CHAPTER 3

Acoustical:
Tone Quality

very musical instrument has its own characteristic timbre, which is determined by its method of sound production, its physical dimensions, and a large number of other, sometimes incalculable factors. No instrument produces a pure tone as such; whatever its mode of sound production it gives rise to vibrations, not only at the frequency of the note which the ear actually perceives, but also at other higher frequencies determined by the modes of vibration open to it. Thus any note produced by the instrument is in fact a compound tone, consisting not only of the note perceived, but also of a series of pure tones of higher frequencies superimposed upon it — tones which are members of a series known as the harmonic series, consisting of a fundamental and a number of partials. In the horn, as in most brass instruments, the ratio of these frequencies to that of the fundamental is 1:2:3:4:5, etc.

For convenience the fundamental is called the first partial, and the second partial therefore has a frequency twice that of the fundamental, and is its octave. The frequency of the third partial is three times that of the fundamental and it sounds as the twelfth above, and so on. The series, as far as the sixteenth partial, based on a fundamental F' and therefore relating to the horn in F is shown in Fig. 2. It is there shown as written for that instrument; the actual

Fig. 2. Harmonic series of the horn up to the sixteenth. The signs before notes 11 and 13 indicate sharpness and flatness respectively of about a $\frac{1}{4}$ tone; that before notes 7 and 14 indicates flatness of rather more than a semitone.

32

sounds will be a perfect fifth lower. It should be noticed that though the F horn can sound its fundamental, as a rule with some difficulty owing to its great length and narrow bore, the wave-length of its simplest habitual mode of vibration is approximately equal to the length of the tube, as opposed to those instruments which commonly use their fundamental, whose wave-length is twice the tube-length. The fundamental is more easily produced on the short horn in B♭, but even this instrument makes comparatively rare use of these pedal notes.

The harmonic series is of significance from two points of view. It is the series which the player, by alterations of his lip tension, can sound on the open tube, and this aspect of the part it plays in horn

Fig. 3. Tonal spectra of the horn. Open notes denote prominent partials and black notes those present in smaller intensity. (Actual sounds.)

technique will be considered later. But the series is also concerned with the tone colour produced by the instrument. It was shown by Helmholtz that this quality depends upon the particular partial tones which are superimposed upon the note sounded, and upon their relative intensities. Seashore[1] and various other investigators have analysed the tone of the horn by determining the distribution of energy in the partials carried by a number of notes of different frequencies, at different dynamic levels. Fig. 3, adapted from Seashore's figures, shows the tonal spectra of these notes. From these spectra it is evident that whatever the frequency of the note actually sounded, a considerable proportion of the energy is expended in producing partials in the region between about 200 to 600 cycles per second, corresponding to the range a to e''. Seashore's own comment is that 'the wide and well-balanced spread of partials in this region gives the rich and mellow characteristic'. Helmholtz came to the general conclusion that notes carrying a series of partials up to the sixth, of moderate intensity, would be rich and splendid. Jeans,[2] more categorically, stated that the second partial adds clearness and brilliance, the third brilliance and a certain hollow quality, throaty or nasal, the fourth brilliance again, and the fifth a rich horn-like quality. Compared with the spectra of

---

[1] *The Psychology of Music*, p. 190.   [2] *Science and Music*, p. 86.

THE INSTRUMENT

most other instruments those of the horn are relatively simple, and it is only the notes in the lower register which carry partials above the fifth in any significant proportion. It should be mentioned, however, that analyses carried out by various investigators have not given entirely consistent results. A. Douglas,[1] for example, states that 'French horn tone contains a complete harmonic series, extending in fact far beyond those shown' — and his diagram for the note f (175 cycles per second) shows nineteen harmonics, the last eleven, admittedly, in low intensity. The presence of these higher partials in notes of the lower register tends to impart a somewhat rougher quality. The general smoothness and mellowness of horn tone in the best part of its range are attributable to the shape of the mouthpiece, the gradually expanding bore, and the widely flaring bell, all of them factors favouring the suppression of the higher partials. It seems possible that these partials are evoked in greater intensity only when a brassy *cuivré* tone is produced by increased wind pressure.

It should be noted that the tonal spectra given in Fig. 3 represent the structure of sustained notes and do not show an important feature which is almost as characteristic of the horn as its tone in sustained notes. This feature is the typical 'attack' of the instrument, which is determined by the relative speeds at which the various partials reach their maximum intensity. Also characteristic of the instrument is its transient behaviour, during which the manner of vibration of the air column changes as it passes from one note to another. Both add to the individuality of the horn.

Returning to consideration of sustained notes, it is clear that the relative intensities of the various partials pertaining to particular fundamentals of different frequencies do not remain constant throughout the compass; in other words, the tone of the horn is not homogeneous throughout its range, as indeed the ear makes obvious. There is reinforcement, not of particular orders of partials, but of those partials which happen to lie within the frequency limits of 200 to 600 c.p.s. In modern terminology, there is a formant in this region, due possibly to some portion of the instrument having its own vibration periods and resonating in sympathy when the air inside the instrument is vibrating with the same frequencies. No doubt analyses of the tone of a number of different instruments would show differences in the relative intensities of the prominent partials corresponding to the slight differences in tone quality noted by the ear, the nature of the formant not being identical.

The analysis shows, too, that there is a difference in the intensities of the partials corresponding to differences in dynamics. In

[1] *The Electrical Production of Music*, p. 28.

other words, a difference in tone quality is to be expected between a horn blown softly and one blown strongly, a supposition which is borne out in practice. When the wind pressure is raised still further, partials higher than the sixth are elicited in significant strength, and the tone becomes coarser and brassier.

Finally, it must be pointed out that the objective analysis of the tone of the horn outlined above does not give the whole picture as far as the listener is concerned. It can be shown that for reasons connected with the structure of the ear, this organ itself modifies the quality of the sound reaching it, creating new tones not already present and reinforcing certain partials which may exist only in relatively low intensities. Thus is explained the fact that below about 150 c.p.s. the note apparently sounded, though shown by objective analysis to be either completely absent or present only in very low intensity, is in fact subjectively to be heard at sufficient strength to create the impression in the listener that the instrument is actually sounding that note.

Basically the art of a designer of a horn lies in his ability to fix the physical measurements of a tube which, when blown with a mouthpiece whose shape and dimensions also require careful designing, will give out a sound in which the partials are present in relative intensities corresponding to the tone quality considered desirable. The number and intensity of these partials depend upon several factors, some of which are beyond the control of the designer. The most important of these factors are:

  (i) The rigidity of the material of which the horn is made;
 (ii) The shape of the tube and the flare of the bell;
(iii) The width of the bore and the length of the tube;
 (iv) The shape of the mouthpiece;
  (v) The position of the hand in the bell, and the presence or absence of a mute; and
 (vi) The skill of the player, the physical characteristics of his lips, facial muscles and oral cavity, and, perhaps most important of all, the ideal of tone quality he aims at.

These may be considered in turn.

(i) MATERIAL

Theoretically the only tone-producing parts are the lips and the vibrating column of air, and the material which encloses this column should be of little or no consequence, provided it is sufficiently rigid. A non-yielding material absorbs little of the energy of the vibrating air and therefore produces a more sonorous sound than an absorbent material, which would lead to a dull and muffled tone.

Horns are almost always constructed of some form of brass —
occasionally of silver or of German silver[1] — and these materials
not only provide the necessary rigidity but also have the advantages of being comparatively light, of wearing well, and of being
reasonably easy to bend into loops. The presence of bends in the
tubing, incidentally, does not appear materially to affect the tone
quality, though the free-blowing properties seem to be sensibly
altered by sharp bends in the first two feet or so, and small defects
in this part of the tubing are particularly liable to cause bad
notes.

In practice there is little doubt that the tubing itself is set in
vibration when its natural frequencies are present as partials of the
notes being sounded; as already explained, each instrument
possesses a formant, and the exact nature of this formant must
depend, among other things, on the material of which the tube is
constructed. There is no doubt that the widespread adoption of the
metal flute in place of the older wooden one has been largely
brought about by recognition of its more brilliant tone quality,
and clarinet players have for long been conversant with the
difference in tone between instruments made of different kinds of
wood. Horn players in general do not show any marked preference,
so far as tone quality is concerned, for instruments made of any
particular material; general opinion is that there is little to choose
in this respect between brass and silver or nickel silver. A brass
containing a high percentage of copper, known as gold brass, is
sometimes favoured as giving a more ringing tone, but it is heavier
and more expensive than ordinary brass. The difference in tone
quality between instruments by different makers is attributable
partly to comparatively small variations in the composition of the
alloys used in their manufacture. The composition of these alloys
usually remains the maker's secret, but it is arrived at mainly by
empirical methods.

With the development in recent years of many new alloys it is
surprising that no real rival has yet appeared to challenge the
supremacy of brass in the construction of horns. Most manufacturers
tend to keep to well-established practices, and innovations are
more likely than not to be introduced at the instigation of players,
who are usually ready to experiment but lack the facilities for such
large-scale investigations.

Valve casings and slides are sometimes made of nickel silver even
when the main tubing is of brass, owing to the greater resistance of
the former alloy to corrosion, to which the valves are particularly

[1] Brass: up to 90 per cent copper, remainder zinc. German or nickel silver:
approximately 50 per cent copper, 20 per cent zinc, 30 per cent nickel.

subject. The rest of the instrument is often clear-lacquered to preserve its polished appearance and to mitigate the effects of constant handling. The lacquer, however, does not last for ever, and a better alternative might be to have the whole instrument silver-plated. Sometimes the bell is made wholly of silver; in any case great attention is paid to its manufacture, and it is usually annealed many times during the spinning operation to condition it for still finer spinning.

Horns are now frequently made with detachable bells. This arrangement appears to have no effect on the tone quality, and its chief advantage is that removal of the bell enables the instrument to be carried in a more conveniently shaped case than the usual type.

A factor which appears to be of some importance in aiding ease of tone production is the degree of smoothness of the inside of the bore; a glass-like surface is said to promote flexibility, and in modern practice it is sometimes obtained by whirling spring-expanding steel balls inside the tube while it is held in a precision mould. This hammering gives a mirror-like finish offering little resistance to the passage of the air.

Mention should be made here of the old belief that a horn must be played in, and that a new instrument reaches its best only after a considerable period of regular use. Conversely, there was a long-held theory that a good instrument could be spoiled by faulty playing. Dauprat, for instance, in his *Méthode*, states that 'in new horns of the best make one sometimes finds a few notes too sharp or too flat; others the tone of which is not sure or the quality not pure. These same imperfections can be encountered for a stronger reason in some instruments which have been played for some time by persons whose ear was neither sensitive nor trained. But if it is possible to spoil a good instrument by faulty playing it is also possible to correct the blemishes in it'. Similarly in Gallay's *Méthode* it is remarked that 'the quality of the instrument which the player uses is more or less responsible for the roundness of the stopped notes and consequently these notes will have more volume on a horn played for a long time than on a new instrument'. The physical explanation of what is an accepted fact among horn players is somewhat obscure, but it must be either a case of the player becoming accustomed to his instrument and learning more or less unconsciously to humour its particular foibles, or less probably the gradual development, after a period of use, of minute changes in the physical structure of the interior of the tube, leading to the eradication of the defects.

THE INSTRUMENT

(ii) THE SHAPE OF THE TUBING

Different authorities give somewhat divergent accounts of the shape of the tubing in the horn. Wood[1] and Richardson[2] say that it is approximately logarithmic or exponential in form; most commonly it is described as conical, which it certainly is not, and a third view[3] is that the tubing 'is neither cylindrical nor conical, but of a shape that has been found by experience to give overtones that are correctly in tune with each other'. In any case, as far as the valve horn is concerned, a proportion of the tubing in the region of the valves and tuning slide is of necessity cylindrical in form, and to this interruption in the expansion of the tube has been attributed the difference in tone, mentioned by early writers on the valve horn, between the open and the valved notes. This supposed difference, which may have been more obtrusive in early valved models, was one of the reasons which led many composers, notably Brahms even to the end of his life, to show reluctance to use the valve horn. Valved notes have been described as 'slightly more resonant and trombone-like', but in modern instruments the distinction is so small as to be negligible, certainly not nearly so marked as between the open and stopped strings of a violin.

Perhaps a more cogent objection to the valve horn was that it involved the loss of what is now regarded as the greatest defect of the hand horn, its unavoidable heterogeneity of tone. Most of the stopped notes, it was declared by the hand horn enthusiasts, have 'a charm which is peculiar to them and which supplies, so to speak, nuances and contrast to the natural notes'. It was, in fact, quite possible to retain these qualities of the hand horn whilst still making full use of the increased flexibility given by the valves, as Meifred showed in his *Méthode* published in 1841. He treated the valves as an addition to the horn which remedied some of its weaknesses while enabling it to retain its special characteristics — a perfectly legitimate view, but one which is not, as in fact the horn has developed, in consonance with present-day ideas.

Neglecting that part of the tubing which is cylindrical in shape, the characteristic tone of the horn may in part be attributed to its expanding bore. An exponential tube is one whose radius of cross-section increases in a constant ratio when measured at equal intervals along its axis, and whose area of cross-section therefore doubles itself at fixed intervals along this axis. The main property of such a tube is that it gives a more efficient radiation of energy

[1] *The Physics of Music*, p. 145.
[2] *The Acoustics of Orchestral Instruments*, p. 75
[3] *Grove's Dictionary*, 3rd Edition, 'Acoustics'.

than a conical tube of the same length and the same initial and final areas. The taper sections of the horn do not conform exactly to this specification; a typical section might follow the general law

$$x_y = \frac{x}{y^n}$$

where x_y is the bore at any axial distance y from the bell-mouth, x is the bell-mouth diameter, and n is a constant known as the flare constant. The numerical values given to the quantities x and n are decided largely by experience; the value of x varies from 10·5 to thirteen inches and a typical value for n might be 0·8. These values are chosen so as (i) to provide a series of partials in strict harmonic relationship with the fundamental, and hence to make correct intonation more certain, and (ii) to ensure that these partials are present in their correct relative intensities in order that the characteristic tone quality shall be available. The values given for the bell-mouth diameter and the flare constant lead to the widely flaring bell typical of the horn. This and the expanding rather than cylindrical bore tend to give broadness of tone quality in place of brilliance.

To some extent, even in single horns, the shape of the tubing cannot conform to the theoretical ideal owing to the length of cylindrical tubing which must be interpolated to allow for incorporation of a valve system and a tuning slide, and in the double horn the matter is complicated still further by the fact that the two sections have a certain length of tubing in common, partly at the proximal but mostly at the distal end of the instrument. Consequently the rate of increase in bore of the shorter B♭ section must be much greater than in the longer F section, while the latter will contain the greater length of cylindrical tubing. This disparity will be even more pronounced in, say, a horn in F and high F, and no doubt it is partly responsible for the difficulties encountered in designing double horns whose two sections will give well-matched tone qualities. Somewhere a compromise must be made between the separate requirements of a single B♭ horn and those of a single horn in F.

The ratio of the cylindrical to the taper length, which is determined by the length of valve tubing and tuning slide required, is usually about 1:1, so that the taper sections constitute a much smaller proportion of the total length of tubing than might at first sight be imagined. The bore of the cylindrical section varies according to its position relatively to the taper sections, for there appears to be no uniform practice among makers with respect to the positioning of the cylindrical part of the tubing. The instruments by various makers shown diagrammatically in Fig. 4 exhibit a wide variation in the position of the valve system and tuning slide as well as in the actual conformation of the tubing. In some cases the valve cluster is placed after a comparatively short length of tapered tubing, and in one of these the airway passes through the valves in the reverse order 3, 2, 1; in the others the valve system is placed much farther on. The exact bore of the cylindrical tubing will depend, therefore, on its position, but a typical value might be of the order of 0·46 inches. The initial bore of the tubing at the mouthpiece end may be as low as 0·30 inches, so that in an F horn there would be a gradual expansion for the first three or four feet until the cylindrical portion is reached; at the farther end of the valve cluster the expansion is resumed, becoming progressively more rapid in the main coil and culminating in the last foot or so in the widely flaring bell. The ratio of the bell-mouth diameter to the effective length of the tubing varies between approximately 1:11 and 1:14 in the F horn and is rather less in the B♭, whose bell diameter is usually not greatly reduced although its tubing is much shorter. Experiments on B♭ horns with detachable screw-on bells, in fact, tend to show that the full-size bell gives better results, and in the double horn, of course, the B♭ section of necessity has the full twelve- to thirteen-inch bell.

The function of the bell requires some explanation. The actual length of an F horn is about 147 inches. Owing to the fact that in an open tube an antinode, or point of maximum vibration, is formed slightly beyond the open end its acoustical length is a little more. The difference is known as the end correction, and it is greatest when the end of the tube is narrow or when it is shaded by some obstruction. This is the reason why occlusion of the bell with the hand can lead to a fall of pitch of as much as a tone, since the antinode is thrown a corresponding distance farther from the end of the tube. If, however, the end of the tube is flared, the end correction is reduced as the vibration of the air is facilitated. Moreover, the end correction is greater for the higher partials than for the lower, and consequently the higher partials will tend to be out of tune with the lower and thus excited less easily. The smaller the end correction the more nearly in tune the higher partials will be, and the greater their intensity, with a corresponding effect on the quality of tone. In the horn, as opposed to other wind instruments, two contrary factors are at work. The flaring bell reduces the end correction and makes for a more colourful tone, richer in the higher partials; the presence of the hand in the bell, however, has the opposite effect of increasing the end correction, thus decreasing the intensity of the upper partials and reducing the brilliance of the tone. Without the flaring bell, therefore, the timbre of the horn would be dull and uninteresting.

The rate of the flare also has some effect on the tone quality. Coar[1] gives some interesting reproductions of the instruments used by the virtuosi Dauprat and Gallay in which it can be seen that Dauprat's (a silver horn by Raoux) has a bell with a much wider throat than Gallay's instrument, giving a correspondingly darker, 'tubbier' tone. The diameters of the bells of these two horns, of course, are smaller than is customary at the present time.

(iii) THE SCALE OF THE HORN

The scale of the horn — that is, the ratio of the width to the length — is small for the greater part of its length, for the bore of the cylindrical section is no greater than that of a trumpet pitched an octave higher. There is, however, a by no means negligible difference between the bore of a modern German-type horn and that of the true French horn. Both may be regarded as narrow-bore instruments, as opposed to the wide-bore tubas and euphoniums, but there is a great gulf fixed, so far as tone quality is concerned, between the two types, and this must be attributed partly to the difference in scale. In the French type, which has the narrower bore, the expansion is very gradual, and the bell diameter may be as small as eleven inches; in some types of German horn, on the other hand, the bore has already increased by one tenth by the time the cylindrical portion has been reached, and thereafter the expansion is much more rapid than in the French type, ending in a bell of diameter perhaps thirteen inches or more. Some Austrian horns lie midway between these two extremes, for the increase in bore up to the valve system is smaller even than in the French type, but thereafter follows the German pattern. These single horns, pitched in F, are still used and are said to give a particularly rich and full tone.

'All German instruments', it has been remarked, 'sound more or less like euphoniums to ears accustomed to the French school,' and it is true that French horn tone is thinner, brighter and more open than the heavier, broader and thicker tone of the German horn. In this connection, however, national traditions and ideals of tone and colour must be taken into account. An American observer, used to the tone quality of the German horn favoured by his countrymen, relates how on hearing a French orchestra he was particularly struck by the small thin tone, accompanied by an uninhibited vibrato, produced by its horn players. On examining

[1] *A Critical Study of the Nineteenth-Century Horn Virtuosi in France*, p. 71.

their instruments, however, he was surprised to discover that they were using comparatively wide-bore double horns not so very different from those he was used to. Though it appears that France, the last stronghold of the narrow-bore instrument, is gradually yielding to the lure of the easier and less fatiguing tone production offered by the German type, yet its ideals of tone colour remain those of the French horn proper, and an approximation to such a tone colour can, it seems, be obtained even with a wide-bore instrument by a player to whom the normal wide-bore tone is anathema. The point is discussed more fully later in this chapter.

The use of the wide-bore horn, then, is now almost universal, but it has not reached its position of supremacy without a struggle. As early as 1892, before the introduction of the double horn, Bernard Shaw was provoked to complain on the occasion of Mahler's visit to London with the Hamburg Opera that 'instead of three distinct and finely contrasted families of thoroughbred trombones, horns and tubas we had a huge tribe of mongrels, differing chiefly in size. I felt', he said, 'that some ancestors of the trombones had been guilty of a mésalliance with a bombardon . . . and that the mother of the horns must have run away with a whole military band.' Sixty years later the wheel had come full circle, for we find an American describing the tone of a narrow-bore small-belled French horn as 'a cross between a saxophone and the bleating of a mountain goat'. Incidentally, this particular French instrument, equipped with piston valves, of which the third was of the ascending type, he regarded as practically a museum piece.

Ideals of horn tone still differ, but the horn of today which, generally speaking, finds favour is not the true French horn of yesterday; the need for greater weight of tone in the orchestra is resulting in the rapid extinction of the French horn proper, and this greater weight of tone has been achieved largely by the increased bore. The term 'French horn' nowadays has little or no significance, though it persists in English-speaking countries to the absurd extent that 'German French horns' are advertised for sale; under pressure of circumstance the instrument is rapidly receding into obsolescence. However much the fact may be regretted by those brought up in the old school of French horn playing, whose voices are still to be heard from time to time, under present conditions the narrow-bore instrument will never regain the supremacy it once enjoyed in certain parts of the world. The odds are too heavily weighted against it, though as often happens in such cases, progress involves some loss as well as gain.

The German horn was adopted in American orchestras mainly because in their early stages these orchestras employed German or

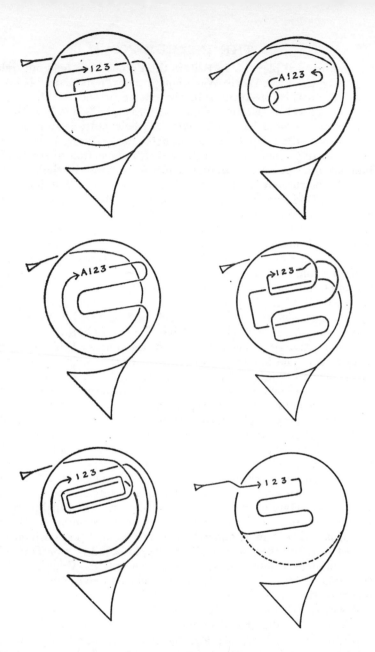

Fig. 4. Conformation of the tubing in single horns by various makers (diagrammatic only). Top: left, in B♭; right, in B♭/A. Middle: left, in B♭/A; right, in F. Bottom: left, in F; right, in high F.

43

German-trained players. In Britain the French horn held out until well after the First World War, though the wide-bore double horn made tentative appearances in the course of the twenties. The influence of Aubrey Brain as principal horn of the B.B.C. Symphony Orchestra (1928–45) ensured that the whole horn section of this orchestra used narrow-bore piston instruments during this period. The visits of foreign orchestras, however, such as that of the Berlin Philharmonic in 1927, stimulated further interest in the German type of instrument, and on the foundation of the London Philharmonic Orchestra in 1932 Sir Thomas Beecham stipulated that wide-bore double horns should be used. It is also said that Sir Hamilton Harty equipped the Hallé Orchestra with similar instruments after hearing the effect of a horn section using German horns. At the present time all the British orchestras use the wide-bore instrument; frequently double horns by Alexander are favoured, but compensating instruments by Kruspe and Knopf are also used as well as single B♭ horns by the same makers. The B.B.C. Symphony Orchestra use British-made instruments by Boosey and Hawkes similar in design to the Alexander double horn.

The effective or acoustical length of the horn in F is about 154 inches; its actual length from the throat of the mouthpiece to the bell is about 147 inches. With all the valves depressed its length is increased to about 210 inches. The corresponding figures for the B♭ horn are approximately 115, 110 and 156 inches. Thus there is a difference of about eight feet between the shortest length of the B♭ horn and the greatest length of the F horn. Other things being equal, a short tube favours the lower harmonics, and a longer tube the higher, so that the tone of an instrument will depend to some extent upon its length. The nineteenth-century hand horn virtuosi were insistent upon the need to cultivate a variety of crooks because of the corresponding variety of tone colour made available. Thus Dauprat affirmed that 'each key of the horn has a timbre of its own which is inherent in it and which is felt even in keys which are closest to each other, such as D and E♭, or E and F'. Consequently between more widely separated keys, such as C and G, or D and A, the difference is so great that 'these might be two different instruments — the one full of force and brilliance, the other of gravity and sweetness'. Domnich (1808) characterized the crooks as follows: high C, brilliant and piercing, like a trumpet; G, A and B♭, shrill; E and F, brilliant; E♭, softer and harmonious; low B♭, sombre, melancholy and religious. In 1886 we find Sullivan complaining at the first performance of *The Golden Legend* that his parts for horns in B♭ were in fact being played on horns in F, and somewhat later Forsyth commented very unfavourably on the tone of the short B♭ horn. One cannot help feeling, too, that the French, particularly, still regret the passing of the different crooks; nostalgic comments appear over and over again in their works on orchestration and in their horn tutors.

There was a very definite difference, then, between the tonal qualities of the various crooks that were in common use, and there was a difference, though the efforts of makers and players have practically succeeded in eliminating it, between the tone of the B♭ division of the double horn and that of the F division. It is probable that in the early days of the double horn difficulties in design and the unfamiliarity of players with the instrument led to differences in tone quality between the two sections sufficiently marked to draw unfavourable comment. Indeed, Anton Horner, who introduced the double horn into the U.S.A., admitted that he himself used the B♭ section only in the upper register 'because the tone is not so mellow and of as good a quality in the middle and lower register, being harsh and hollow', and it is certainly true even now that in the hands of the beginner the B♭ horn can sound unsympathetic. If, however the player has had long experience of the F horn and the sound it produces he instinctively matches his tone on the B♭ instrument to that which he is accustomed to produce from the F horn, and with practice consolidates the tone in the middle register until it is indistinguishable from the sound of a horn in F. When this is accomplished, as it is by good players, the case so frequently argued against the B♭ horn falls to the ground.

Theoretically a horn pitched in a key even lower than F would provide a still richer tone, but in practice its use would rarely be feasible for modern horn parts with their high tessitura, since the necessary lip tension would be very difficult to attain, and in any case the lower-pitched horns do not take kindly to valves. The horn in F was a compromise, and one which in modern conditions does not always prove satisfactory. The double horn is one answer to the problems posed by modern horn parts, the B♭ horn is another, and the high F horn is a third. All, in the hands of experienced players, are capable of meeting most reasonable demands, and there is no doubt that the longer, lower-pitched horns have disappeared, never to return. The present tendency, in fact, is towards the shorter instruments.

(iv) THE MOUTHPIECE

The traditional form of mouthpiece used with the horn is of a narrow funnel-like shape merging more or less imperceptibly into the narrower end of the crook or into the mouthpipe. Such a

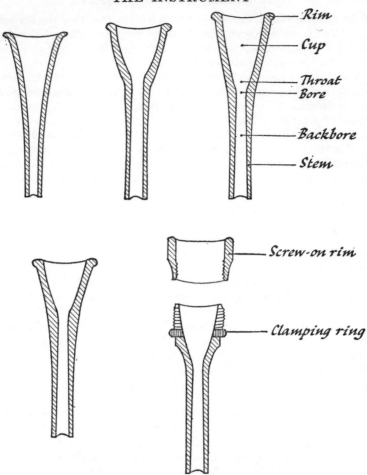

Rim

Cup

Throat
Bore

Backbore

Stem

Screw-on rim

Clamping ring

Fig. 5. Horn mouthpieces. Top: left, obsolete funnel shape.
Bottom: right, adjustable mouthpiece with screw-on rim.
Remainder: typical modern shapes.

mouthpiece is shown in longitudinal section in Fig. 5, and it makes a sharp contrast with the cup-shaped mouthpieces of most other brass instruments. Its shape is yet another factor tending to give a smooth and mellow tone quality, probably owing to the absence of any sharp flange and hence of any definite edge tone such as is generated, for example, in the trumpet. A conical mouthpiece enables the tone to be produced with a smaller expenditure of energy, and renders the correction of small faults of intonation comparatively easy. The smaller the diameter of the cone at its wider end — that is, the end applied to the lips — the more easily are the high notes produced, though the tone is likely to be thinner than with a mouthpiece of greater diameter.

This funnel-shaped mouthpiece, however, is now obsolescent. The modern tendency is to use one which is slightly cup-shaped, though the cup is very much less marked than is to be found in a modern trumpet mouthpiece.

The horn mouthpiece is made from brass rod, with a gold or silver plating, or of silver alone, or of a composite white metal,[1] though in earlier days ivory, horn or even hard wood was sometimes used. It consists of a flat or slightly curved rim surrounding the cup, which itself converges through the throat or *grain* to a region, known as the bore, where the internal diameter of the mouthpiece is at a minimum. Beyond this region the stem expands internally to a greater or lesser degree to form the backbore. The dimensions of these various component parts influence both the tone quality and the ease with which notes at either end of the range are produced. The mouthpiece has yet to be produced, however, which combines all the more desirable qualities in full measure to the exclusion of the less desirable, for a significant variation in any one dimension designed to effect improvement in one respect is bound also to introduce other characteristics which are not required. Thus the ideal mouthpiece will produce a rich, full, pure, well-focused tone; it will allow both of smooth slurring and a clean, sharp attack; it will permit both high and low notes to be obtained in good volume and with equal facility and security of pitch; and it will do all this without inflicting punishment on the sensitive muscles of the embouchure. But unfortunately such requirements are mutually incompatible so far as the dimensions and shape of the mouthpiece are concerned. This is shown by consideration of the playing characteristics resulting from differences in the size and shape of the various parts of the mouthpiece.

(i) *The rim.* The width of the rim may vary from as little as 2 mm. (a width which was commonly used by first hand horn players) to as much as 4 mm., which is a little greater, perhaps, than the average width of a modern rim. The narrow rim allows of greater control of the embouchure muscles, but is tiring to use and detrimental to the endurance; the wide rim is easier on the embouchure but does not give as good control. A sharp inner edge to the rim makes for a good clean attack and well-produced staccato, while a rounded edge, though promoting smooth slurring, tends to

[1] Mouthpieces of plastic material, or with plastic or ivory rims, are also available.

blur the attack.

(ii) *The cup.* The shape of the cup is determined by its diameter at the rim, its depth, the degree of curvature of its sides, and the bore at its base. The internal diameter of a modern mouthpiece at the rim varies from 16 mm. to 18·5 mm. or more, measurements which are not markedly different from the 17 mm. of the old *cor alto* and the 19 mm. of the *cor basse.* The larger diameter favours the production of the low notes, the smaller of the high. Similarly a deep cup more nearly approaching the obsolete funnel shape results in more readily produced lower notes and a richer tone, while a shallow cup gives easier higher notes and greater incisiveness at the expense of the tone, which becomes harder and more trumpet-like. Markedly curved sides to the cup give greater resonance, straighter sides a smooth quality. A narrow throat and bore at the base of the cup aid the production of high notes, but the tone is likely to become small and choked and the intonation uncertain if the narrowing process is carried too far. It is quite possible that early opposition to the short wide-bore instrument in this country was partly due to the use of cupped mouthpieces which were too heavily choked at the throat. The open-throated mouthpiece gives a fuller, freer tone and easier low notes, but this, too, can be carried to excess, leading to too woolly and dispersed a sound.

(iii) *The backbore.* This is usually more or less flared to give better tone and volume, but the flare can be carried too far and lead to woolliness. A cylindrical backbore, on the other hand, is a help with the high notes but is inimical to good tone and volume. It is said that a compromise in the form of a short straight section immediately following the bore leads to better control of pitch and greater steadiness of tone.

It is clear that the perfect mouthpiece is an unattainable goal. In any case, the choice of a mouthpiece is a highly individual matter, depending upon the player's lip and facial structure, his predilections with regard to tone quality, his position in the orchestra, and so on. Most players would advise that the best procedure is to find a model that appears likely to satisfy one's demands reasonably adequately, having regard to the particular qualities considered desirable, and if, after an extended trial, it proves comfortable and no overwhelming disadvantages become apparent, to stick to this model through thick and thin, steadily resisting the natural tendency to experiment in the hope of finding something better. 'One of the player's most valuable possessions', it has been said, 'is his *own* mouthpiece, for it has a radical influence on his whole style of playing; it can almost be said to have a soul of its own and a first-class player will decline to change to another.'

A wide variety of mouthpieces is available from manufacturers. The catalogue of a continental maker offers nine basic types: shallow, medium or deep cup, each of small, medium or large diameter in varying widths of rim. Many makers will copy a player's own mouthpiece if required, either from the actual model or from a plaster cast, or will manufacture experimental models to his own specification from accurately dimensioned drawings. Some makers are now producing mouthpieces with detachable screw-on rims. By this means once a rim of suitable width and inside diameter has been chosen, experiments may be made with different cup shapes. For example, a rim may be supplied with up to ten different cups. A further refinement is found in the mouthpiece with adjustable cup (Fig. 5). It consists of three parts: a stem and cup, an adjusting and clamping ring and a screw-on rim. By altering the position of the clamping ring the rim can be screwed up or down, thus altering the depth of the cup. This mouthpiece can be supplied in four different cup diameters (16·5 to 18 mm.) in small, medium or large bore, giving a choice from which the player should be able to select a shape suited to his own particular requirements.

In this country most players use German mouthpieces, and the tendency is towards a larger diameter both for high and low players. Abroad there is considerable variation. In a well-known German orchestra the high horns, using single B♭ instruments, favour a medium cup with a fairly open throat in pursuit of their broad blending tone, and the lower players, with double horns, a deeper, more funnel-shaped cup also not choked at the throat. The French incline generally to a large mouthpiece with a wide rim and deep cup which is much more heavily choked. Elsewhere much smaller mouthpieces are to be found than anything in use in this country.

Since the mouthpiece is the part of the instrument in most intimate contact with the player, it should sit on the lips in so natural and comfortable a manner as almost to become part of him. How this is achieved is largely a personal matter, but there are certain general principles to be observed in the placing of the mouthpiece and these are dealt with in Chapter 6.

(v) The Effect of Hand and Mute

It has been known at least since the middle of the eighteenth century that the partial closure of the bell with the hand lowers the pitch of the note emitted, and at the same time converts the normal open tone into a dull repressed sound. The reason for this, in terms of the displacement of the terminal antinode and the consequent increase in the end correction, has already been given. The horn is nowadays usually played with the hand in the bell, so that the pitch is always slightly flatter than the length of the tubing itself would indicate. For this reason some horns are purposely built slightly sharp.

With the invention of the valve the practice of stopping as a means of obtaining additional notes not available on the natural horn became unnecessary, but was retained as a means of varying the tone colour. The extent of the difference in tone between the normal open note and, say, the half-stopped note a semitone below has been the subject of much debate. One view is that the stopped note was at best a makeshift, better than nothing in that it filled in some of the gaps in the natural horn's very restricted series of notes, but that the stopped notes were of so inferior a quality that they sounded as though they were played on a different instrument; others hold that the stopped notes could be made to sound sufficiently like the open notes as not to offend the ear if the open notes were blown softly and the contrast between the two types of tone colour was thus modified. A third opinion cherished the stopped notes to the degree that their use was advocated even on the valve horn, a perfectly logical idea if variation in tone colour is the aim. Nowadays stopped notes as understood by the hand horn players — that is, notes in which the pitch is lowered — are rarely, if ever, used except perhaps in France. A stopped tone quality is, however, frequently required by modern composers, though it is produced in a different way. If the bell is closed completely with the hand, and the wind pressure slightly raised, a note about a semitone *above* the fingered note is emitted. It is not altogether clear when this different technique was first discovered, though in his tutor it is stated by Domnich, a pupil of Punto, who in turn had been taught by Hampel, that during his experiments on muting with a cotton stopper Hampel himself was surprised to find his instrument *raised* a semitone. If this was so, he did not appear to pursue his investigations upon these lines. Even now, Koechlin and other writers have denied that such raising of the pitch is possible. 'Certain works', writes Koechlin in his *Traité de l'Orchestration*, 'state that stopping lowers the notes a semitone in the low and medium registers, and then raises them a semitone in the high register. This would be completely illogical and is quite incorrect.' It must be said, however, that the technique of stopping and raising the pitch is commonly used by orchestral players with good effect, and however illogical it appears must be accepted as an accomplished fact.

D. J. Blaikley's explanation was in terms of a flattened harmonic series; he held that these notes are in fact higher harmonics of a disturbed lower fundamental, the presence of the hand in the bell sufficiently altering its form to give rise to this disturbed series. He argued, for example, that the notes c'', d'', e'', harmonics 8, 9 and 10 from a fundamental C', become $d''\flat$, $e''\flat$, f'', harmonics 9, 10 and 11 from a fundamental $C'\flat$. This explanation, however, will not cover the observed facts that (i) when full muting is applied gradually from the bell, a gradual rise in pitch is found to occur, incompatible with the possibility of a jump from one harmonic to a higher, and (ii) with full muting, notes a semitone high in pitch can be obtained over the whole range of the instrument, and not only in the region where the harmonics lie a tone apart. If Blaikley's theory were correct, gradual full muting from the bell would lead to a corresponding gradual lowering of the pitch, until the full flattening of a semitone was achieved; it would then be necessary to jump to a harmonic a tone higher in order to obtain a net rise of a semitone. Moreover, this could only be done for those harmonics which are a full tone apart.

An alternative explanation has been advanced by Dr. Birchard Coar.[1] He attributes the fact that the raising of the pitch has hitherto been described, by those who accept it at all, as exactly a semitone, to the accident that the human hand happens to be the size it is, and describes experiments in which he gradually introduced a large pad into the bell. No alteration in pitch was observed when the pad was at the bell-mouth, but a gradual rise took place as it was pushed farther and farther into the bell, provided that full muting was continuously maintained, until eventually, with the pad at a distance of approximately six and a half inches from the bell-mouth, a rise of a semitone was achieved. He goes on to say, 'It is more than mere coincidence that if this six and a half inches be taken from the total length of the main tubing, the instrument becomes a semitone higher in pitch.' When the hand is placed at this distance inside the bell, he argues, its effect is to render the last six and a half inches of the tubing inoperative. In effect, the hand cuts off the last section of the tube as if it were operating as a semitone ascending valve, provided it is in the correct position and is fully muting the instrument. He gives further support to his theory by describing experiments in which the 'stopper' was pushed in twice as far, when the pitch was raised a full tone, and the valve notes were perceptibly flat since the valve slides were now adjusted to suit a length of main tubing thirteen inches greater than in fact was operating.

The instrument on which these experiments were carried out was

[1] *The French Horn*, p. 71.

a horn in F provided with a fourth valve lowering the pitch a semi-tone to E. Thus with the hand in position at six and a half inches, raising the pitch a semitone, and the fourth valve in operation, lowering the pitch by the same amount, the horn was restored to F — which is, of course, the main purpose of the fourth valve — and the valve notes were in tune. With the 'stopper' pushed in to thirteen inches, the pitch was raised a whole tone to G, the length corrected by the fourth valve to a value corresponding to a horn in G♭, and the valve notes were then flat.

Attractively simple though this explanation appears at first sight, it is not acoustically sound. In order to raise the pitch of a horn in F by a semitone, the tubing must theoretically be shortened not by six and a half inches, but by between eight and nine inches. For a rise of a full tone the distance is almost seventeen inches. The corresponding figures for the horn in B♭ are six and a half inches and twelve and a half inches respectively. Thus if the effect of full muting is merely to shorten the tube, the position of the hand at six and a half inches would be sufficient to raise the pitch of a B♭ horn by a semitone, but not enough to do the same for a horn pitched in any lower key. The reduction in length required varies according to the length of tubing in operation at any given moment, and the amount of stopping required would therefore alter according to the pitch of the instrument, and indeed, to a lesser degree, with the valves being used. In practice it is found that full stopping on the B♭ horn raises the pitch by considerably more than a semitone, so that stopped notes tend to be sharp on this instrument unless a stopping valve is fitted whose slide can be accurately tuned. In addition, experiments on a Kruspe horn with a detachable bell gave conflicting results; removal of the bell — some four inches of tubing — appeared to have comparatively little effect on the pitch, and certainly nothing of the order of a semitone rise was observed when the F section was in use.

Experiments with a pad carried out on the lines indicated by Coar appeared to confirm his results; his interpretation of these results, however, is open to question. In any case it would seem that when the hand is used for muting, a great deal will depend upon its size and upon the bore of the instrument. If, for example, a normal-sized hand could produce full muting on a B♭ horn at a distance of six and a half inches when the throat of the bell is comparatively narrow, the same hand in an instrument with a wider throat would have to be introduced rather further into the bell to effect full muting, and all stopped notes would then be sharp. This is, in fact, in accordance with actual experience. For a player with a small hand the effect would be still more pronounced.

The problem is equally inexplicable when approached from an acoustic standpoint. The acoustical length of an F horn is about 154 inches, the terminal antinode lying about seven inches beyond the bell-mouth. If, however, full muting is applied about six inches up the tube, it might be expected that a node would form at this point, and the tube be converted from an open pipe of acoustical length 154 inches into a closed one of acoustical length about 141 inches — 154 inches less the end correction now no longer operative, less six inches actual shortening of the tube by the hand. If a horn in F fully muted were to operate as a closed pipe of this length, mathematical analysis[1] shows that it would give, not the normal harmonic series of frequency ratio $1:2:3:4$ etc., but an inharmonic series of ratio $1\cdot43:2\cdot46:3\cdot47:4\cdot47$ etc., resulting in notes bearing no obvious relation to the normal series and certainly exhibiting no constant difference of a semitone from it. In fact the horn is not, of course, a truly conical tube, for which the above series is calculated, but one of a complicated shape which does not lend itself to rigorous mathematical treatment. It is, too, so flexible an instrument that experiments on pitch are not easily carried out if the primary vibrating agents are the human lips. Much carefully planned and strictly controlled experimentation will be necessary before this problem can be fully and finally solved. The answer, said the late Professor Bernard Hague, an authority on the acoustics of wind instruments, will probably involve 'considerable redistribution of the nodes and antinodes at the bell end of the instrument. In other words, it is a question of the terminating acoustic impedance.' It is to be hoped that some well-qualified scientist who is also a musician will be able to find the solution to a problem which has provoked as much controversy in the recent history of the horn as any.

To return, after this somewhat lengthy digression, to the question of tone colour. If the horn is fully stopped, so that the pitch is raised, and at the same time the wind pressure is forced, causing the metal to vibrate, yet another variety of tone quality is produced, explained by Richardson as due to the setting up of the inharmonic series of partials mentioned above. In the narrow-bore horn this occurs suddenly at a comparatively low dynamic level, but in the wide-bore instrument more gradually and at a higher dynamic level. The clanging strident sound so produced is described by the term 'brassy' or more often by its French equivalent *cuivré*. It is also possible to produce a brassy tone by overblowing without stopping, giving a greater volume of sound than a stopped *cuivré* note, but of a rather different tone quality.

Some of the effects which can be obtained with the hand can also

---

[1] A. Wood, *Acoustics*, p. 399.

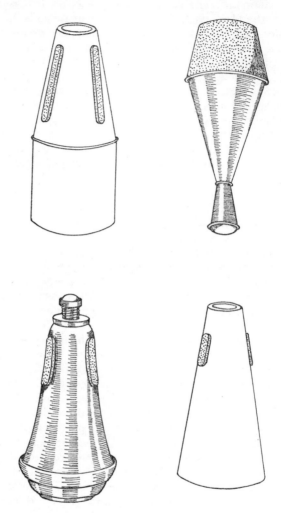

Fig. 6. Different types of mute. Above: left, non-transposing mute (papier-mâché); right, transposing mute (spun brass). Below: left, tunable non-transposing mute (aluminium); right, non-transposing mute of fibre, compressed cardboard or thin wood covered with leather substitute.

be produced with a mute, though there may be a slight difference in tone quality. Horn mutes are either truncated cones or pear-shaped stoppers (Fig. 6), made of wood, cardboard, *papier-mâché*, or of metals such as spun brass or aluminium, which are placed in the bell. They are of two general types, known as transposing and non-transposing. The non-transposing mute is either bored with air passages, or has some other arrangement such as cork wedges fixed to the body of the mute which keep it out of contact with the bell, so that air may pass and the tone colour be altered without changing the pitch. It is rare to find a mute of this sort which is perfectly in tune. The reason for this is not at all clear, for there appears to be no obvious connection between the size of the mute or the distance it projects up the bell and the amount of sharpness or flatness that it produces. Most players experiment until they find a more or less satisfactory mute, but few would claim to be entirely content with such empirical methods, or with the results achieved. It may sometimes be possible to correct faults of intonation produced by the mute by adjustment of the tuning slide, or the pitch may be altered by shortening or lengthening the piece of cylindrical tubing which projects inside the mute. This must also be done empirically, and since a small difference in length makes a considerable difference in pitch, it is best to proceed in small stages. The same process is carried out more expeditiously in a tunable non-transposing mute now manufactured. This is provided with a tuning screw regulator to be turned inward if the sound of the muted note is too sharp and outward if too flat. It is claimed that once it is adjusted all muted notes are in perfect tune.

The tone quality of a mute is determined by the size of the air passage allowed when the mute is in position. A comparatively wide passage gives a more open sound and greater volume. The volume can be reduced and the tone quality closed up by decreasing the thickness of the cork strips which keep the body of the mute away from the inside of the bell.

The transposing mute produces a rise in pitch when inserted in the bell in much the same way as does the hand in full stopping. In conjunction with a stopping valve such as is fitted to many modern instruments stopped passages can then be played without transposition. In this case the slide of the stopping valve should be tuned with the mute in position. These mutes raise the pitch by a semitone on the F horn, but by rather more — about $\frac{3}{4}$ tone — on a B♭ instrument. They are especially valuable for use in the low register, where hand stopping is difficult and rarely gives a satisfactory result. Here the transposing mute gives an altogether firmer and better-defined sound.

The insertion of the mute takes a little time, even if some such expedient as slinging the mute from the wrist by a cord attached to the base of the mute is employed. Composers do not always allow for this fact. Britten, for example, in the 'Nocturne' from his *Serenade for Tenor, Horn and Strings*, asks for the mute to be inserted while a note is actually in progress, and Bartók, in the 'Elegia' of his *Concerto for Orchestra* writes:

(*By permission of Boosey & Hawkes, Ltd.*)

If these examples were to be played as written the mute would have to be held in the hand ready to be put in before the first note was sounded, leading to difficulties in control of tone and intonation. In practice the hand would be used instead of the mute. There is not a great deal of difference in tone quality between a muted horn and one stopped by hand; little more, in fact, than there is between the sounds produced by the various types of mute in common use. The mute perhaps gives a slightly more disembodied sound when *pp*; it has been described as intermediate between clarinets and muted strings, and a little more metallic than very soft bassoons. In *ff* both muted and stopped notes sound *cuivré*, the volume of tone being slightly greater with the mute but the stopped note having the greater tang and penetration.

There are, therefore, four basic types of tone colour in addition to the normal open quality, but composers are often casual in indicating exactly what they require, and sometimes their demands are not feasible from a practical point of view. These tone qualities are denoted in the parts as follows:

1. Terms used to indicate that the insertion of a mute is required: Muted, *con sordino, avec sourdine, gedämpft* or *mit Dämpfer*. If the dynamic level is high, the sound will automatically assume the *cuivré* character.

2. Terms indicating that hand stopping is required: Stopped, closed, *sons bouchés* or *bouchez, chiuso, gestopft*, and the sign +. The latter is usually used for single stopped notes, when it may or may not be cancelled by O or *ouvert*. A passage marked *sons d'écho* or *Echoton* can often be played with good effect by hand stopping. In France the term *sons bouchés* or the sign + implies stopping by hand and fingering the notes a semitone *above* those written; for example, near the beginning of *L'Apprenti Sorcier*

56

Dukas specifically asks for this method of playing a stopped passage to be employed. It is doubtful whether in practice many players would perform it in this manner, for the same effect can be obtained with more certainty by stopping and *raising* the pitch by exactly a semitone on the F horn.

Hand stopping can be carried out much more rapidly than muting; nevertheless, a passage like the following from Debussy's *La Mer* (*Jeux des vagues*) demands a good hand technique owing to the speed at which it must be played. This is a case where a stopping valve might well prove useful:

(*By permission of Durand et Cie., copyright owners*)

3. Terms used to indicate that a brassy tone is required:
Brassed or brassy, *cuivré* or *cuivrez*, *schmetternd*, *blechern*.

Strictly speaking these terms by themselves imply a brassy sound obtained without stopping or muting, the tone quality produced rather resembling that of the old *trompe de chasse*. Such a sound can only be obtained in *forte* above, and it becomes a problem to decide, for example, what Debussy intends near the end of *L'Après-Midi d'un Faune* when he marks a single *piano* note *cuivré* and the first few notes of the next phrase (still *piano*) *sons bouchés*. Presumably what he requires, since the note is accented, is a slight momentary edge on the sound, and it is possible that he had in mind the narrow-bore French horn whose *cuivré* tone can be obtained at a lower dynamic level than with a wide-bore instrument. With the modern horn the necessary edge can only be imparted by playing the note stopped and *fp*.

4. Terms used to indicate that a stopped brassy tone is required:
Any of the terms having the same meaning as stopped, together with the word *cuivré* or the dynamic markings *ff*, *sf* or >, and sometimes *mit Dämpfer und stark anblasen*. Here again Debussy sets a problem with a note marked *piano*, *bouchez et cuivrez*, in his *Rondes de Printemps*. Again it seems that it is the initial tang that is required.

For various reasons, some of which have already been mentioned, these indications cannot always be strictly adhered to, and in practice the player is guided by the following general principles:

(i) Hand stopping is effective down to about *g*; below this limit the sound is not really powerful enough to tell, even in *forte*,

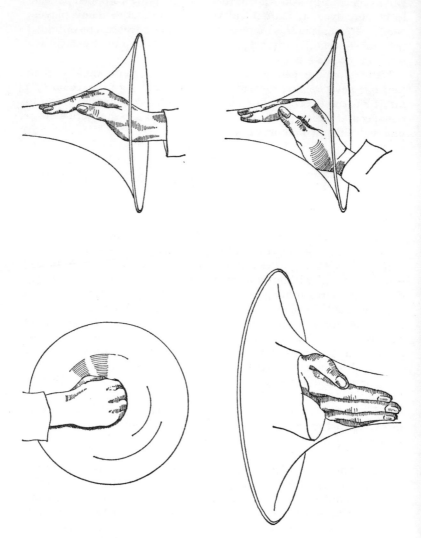

Fig. 7. Positions of the hand in the bell. Above: left, normal position from above; right, closed position from above. Below: left, closed position from behind; right, closed position from the side.

especially as composers often overload the accompaniment. More often than not a loud note in the lower register would be played open without any very great difference in effect, except that the note would come through better. The held *fortissimo* c♯ near the end of Tchaikovsky's *Pathétique* symphony — scored for second and fourth horns *chiuso* — is often actually played by all four with one or two stopped or muted and the others open, as a matter of balance decided by the conductor. In a chord or passage for four stopped horns, the fourth will provide a slightly firmer bass if he uses the transposing mute instead of the hand; a *pp* chord in Ravel's *Rapsodie Espagnole* is actually marked to be played in this manner. For a single *sfz* note b♭ is about the lowest practicable limit for stopping, and even here the mute gives a clearer sound.

(ii) The composer sometimes marks a muted passage without providing sufficient time for the insertion of the mute. Elgar is particularly inconsiderate in this respect. In these cases the hand must be used.

(iii) The hand offers more resistance than the mute and it is therefore safer to use it for a very soft exposed held note which can then be reduced to almost nothing.

(iv) Although the hand is less trouble to use than the mute, hand stopping involves transposition unless a stopping valve is available. In any case, the stopping valve is usually tuned to be in correct intonation for the unvalved notes, and will therefore tend to be flat when used with valved notes. The mute is thus a little more reliable for any complicated or rapidly moving stopped passage.

One further variation in tone colour may be mentioned. A few composers, of whom Mahler was most addicted to the practice, sometimes indicate that the bell of the instrument is to be raised (*Schalltrichter in die Höhe, Campana in aria*). It is not clear from the bare indication exactly how this is intended to be carried out: whether the hand is to be removed entirely from the bell when this is raised, or whether the right arm is to be lifted to shoulder level with the hand still in the bell. The former procedure would lead to a blaring uncontrolled tone, which is possibly what the composer requires, but without the hand in the bell intonation is likely to be impaired and time is rarely allowed for adjustment of the tuning slide to compensate for this. The indication is not popular with players. They are unconvinced that its employment makes much difference to the volume of sound, and they dislike having to alter round the embouchure and the feeling of unsteadiness which results.

In practice there is considerable variation in the method of carrying out this instruction. Some German players, accustomed to playing with the bell resting on the thigh, do little more than lift the instrument off it without altering the hand position. A possible compromise is to raise the bell to shoulder level while spreading the fingers across it so that the pitch remains unaltered but the sound can emerge more freely than with the hand in the normal position.

In his first symphony Mahler instructs his seven regular horn players, together with any others who may be available, to stand up in their places. The value of this device, which has occasionally been employed by other composers, probably lies more in its psychological effect on the audience than in its physical impact. In Mahler's symphony it is used at a climactic point in the last movement where as many horns as possible deliver the chorale theme in such force as to ring out triumphantly above the whole of the rest of the orchestra, and the listener's attention is particularly focused on this theme by the sight of a long row of horn players seeming to dominate the orchestra.

In addition to the special effects obtainable by the use of the hand, the very fact that the normal method of holding the horn involves the presence of the hand in the bell is bound to have some effect on the quality of tone. If the horn is played without the hand in the bell its tone is somewhat coarse and brassy, though this can be mitigated to some extent by holding the instrument so that its bell points towards the body of the player, and this method of playing appears to be employed by some players, though not of the first class, in America and in Central Europe. Placing the hand in the bell, however, has a refining effect on the tone, giving it a slightly veiled and quite characteristic colour unlike that of any other instrument. It was Hampel's search for a means of modifying the coarse tone of the open instrument that led to the new method of holding the horn which eventually became generally accepted as normal. The technique of the hand horn followed, involving subtle and sensitive manipulation of the hand in controlling tone and intonation. With the coming of the valve, this technique was gradually lost, though its acquisition is recommended by many modern writers as a very desirable addition to the horn player's technical equipment, which can be usefully employed in special circumstances. For example, in the slow movement of Beethoven's fourth symphony the first horn (in E♭) has a *pianissimo* entry on a high c'''. This can be taken as an open note on the B♭ horn, but as the eleventh harmonic it will be sharp. Discreet use of the hand will not only bring it into tune but make it easier to play softer, with no appreciable difference in the quality of sound. Apart from cases such as this there should be no need to use the hand for the control of intonation with the flexible wide-bore horn.

The position of the hand in the bell should be, generally speaking, such as to allow almost unimpeded passage of the sound between the palm of the hand and the inner side of the bell. If the sound is completely unobstructed, the tone, as already mentioned, is apt to be hard and coarse. If, on the contrary, the hand interposes too great an obstacle to the passage of the sound, not only is the pitch altered, but the tone becomes dull and uncharacteristic. The ideal to be aimed at, therefore, is a position somewhere between these two extremes, so that the asperities and edginess of the wholly open instrument are softened and rounded off and a slightly veiled quality is imparted, without carrying the process so far that the tone is at all muffled.

The exact position of the right hand can only be determined by trial and error; almost everything depends upon the size of the hand, the bore of the instrument, and the ideal of tone quality which is aimed at. The most common method adopted is for the hand to be kept open or slightly cupped, the fingers and thumb lying parallel to each other against the inside of the bell on its far side, away from the body, with the knuckle of the thumb roughly level with the bell-stay. Thus the bell is resting mainly on the thumb and there is an opening of about one and a half inches between the ball of the thumb and the near side of the bell, sufficient to allow free emission of the sound and yet to soften it without muffling it (Fig. 7). A slightly different method, described by Ceccarossi in *Il Corno*, advises that the thumb should lightly touch the first and second fingers, giving the hand the shape of a shell. This position, he claims, allows the production of a round, homogeneous tone, and permits intonation to be regulated by small movements of the wrist at pulse level, keeping the original position of the hand itself unchanged. Movement of the wrist away from the body slightly raises the pitch; movement in the opposite direction flattens it, until when the wrist is in contact with the near side of the bell the closed position is reached.

No rigid rule, however, can be laid down, for so much depends upon the individual idiosyncrasies of the player and his instrument. The most that can be said is that the position of the hand must be such that the closed position can be easily reached by a flexing movement of the wrist and knuckles, not of the whole hand, for stopping often has to be carried out very rapidly. Each player must experiment to find the position which suits him best, for hands are not of the same size or shape and different instruments respond differently.

THE INSTRUMENT

(vi) THE INFLUENCE OF THE PLAYER

The various physical factors affecting horn tone have been dealt with above. More important, however, in the last resort than any of these is the somewhat intangible and indefinite influence exerted on the tone by the player himself. It is not easy to say exactly what this influence is, for it is compounded of a large number of personal factors, both physical and mental. It is certainly true that a first-class instrument in the hands of a second-rate player is capable of producing a tone of poor quality, and conversely a skilful player will coax a good tone from a poor instrument. The skill of the expert player consists basically of perfect control — of embouchure, breath, hand and fingers — and the complete co-ordination of the various muscular activities which result in the production of tone. Physically, the conformation and flexibility of his lip muscles and his control of them are of the utmost importance. A further factor of physical significance is the shape of the oral cavity, and not enough is known of the effects of this factor on tone quality. A close study of the applied anatomical, physiological and clinical problems of the embouchure has been made by M. M. Porter,[1] who has published radiographs showing changes in the embouchure and oral cavity during the production of tone. G. Gorgerat[2] states that a high vaulted palate favours a more ample tone, while a flatter palate results in a thinner and less well-nourished quality, and produces evidence to support this view from players who have found it necessary to be fitted with certain types of dental appliance. They have noticed that this has led to a deterioration in their tone quality, presumably owing to the reduction in volume of the oral cavity, and the partial obstruction offered to the free passage of the air-stream through the mouth. In the same way, if the tongue, after the emission of the sound, is kept in a hunched retracted position towards the back of the mouth, a dull and uninteresting tone results, and the same effect of a partially strangled and under-nourished tone is detected if the throat muscles are not completely relaxed. The general principles underlying the production of a good singing tone apply equally well to the playing of the horn. The acoustic system producing tone consists not only of the lips coupled to the air column inside the tubing of the instrument, but also of the cavities of the mouth, throat and chest through which the air-stream passes, though the exact part they play in tone production is far from clear.

Apart from such physiological considerations, there is the player's mental attitude to be taken into account as a factor influencing

[1] *The Embouchure.*

[2] *Encyclopédie de la Musique pour Instruments à Vent.*

tonal quality. He should continually carry in his mind's ear the ideal of tone he wishes to attain to; 'his ear, mind and heart', said Anton Horner, 'are as much the instrument as the horn itself.' It is claimed by some writers that national differences of character, tradition and language are more to be held responsible for national differences in tone quality than are variations in the design of the instruments in use. The tone quality, they declare, is determined very largely by the player's attitude to life and to vocal and instrumental art generally, by physiological causes due to his methods of forming the sounds of his own language, and by psychical factors ingrained in the national outlook and temperament. The German produces his broad, massive tone not because of the type of instrument he uses, but because this is the sort of tone he wishes, perhaps sub-consciously, to produce; one might even say he is constitutionally pre-disposed to such a tone quality. The Italian will still emit his slightly oily quality on a German instrument, and the Frenchman, as already mentioned, his narrow-bore tone even when using a wide-bore horn. This is one of those points on which theory and fact diverge most widely. Doubtless it is easier to produce 'wide-bore' tone on a wide-bore instrument; but theory takes too little account of the man behind the instrument, and the influence he will inevitably exert on the tone quality. It is the quality he has grown up with and has known all his life which he believes to be true horn tone, and willy-nilly this is the quality he will produce. Hence most of the arguments[1] which frequently arise about 'real horn tone' lose their meaning, for they are based on the false premise that there is one, and only one, quality which is permissible. In fact, there are as many types of 'true horn tone' as there are players who are satisfied with the sounds they produce. Each has his own ideal, determined by factors already mentioned, and provided he attains this ideal then he is producing what is for him 'true horn tone'.

In a narrower way, an individual player's tone will depend upon personal factors within the national framework; his own particular predilections, habits and temperament, the type of musical company he keeps and the music he plays. The orchestral player, for example, becomes accustomed to the need to blend with strings and woodwind, and modifies his tone accordingly; he learns to listen to other instruments and to develop a style, including a type of tone quality, which conforms to that of the rest of the orchestra. The final result is due to a highly complex conglomeration of factors, physical and

[1] 'The various viewpoints on horn tone are held with a fierce devotion that one encounters otherwise only in religious controversies.' Schuller: *Horn Technique*, p. 14.

psychical, whose separate effects are impossible to disentangle.

A large part of the skill of the player lies in his ability to 'hit' each note in the very centre with absolute certainty. This process is impossible unless, as in singing, the performer has a mental image of the note to be sounded a fraction of a second before it is emitted. Muscular reflexes then bring into play the minute adjustments of the embouchure necessary to sound the particular note required. For this reason the nineteenth-century pedagogues insisted upon a course of *solfège* for all aspiring horn players. Poor tone and split or cracked notes are the inevitable result of incomplete mental realization of the note to be sounded with its consequent maladjustment of the muscles of the embouchure. Even if the correct harmonic is found, it may well be that the lips are not vibrating at the start with exactly the right frequency, so that the coupled acoustic system is not operating at maximum efficiency, with the result that the sonority of the sound is, at any rate momentarily, impaired. This principle applies, of course, to all lip reed instruments, but is of particular importance in connection with the horn, since the harmonics in the upper part of the compass are so close together.

Next, the air column must be kept steadily in vibration by a well-controlled air-stream, giving it a firm foundation devoid of any quavering or involuntary vibrato. Finally, some control of the tone may be necessary by the judicious use of the right hand.

The watchword, then, for the player of the horn is control, and this is only achieved if the whole body is in a state of relaxation. The muscles, whether of embouchure, tongue, abdomen or diaphragm, must be firm but not tense; any degree of tenseness has an immediate and inevitable effect on tone quality, which becomes pinched and thin. This state of relaxation is conditioned partly by the posture adopted, and partly by the player's mental approach. For the first, an erect position with a straight back is essential so that the chest and abdomen are capable of the required degree of expansion. The legs must not be crossed, for this impedes the action of the abdominal muscles. The instrument must not be held too close in to the body nor in the lap as the sound is then emitted directly towards the coat, giving it a muffled quality and diminishing its carrying power. It may, however, be held with the lower edge of the bell resting on the outside of the thigh; this is a widespread practice on the continent and in America, introduced owing to the greater weight of the modern instrument, and is beginning to be adopted here. Its advantages are that it relieves the arms of much of the weight, and gives a steadier position for quick right-hand work in stopping, since this hand is now hardly concerned with supporting the horn. Whatever posture is adopted, the ideal to be aimed at is a position in which the muscles are capable of performing the work they are called upon to undertake without being constricted in any way, while at the same time the whole body is in a natural and easy state of relaxation without being limp or flaccid.

Such a state of relaxation is most easily attained if the player has complete confidence in himself. Nervousness often leads to loss of control of the muscles; the embouchure, particularly, is subject to an involuntary quivering which leads inevitably to unsympathetic and badly controlled tone. On the other hand, some degree of nervous excitement, mental rather than physical — a sort of emotional tension unaccompanied by muscular tension — is essential if the playing is not to lack warmth and to become dull and lifeless.

It should be obvious that the state of physical health of the player will have a considerable bearing on the quality of tone he produces, and insufficient allowance is made for this fact by those who do not themselves play wind instruments. Wind players are frequently conscious that their tone quality does not always reach the standard they would wish, nor match the ideal they carry in their mind's ear; it varies, though perhaps only slightly, from day to day, and the reason is impossible to pin down with any certainty. The smallest maladjustment of his mental and physical reflexes, due to any one of a number of factors, internal or external, physical or mental, may affect for the worse his tone and intonation.

Finally, the acoustics of the room in which he plays make a great difference to a player's quality of tone. Every man imagines himself to be a potential *Heldentenor* or *basso profondo* in the privacy of his bathroom, because the hard reflecting surfaces secure a longer time of reverberation, providing a sense of ease and power in the production of tone. The same is true of playing a wind instrument, particularly of one which is played with the bell pointing, not towards the auditorium, but towards the back of the stage. If the surface here is absorbent, the tone seems to be dull, and the effort required to produce even this under-nourished tone is disproportionately great. All players will readily have noted the deleterious effect on their tone of an acoustically dead concert-room, and the converse effect in a reverberant one.

A point to be borne in mind, however, is that very often the player cannot tell exactly how he sounds to the listener in the body of the concert-room, for much depends upon his exact position on the platform, the presence and proximity of baffle boards, and so on. What sounds satisfactory to the player may well sound thin from a distance, and conversely tone which sounds coarse from close to may reach the listener farther away as a pleasantly full and rounded sound.

E   G.T.H.

CHAPTER 4

Acoustical:
The Valve System

U ntil the invention of the valve in the early nineteenth century the horn consisted of a fixed length of tubing, and this length determined the particular fundamental whose harmonic series could be obtained as a playable set of notes. The technique of stopping helped to fill in some of the gaps in this series, particularly in its upper reaches, though rendering the expanded series somewhat heterogeneous in tone quality. The only method of obtaining a different harmonic series was to insert a crook at some point in the main tubing. By this means the horn could, to some extent, follow modulations in the music or, at any rate, suit itself to the keys of different movements. The disadvantages of the system were (i) that it involved the insertion of a considerable length of cold tubing into an instrument that was already warm, causing difficulties of intonation, and (ii) that this insertion could not be made instantaneously. The handicaps under which the player laboured are obvious, and the composer was forced to cut his coat according to his cloth or else involve his players in difficulties which might well lead to disaster.

With the coming of the valve these difficulties were largely swept away, for the introduction of a three-valved horn enabled the player to produce a complete chromatic scale over the whole compass of the instrument without having recourse to stopping. The valve system, however, is by no means acoustically perfect, for it embodies (i) the introduction of lengths of cylindrical tubing into an otherwise exponential tube, though the tuning slide already fitted was of necessity cylindrical also, and (ii) sharper bends in the tubing than are necessary in the natural horn. Both of these modifications led to changes in the character of the tone whose magnitude was the subject of considerable controversy at the time, but which were probably exaggerated by those diehards who regarded the

66

valve as an invention of the devil. In addition, the valve system is imperfect for another reason. In the standard three-valved instrument the valves extend the tubing in such a way as to lower the fundamental, and hence its attendant harmonic series, by a tone, a semitone, and a tone and a half respectively. When the finger plate or valve button is depressed the requisite length of tubing is automatically thrown in. To lower the fundamental of a given length of tubing by a semitone an additional length is required which is a fixed fraction of the original length. If the main tube has already been lengthened by depressing one of the other two valves, the semitone valve tube will no longer be that specified fraction of the length of the elongated tube, but a little less, and the resulting series will be too sharp. This deficiency in length will inevitably be

TABLE I. *Errors of intonation due to valves:
unmodified third valve.*

Valves in use	Fundamental (Actual sound)	Length of tubing added (inches)	Length of tubing required (inches)	Error (inches)	Error of intonation	
					c.p.s.	Semitones
2	E′	9·16	9·16	—	—	—
1	E′♭	18·87	18·87	—	—	—
3	D′	29·14	29·14	—	—	—
1 +2	D′	28·03	29·14	−1·11	+0·22	0·11♯
2 +3	C′♯	38·30	40·02	−1·72	+0·30	0·15♯
1 +3	C′	48·01	51·54	−3·53	+0·58	0·30♯
1 +2 +3	B″	57·17	63·78	−6·61	+0·97	0·52♯

evident whenever any two valves are used in combination, reaching its maximum when all three are in use, and being least for the combination 1 + 2.

The figures in Table I, calculated for the F horn, illustrate this point. The values have been calculated for intervals of equal temperament, and show that the instrument will give correct intonation only on the open (unvalved) notes and those obtained by using the valves singly. The combination 1 + 2, giving a series of notes a tenth of a semitone sharp, need not be used as the third valve alone will give the same series correctly in tune, but all other combinations give series which are from about a sixth to one half of a semitone sharp. Fortunately these combinations need not be frequently used; the fingering 1 + 2 + 3 is required only for the written notes F♯ and c♯, and 1 + 3 only for G and d, though the combination 2 + 3 is the sole means available for obtaining A♭, e♭, a♭ and a′♭.

It is possible to use a system in which extra knuckles of tubing are automatically introduced into the valve tubing whenever the third valve is used in combination with the other two, singly or together; then all the notes except those obtainable only with all three valves would be properly in tune, and the error in these two exceptions would be only one tenth of a semitone. Such an arrangement, however, adds considerably to the complication and expense of manufacture, and is not normally employed except on four-valve instruments such as the tuba, where it is practically essential. There is, nevertheless, a means of mitigating the errors inherent in the valve system by making the third valve tube rather longer than its correct acoustical length, so that when it is used in combination with either of the others the total length of the tubing more

TABLE II. *Errors of intonation due to valves:*
modified third valve.

Valves in use	Funda-mental (Actual sound)	Length of tubing added (inches)	Length of tubing required (inches)	Error (inches)	Error of intonation	
					c.p.s.	semi-tones
2	E′	9·16	9·16	—	—	—
1	E′♭	18·87	18·87	—	—	—
3	D′	31·14	29·14	+2·0	−0·40	0·19♭
1+2	D′	28·03	29·14	−1·11	+0·22	0·11♯
2+3	C′♯	40·30	40·02	+0·28	−0·06	0·03♭
1+3	C′	50·01	51·54	−1·53	+0·25	0·13♯
1+2+3	B″	59·17	63·78	−4·61	+0·67	0·37♯

nearly reaches its correct value. This compromise reduces the errors of intonation, but spreads them more widely, as may be seen from the figures in Table II, which have been calculated on the basis of increasing the length of the third valve tube in the previous table by an arbitrary figure of two inches.

Thus with the third valve slide modified as suggested, all notes played on the open tube, or with the first or second valve alone, will be correctly in tune. The first and second valves in combination will give notes one tenth of a semitone sharp; on the third valve alone the same notes will be one fifth of a semitone sharp, and on an instrument modified in this way it is therefore usual to use the first and second valves together rather than the third alone, and correct the intonation if necessary by 'lipping'. The third valve is better not used by itself, at any rate for sustained notes. On the other hand, all notes played on the second and third valves together are now very nearly in tune; the combination 1+3 gives notes capable of correction by the player, but the combination $1+2+3$ gives a series which is still about a third of a semitone sharp. As already explained, this defect is not of great consequence, for it affects only two notes which occur comparatively rarely.

It can be seen from the table of fingering (Table III) that in the unmodified instrument there are eight notes out of the forty-three in the compass of the horn which are affected by the inherent deficiencies of the valve system; all are sharp in degrees ranging up to half a semitone. In the modified type fourteen notes are to some extent out of tune, but of these five have a negligible error, and of the remaining nine, only two are subject to an error of more than about one tenth of a semitone. It should be noted that the player, by calculation or by empirical methods, can alter the length of his third valve slide to suit his own style of playing and his own instrument, and that the figure of two inches increase used in the above calculations is a purely arbitrary one used solely for illustration. Generally speaking the combination of first and second valves is satisfactory even on the less flexible narrow-bore horn, and should present no difficulty at all with the wide-bore instrument. Hence, in tuning the valves of a single F horn, the player would probably proceed as follows: the instrument is first tuned on the open notes to the pitch required, using the main tuning slide. The open c'' is now sounded, and then in succession the first valve, and the combination of second and third, are tuned to the same note. It will then be found that a note played with the third valve alone (e.g. a') is slightly flatter than the same note played with the first and second valves together. By this means the third valve has been tuned exactly for the combination $2+3$.

An alternative method is as follows: (i) Tune the horn on the open notes with the main tuning slide as before. (ii) Tune the first valve slide exactly for whole tone flattening, and the second for semitone flattening. Mark the positions of each — the settings giving correct intonation for the valves used singly. (iii) The combination $1+2$ will now be slightly sharp. Tune to get this combination in correct intonation, lengthening the first and second valve slides as nearly as possible in the ratio $2:1$. Valves 1 and 2 used singly will now each be slightly flat. (iv) Set the first and second valve slides halfway between these two extremes, giving a compromise in which the valves used singly are very slightly flat, and together very slightly sharp. The minute errors now involved can be corrected without difficulty by 'lipping'. (v) Tune the third valve slide, which it will never be necessary to use alone, for the few notes in which it will be used in combination; that is, $a\flat$ and $a'\flat$ $(2+3)$, and d and G $(1+3)$.

TABLE III. *Chart of fingering and inherent errors in intonation, horn in* F.

Harmonic number	VALVE COMBINATIONS							Temperament Error in Semitones
	Open	2	1	1 & 2	2 & 3	1 & 3	1 & 2 & 3	
16								—
15								0·12♭
14 } 13 }	Not used							
12								0·02♯
11	Not used							
10								0·14♭
9								0·04♯
8								—
7	Not used							
6								0·02♯
5								0·14♭
4								—
3								0·02♯
2								—
1	Practically unobtainable							

	Errors due to valve combinations (semitones)							
unmodified 3rd. valve	—	—	—	(valve 3)	0·15♯	0·30♯	0·52♯	
modified 3rd. valve	—	—	—	0·11♯ (valves 1&2)	0·03♭	0·13♯	0·37♯	

ACOUSTICAL: THE VALVE SYSTEM

A further problem of tuning, the concern of the manufacturer rather than the player, arises in connection with the double horn in F and B♭. The operation of a thumb valve on this instrument automatically cuts out over three feet of the main tubing and thus converts it into a nine-foot horn in B♭. The lengths of tubing necessary to lower the pitch of the B♭ horn by a tone, a semitone, and a tone and a half are not the same as those required to perform the same operations on a horn in F, being only 14·18, 6·88 and 21·83 inches respectively. Some arrangement must therefore be made to replace the lengths of tubing added by the valves in the longer horn by the shorter lengths necessary when the thumb valve is in use. The mechanism usually employed provides a duplicate set of valve tubes of the correct length which are automatically brought into play whenever the thumb valve is depressed. The addition of a second set of tubes adds, of course, both to the weight of the instrument and to the complications of its manufacture. A slightly different expedient sometimes used is to provide valve tubes for the B♭ section which are lengthened by the correct amount when the F section is used, instead of using completely separate slides, an arrangement found on the so-called compensating double horn.[1] Any double horn is, of course, subject to the same errors of intonation as the single, and the same compromise of increasing the length of the third valve tube can be effected on the B♭ section.

A further source of errors in intonation inherent in the instrument derives from the fact that the horn utilizes partials of a higher degree than the fundamental for the production of practically all the notes within its compass. For any given fundamental these partials form a series most members of which are in just intonation, whereas the horn is normally required to give equal temperament intervals. Of the partials up to the sixteenth, the highest normally used on the horn, the second, fourth, eighth and sixteenth are theoretically in correct intonation. The seventh, eleventh, thirteenth and fourteenth are not often used on the valve horn, though on the natural horn the technique of stopping rendered them too valuable to be rejected. Of the remainder the fundamental is unobtainable for all practical purposes on the F horn, leaving seven partials subject to some error in relation to the scale of equal temperament. The fingering chart (Table III) shows all the errors of intonation to which the horn in F is subject. Semibreves indicate fingerings normally used; black notes are alternatives which may be used in particular cases where their employment might simplify

[1] The main advantage of this type of double horn is its reduced weight compared with that of the full double horn.

71

the execution of a passage. On an instrument with a third valve tuned for the combination 2 + 3 the first and second valves would be used together in preference to the third alone.

Certain other factors, which are briefly discussed below, also affect intonation. Strict accuracy would demand that whenever the position of the main tuning slide is altered, the valve slides should be adjusted. In practice, however, this is hardly necessary, for if the tuning slide is drawn by the comparatively large distance of one inch, thus adding two inches to the length of the main tubing, the required increase in the length even of the longest of the valve tubes would be a small fraction of an inch. If, however, the crook is changed, say from F to E♭, approximately eighteen inches of extra tubing have been added, and the adjustment of the valve slides is no longer negligible. For this reason the slide positions are often marked on F horns equipped with E♭ slides or crooks. When using the fourth, A, valve on the B♮ horn it is not necessary to adjust the slides in normal orchestral work, but for a long solo passage, such as the 'Quoniam' from Bach's B minor Mass, played on the A horn, slight lengthening of the slides would give better results.

The effect of temperature on pitch needs to be borne in mind. Any wind instrument will play flatter when cold than when warmed up by the player's breath. A rise in temperature of 5° C (9° F) causes a rise of pitch of about 1 per cent, or rather less than a twelfth of a tone. This alteration in pitch as the instrument warms up is by no means negligible, for a change of temperature of 20° F until the instrument reaches a more or less constant temperature is within the bounds of possibility. The temperature suggested by the British Standards Institution as suitable for fixing a standard of pitch is 68° F and most instruments made in this country are constructed so as to be in correct intonation at this temperature.

A factor whose effect on intonation should not arise in an instrument which is properly cared for may, however, be mentioned in passing. Any constriction in the tube, altering its shape from the acoustical design, will change the pitch of the note emitted, though only slightly unless the dent is a deep one. Its effect will be to put notes out of tune with one another, for the constriction, though fixed in position in relation to the tube, will occupy a varying position in relation to the vibrating segments according to the harmonic being sounded. If it lies near the centre of one of these segments, the pitch will be lowered; if it is near a node, the pitch will be raised. Damage to an instrument caused by careless handling will do more than spoil its appearance; it will also spoil its intonation.

However good the design of an instrument and however accurate its manufacture, in the last resort perfect intonation is to a large extent in the hand of the player. A well-designed and carefully made horn will make it easier for the player to secure correct intonation, but all this will be of little avail unless he has an ear capable of distinguishing between accurate and inaccurate intonation, and the ability to correct small imperfections by positive action on his own part. Too often it is assumed that all the player of a wind instrument has to do is to press the right keys or valves and an accurately tuned note automatically follows. This is very far from being the case, but with the horn two methods are open to the player of correcting his intonation. One, the manipulation of the right hand in the bell, has already been described, but is rarely necessary on the wide-bore instrument. The other, possible only when a small correction is required, since it will otherwise have an adverse effect on the tone quality, is to force the air column, by slight contraction or relaxation of the lip muscles, to vibrate at a frequency slightly different from that determined by its dimensions. Such a process, known as 'lipping', is employed by expert players to bring into correct intonation those notes in the instrument which are inherently slightly out of tune, and the adjustment eventually becomes automatic. Inadvertent lipping where it is not required is more than likely in the case of the inexpert player with a faulty embouchure and inadequate muscular control.[1]

Finally, it appears to be a fact verified by experiment that players of wind instruments in which small modifications of intonation are possible do not actually keep to any one of the standard scientific systems of intervals, any more than players of stringed instruments do. Though in theory the pitch of any particular note is absolute, in practice this is not so, for much depends upon its context. Playing in tune, then, is not so much a question of adhering to a fixed system as of careful adjustment to the sounds of other instruments. In the last resort, what sounds right is of greater importance than the exact frequency of the note sounded.

Generally speaking, a given note, particularly in the upper register, is produced with greater ease when taken as a lower harmonic from a higher fundamental rather than as a higher harmonic from a lower fundamental. In consequence, the best fingerings, when a choice is available, are those in which the open tube or single valves

---

[1] A recent book puts these points somewhat infelicitously as follows: 'It is possible to force the natural resonance a little one way or the other by the lips, and the pitch range can be slightly altered by the insertion in the mouth of a large pear-shaped mute, or even the hand.'

are used, for these will employ the higher fundamentals. Owing to the general rise in tessitura of modern horn parts and the more frequent use of notes above the staff some players have adopted the horn in B♭ in place of the lower pitched F horn, thus making use of these higher fundamentals. On this instrument the high c''', for example, sounding f'', is taken as the twelfth harmonic from a fundamental $B'♭$ instead of as the sixteenth from a fundamental F'. A minor disadvantage of the higher-pitched instrument is that the lowest fourth of the compass of the F horn is not, of course, available; more important, perhaps, is the fact that, except in expert hands, the shorter instrument tends to lack something of the characteristic colour of the other, particularly in the middle and lower parts of the range. The double horn in F and B♭ makes the best of both worlds, providing the richness of timbre of the F horn in its best register with the ease of production and, it is claimed by some, a better tone in the high register, which are the most valuable properties of the B♭ horn.

No hard and fast rule can be laid down for deciding when to switch from the F to the B♭ side of the double horn, though normally passages in the high register will obviously be easier to perform on the shorter tube, and for certain lower notes, from f down to $c♯$, which speak readily, the ease of emission will be of great value. A rough guide to general practice is: (i) from $F♯$ to c the F side is used; (ii) from $c♯$ to f, the B♭ side for single notes or slow-moving parts, otherwise played on the F horn; (iii) from $f♯$ to g', almost always on the F section; (iv) from $g'♯$ to c'', on the F side if passing through this range from below, but with the same fingering on the B♭ side if entering it from above, where (v) the B♭ section is almost exclusively used. Employing this method it is rarely necessary to utilize higher harmonics than the twelfth, giving c''', on the B♭ side, and the eighth, giving c'', on the F side. The double horn is nearly always of the wide-bore type, enabling the instrument to hold its own more easily in a modern tutti besides making it perhaps less fatiguing to play.

A fingering chart for the B♭ horn is given in Table IV. The fingering on the B♭ section of the double horn will be identical except that the valve combination at the head of each column will include the thumb valve which switches the horn into B♭.

Certain problems of intonation arise with the wide-bore B♭ instrument, whose solution depends to a large extent upon the individual player. R. Morley-Pegge has pointed out that 'the shorter the crook the more marked is the tendency for the fifth, eighth and tenth harmonics to be flat: this tendency is especially noticeable in the case of the large-bore German type of horn'. A

74

TABLE IV. *Chart of fingering, horn in B♭ and B♮ side of double horn.*
(Notes as written for horn in F)

		VALVE	COMBINATIONS				
HORN in B♭	OPEN	2	1	1+2	2+3	1+3	1+2+3
DOUBLE HORN B♭ Side	THUMB	THUMB +2	THUMB +1	THUMB +1+2	THUMB +2+3	THUMB +1+3	THUMB +1+2+3

HARMONIC NUMBER: 12, 11, 10, 9, 8, 7, 6, 5, 4, 3, 2, 1

NOT USED (at harmonic 11)

NOT USED (at harmonic 7)

PEDAL NOTES : lowest rarely needed.

75

scientific explanation is not easy to find. In the case of the fifth and tenth harmonics the temperament error is towards flatness, though it is not clear why it should become more obvious in the shorter wider instrument, but the eighth is theoretically exactly three octaves above the fundamental. Whatever the explanation, most players find that an open a' (fifth harmonic) is not satisfactory, while $a'\flat$ (second valve) and g' (first valve) are also flat. The a' and $a'\flat$ can be played as sixth harmonics (first and second, and second and third valves respectively), but the alternative g' (first and third valves) will then tend to be sharp if the third valve is tuned for the combination of second and third. Hence for this note the player must choose between two alternatives, neither of which is completely satisfactory. If a fourth valve is available, the note could be played as a sixth harmonic on the A horn — thumb, second and third valves. On the double horn the problem does not really arise since the g' can be played as an open note on the F section, and the combination of first and third valves is nowhere necessary except for the easily manageable low G played on the F horn. Hence the valves can be tuned for the combination of second and third.

In tuning the valves of a B♭ horn the player will therefore be guided by his fingering habits. He can tune as for the F horn — i.e. with the third valve tuned for the combination of second and third, when the g' will be sharp, or for the combination of first and third to get this note in tune, when notes played with the second and third together will be flat. In the latter case a possibility would be to use the fourth valve (tuned accordingly) together with the first and second instead of second and third, though this would probably prove somewhat clumsy in rapid passages.

In the upper octave the a'' and $a''\flat$ can be taken as twelfth harmonics with the same fingering as in the lower, or as more easily blown tenth harmonics (open and second valve respectively) when they will probably tend to be flat, though this depends largely upon the instrument and the player.

In tuning the full double horn the sections can be tuned separately as each side normally has its own tuning slide. Thus the procedure would be as follows: (i) Tune the F side to concert pitch on open notes — say e'', c'' and g'. (ii) Tune the B♭ side to the F side by playing the open notes c'' and g'' on both sections, adjusting the B♭ tuning slide as necessary. (iii) Tune the valves according to the fingerings favoured for each side, as already described for the single F and B♭ horns. This will probably be for the combination $2 + 3$ on the F side, and for $2 + 3$ or $1 + 3$ on the B♭ side; or (iii) adopt the compromise tuning for the valves halfway between the 'long' and 'short' settings on both sides.

Some players prefer to tune the Bb side fractionally higher than the F, since the Bb horn is used largely in the upper register and the tendency here, especially with a tiring embouchure, is to play flat. Generally speaking, it is easier to lip a note down than up; the effort to lip up often results in thin tone, whereas a more relaxed embouchure is more likely to give the fuller tone required.

In many double horns built on the compensating principle no provision is made for a tuning slide on the Bb side, since the whole of the Bb tubing is incorporated in the F section, and in some of them it is not possible to tune the second valve on the Bb side, though this is a matter of only minor importance. In these instruments the Bb side must first be tuned by means of the main tuning slide, and the F section can then be tuned to the Bb. In the Kruspe instrument and some others, however, there is a small section of tubing on the Bb side which is cut out when the F section is in operation and thereby provides a separate Bb tuning slide (Fig. 16). In theory the first scheme should be adequate, but players usually have a preference for the second. This type of compensating horn is tuned in the same way as the full double horn.

In practice the player of the double horn treats it as an instrument providing more numerous alternative fingerings than the single F or Bb horn. Playing, as will usually be the case, from parts for horn in F, and using the Bb section in the manner already described, he does not transpose the part down a fourth and then utilize fingerings as for the single Bb horn, but instead makes use of the fingerings given in the chart as alternatives for the normal F horn fingerings. Thus the notes

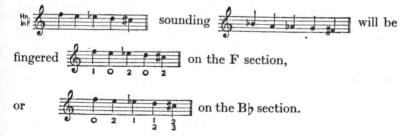

sounding ... will be fingered ... on the F section, or ... on the Bb section.

THE ASCENDING VALVE

The valve system as applied to brass instruments usually involves the addition of subsidiary lengths of tubing to the main tube; that is, the valves are 'descending'. In one system which has found favour, particularly in France, the third valve is of the 'ascending' type. The main tubing of this instrument is in G, but the third valve is so arranged that its tube forms part of the main tube when the valve is not in use, thus putting the horn into F. When this valve is in operation its tube no longer forms part of the main tube, and the horn is then in G. The second valve is of the usual descending type, so that in combination with the third it raises the pitch by a semitone to G♭. The tone valve is also descending, and with the third gives the same effect as the open tube, cancelling the rise of a tone given by the ascending valve. This arrangement has certain advantages in the higher register and in remote keys, and is often used by first and third players in France. It involves the inevitable absence of the notes F♯, G, A♭, and e♭ (written) from its compass as compared with the normal F horn. This, however, is comparatively unimportant, and the advantages in the upper register outweigh these minor defects. Chief among these advantages is the ability to take the notes f″♯ and f″, twelfth harmonics on the descending F horn, as tenth harmonics, and a″, a″♭ as twelfth harmonics instead of fifteenth. In Table V the normal fingerings are represented by semibreves, and the black notes are alternatives, but in many cases these are equally good, and in certain circumstances depending on the key of the piece may even be easier.

OTHER SYSTEMS

Horns utilizing various other valve arrangements, usually in addition to the normal three valves, are in current production, and some of these are listed below.

1. *Single horn in F.* This may be supplied with a detachable F crook, in which case an E♭ or an E crook, or both, are often available. If the instrument has a fixed mouthpiece an E♭ slide or a D slide is sometimes provided, and in both cases the valve slides are marked for E♭ or D positions, since they will need pulling out when the longer crook is used. Sometimes a quick-change key is fitted, as on many trumpets, so that the switch from F to E♭ may be made without removal of crook or slide, though the main valve slides must still be adjusted. Alternatively a fourth valve operated by the thumb puts the instrument into E or sometimes into E♭; that is, it operates as an additional semitone or tone valve. If this extra valve is a semitone one it is used especially for stopped passages, enabling them to be played without transposition.

Like the Zuleger oboe, the Viennese horn still used by some Austrian players has several unique features. Its bore, unusually wide at the mouthpiece end, but expanding appreciably only after leaving the valve system, has already been mentioned. Normally the instrument is pitched in F, with a detachable crook, and it is

TABLE V. *Chart of fingering, horn in* F *with ascending third valve.*

HARMONIC NUMBER	VALVE COMBINATIONS					
	3	2 + 3	OPEN or 1+3	2	1	1 +2
15						
14) 13)	NOT USED					
12						
11	NOT USED					
10						
9						
8						
7	NOT USED					
6						
5						
4						
3						
2						
1	NOT USED					

fitted with Vienna valves based on the old principle of the double piston (see Chap. 5). Occasionally it is converted into a B♭ horn (e.g. for high parts in some Haydn symphonies) or into an A horn (e.g. for the first and last movements of Beethoven's seventh symphony) by substituting for the F crook either a short tuning bit (for B♭) or the short A crook, and changing the valve slides. The tone of these high-pitched horns is not considered to be so broad or expressive and the F crook is used for all modern works. The Viennese horn is still made by a few firms, but only to special order.

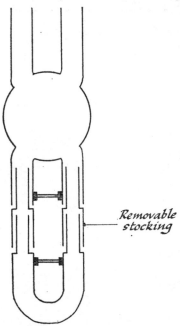

Removable stocking

Fig. 8. A-valve with stockings, giving flattening of ⅛ tone, shown in the ¾ tone position for stopping.

2. *Single horn in B♭*. This instrument is almost invariably fitted with a fourth valve, operated by the thumb, to serve one or more of the following purposes.

(*a*) It may be a straightforward semitone valve, giving a horn in A. If this is used for long solo passages, the other valve slides will need to be slightly pulled.

(*b*) It will usually be provided with a slide so that it can be extended to lower by ¾ tone and thus function as a stopping valve. The two functions can be combined by fitting a rotary key change from semitone to ¾ tone flattening, or the valve tubes can be

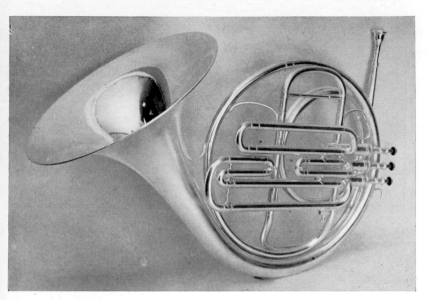

I. Single horn in F, with crook, piston valves, *Boosey & Hawkes*
(*Photograph by courtesy of Boosey & Hawkes Ltd.*)

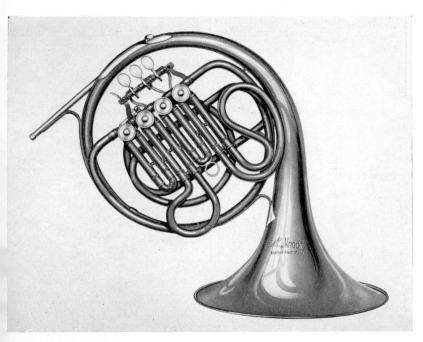

II. Single horn in F and E, fixed mouthpipe, rotary valves, *Knopf* (Model 10)

(*a*) without crook

(*b*) with B♮ bit

(*c*) crooks and valve tubes:
above, A crook, B♭ bit, B♭ valve
tubes; *below*, F crook and valve
tubes

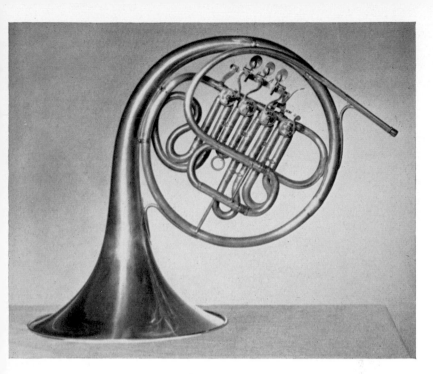

IV. Single horn in B♭, with stopping valve, *Börner*

V. Single horn in B♭ and A, *Alexander* (Model 90 II)

VI. Single horn in B♭ and A, *Kruspe*

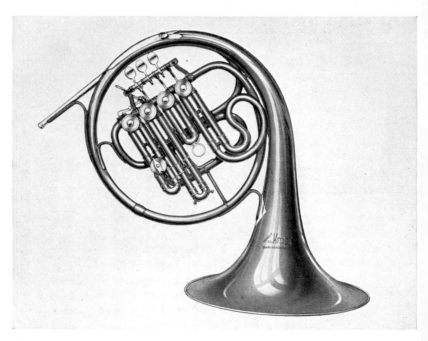

VII. Single horn in B♭, with combined A and stopping valve, *Knopf* (Model 6)

VIII. Single horn in B♭, with combined A and stopping valve and little finger extension to F, *Geyer*

(The player is Harold Meek of the Boston Symphony Orchestra)

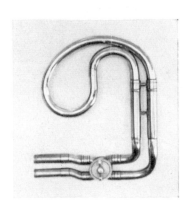

IX. Four valve single horn in Bb, Schöpf

above, left, fourth valve as A valve; *right,* with stockings, as stopping valve

XI. Full double horn in F and B♭, *Conn* (Model 8 D)

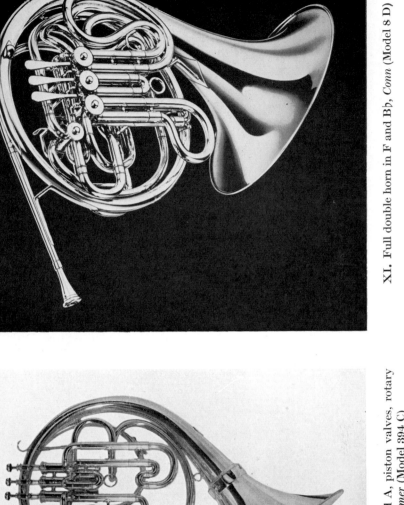

X. Single horn in B♭ and A, piston valves, rotary change to A, *Selmer* (Model 394 C)

XII. Full double horn in F and B♭, *Alexander* (Model 103)

XIII. Full double horn in B♭ and F, piston change to F, *Rampone & Cazzani*

XIV. Compensating horn in B♭ and F, *Rampone & Cazzani*

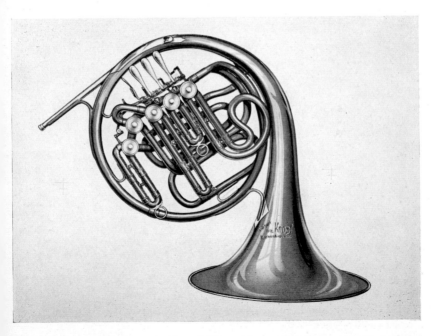

XV. Compensating horn in F and B♭, with combined E, A and stopping
valve, *Knopf* (Model 14)

XVI. Compensating horn in B♭ and F, with combined A, E and stopping valve, *Monke*

XVII. Compensating horn in F and B♭, with stopping valve, operated by second thumb lever, situated behind main valve system, *Kruspe*

XIX. Compensating horn in B♭ and F, piston valves, rotary change to F, ascending third valve, *Selmer* (Model 396)

XVIII. Full double horn in F and B♭, thumb change operating behind the valve system, *Knopf* (Model 16)

XX. Triple horn in F, B♭ and high F, with fully independent tuning. The instrument stands in B♭; one thumb lever gives the change to F basso and the other to F alto. Alternatively, it can be converted to stand in F basso, with one lever for B♭ and the other for F alto, *Paxman*

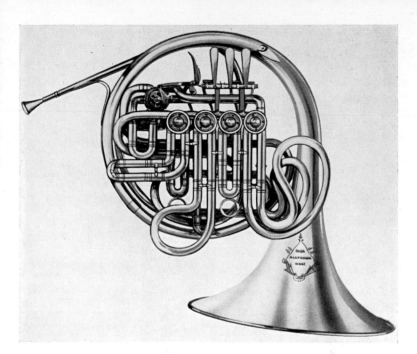

XXI. Full double horn in F and E, B♭ and A, change to E and A by second thumb lever, *Alexander* (Model 104 E)

XXII. Descant horn in high F, *Alexander* (Model 105)

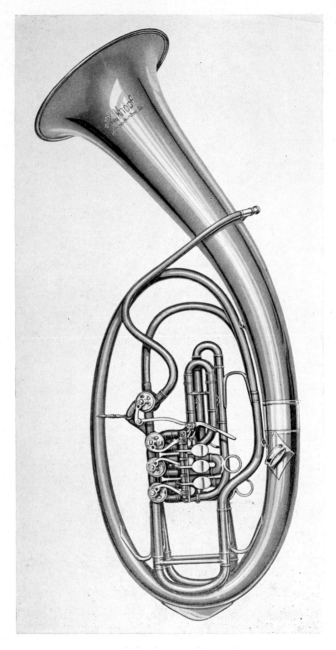

XXIII. Double Wagner tuba in B♭ and F, *Knopf*
(Model 22)

XXIV. Horn section of the B.B.C. Symphony Orchestra. Instruments: *Boosey & Hawkes.* The instrument of the first player is fitted with a rotary switch giving a quick change to A on the B♭ section
(*Photograph by courtesy of the B.B.C.*)

XXV. Horn section of the Berlin Philharmonic Orchestra. Instruments: three single B♭ and three double horns by *Alexander*
(*Photograph: Carl Ullman*)

XXVI. Horn section of the New York Philharmonic Orchestra. This photograph was taken in Moscow during a rehearsal of Stravinsky's *Le Sacre du Printemps*. The third, fourth and ninth players from the left are Russians; the American players, reading from the left, are using instruments by *Schmidt* (hidden), *Wunderlich*, *Kruspe*, *Conn*, *Conn*, and *Reynolds*, respectively
(*Photograph: Don Hunstein*)

XXVII. Horn and Wagner tuba section of the Vienna Philharmonic Orchestra
(*Photograph: Brigitte Freiberg*)

equipped with a set of stockings (Fig. 8). When these are pulled out to the maximum the valve lowers the pitch by $\frac{7}{8}$ tone. This gives a good g' as a fifth harmonic from the flat a' and also a good top a'' from the sharp eleventh harmonic. With the stockings pushed in the stopping position is reached, and with the stockings removed the valve gives a horn in A.

(c) A long extension may be fitted to give low notes not available on the Bb horn. This is usually made to lower the instrument by a fourth to F, but in conjunction with the other valves will of course give notes that are sharp. A common design for this extension is in the form of a double loop, but if it is this shape it must be pushed

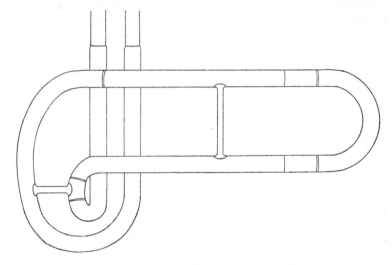

Fig. 9. Extension for low notes for use with fourth valve of Bb horn.

right home on account of its weight, and it cannot therefore be tuned. A better design (Fig. 9), due to Mr. Raymond Bryant, lowers the instrument by rather more than a fourth and thus gives a good Bb, the first note for which it is required, in conjunction with the first valve. The tuning slide of this extension pulls out by a maximum of about four and a half inches so that A, Ab and G are available with fingering as for the F horn. In another design the extension is folded back twice upon itself, and this type can also be tuned. Sansone makes a Bb instrument with an A thumb valve as well as a looped F extension operated by the little finger, while Alexander and others make a similar horn with a built-in extension worked either from a second thumb lever or by the little finger.

Alexander also makes a B♭ horn with three piston valves and a fourth, rotary, thumb valve for A. The piston valves, however, are positioned, not as in the ordinary piston instrument, but on the slant so that the fingers of the left hand, in operating them, move in what is perhaps a slightly more natural manner towards the palm of the hand. A French B♭ piston instrument is made with a rotary A valve and an ascending third valve.

3. *Double horn in F and B♭.* As already explained, this instrument is often built with a double set of valve slides which are quite independent of each other — the so-called 'full' double horn. In this case the slides of the F section usually lie above those of the B♭ section. The lower set, being the shorter, are not easy to remove without first removing the upper. There seems no obvious reason for this arrangement (except, possibly, to preserve the traditional look of the slides), and Sansone makes a double horn with the B♭ slides uppermost.

Some full double horns are fitted with a stopping valve, operated from a second thumb lever or more rarely by the little finger. If this has two slides, so that it operates on both sections, it makes an already heavy instrument weightier still. This question of weight is an urgent one, for the full double horn, fitted with such extra valves and probably made of heavier gauge brass, may be nearly twice the weight of the old single F horn. Any expedient, therefore, which can help to lighten it will make the player's task easier. For example, in *The Art of French Horn Playing* Farkas suggests that when playing high parts in which the B♭ side only will be used, the horn will respond more freely if all the valve slides on the F side, and even the third valve slide on the B♭ side, if not required, are removed.

The extra valve on a double horn may therefore be made to operate only on one section. If on the F side, it gives a horn in E and can also be used for stopping. If on the B♭ side, it gives a horn in A, or with the slide pulled, can be used for stopping on the B♭ side. Before the use of such a valve became comparatively common, stopping was always carried out on the F side, since it was impossible to correct for the ¾ tone rise in pitch on the B♭ horn by transposition, except by the somewhat dubious device of pulling the main tuning slide of the B♭ side (if such a slide was fitted) by about two inches.

An alternative arrangement places the fourth valve in that part of the tubing common to both sides — that is, shortly after the mouthpiece and before the tubing enters the valve effecting the change from F to B♭. It can then be used (i) as an A valve, or (ii) with a longer slide, as an E valve or stopping valve for use with the F horn, or as a stopping valve for the B♭ horn. Sometimes (Fig. 15) this extra length of slide is permanently incorporated and can be thrown in or out at will by a hand-operated quick-change key.

As with single horns, the double horn is occasionally made with an ascending third valve, and instruments of this type are still made in France. These often employ piston valves, which elsewhere are rarely used, though a few models use a piston for the change from F to B♭ even when the rotary mechanism is used for the remaining valves.

4. *Descant or piccolo horns.* A short-tubed instrument, built in high F, or in high G with an F crook, is sometimes used for high parts in works by Bach and Handel, and at least one leading German horn player uses a single four-valve horn in high F for all purposes. The instrument is by no means easy to play, either from the point of view of intonation or of tone production. Its advantages are, of course, that the harmonics are more widely spaced and that for normal parts it is not necessary to go higher than the eighth. It is said that if the instrument is properly designed it is capable of producing a sound indistinguishable from that obtained with the standard lower-pitched instruments. Acoustically this would appear to be improbable, but it has already been pointed out that in horn playing the human element seems to transcend acoustical theory.

Descant horns are also made as duplex instruments; for example, double horns in B♭ and high F, with or without a second thumb valve for A on the B♭ section, and in F and high F, are available, and horns in B♭ and D, and in B♭ and G, have also been tried out. A triple horn in F, B♭ and F alto has also made its appearance. An American maker advertises a piccolo horn in high B♭, an octave higher than the normal B♭ horn and at the same pitch as the B♭ trumpet. A special mouthpiece with a shallow cup is used. Even if acoustical theory is entirely disregarded, however, one's instinct is to deny that such an instrument can rightly be classed as a true horn.

Many other valve arrangements have been introduced from time to time, but few have found general favour. The Prager system, for example, employed six valves, five of which could be used as ascending independent valves. Acoustically this is the best system, for the valve slides can be accurately tuned without any compromise. The operation of the sixth, thumb, valve, changed the instrument to a descending, dependent one. Probably, however, these complex systems defeat their own ends, for the number of possible fingerings becomes very large without providing any overwhelming compensating advantage. This may appear to be a paradoxical statement, for at first sight it would seem that the greater the number of alternative fingerings the better. But it has been truly remarked that 'the chances of accuracy are much greater if one knows that with a certain fingering a certain note will result — as with most instruments — instead of being able to help oneself to half-a-dozen or so in the vicinity, with the same fingering'.[1] As it is, almost any note in the highest register can be obtained with almost any fingering on the F horn, and this fact increases rather than diminishes the difficulties encountered in playing the horn.

Some players have had instruments made with valve systems to their own specifications, but all without exception advise the beginner to start with the F horn, and to change to the B♭ instrument or to the double horn only when he has learnt the art of tone control so necessary in playing these shorter instruments.

[1] Dennis Brain: *The French Horn.*

CHAPTER 5

Mechanical:
The Valve Mechanism

T he object of any valve system is to enable an instantaneous extension of the main tubing of an instrument to be effected, so as to lower its pitch by specified intervals. The extra lengths of tubing required are attached to the main tubing at some point which varies according to the particular maker's design, and they are brought into circuit by valves which close the direct route and cause the sound waves to travel through the extra tubing instead. The only exception is to be found in the ascending valve described in Chapter 4, and in the shortening system employed in the double horn to cut out a length of the main tube and raise the fundamental from F to B♭.

Two types of valve mechanism were in common use — the piston and the rotary — but the rotary has gained considerable ground almost everywhere during the last twenty or thirty years, and may now be considered the standard type. Piston valves are still fitted to some French and English single horns; American and German instruments almost invariably employ the rotary type. The latter are always used on double horns, except in some French instruments, though the change from F to B♭ is occasionally made by a piston valve even when the remaining valves are of the rotary type. The change from one section to the other is nearly always effected by the thumb; the little finger is rarely used.

Before discussing the relative merits of the two types of valve mechanism it will be necessary to give some description of their mode of action. The piston valve, in its present form, is an improved version of the type invented by Périnet. The two ends of the valve tubing open into the cylindrical casing in which the piston moves, the one above the inlet and outlet of the main tube, and the other below. Thus there are four ports in the valve casing. The piston itself is bored with three airways. The top two serve to lead the air-stream from the main tube into the valve tube, and from this tube back into the main tube, and take effect only when the piston is depressed, not otherwise being opposite the openings of the valve tube into the casing. The lowest passage makes a direct connection between the inlet and outlet of the main tube, so that the sound

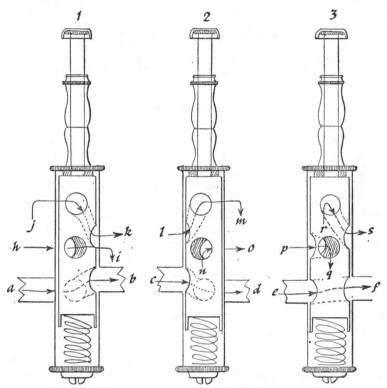

Fig. 10. Valve action: piston valves. a–f: *airway through pistons when none is depressed.* a–h–i–j–k–b: *airway through first piston when in use;* c–l–m–n–o–d: *through second piston;* e–p–q–r–s–f: *through third piston.* i, m, q *lead into their respective valve tubes;* j, n, r *lead from the valve tubes back into the pistons.*

waves pass straight through the piston without entering the valve tube, and this passage is in operation when the piston is up. This is illustrated in Fig. 10. The passages through the pistons are necessarily curved, and their positioning requires great exactitude. In addition, the aim of the designer is to make all curves as gentle and the bore as uniform as possible, so that there are none of the sharp

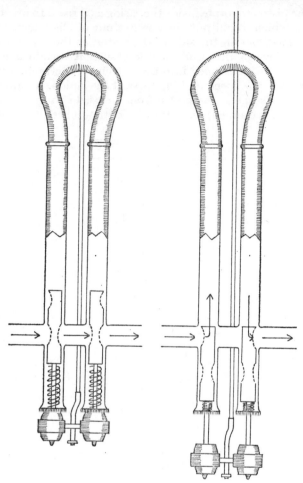

Fig. 11. Valve action: Vienna valve. Left: closed. Right: open.

turns and narrow passages which affected the quality of tone of the early valved instruments.

As soon as the pressure on the valve finger-top is released, a spring causes the piston to return to its original position. This is an open helical spring usually situated in the piston casing below the piston and resting on the lower·valve cap. Depressing the piston compresses the spring, and on releasing the pressure the spring expands and pushes the piston up. The spring has a tendency to

87

cause the piston to rotate inside the casing as it rises; to prevent this rotation, which would put the airways out of alignment with the ports, a small pin on the side of the piston at the top moves in a shallow groove in the inside of the casing. A certain amount of friction is thus introduced into the movement, detracting in some measure from the speed and lightness of the action. An alternative method is to suspend the piston from a closed spring; this type of springing, it is claimed, obviates the friction inherent in the other

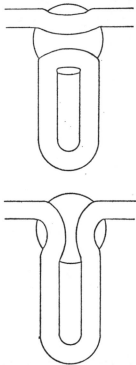

Fig. 12. Valve action: rotary valve. Above: closed. Below: open.

type, and provides a quicker and quieter action. It does not appear, however, to have been extensively applied to the horn. A cork buffer at the top of the piston and a felt washer below the finger-top serve to reduce noise and jarring as the piston moves to either end of its vertical traverse. Special lubricating oil may be used to render this movement more smooth, but most players seem to prefer the old-fashioned method of lubricating the piston lightly with saliva.

Another type of piston valve, the so-called Vienna valve, is still to be found fitted to instruments made in the city of its origin. Its principle is illustrated in Fig. 11. The valve is worked by a long lever operated from a finger-plate similar to that of a rotary valve. The greatest virtue claimed for this mechanism is the perfectly straight airway available on the unvalved notes, and the absence of any sharp curves or constrictions in the airways such as are found in other types of piston valve.

In the rotary or cylinder valve a more or less rectilinear movement of the finger-plate is converted, by means of a system of cranks or by a cord, into the circular motion of a rotor enclosed in a cylinder lying in the plane of the instrument. As with the piston valve, this casing receives four tubes, the inlet and outlet of the

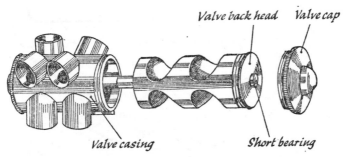

Fig. 13. Rotor and cylinder of the double horn.

main tubing and the two ends of the valve tube (Fig. 12). The four ports are equally spaced round the casing. The rotor itself has two curved airways, and when the valve is not in use one of these makes direct connection between the inlet and outlet tubes. When the finger-plate is depressed, the rotor moves through 90°, so that one of the airways connects the inlet tube with one end of the valve tube, while the second provides a path between the other end of the valve tube and the outlet tube.

In the double horn with its separate B♭ and F valve tubes each rotor has four airways, one pair for each valve tube (Fig. 13). The switch of the whole instrument from F to B♭ is usually carried out by a rotary valve whose cylinder has six equally spaced ports (Fig. 14, a–f). The air-stream must enter the valve at port a and leave by port d to enter the tubing common to both sections. The rotor has two airways, and if the F section of the horn is in use (thumb valve not depressed) these connect ports a and c, and f and d respectively. For the change to B♭ a is connected to e and b to d. The effect is therefore for the sound to travel through one of two completely separate lengths of tubing before returning to the rotary

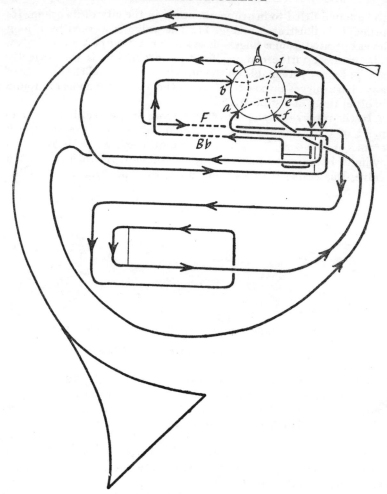

*Fig. 14. Windways of the full double horn. (Diagrammatic
only, valve system not shown.)*

change, according as the F or B♭ section is in use. The rotor of this
valve moves only through 60°, and is consequently very rapid in
action.

The compensating double horn may be one of two basic types. In
the first (Fig. 15) the two sets of valve tubes lie one on top of the
other, as in the double horn with independent slides just described.
The air passes from the mouthpiece (which in the model depicted is

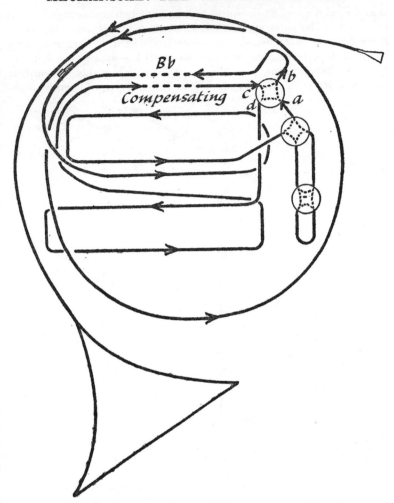

Fig. 15. Windways of the double horn, compensating type. (Diagrammatic only, valve system not shown.) This instrument has an A valve with quick change ¾ tone extension for stopping.

somewhat unusually but most usefully provided with a water-key) by way of an A valve to the rotary change which determines which section of the horn is to be used. This valve has two airways. When the first thumb lever is not depressed, ports *a* and *b* are connected and the air passes through the B♭ valve system to the main loop of tubing. If the first thumb lever is depressed, however, ports

91

a and *d*, and *c* and *b* are connected, so that before passing through
any part of the valve system the air must travel through the extra
three feet of tubing which put the instrument in F, thence by way
of the compensating valve tubes through the airway *c–b* back to
the B♭ valve system and the main loop. Thus this instrument
stands in B♭ with a rotary change to F. This type of horn is some-

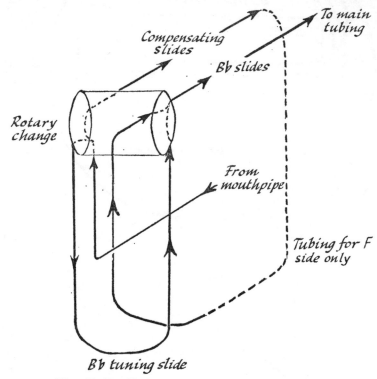

Fig. 16. Double horn, compensating arrangement.

times fitted with a simple device which, involving only the alteration of a single screw at the end of the lever action, enables the
player either to use the instrument as above, or as an F horn changing to B♭.

A slight variation in this basic design includes a short section on
the B♭ side which is cut out when the F section is in operation, thus
providing a separate B♭ tuning slide (Fig. 16).

In the second type of compensating instrument (Fig. 17) one long
horizontal rotor lying in the plane of the main coils is connected to
the ends of the B♭ valve tubes and is operated from the thumb

lever. This rotor has eight airways; the first two control the length of the main tubing in circuit, while the other three pairs do the same for the valve tubes. The action of the thumb valve is to cut out (or include, according as the basic key of the instrument is F or Bb) three feet of main tubing and simultaneously to shorten the valve tubes by the appropriate amount. In this type the air passes through the valve set once only, whereas in the first it returns to the valve system when the F section is in use. This principle, it is

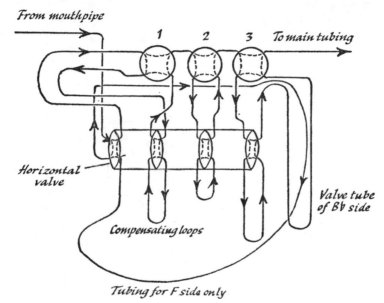

Fig. 17. Windways of the double horn, compensating type with horizontal valve.

claimed by the makers, gives freer blowing properties than are possible with the more conventional design. A minor disadvantage of this type of compensation is that the second (semitone) valve cannot be tuned on the Bb section.

A variant, now almost obsolete, substituted three separate rotary valves at the ends of the Bb valve tubes, in place of one long one. Altogether four separate rotors were actuated from the thumb lever. The effect was exactly the same as in the previous instrument, but the first is probably the more reliable mechanically, Both, however, involve rather heavy work for the thumb in comparison with the conventional compensating instrument.

In any rotary valve, the two ends of the cylinder are closed by screw-on caps. Inside each of these is a second cap, through which passes the end of the rotor spindle. This is actuated from the finger-plate by one of two types of mechanism — the so-called mechanical and string actions. In a common type of mechanical action (Fig. 18) the finger-plate is prolonged, in the plane of its motion, into an

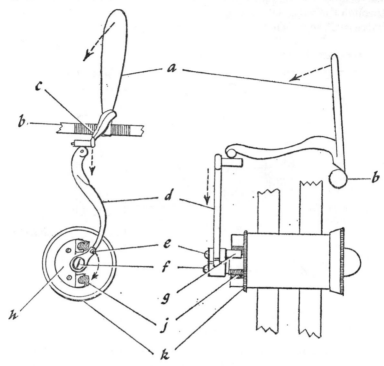

Fig. 18. Rotary valve: mechanical action. Left: view of action from underside of finger-plate. Right: view from side. a, finger-plate; b, finger-plate axle; c, finger-plate spring; d, crank; e, pivot; f, stop arm retaining screw; g, stop arm; h, 'horseshoe' plate; j, cork stop; k, valve front head.

arm which in turn is rigidly connected to a crank lying in a vertical plane, so that movement of the finger-plate is converted into motion in a plane parallel to the end of the rotor. The end of this crank is pivoted to one end of a stop arm whose other end is itself pivoted to the rotor spindle. The crank is sometimes connected to the stop arm through a ball-and-socket joint to which is attached a small threaded tube which receives a screw from the stop arm (Fig. 19).

By this means any play in the action which develops through constant use can be taken up. The end of the spindle lies between the arms of a horseshoe-shaped plate bearing two cork buffers whose function is to act as stops to a small projection on the underside of the stop arm. Theoretically the thickness of these buffers is a matter of some importance, for if either of them is too thin or too thick the airways of the rotor will not be in exact alignment with the ports in the cylinder. Correct alignment may be checked by noting

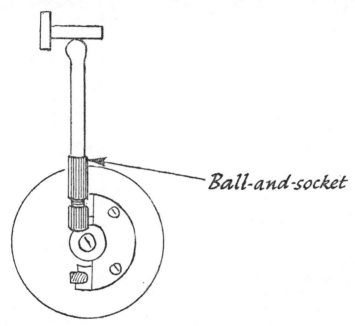

Ball-and-socket

Fig. 19. Rotary valve: ball-and-socket joint.

whether two notches in the rotor spindle coincide with corresponding notches in the cylinder, visible when the cap is removed. Adjustment is made either by compressing the corks or by replacing them with thicker ones. In practice, however, accurate alignment does not seem to matter as far as tone quality is concerned, and some players intentionally make their corks larger than is theoretically correct, with the aim of shortening the travel of the valve, thus making rapid fingering a fraction easier, and reducing the possibility of a valve sticking.

The finger-plate works on an axle and is fitted with a spring which returns it to its original position when the pressure on the plate is released.

In the string action valve (Fig. 20) a loop of gut or nylon fishing line, attached at its two ends to a vertical crank worked from the finger-plate, passes round the rotor spindle, being retained in position by a small screw at the end of the reciprocating driver. When the finger-plate is depressed, the rotor is pulled through 90° by the

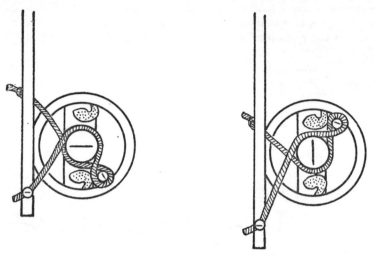

Fig. 20. Rotary valve: string action.

string, further movement, as before, being prevented by cork buffers.

In assessing the relative merits of the piston and rotary valves the following points need to be considered: rapidity, ease and quietness of the action, ease of maintenance and the frequency of examination and overhaul required. A comparison is made in Table VI. On balance the rotary type is the better mechanism; it is slightly more complicated than the piston, but it is mechanically sounder and its greater rapidity of action tells heavily in its favour.

TABLE VI. *Comparison of Piston and Rotary Valve Actions.*

	Piston	Rotary	
		Mechanical	String
Rapidity	Fair.	Good.	
Smoothness	Fair: some friction due to tendency of piston to rotate. Liable to stick but fault easily remedied.	Good: little friction.	
Quietness	Fair.	Becomes noisy with wear in moving parts.	Practically noiseless.
Reliability and robustness	Normally high. Piston subject to uneven wear, since few hands will take up a position in which the piston is pressed down quite straight.	Internal moving parts rarely need examination.	
		Cranks wear and then require expert adjustment.	String subject to wear and may break at inopportune moment. Retaining screw may work loose with use and is then easily lost.
Maintenance	Piston open to dust and dirt: requires removal for cleaning and lubrication. Spring and washers need only infrequent renewal.	Sealed by valve caps from dust and dirt, which can reach rotor only through mouthpipe. Lubrication possible *in situ* through valve tube. Cork buffers require periodical examination to check alignment of airways in rotor.	
			String requires examination, e.g. every six months. String easily replaced.

Part II

THE PLAYER

CHAPTER 6

Physiological:
The Embouchure

'God makes some people horn players — others are not so fortunate.' In making this remark Anton Horner, himself a famous exponent of the art of horn playing, intended to convey the fact that ability to excel at this instrument is, ultimately, a gift of Nature. Just as no amount of training and practice, even if allied to consummate musicianship, will make a fine voice from a mediocre one, so the physical conformation of the facial muscles and lips of the potential horn player will almost make or mar him before he has ever taken his instrument into his hands. The embouchure is to the horn player what the vocal cords are to the singer — the raw material of his art, capable of development and ever-increasing control, but in the last resort a physical accident whose possession in itself confers no credit on its owner, but only the use he makes of it. It is a small area of the lips, and the muscular control of this area, which is the greatest single factor in horn playing — a factor of paramount importance in the proper production and control of tone.

In its literal sense the word 'embouchure' means 'putting to the mouth'; its connotation in the playing of wind instruments is rather wider, for it indicates not only the mode of application of the instruments to the lips, but also the use and development of the muscles involved in controlling the pitch and quality of the sound produced. A player will speak of his embouchure, or less formally of his 'lip', and thereby indicate something that is personal to himself. If he earns his livelihood by his playing, his instrument and his embouchure will be equally treasured possessions; if anything, the embouchure will be the more valuable, for an instrument can be repaired or replaced, but the lip is much less amenable to treatment. In *The Orchestra from Beethoven to Berlioz* Adam Carse quotes the story of Heinrich Gugel, one of two brothers who were both horn virtuosi. In 1823 he found that his lips, 'which up to that time had been remarkably flat (and this he said was the great secret of his success) took another shape. They bulged, probably from age. He was much distressed as he now lost some of his highest notes. He was sure he would recover his powers if he could get a skilled surgeon to pare his lips down flat as before. Unable to prevail on any surgeon to undertake such an operation, he performed it himself with a razor! This ruined him.' Modern developments in surgery and dentistry, however, may sometimes render injury to the embouchure less disastrous. A few years ago a trumpeter in a famous American orchestra was involved in a motor-car accident, as a result of which he suffered six broken teeth and severe lip cuts. Fortunately a year or two earlier his brother, as a student of dentistry, had made a practice cast of the player's teeth, and owing to this circumstance it was agreed by surgeon and dentist that his teeth could be rebuilt to their original shape, while the lips would heal so that his embouchure would eventually be as good as before. Famous players have gone to great pains to preserve their embouchures; Brémond, for example, counselled against smoking, alcohol and oily foods and, himself the possessor of a luxuriant moustache, even against shaving the upper lip. The lips may as legitimately be regarded as part of the instrument as may the reed of an oboe, with the important difference that on the horn one cannot change one's reed, as with the oboe, if it proves unsatisfactory or deteriorates.

The passage of an air-stream through the almost closed lips causes them to vibrate. They are forced further apart by the air, but their elastic tension immediately pulls them together again, and the process is rapidly repeated. The rate at which they vibrate is determined by their state of tension; the tauter they are the more rapidly they vibrate, and the greater the wind pressure required to set them in vibration. As a result, a series of impulses is set up which is transmitted to the column of air enclosed by the instrument. The rate of vibration of this column depends upon its natural frequency, which in turn depends upon its length. If the tension of the lips is increased, and the generating air pressure raised, the air column is caused to vibrate in a slightly more complex manner, and the note emitted jumps to the octave, and with further increases in the lip tension and wind pressure successively to the twelfth, the second or super-octave, and so on up to the twelfth harmonic or higher, the exact limit being determined by the degree of tension capable of being imposed upon his lips by the individual player. Together the lips and air column form a coupled acoustic system, in which the lips act as a generator of vibrations and the air column as a resonator which to some extent is able to impose its natural vibrating period upon the generating system.

It should be added that this explanation of the generation of sound waves in the horn is not universally accepted. Some writers[1] hold that the lips do not vibrate, but that the air column is set in vibration as the result of the formation of an edge tone whose frequency depends upon the position of the lips with respect to the mouthpiece and the velocity of the air-stream that passes between them. To some extent this is probably true with the trumpet and other instruments using a more or less cup-shaped mouthpiece, but in the horn this condition does not obtain. It is true that whenever air passes through a narrow slit (e.g. the slightly parted lips) vortices are formed giving rise to a note which is, however, very feeble and indecisive — the so-called slit tone. In any event, photographs have been taken of the lips while a note was being sounded, and show unmistakably that they do vibrate, so that the theory first outlined above seems the more likely to be correct.

To some extent the player, by relaxing or tautening his lips, can force the column to vibrate slightly out of its natural frequency. The pitch of notes low in the harmonic series can be flattened by this method; for example, by the use of very low lip tension the five semitones below the second harmonic — the so-called factitious notes which theoretically do not exist on the natural instrument at all — may, with luck, be sounded. Their quality, however, is not such as to call for their frequent use, and in any case on a valved instrument they may be obtained with certainty by using the valves.

It is impossible to lay down with exact accuracy the conditions under which the perfect embouchure may be formed, for so much depends upon individual differences in the physical characteristics of the parts concerned. Generally speaking, however, a small mouth, thin narrow lips and even teeth of moderate size are favourable prerequisites. A large mouth makes more difficult the muscular control of that area of the lips actually under the mouthpiece. Thick lips, as poor Gugel found, are less sensitive and flexible than thin, entailing more difficulty in adjusting and maintaining their tension when producing notes in the higher register, while uneven teeth make a satisfactory embouchure very unlikely, since a projecting tooth, even if the pressure employed is kept to a minimum, is almost certain to cause pain and thus prevent the lips from performing their function efficiently. Preservation of the evenness of the front teeth, indeed, ranks second only to the tone and

---

[1] E.g. G. Gorgerat: *Encyclopédie de la Musique pour Instruments à Vent.*

flexibility of the lip and facial muscles in maintaining a satisfactory embouchure.

Since the technique of the horn involves the use of harmonics at least up to the twelfth, the uppermost of which lie very close together, the harmonic required must be picked out by the player by the exercise of minute alterations in the state of contraction of the muscles concerned. Such adjustments call for a high degree of muscular control and sensitivity. The importance of the muscles concerned in this exact control cannot be overstressed. Until they have been developed a feeling of strain and probably of discomfort is almost certain to be experienced after any prolonged period of practice, and from this point of view 'little and often' is a desirable maxim so as to allow fatigued muscles time to recover. M. M. Porter makes the distinction between 'normal tiring' of the embouchure muscles, due to the opposing action of the involuntary muscles tending to close the mouth and those of the embouchure which keep it open, and 'rapid tiring' which is caused if pain occurs in the lips, when still more effort is required to keep the lips open. Thus excessive pressure is likely to lead to rapid tiring, but there is no doubt that continuous playing without adequate rest is detrimental even to the player who has kept his embouchure muscles in proper trim by regular practice. This is illustrated by the story of Anton Horner, who while rehearsing the Strauss wind serenade asked for a rest after having repeated a passage several times. When later the conductor, Gabrilowitsch, asked for an explanation, Horner grasped one of the conductor's fingers and held it in a vice-like grip. As the finger grew redder and redder, Horner pointed out that the same effect was produced in the embouchure if it was allowed no rest — a demonstration which completely convinced Gabrilowitsch. Though the ideal is to use as little pressure as possible, some compression of the lips between the teeth on one side and the rim of the mouthpiece on the other can hardly be avoided, if only to prevent the escape of air between mouthpiece and lips. The result is a restriction of the circulation of the blood in this region, with consequent dilation of the vessels and hence of the lips, which therefore do not receive the oxygen necessary if the muscles are to do their work without becoming too fatigued. In these conditions loss of control becomes inevitable; most players will be familiar with the discomfort, even disaster, that ensues when tired lip and facial muscles will no longer obey the dictates of the brain. It is for this reason that most orchestras include an assistant first horn to take over in tutti passages and allow the principal player time for his lip muscles to recover their tone.

The various factors concerned in the formation of a satisfactory embouchure cannot really be considered in isolation, for it is only by their controlled and integrated interaction that the required results will be obtained. Though players may differ to some extent on matters of detail — as they are bound to, since an embouchure is a personal and individual affair — there is fairly general agreement on certain basic fundamentals. These involve (i) the muscular complex of the face and lips and its proper control, (ii) the degree of mouthpiece pressure employed, (iii) the position of the lower jaw, with which, together with (i), is associated (iv) the size and shape of the aperture between the lips, and (v) the exact position of the mouthpiece on the lips.

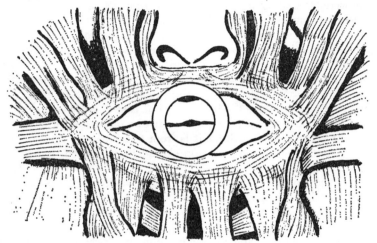

Fig. 21. Musculature of the embouchure.

The muscles involved are shown in Fig. 21. Viewed from the front, the embouchure is convex, though the lips are slightly compressed inwards by the pressure of the mouthpiece upon them. Basically the complex consists of an oval muscular ring, from around which radiate, like the spokes of a wheel, a number of other muscles. This ring, of complicated structure since it consists partly of its own fibres and partly of fibres derived from the other oral muscles, is called the orbicularis oris. Its action, on contracting, is to purse the lips, as in whistling, making them thick and soft. In this condition they are incapable of vibrating satisfactorily; their mass is too great and they are not resilient enough. The muscles of the cheek, pulling laterally, stretch the lips tightly over the teeth, as in smiling, making them thinner. They are now capable of vibrating, but only to produce a thin, pinched tone, and, moreover, they are much more subject to punishment by pressure. These are the two extremes of embouchure muscle settings, and neither, on its own, provides a satisfactory lip condition. If, however, the orbicularis is made to contract to produce a slight pursing of the lips, and simultaneously its action is opposed by contraction of the cheek muscles, the lips become taut and resilient and in an ideal state for vibration by an air stream passing between them. A small area at each corner of the mouth is now in a state of considerable tension, and there is general agreement that the distance between these two areas should remain more or less constant, whatever the pitch of the note to be sounded. The lips, as it were, are slung between these two points, which are firmly anchored against the teeth. The changes in lip tension required for ascending passages are effected by increased contraction from opposite directions, the attempt of the cheek muscles to stretch the lips into a more smiling condition being exactly counter-balanced by increased contraction from the orbicularis, and for descending passages these opposing pulls are decreased, again in equal proportions. Thus the lips in the one case do not become more tightly stretched over the teeth, and in the other are not allowed to sag or become flabby. Since it is from these areas at the corners of the mouth that the lip tension should be regulated, it is here, and not in the lips themselves, that the first signs of fatigue should appear if a proper embouchure has been formed. If tiring occurs first in the lips, then either the embouchure has too much of the smile in it, or too much mouthpiece pressure is being used, or both.

Excessive pressure, since it bears upon the fibres whose tension should be controlled from the corners of the mouth, inhibits their freedom of action and instead imposes upon them an artificial tension from outside. The tendency to use undue pressure is most pronounced in the high register, and the upper lip is usually more affected than the lower. The pressure originates largely from the left arm and the little finger hook. Some teachers suggest dispensing with the use of this hook during part of the daily practice; others advocate playing a few minutes each day with the instrument placed upon a flat smooth surface without being held or touched by the hand. This does not mean that no pressure at all will be used, but that it will be kept to a limiting value determined by the amount of friction set up between the instrument and the smooth surface. Such practice gives the embouchure muscles the chance to develop the required flexibility unhampered by any increase of pressure involuntarily exerted if the muscles are not in good trim. As the muscles become more pliable it should be possible to reach the eighth harmonic or even higher, but this flexibility, only to be attained by practice over a period of weeks or even months, is quickly lost if practice ceases.

The muscles of the chin also play a part in the formation of an embouchure. Some of them are able to pull the lower lip upward and outward, raising the fleshy part of the chin towards the mouth; others pull the lip downwards, while still others depress the corners of the mouth. Farkas[1] lays considerable stress on the proper employment of these muscles to produce a downward arched chin whose visible sign is a U-shaped indentation running in a wide sweep from the corners of the mouth to the middle of the chin. This depression is the result of a strong downward pull whose aim is to tense the lower lip and to maintain the aperture between the two lips.

It is generally agreed that the upper and lower teeth should lie in line in a vertical plane, so that the lips are correspondingly in line. Since in the normal mouth the upper teeth slightly overlap the lower, a conscious forward movement of the lower jaw is usually necessary to bring the lower teeth into the required position. Unless this movement is made, the flow of air between the lips will be below the horizontal, and two faults will become evident: the air will not pass straight into the mouthpiece, and pressure on the two lips will be unequal. To correct these faults the mouth-piece angle must be adjusted downwards, and now any increase in pressure will cause the mouthpiece to ride up towards the nose. If, however, the mouthpiece is almost horizontal, as it must be if the teeth are in line and equal pressure is exerted on each lip, the air-stream is also horizontal and increased pressure will have no sliding effect. Some players hold that the mouthpiece angle may need to be slightly altered as the pitch changes, but agreement on this point is not universal. Schuller,[2] for example, recommends for ascending pitches (i) slight pressure on the upper lip, (ii) increased lip tension, and (iii) a backward and upward movement of the lower jaw whose effect is to decrease the size of the lip aperture and to deflect the air-stream slightly downwards so that it impinges on the mouthpiece closer to its rim. The reverse procedures are adopted for descending pitches.

The lower jaw, in conjunction with the muscles of the em-bouchure, regulates the lip aperture. Since it is through this aperture that the air-stream passes, causing the lips to vibrate and thus produce the sound, its size and shape are vitally important.

---

[1] *The Art of Brass Playing*, p. 16.
[2] *Horn Technique*, p. 19

If it is too narrow and slit-like the sound is constricted, often sharp in pitch, and speaks with difficulty at a low dynamic level. The opposite fault — a too nearly circular opening — leads to a dull fuzzy tone quality. The ideal shape lies somewhere between these two extremes. The brass instruments are commonly known as lip-reed instruments for just the reason that the lips function in the same way as the double-reed of a woodwind instrument, giving intermittent access to the column of air which is to be made to vibrate, and it is logical to suppose that in playing a brass instrument the opening between the lips should assume the same shape as that between the lamellae of a double-reed in a woodwind instrument. The size of the aperture must vary both with pitch and dynamic level, being largest for a loud note of low pitch and smallest for a high note of small volume, but the same general shape must be maintained throughout. Changes in size are effected by small up-and-down movements of the lower jaw, carried out in conjunction with adjustments in the tension of the orbicularis oris, cheek and chin muscles of such a kind that the corners of the mouth remain unchanged in position.

The position of the mouthpiece on the lips must, of course, play a considerable part in the formation of a satisfactory embouchure. It will inevitably vary from player to player, for in no two players will the combination of factors producing the best results be exactly the same. Generally speaking, however, a position in which about two-thirds of the mouthpiece rests upon the upper lip and the remaining third on the lower is found to be satisfactory. Normally the mouthpiece should be placed centrally, but cases have been known where players have developed successful embouchures which are not central owing, for example, to a projecting front tooth.

Some players prefer, or have unconsciously developed, an embouchure in which the rim of the mouthpiece lies *in* rather than *on* the red part of the lower lip; whether the setting should be *einsetzt* or *ansetzt*, as the Germans term these two positions, is a matter which can be decided only by the individual, since his choice will depend upon the physical conformation of his teeth and lips (Fig. 22). The settings of many players, in fact, though technically *ansetzt*, carry about them a suspicion of the *einsetzt* character. Occasionally a player will be found who even insets in the upper lip, though this position is much rarer.

To obtain the very lowest notes, and even the fundamental, the French *trompe de chasse* players practise a technique in which the lower lip is drawn right out from under the mouthpiece and brought back again on to its outside surface, so that the opening between the lips is increased to the maximum and is, in fact, between the edge of the upper lip and the flesh situated near the bottom of the inside of the lower. Notes produced by this technique of *débouchant*, though certainly easier of emission, tend to be rather harsh in tone.

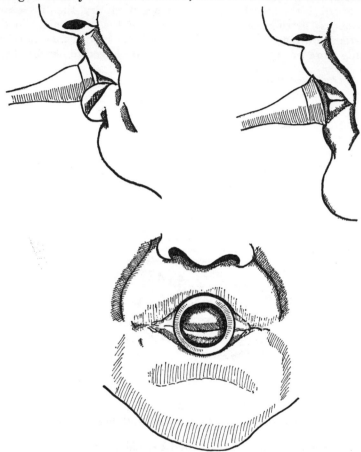

Fig. 22. Types of embouchure. Above: left, rim in the lower lip; right, rim on the lower lip. Below: typical embouchure from the front.

The question whether the lips should be dry or moist when the mouthpiece is placed in position is a vexed one on which there is no general agreement. It is maintained by some players that a moist lip engenders the feeling that the mouthpiece may at any time begin to slide about on the mouth, even if it does not actually do so. This sense of insecurity, they claim, is a further and unnecessary hazard to be added to those that already beset the horn player. On the other side it is pointed out that if the lips are moist the mouthpiece is able to settle itself in the most natural and comfortable position. In addition, since the lips are no longer anchored to the mouthpiece as they are when dry, such necessary actions as getting some of the lip out of the mouthpiece in the extreme low register are facilitated, while the embouchure muscles, being more free to move under the rim, are forced to perform their

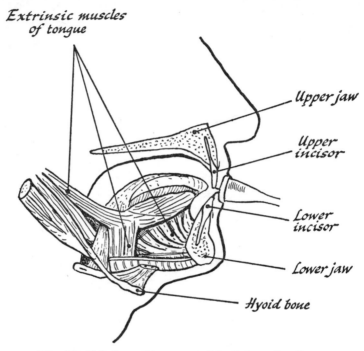

Fig. 23. Relation of tongue and teeth to embouchure.

function more efficiently, provided excessive pressure is not used.

A typical position of the mouthpiece is shown in Fig. 23, which also illustrates the relation of the tongue and teeth to the embouchure. The lower rim rests on the lip, its lower edge a little above the top of the gum which encloses the lower incisors. The small opening between the lips allows for the passage of air into the instrument, and the area of the lips under the mouthpiece is free to vibrate. When the tip of the tongue is resting against the top of the upper incisors the passage of air is prevented, but as soon as it is withdrawn by sounding the syllable 'too' or 'tah' a stream of air is able to pass through the lips if there is sufficient pressure, thus setting them in vibration.

The development of a suitable embouchure is a slow and often frustrating affair, and diagnosis and correction of faults is rarely easy. When such an embouchure has at length been achieved, it must be kept in trim by continual and regular practice, constant watch being kept to ensure that insidious flaws do not creep in unnoticed. 'God makes some people horn players' because they have been blessed with the lips, teeth and facial muscles which form the basis of a good embouchure; 'others are not so fortunate' because the conformation of these organs is not so favourable. Nevertheless, provided there is no gross malformation of teeth or lips, these others can usually reach their goal if they are prepared to put in a great deal of analytical and self-critical practice. Farkas,[1] indeed, goes so far as to say that in some respects the 'natural' player may be at a disadvantage in that he has never had to deal with flaws of embouchure, as most players have, and is therefore less well equipped to diagnose and deal with one if ever it does arise.

[1] *The Art of Brass Playing:* Introduction.

CHAPTER 7

Physiological: Breathing

T he air pressure necessary to set the lips in vibration is developed from the inflated lungs, but in playing wind instruments the natural mode of breathing may have to be adapted so as to produce and maintain a well-controlled air pressure for some considerable time. The normal rate of breathing is about fifteen inspirations per minute, but in playing the horn it may be necessary, for short periods, to reduce this to three or four. Deeper breathing than normal is then required, both to maintain the requisite pressure and to keep the working muscles supplied with the oxygen without which they cannot function. As one writer has put it, the air must be taken in in the form of a sphere, and let out as a thin thread. If an even and continuous flow of air at a given pressure is to be passed through the lips, the muscles concerned with respiration must be capable of fine and sensitive adjustment. These muscles are shown diagrammatically in Fig. 24. They are (i) the muscles of the diaphragm, which flatten its dome during inspiration, and the abdominal muscles which help to push it back to its relaxed position in expiration; (ii) the scalene muscle and the intercostal muscles between the ribs. The external intercostals help to raise the ribs upwards and outwards and thus enlarge the cavity of the chest, the internal intercostals pull them down again. (iii) It is also possible to use the muscles of the larynx to help to control the pressure of the air stream by altering the shape and size of the glottis. This practice is often deprecated as tending to lead to thin and unsteady tone, but some teachers hold that many players consciously, and most others unconsciously, make use of the laryngeal muscles during expiration. If they are to be employed, it is obviously necessary that they should be exercised by practice until complete control is attained.

During the inspiration of a deep breath the ribs, but not the shoulders, should rise while at the same time the diaphragm is lowered. The result of the latter action is to cause the upper part of the abdomen to protrude slightly as the abdominal muscles relax and the organs below the diaphragm are compressed. The air in the

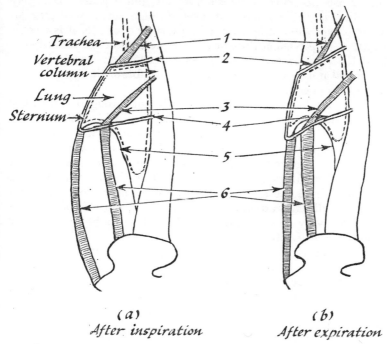

(a)
After inspiration

(b)
After expiration

Fig. 24. Action of the breathing muscles. (a) after inspiration;
(b) after expiration.

		(a)	(b)
1.	Scalene muscle	contracted	relaxed
2.	First rib	raised	lowered
3.	Intercostal muscle	contracted	relaxed
4.	Seventh rib	raised	lowered
5.	Diaphragm	lowered	raised
6.	Abdominal muscles	relaxed	contracted

lungs has now to be let out in a steady stream at a regulated pressure, though the volume of air passing into the instrument is comparatively small. The elasticity of the lungs themselves plays some part in promoting the flow of air at the beginning of an exhalation, but the force that this exerts cannot by itself sustain the flow for long. The greatest delicacy of control is attained if the

H
G.T.H.

abdominal muscles whose function it is to compress the abdominal contents and help to force the diaphragm upwards are used as the primary means of regulating the pressure. The ribs may be lowered, if necessary, to maintain the pressure at the end of a very long phrase. Good breathing is almost invisible because it is largely abdominal and diaphragmatic; even on high notes taken *forte* an expert player will not appear to be exerting effort, for it is a combination of lip tension (but not great pressure of the mouthpiece upon the lips) and high air pressure generated largely by the abdominal muscles which enables him to obtain these notes with such apparent ease.

The air is taken in through the mouth, not through the nose nor through the instrument. There are occasions when little time is available for breathing, but even under these conditions it is desirable to breathe through the sides of the mouth by a momentary relaxation of the embouchure into the 'smile' setting, rather than to keep the mouthpiece firmly in position in the hope of retaining the embouchure undisturbed, and to use the nose. This relaxation has the additional advantage of giving the muscles of the embouchure a very short rest, during which they can begin to recover their tone and sensitivity.

The air pressures developed in playing the horn are shown in the graph (Fig. 25). These were measured by the writer, using a water manometer attached to a small tube held in the player's mouth during the sounding of notes covering the range of the compass. It will be seen that, as expected, the pressure developed increases with loudness, and also with the frequency of the note. The pressure is not, however, directly proportional to the frequency, for it rises more rapidly at the higher than at the lower frequencies. For a given lung capacity, therefore, it is much more difficult to maintain the pressure required for a *forte* passage in a high register than it would be if the same passage were to be played in a lower register. Widor[1] gives the times that holding notes can be sustained as follows: lowest register, 10 seconds in *f* and 14 seconds *mf*; medium register (4th to 8th harmonics) 22 seconds *f*, 28 seconds *mf*, and 50 seconds *p*; above the 8th harmonic, much less owing to the high pressure required. These figures are on the conservative side, and could doubtless be exceeded, though at the expense of tone quality and control towards the end of the expiration. At the end of the *Siegfried Idyll* Wagner writes a very long low B (about 45 seconds) for the second horn, which in practice is impossible without a quick breath at the point where the 'cello enters. A low D earlier in the

---

[1] *The Technique of the Modern Orchestra*, p. 61.

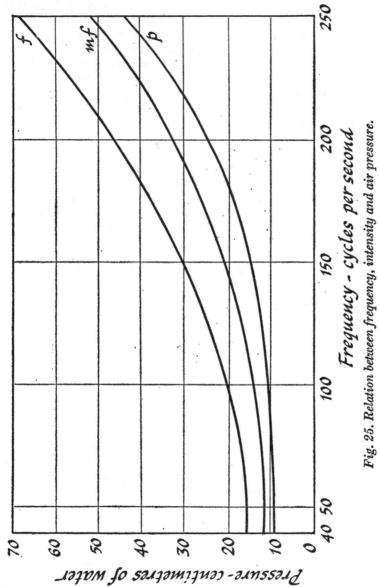

Fig. 25. Relation between frequency, intensity and air pressure.

THE PLAYER

same work is just manageable (30 seconds) in spite of the fact that it ends with a *crescendo*. It will be noticed that although a low pressure is required for the bottom register, a note can be held at the same dynamic level for a shorter period than in the medium. This is explained by the fact that the lower notes, produced with the lips in a comparatively relaxed state, involve a greater expenditure of air. For the high harmonics little air passes into the instrument, so that it may happen that though the reserve of air is adequate the player feels the need to take a new breath, the old supply having become vitiated. The muscular actions involved in playing use up oxygen, which must be renewed by the exhalation of stale air containing excessive carbon dioxide, and the intake of a new breath, even though the pressure of air in the lungs is sufficient.

It is important to gauge the correct volume of air to be taken in to perform a particular passage; the determining factors are the pressure required, the length of the passage, and the amount of air that will pass through the instrument during its performance. Too much air is almost as bad as too little; it may cause a feeling of discomfort and is likely to lead to deterioration in tone quality in the form of 'breathiness'. If too much air is inadvertently taken in, it is sometimes possible to let out any excess through the nose while still playing, especially if on a single held note. Control of the air-stream is most easily attained midway through an exhalation; at either extreme — that is, when the lungs are expanded to their maximum capacity, and when they are almost empty — it becomes much more difficult to maintain the steady pressure which is one of the essentials in the production of good tone. The basis of good breathing is, first, accurately to judge the optimum volume of air required, and secondly, the ability to dispose of the vitiated air and inhale a new supply in the shortest possible time.

To attain this control, many teachers advocate continual practice of long-held notes ranging over the whole of the horn's compass, starting *pianissimo*, swelling to *fortissimo* with a perfectly graduated *crescendo*, and then dying away again with an equally well-graduated *diminuendo*. Practice of sustained notes, it is claimed, gives firmness and durability to the lip muscles, improves the tone quality, and leads to better control of the breathing muscles and hence to more even and precise command of dynamic gradations.

In Britain, Germany and America the ideal tone is generally accepted to be one that is steady and unwavering, without a trace of vibrato. It is possible, however, to obtain a vibrato, if wished, by rapidly varying the wind pressure so that pulsations are imparted to the air-stream. The note may vary both in pitch and in intensity as a result of the pulsations, which can be effected by small but rapid contractions of the abdominal muscles acting in conjunction with the diaphragm. The rapidity of the pulsations determines the width of the vibrato.

It is also possible to produce a vibrato by using the throat muscles to force the air in small gusts through the instrument, and methods have also been described in which the lips are used or the instrument is moved on the lips by the action of the left hand and forearm. None of these ways is to be recommended; a throat vibrato is likely to lead to too much extraneous noise and is difficult to control, while any method involving movement of the instrument is apt to upset the embouchure.

A vibrato, then, is a perfectly feasible addition to the technique of horn playing. On the other hand, whether it is ever a desirable one is open to doubt. When the horn section of an orchestra is used as a group a vibrato is certainly not only unnecessary but out of place, for it would have a disrupting influence on the section as a whole. The orchestral horn player must continually be listening to his colleagues in the section, so that small but essential adjustments in intonation may be made. A vibrato produced by any one of the section would make such adjustments impossible, and would ruin the homogeneity of the group. Similarly, any unsteadiness in horn tone would fatally mar the blend with woodwind and brass.

There remains the possibility of employing the vibrato in solo work, or in solo passages in orchestral pieces. It must be admitted that the vibrato seems foreign to the nature of the horn, whose tone, warm and rich, and whose function as a cohesive element require absolute steadiness to be effective. The slightest variation in pitch, however artistically produced, tends to impair its characteristic qualities of tone, and in their place to substitute an emotionalism ill-suited to the genius of the instrument and usually to the style of music for which it is best fitted. It is noteworthy that French players, who in general favour the brighter tone of the small-bore instrument, often play with a marked vibrato which assaults the ears of those accustomed to the steady tone of German, British and American players.[1] This national predilection, though it may in occasional cases be justified, more frequently proves to be an error of style, for it devitalizes what is strong, and sentimentalizes what is beautiful. It is only necessary to imagine the effect of, say, the opening of the overture to *Oberon*, or the great horn theme

[1] An interesting discussion of this point by Malcolm Macdonald is to be found in a review of the gramophone record *The French Horn* (Decca LX 3143) in *The Gramophone*, Dec. 1955, pp. 272–3.

from Strauss's *Don Juan,* played with a vibrato. In the one case we are immediately transported from fairyland to a cinematic world of synthetic emotion, and in the other Don Juan is transformed from the virile idealist of Strauss's imagination into an emasculated and whining caricature of a man.

Part III

THE INSTRUMENT
AND THE PLAYER

CHAPTER 8

Technical: General

The horn is popularly regarded as one of the most difficult of all instruments to play well, and there is much truth in this contention. Most of the difficulties of technique stem from the physical facts that (i) the narrow bore makes the actual emission of sound less easy than in a wider-bored instrument, (ii) the small diameter of the mouthpiece leaves only a small area of lip muscle available for control, and (iii) the instrument utilizes an exceptionally wide range of harmonics — from the second to the twelfth or higher as compared with an upper limit of the eighth or ninth in other brass instruments — and the harmonics in the upper part of this range lie uncomfortably close together. The combination of these last two factors puts the player in the position, in common with the players of other brass instruments, but to a greater degree, of having to pick out the required harmonic by the extremely fine adjustment of his lip tension, with the knowledge that the slightest miscalculation may well end in disaster. The wonder is, therefore, that 'cracked' notes are not more common than they are. The problem of sounding the right note is even more acute when an unprepared attack is required on a high harmonic — say the twelfth or above. High harmonics are always more easily attained if they arrive at the end of a rising phrase, or, as in Siegfried's horn call, when the music moves step by step with increasing intensity towards its ultimate goal. With no landmark to serve as a guide the unprepared high note is bound to be a hit-or-miss affair except for the player who has the niceties of lip tension under control to a marked degree.

Large intervals are awkward on the horn, particularly if they are to be produced with the lips alone. Nevertheless, in the days of the hand horn they were frequently written, especially for the second of a pair of horns (the *cor basse*), owing to the lack of a complete scale in the lower register. A well-known example from Beethoven's sextet, Op. 81b, for two horns and string quartet demands a virtuoso technique:

But even in a simple leap of an octave from the fourth to the eighth harmonic, especially if slurred, it is only too easy for an inexperienced player to touch on one of the intermediate harmonics, or even to misjudge to the extent of leaping a trifle too high to the ninth. A good player will slur an interval of an octave without difficulty, but larger intervals present more of a problem, at any rate in the upper part of the compass, owing to the number of intervening harmonics. More troublesome still are alternate ascending and descending intervals of an octave or more, especially if they are to be played legato. A typical example occurs in the second horn part of Haydn's *Oxford* symphony, and the problem is accentuated here owing to the slowness of the lower note to speak readily:

This is a case where the B♭ section of the double horn may be used with advantage, since the low C, read as a D, is emitted more easily on the shorter tube, which will, in fact, be the horn in G that Haydn envisaged. Relaxation of the lip muscles seems to take place a fraction less readily than contraction, and as a consequence a large descending interval at a rapid pace leaves little time for adjustment of the tension, or for overcoming the inertia of the tube.

Arpeggios, especially if rising and based on an harmonic series, are in the character of the instrument as a relic from the days of the natural horn. The opening theme of Strauss's *Heldenleben*, for example, covers a very wide range in its first two bars, but it is based almost entirely on the harmonic series of E♭, and if written for horn in E♭ would have aroused no great apprehension in the mind of the hand horn player. Paradoxically enough, however, this passage, apart from its first note, would be tackled by the modern player on the B♭ horn, where the changes in valve fingerings which are then needed in a sense aid the lips in making the move from one note of the arpeggio to the next. Much the same is true of the prelude to *Das Rheingold*.

Rising arpeggios in detached notes are also effective, but if descending are a little more difficult, for the reason already explained, although they were often written by the classical composers. Legato descending arpeggios at a moderate speed are also possible.

Passages based on diatonic scales in all keys, legato or detached, or in a variety of articulations, are made possible by the valves, as are also passages based largely on the chromatic scale. The nineteenth century horn idiom, still retaining a suggestion of hand horn technique, has now almost disappeared. Though perhaps not yet fully able to compete with the woodwind on its own ground, the horn is capable of taking its turn with quite complicated passages. This extension of its technique has been effected in part by mechanical improvements in the instrument itself, and in part also by the composer's demands for an ever wider range of expression. No doubt the influence of jazz has also been felt, even if not at first hand. The horn rarely forms part of a jazz group, but the prodigious technique of the jazz trumpeter must have had its effect on the orchestral trumpeter and through him on the horn player. Thus a well-known American horn player, Gunther Schuller, who has played and composed for jazz groups, has put on record his view that 'the members of the brass family are not limited to the stereotypes of expression usually associated with them. Thus, there is more to the horn than its "heroic" or "noble" or "romantic" character. . . . Indeed, these instruments are capable of the entire gamut of expression.' In his symphony for brass and percussion, written partly with the aim of exploiting these potentialities, he presses the technique of the horn (and the rest of the brass) to its limits, and asks it to perform feats unimaginable even a mere twenty or thirty years ago. It cannot be denied that the result, as a practical demonstration of his assertion, is both effective and impressive, though it would cause the hand horn player to turn in his grave.

Less difficult technically, perhaps, Britten's setting of Middleton's little poem in his *Nocturne*, Op. 60, provides in less than thirty bars a miniature compendium of modern horn technique from the colouristic viewpoint. Set for tenor, obbligato horn and strings, the poem offers obvious opportunities for illustrative writing, although the horn is not, perhaps, the instrument which would first come to mind. With his usual imaginative insight, however, Britten uses the full resources of the modern instrument to portray in quick succession the midnight bell, the howling of dogs and twittering of nightingales, the hooting of owls and croaking of ravens, the cricket's chirpings, the mouse's squeaks and the mewing of cats. In this series of minute tone-pictures he instructs the player to use the mute; to play stopped and *sf*; stopped and flutter-tongued *pp*; muted and very short; and muted, *mf* and nasal.

Whether such extensions of the horn's expressive powers have all resulted in gain and none in loss is a debatable point which cannot be fully argued here. Certainly the instrument has lost something of its individuality, to the regret of the more conservatively minded. Thus when Schoenberg, as early as the second decade of the century, wrote passages like the following, from his *Erwartung*,

(*By kind permission of Universal Edition* (*Alfred Kalmus, Ltd., London*))

or this, from *Die glückliche Hand*,

(*By kind permission of Universal Edition* (*Alfred Kalmus, Ltd., London*))

it moved Koechlin to shake his head sadly and say, 'Ce n'est pas du cor.' But Schoenberg, though he notoriously set his performers some awkward technical problems, was enough of a realist, on the one hand, to believe that they would eventually be solved, and a sufficiently skilled orchestrator, on the other, to know that the effect he wished to obtain could only be achieved by these particular means. For better or for worse, parts like these are now almost commonplace, and the modern player accepts them and takes them in his stride.

CHAPTER 9

Technical:
The Left Hand

I f the lips and embouchure are the most important part of a
player's equipment, the hands run them a close second. The
function of the right hand in controlling the tone and intonation has already been described; to the left hand falls the
double duty of holding the instrument steady and of operating the
valves. In the latter respect it is unique, for in all other valved brass
instruments it is the right hand which performs this function. This
peculiarity is a relic from the days of the hand horn. Both right-
and left-handed natural horns were in common use, but when the
technique of stopping was developed the task of carrying out the
intricate movements necessary was usually and naturally delegated
to the right hand, and most of the great hand horn virtuosi played
the instrument with this hand in the bell. With the coming of the
valve, this procedure was continued, and the left hand, which pre-
viously had done no more than hold the instrument steady, was
now also given the task of manipulating the valves. From time to
time attempts have been made, notably by Brémond, to bring the
horn into line with other valved instruments, but they have met
with little success. Horns with valves operated by the right hand
are still to be had to special order in France, but players in general
have retained the traditional practice, and the horn is now practically always constructed so that the right hand is to be placed in
the bell, with the left hand working the valves.

In all three-valved horns, the first finger operates the tone valve,
the second the semitone and the third the tone and a half valve, but
the exact position of the left hand varies with the type of valve
fitted. In piston-valved instruments the direction of motion of the
piston is in the plane of the coils, and the fingers must therefore be
slightly bent so that the soft part of their tips rests lightly on the
valve buttons, ready to depress any combination of valves by a

125

rapid downward movement. If the fingers are not actually in contact with the buttons, or at most not more than a fraction of an inch above them, time will be wasted while the fingers search for them, and the jerky movement may be communicated to the instrument with the possibility of disturbing the embouchure. The thumb is either provided with a shaped rest, or is placed in position against the casing of the first valve chamber. The little finger anchors itself by its end joint to a ring or hook soldered to the top of the tubing. This provides the firm grip necessary if the instrument is to be held steadily in position without disturbance of the embouchure. The finger stretches of different individuals, however, vary considerably, and it would be an advantage both on piston and rotary valved instruments were this hook to be made adjustable. For a large hand some expedient such as fitting the hook with a cork of the requisite thickness may be employed, but for a small hand there is little that can be done.

On the horn with rotary valves, the movement of the fingers in depressing the finger plates is at right angles to the plane of the instrument, since the finger plates themselves lie in this plane. The left hand must therefore be positioned so that the fingers project over the main tubing on to the upper face of the instrument where the valve system is situated. Here again the finger tips must be in contact with or very close to the finger plates. To accommodate the altered position of the hand the little finger hook is fixed, not to the top, but to the side of the tubing. If the horn is fitted with a fourth valve — either a stopping valve, an A valve, or the one which makes the switch from one section of a double horn to the other — this is usually operated by the thumb, moving in a direction away from the player. Normally this valve is also of the rotary type, and is provided with a curved lever into which the thumb fits. It is sometimes found that the position of this lever entails a wide stretch between thumb and first finger, and it may need some adjustment to suit the individual player. In any case its position must be such that the thumb and fingers are capable of free and independent movement. If a fifth valve is fitted, for example a stopping valve on a double horn, it is usually operated from a second thumb lever, but when the little finger is used a right-angled rest, adjustable by a screw collar, may be attached to the instrument to project forward and come up between the thumb and first finger, giving the required degree of support and leaving the little finger free to operate the valve.

Theoretically a change may be required from any valve combination to any other, but in practice few of those possible are needed at all frequently. The most awkward to execute smoothly are those

126

involving the second and third valves together, especially if the thumb is also in use. A knowledge of alternative fingerings, however, will sometimes enable the player to by-pass these difficulties without any musical loss. Perhaps on the four-valve B♭ instrument a more enterprising thumb technique could be worked out; players might at first find it cumbersome, but they have the example of bassoon players to show them what can be done with the thumb.

Perfect control of the fingers is necessary. They must be capable of moving quite independently, smoothly and rapidly, but not violently. Precise co-ordination must be achieved, or unwanted notes may be momentarily sounded. Moreover, the finger movements must be carried out in such a manner that each phrase is musically shaped and does not progress mechanically from note to note. The musical mind must be at work behind the muscular actions of the fingers, directing and controlling their motion.

Finally, exact synchronization between tongue and finger movements, especially in staccato passages, is absolutely essential. This is no easy matter when it is necessary to employ double or triple tonguing to articulate scales or arpeggios where valve changes are required. Fingers, tongue and lip tension have all to be exactly co-ordinated, and at the same time air pressure carefully gauged to give the desired dynamic level or shading. These problems are common to all players of valved lip reed instruments, but they are present in a particularly acute form for the horn player. The coming of the valve, though it has rendered his task easier in some respects, has also brought in its train additional problems of technique, and these are largely bound up with the muscular actions of the left hand.

CHAPTER 10

Technical: Articulation
and Phrasing

The tongue is to the horn player what the bow is to the violinist. By its means all degrees of articulation from the almost explosive *sforzando* to the gentlest attack corresponding, say, to the *louré* bowing of string instruments are possible. Two factors, however, make clear articulation more important on the horn than on any other wind instrument. It is, in the first place, the only one of these instruments which is normally played with the bell facing away from the listener and with the hand in the bell. In consequence, the sound never reaches the hearer directly, but always by reflection, with the result that the attack may easily appear to be blurred and the articulation lacking in precision. Moreover, the sound reaches the listener a fraction of a second later than from other brass instruments similarly articulated. Hence conductors' constant admonitions to the horns not to drag.

In addition, the length of the tube precludes so crisp and sharp an articulation as is possible, for example, on the trumpet with its shorter tube and cup-shaped mouthpiece, and this is particularly the case in the lower register, where the instrument speaks appreciably less promptly. For these reasons the attack must be made with what may sound to the player an exaggerated degree of accentuation, and exactly on the beat. Sitting to the rear of a first-class player a listener would gain the impression that his articulation was over-accentuated; to the listener in front the effect would be of clean and clear articulation without any suggestion of the imprecision and slovenliness which would accompany a less pronounced attack.

The tongue is the means whereby the player articulates the rhythmic pattern of the music, and sensitive control of its muscular system is therefore essential. The shape of the tongue is maintained by its intrinsic muscles; its movement is effected by a number of

128

extrinsic muscles attached to the middle of the lower jaw, the hyoid bone in the floor of the mouth, and the under side of the skull (Fig. 23). Upon the efficiency of these muscles depend the accuracy and rapidity of the tongue movements. The movement of the tip of the tongue releases the air-stream and the lip reeds are thus set in vibration. When the mouthpiece is in position, the lips are slightly parted and the tongue rests with its tip either almost touching the upper gum line or against the back of the upper incisors. Silent pronunciation of one or other of the syllables Tu (almost a Thu sound at times), Tee, or Du, Dee automatically brings about a tongue movement which releases the air-stream. This movement is a rapid lowering and slight withdrawal of the tip of the tongue which allows air to pass between the lips and set them in vibration. Several advantages are apparent if the backward movement of the tongue is not carried too far. The shorter stroke required for the succeeding attack ensures that (i) the tongue can carry out this attack more rapidly, (ii) there is less chance of inaccuracy, and (iii) over a period of time the tongue will become less fatigued. In addition, it is easier to maintain a steady flow of air, supporting the tone from one note to the next, if the tongue movements are restricted in scope and there is less chance of these movements — or their effects on the air-stream — disturbing the embouchure.

The exact position of the tongue prior to the attack depends upon the type of attack required, and also probably upon the pitch of the note to be sounded. If the consonant T is sounded, with the tip of the tongue starting hard and low down against the back of the teeth, or even between the lips, and making the most rapid downward movement possible, a hard and almost percussive attack is produced, suitable for *sforzando* or strongly staccato notes. With D the tongue may or may not begin with its tip low down on the teeth, but its movement is less rapid and forceful and the resulting attack is softer and less marked. Thus by varying the starting position of the tip of the tongue, low down for a hard attack, and higher up for a soft, and sounding a harder or a softer Tu or Du, a wide variety of different attacks can be produced.

If two or more notes are to be slurred together, a smooth legato will be facilitated by silently forming, after the initial attack, a second vowel as the slurred notes are approached. In an ascending interval, for example, the movements of the tongue and larynx involved in sounding the syllables Dooee have the effect of increasing the wind pressure as the upper note is approached, and the reverse effect is obtained with the syllables Deeoo.

The rate at which fast staccato in single tonguing can be achieved varies with the register, being much slower in the lower part of the compass. The exact speeds attainable will depend upon the individual player and the flexibility of his tongue. A large or heavy tongue makes rapid staccato articulation almost impossible, even with constant practice.

If a fast rate of articulation is required recourse may be had to double or triple tonguing. Neither of these techniques is easy or effective in the low register, and they are not normally employed nor, in good horn writing, required below the third or fourth harmonic. A reasonable upper limit would be the ninth or tenth harmonic. The double or triple articulation is made by the interpolation of the consonant K. The stroke is made in this case not by the tip of the tongue in retreat from the teeth, but by the withdrawal of its base from the hard palate. This movement results in the release of air at the back of the mouth, and at the same time brings the tip of the tongue forward into a position where it is ready to sound the following T. Similarly the T stroke takes the tongue back to the K position. This economy of movement must lead to a higher possible rate of articulation than could be achieved by single tonguing, when the tip of the tongue has to make both a backward and a forward movement in each stroke, but the device cannot be used artistically at low speeds owing to the less accurate control of the air-stream attainable on the K stroke formed at the back of the mouth.

In double tonguing T and K are sounded alternately — T-K, T-K, etc. For passages in fast triple rhythm there are three possible methods. These can be represented as T-T-K, T-T-K, etc., T-K-T, T-K-T, etc., or an adaptation of double tonguing to this rhythm, T-K-T, K-T-K alternately.

As a special effect a system of tonguing known as *Flatterzunge* or flutter-tonguing is sometimes used. It is said to have been originated by Richard Strauss, and is more commonly used by the flute than by brass instruments. It is a type of tremolo obtained by rolling an R. In the second variation of *Don Quixote* Strauss depicts the sheep by woodwind and brass in detached notes in tremolo notation, with a footnote explaining that this notation indicates that such notes are to be played *mit Zungenschlag*. The tongue tremolo thus notated is not specifically designated as fluttertonguing, a term actually used later in the same work in the flute part, but in practice the passage is played in this manner. Bax, in his fourth symphony, has two single bars of this type of tonguing, marked as such, for muted horns, and Walton, in the Foxtrot, 'Old Sir Faulk', from his Suite *Façade*, and Britten, in his *Sinfonia da Requiem,* use the same effect. Flutter-tonguing, however, is of very limited application in horn technique, and suitable opportunities for its use do not occur very frequently.

The composer indicates the articulation he requires by means of slurs. The player tongues every note except when it is slurred from a preceding note or notes. An exception is made to this rule in the case of the long slur, which is a phrasing rather than an articulating sign. Repeated notes are often included under this type of slur, and must obviously be articulated, even if not marked with dots or lines, for otherwise they will sound as if tied. This is shown in the following example from Bax's third symphony, where the notes which must be tongued are marked with asterisks:

(*By permission of Chappell & Co. Ltd.*)

Dots under a slur indicate that the notes concerned are to be half-tongued, that is, without a sharp attack, and with the notes held and only just separated from each other, as in the opening of Brahms's second pianoforte concerto:

Lines associated with notes under a slur denote a slight degree of accentuation or emphasis, only to be obtained by tonguing, though the notes are well held and only just detached from each other. Another quotation from Bax's third symphony gives an example of this type of tonguing:

(*By permission of Chappell & Co. Ltd.*)

131

Where the last of two or more notes under a slur has a dot over it, the note concerned is not tongued but merely cut off short. This is shown in the following phrase from the *Larghetto* of Elgar's second symphony:

(*By permission of Novello & Co. Ltd.*)

Similarly notes marked with accents under a slur are not intended to be tongued; the accentuation is provided by the breathing rather than the tongue.

These rules in theory should give the player all the guidance he requires in respect of tonguing; within their framework he is free and able to exercise his discretion and innate musical feeling in shaping the phrases of his part. In practice, however, it is not always possible to obey them, for composers' markings are often unrealistic, paying too little regard to the player's physical capabilities and to the limitations of his instrument. Frequently, too, there may be ambiguity as to the meaning of the markings, leaving the phrase open to more than one interpretation. This is often the case with the slur, which may be intended to define the limits of a phrase or to indicate that the passage is to be played legato, without tonguing.

Many of the difficulties of phrasing are connected with the problems of deciding where to tongue and where to breathe. Points of attack should be marked by the composer, but caesuras for breathing are rarely shown and it is left to the player, using his own musical sensitivity, to choose points at which to take breath in such a way that the melodic and dynamic design of a passage is brought out to the best effect. Scherchen[1] goes so far as to assert that it is part of the duty of a conductor to mark the wind parts with breathing and phrasing signs; they are, he says, 'as vitally important as indications of bowing for the strings'. In certain cases, as, for example, when the whole of a wind section is allotted a chord progression in the same rhythm, it is essential that the conductor, in consultation with the players, should give a ruling on this point, but in a solo passage such as the following from Roussel's fourth symphony it may safely be left to the player to make his own

[1] *Handbook of Conducting*, p. 102.

decisions, which might well be as shown in the example by commas:

If all four horns are playing in unison, as in the *fugato* passage from the last movement of Malcolm Arnold's second symphony (Ex. 12), the four players must agree between themselves which are the most suitable places to take breath and thus ensure the uniformity necessary if the group is to sound as a single voice:

In the next example, from the first movement of his ninth symphony, Mahler sets his first horn player an awkward problem. It would be easier to execute this long passage artistically if a break could be made somewhere for a quick breath, but no obvious place presents itself. It *can* be played, with some discomfort, in a single breath, but needs a high degree of control, and a reserve of air must be kept for the *crescendo* at the end.

Ex. 13.

(*By permission of Universal Edition (Alfred A. Kalmus Ltd.)*)

When a breathing space has to be found in a long solo, it must be contrived by slight shortening of the time value of the note it follows, and on no account at the expense of the succeeding note, for this would lead to untidy attack and imprecision in the rhythm.

New attacks can be made either with or without taking a fresh breath. In long passages such as have been quoted so far, it has been a physical necessity to find points at which breath can be taken, and this is done without impairing the continuity of the melodic line more than is necessary. On the other hand a breathed attack can often be usefully employed even in places where the reserve of air available to the player should be adequate to complete the passage. An attack of this type is more decisive than one in which the breath is not interrupted; the minute break during which the breath is inhaled gives the phrase which follows added significance. Thus in the following example from Strauss's *Don Juan* a breathed attack after the first minim gives impetus to the succeeding triplets. This is obviously one of those cases where all four players must conform:

(*By permission of Hinrichsen Edition, Ltd., London, copyright owners*)

Two other well-known themes for horn from the same work provide examples of the breathed attack being used to secure greater definition and emphasis:

(*By permission of Hinrichsen Edition, Ltd., London, copyright owners*)

(*By permission of Hinrichsen Edition, Ltd., London, copyright owners*)

Towards the end of the first part of his *Konzertmusik* for strings and brass, in a long unison melody for horns and strings, Hindemith adopts an unusual expedient in phrasing the parts for first and third horns in a different manner from those for second and fourth, though all four are playing the same part. The aim is probably to ensure that the players shall not interrupt the broad even flow of the melody by all taking breath at the same points; the momentary pauses made by the first pair are covered by the other two, who make their caesuras while the first pair are in mid-phrase. A smooth continuous flow of sound is thus achieved:

(*By permission of Schott & Co. Ltd., London*)

TYPES OF ARTICULATION

The choice of a suitable articulation, when this is not specified by the composer, is perhaps more important on the horn than on any other brass instrument. It is also true to say that composers do not always indicate the articulation best suited to secure the effect they require. The discerning player recognizes this fact and discreetly amends the composer's markings, when necessary, to a pattern which his experience tells him will prove more effective.

Practically all types of rhythmic pattern are possible on the horn, but not all are equally effective. When the horn is playing quick scale or arpeggio passages, it is fatally easy, unless the player takes positive steps to avoid it, for these passages to sound blurred and woolly. In order to give them sharp definition the tonguing must be very carefully considered. The solution nearly always involves using the tongue more rather than less often. Frequently to 'slur-two, tongue-two' gives much crisper definition than to slur all four of a group of semiquavers, in passages such as the following from the last movement of Mozart's quintet, K. 407:

and

In the last example it might even be preferable to tongue all four semiquavers for the sake of clarity, as it certainly will be in the arpeggio figures at the end of the same work:

This is largely a matter of style; in Mozart the aim is at all costs to be precise and clear-cut, for the slightest suspicion of slovenliness spoils the whole effect. For the same reason the 6/8 quaver figures in the *Rondo* of Mozart's fourth horn concerto, K. 495, could well be tongued as shown below:

EX. 21

HornInEb

TECHNICAL: ARTICULATION AND PHRASING

One of the outstanding features of the playing of Dennis Brain was the sensitivity and clarity of his phrasing. Careful analysis shows that this was achieved largely by discreet and judicious use of the tongue, allied, of course, to consummate musicianship. Though he was a master of delicate rapid staccato playing, and capable, too, of an aggressive and almost percussive attack when required, his greatest asset was perhaps his ability to impart clarity and definition to a melodic line without destroying its legato character, by carefully considered but well-nigh imperceptible half- or legato-tonguing at appropriate points, not necessarily obeying the letter of the composer's marking, but always the spirit. Slavish adherence to printed phrasing and tonguing indications does not always produce the most effective result; much depends upon the composer's understanding of the instrument and its foibles, and chief among the latter is its tendency to sound woolly unless meticulous attention is paid to the tonguing. In general, it is true to say that composers are not sufficiently alive to this idiosyncrasy of the horn when playing rapidly moving parts. If such parts are safely doubled by other instruments the matter is of no great moment, but in solo passages when the horn is exposed it assumes considerable importance. If Strauss had phrased the well-known solo at the start of *Till Eulenspiegel* like this,

(*By permission of Hinrichsen Edition, Ltd., London, copyright owners*)

instead of this,

(*By permission of Hinrichsen Edition, Ltd., London, copyright owners*)

not only would the whole character of the theme have been altered, but it would have appeared with blurred edges, like a figure seen through a translucent screen.

137

CHAPTER 11

Technical: Trills, Tremolos, Glissandi, Chords

TRILLS

Owing to the limitations imposed on the natural horn by its inability to sound notes not forming part of its harmonic series, trills on this instrument were possible only in that region where the harmonics lie a second apart, i.e. from the seventh harmonic upwards, and even then, only major shakes were feasible unless high harmonics above the twelfth were used.

There was some difference of opinion among nineteenth-century players as to the exact method of producing the trill. Most of them advocated using the lips; rapid changes in their tension, though of a minute degree, caused a rapid alternation between a particular harmonic and the one adjacent to it. Other players, however (for example, Gallay), advocated the use of the tongue, which 'makes light strokes on the inside of the lips', and still others made a movement of the horn on the lips by the action of the left hand. There seems no doubt, however, that a clean-cut trill must involve some change in lip tension, whether tongue or hand is used in addition or not, and movement of the left hand would be liable, in any case, to impart an unpleasant vibrato-like quavering to the tone.

The fact that some of the trills involved one or other of the 'out-of-tune' harmonics was not necessarily a defect of great moment, for the false intonation, only too obvious in slow-moving passages, passes almost unnoticed when occurring in rapid alternation with another note.

Trills on notes lower than the seventh harmonic were written in the days of the natural horn, but must have been 'faked' in performance. In his horn concertos Mozart writes this shake:

138

On the hand horn, the A is a stopped note from the flat seventh harmonic above, and the B is also stopped from the true-tuned eighth harmonic. A trill of this sort, alternating between stopped notes lying a little more than a major second apart, would have a poor effect except perhaps in the hands of a virtuoso player such as Leutgeb, for whom the concertos were written. Again, in Handel's *Water Music* there occurs a trill on *e'* which can in practice have been no more than a 'wobbling' between two notes a minor third apart. Taking it all in all, it may seem surprising that so much attention was paid to the technique of horn trills by the eighteenth- and nineteenth-century pedagogues, for the results might appear to be hardly worth the time and trouble involved in learning and perfecting it. It should be remembered, however, that the practising of lip trills is an extremely valuable exercise for developing the lips, and it was probably for this reason, rather than for its musical value, that the trill received so much attention.

With the advent of the valve horn, the number of shakes obtainable with the lips was greatly increased, for the number of harmonic series available was now seven, and trills derived from those on the open tube were playable in each of the six extra series. This made possible whole tone shakes as low as that on *e'*. But modern composers ask for both semitone and whole tone trills on notes as low as *b*, and what composers ask for from their players they usually obtain. The statements, therefore, made in many works on orchestration that the valves are never used in performing trills are quite incorrect. In practice trills are performed either with the lips or with the valves, whichever is more convenient. If a valve is used, it will give best results when it is the second, owing to the shorter length of its tube, and it is probably true to say that a semitone trill of this type is as effective as any whole tone lip trill. On the other hand, trills involving the movement of more than one valve will be very awkward and unlikely to give good results. With a modern four-valve instrument it should be possible to devise some method of playing practically any semitone trill without recourse to such unsatisfactory expedients. For example, shakes like the following cannot be played as lip trills:

On the F horn the only fingerings are so clumsy as to be useless, but the first can be obtained on the B♭ horn with the fingering 2 + 3/3 and the second with the A valve, 2/ open. Even if his double horn is not fitted with an A valve, the player will probably possess a long

A slide to replace the B♮ tuning slide, as already described. Whatever fingerings are used, they will obviously produce the best effect if both notes of the trill are obtained as the same harmonic from fundamentals a semitone apart.

Generally speaking, whole tone shakes are less satisfactory when played with the valves, and it is wiser to confine them to first horn parts, where they can usually be played with the lips.

TREMOLOS

Tremolos are possible on the horn, if they are close, and can be obtained either with the lips alone or by the operation of a single valve. In practice they are thus restricted, if they are to be at all effective, to major and minor thirds in the middle register; but a more suitable method of obtaining the same result would be to give the notes of the tremolo to two horns playing rapidly repeated notes or even flutter-tonguing them.

GLISSANDI

By rapidly sounding, with increasing lip tension, all the harmonics from the fourth or even the third upwards to the fifteenth or sixteenth, a sort of glissando may be obtained. In *The Rite of Spring* Stravinsky writes such glissandi extending from the fifth to the fourteenth harmonic, and later from the eighth to the sixteenth. Thus, using different valve combinations, glissandi within the range of the following are possible.

Glissandi are a feature of the playing of the *trompe de chasse*; a flourish will often be ended by an upward 'scoop' to a high harmonic appearing to be expressive of a certain *joie de vivre* on the part of the player. Horn players also enjoy executing glissandi; they are often well supported or covered by other instruments, and for once they can let themselves go without fear of the consequences. They prefer them, however, to cover a shorter range than those quoted. The well-known horn 'whoops' in the introduction to Act I of *Der Rosenkavalier* (which are not actually notated as glissandi, though they must be played as such) lie within the limits of an octave, from b' to b'', and are very effective. An all but true glissando is possible over an interval of a fourth or fifth, up or down, by making use of as many valves as possible as rapidly as possible. Such glissandi occur frequently in light music, most effectively when of a beat's duration and often quite solo for four horns in unison.

Ceccarossi[1] mentions a quintet for horns by Gunther Schuller in which quarter-tone glissandi are used, performed by movement of the hand in the bell. He describes the effect as unreal and astonishing, as well it may be.

CHORDS

The phenomenon of the apparent production of chords of three or four notes on the horn has been familiar since the late eighteenth century at least. The virtuoso Punto, as Dauprat mentions in his *Méthode*, 'confessed the ease and worthlessness of their performance', and Dauprat himself makes it plain that he knew of the technique and was indeed somewhat scornful of what he looked upon as no more than a parlour trick. Nevertheless, that remarkable character Vivier (1817–1900) astonished his contemporaries by the facility with which he sounded chords, using a technique whose secret he would never divulge and which remained a source of mystery to those who heard him.

The musical value of the trick is doubtful, and horn chords have been used but rarely in serious music — by Weber in his concertino, Ethel Smyth in her concerto for violin and horn, Norman Del Mar in a sonatina for two horns, and Birchard Coar in his concerto.

The acoustical explanation seems to be comparatively simple. The horn, being at any particular moment a tube of fixed length, can sound only one note at that moment. If, however, another note is hummed at a fixed interval above or below the note of the horn, there may be noticed, besides the hummed and blown notes, two others, one below and the other above both of the generators. These are the so-called difference and summation tones, whose frequencies are respectively equal to the difference between the frequencies of the two generators and to their sum. Thus, by

[1] *Il Corno*, p. 35.

playing g' (sounding c') and humming g' (actual sound), a fifth above, this chord

may with luck be elicited — with luck because much depends (i) upon the facility with which the player can maintain both blown and hummed notes at a steady pitch, at the true interval, and at approximately the same dynamic level, and (ii) upon the timbre of his voice, which should match that of the horn as nearly as possible. It follows that not all players will find the production of chords equally easy, and that chords will be sounded most readily in that region of the player's vocal compass whose timbre most nearly resembles that of the horn.

It is generally found that of the two combination tones the lower is the more prominent, but neither is likely to be heard at a much higher dynamic level than *mezzo forte*. Quite apart, therefore, from aesthetic considerations, the use of the technique must perforce be limited to cases where the horn is playing solo, or at most very lightly accompanied.

Other chords besides that shown can of course be obtained by varying the interval between the two generators, and some of these are given below. The resultant tones produced can easily be determined from the relative frequencies of the generators, as shown against each chord. The same chords, transposed, will be given if the generators are transposed, the interval between them remaining the same. The notes in brackets are not quite in tune:

Whether the higher or the lower of the two generators is the one to be hummed depends upon the character of the player's voice, though humming the lower of the two notes usually proves more difficult. It would be interesting to know whether any of the increasing number of female players has experimented with horn chords, and if so, with what results.

It should be pointed out that the interval between the generators must be played and hummed in just rather than in equal temperament, since the frequency ratios shown against each pair of generators are those of just intonation.

142

CHAPTER 12

Technical: Notation
and Transposition

NOTATION

In the orchestral full score, the horn parts are nowadays placed immediately after those of the woodwind — possibly because the horns are so frequently to be found playing in combination with that group — and are followed by the trumpet parts which would precede them if the pitch of the brass were the sole determining factor. Wagner sometimes placed the horns before the bassoons, and Reger the trumpets above the horns. The usual arrangement, if only because it is now the most familiar, is probably the best. When the normal four horn parts are provided, they are arranged two to a stave, occasionally paired 1 + 2 and 3 + 4, but more often 1 + 3 and 2 + 4. The latter arrangement is more convenient if, as is often the case, the horns are playing in two parts, since the first and third players will be playing the higher lying part, and the second and fourth the lower. If more than four horns are used, as in many of Mahler's symphonies, the parts are printed on three or four staves, e.g. 1 + 3, 2 + 4, 5 + 7 and 6 + 8. The players themselves should be provided with separate parts, one to each player, but sometimes the first and second will share one printed part and the third and fourth another. Such an arrangement is most unsatisfactory, for two reasons, and should be avoided at all costs. First, confusion is caused if the two parts cross or if it is necessary to employ different clefs for the two parts unless these parts are on different staves; and secondly, with a large bell to be accommodated between them the two players are unable to sit as close together as, say, two oboists can. For this reason most large orchestras will provide two copies of parts printed in this way, if they are obtainable.

Horn parts are normally written in the treble clef, and until recently have been without key signatures, accidentals being inserted as they occurred. This was a relic of the days when the horn part was always in C, the necessary crook being specified at the start. There is no logical reason why this practice should be perpetuated, and increasingly often composers now provide their parts for horn in F with a suitably transposed key signature. The advantage of this procedure is that it gives the player a surer sense of the tonality of the piece, and also avoids a large number of accidentals in the part. Nevertheless, some players prefer to do without a key signature, particularly when they may be using an instrument in a different key from that designated, and carrying out the necessary transposition at sight. Efforts to modernize classical parts by transposing them for F horn, but without key signatures, are misguided and prove an unsatisfactory compromise, especially as the parts will often not be played on the F horn. It would be better either to leave them as they are — (why not? an essential part of the horn player's technical equipment is the ability to transpose at sight) — or, if they must be transposed for F horn, to provide them with the proper key signature. A plea for the continued omission of key signatures in the full score has been made, perhaps lightheartedly, on behalf of conductors, who are thereby quickly enabled to spot the horn parts as the eye runs down the page.

The lower notes of the horn's compass are written in the bass clef. Usage in this respect has until recently been illogical, since by custom for which it is difficult to find any compelling reason notes in the bass clef have been written an octave too low. Hence for a horn in F the notes sound a fourth higher instead of a fifth lower. For very low notes such as are sometimes to be found in the scores of Mahler, for example, this has involved the use of large numbers of unnecessary leger lines. Efforts by composers to revert to a more logical procedure are gradually having more success, though when they use the so-called new notation for the bass clef they may deem it necessary to call attention to the fact by some sort of footnote. In most cases the context makes it clear whether the old or the new notation is in use, but there are occasions when misunderstanding may arise. The classical composers, almost without exception, employed the old notation, so that a modern player must be prepared not only to transpose his part according to the crook specified, but also to carry out a further octave transposition when the music goes into the bass clef. The fact that players are skilful enough to do this without difficulty is small reason for continuing a convention which has no logic behind it.

In other respects the notation of the horn is straightforward, apart from the question of stopped and muted notes which has already been dealt with in Chapter 3.

TRANSPOSITION

Since horn parts are now almost always played on the instrument pitched in F or in B♭, or on the double horn combining these two keys, the ability to transpose at sight is an essential part of the player's technique. In the performance of music composed up to the time of Richard Strauss he may be called upon to play from parts for horn in C or B alto (rarely), B♭ alto, A, A♭, G, G♭ (rare), F, E, E♭, D, D♭, C basso, B basso and B♭ basso. The transpositions involved are shown in Table VII. Various methods can be employed to carry them out.

TABLE VII. *Transpositions*

Part for horn in	Played on horn in F transpose	Played on horn in B♭ transpose
Low B♭	Down a perfect 5th	Down an octave
Low B	Down a diminished 5th	Down a diminished octave
Low C	Down a perfect 4th	Down a minor 7th
D♭	Down a major 3rd	Down a major 6th
D	Down a minor 3rd	Down a minor 6th
E♭	Down a tone	Down a perfect 5th
E	Down a semitone	Down a diminished 5th
F	As written	Down a perfect 4th
G♭	Up a semitone	Down a major 3rd
G	Up a tone	Down a minor 3rd
A♭	Up a minor 3rd	Down a tone
A	Up a major 3rd	Down a semitone
B♭ alto	Up a perfect 4th	As written
B alto	Up an augmented 4th	Up a semitone
C alto	Up a perfect 5th	Up a tone

(*a*) All written parts can be referred to concert pitch; that is, the player thinks in terms of the notes actually sounded. Thus

actually sounds and is fingered with first and second valves on the F horn. The same fingering would then be required to play any of the following:

Horn etc.

This method, involving a kind of double transposition, from the written note into concert pitch, and from concert pitch to the note to be fingered, would appear to be cumbersome and difficult, but suits some players — particularly, perhaps, those with absolute pitch who experience a sense of discomfort if the note actually

THE INSTRUMENT AND THE PLAYER

sounded does not correspond to their mental idea of the written note in front of them. Unless, however, such players are reading from a part in high C, at least one transposition is required if the fingering is always to be related to concert pitch; even a part in F must first be transposed down a fifth if played on the F horn.

(*b*) Another method, which might be called a movable clef system, is not conveniently applicable to all crooks, and is of value only to those who are conversant with, or are willing to learn to read from obsolete or unfamiliar clefs. A different clef and the appropriate key signature are substituted mentally for those printed, and the part may then be read as for horn in F. Thus the E horn is read in the tenor clef with a key signature of five sharps. Other transpositions can be made in a similar way, e.g.:

horn in Eb: tenor clef, with two flats;
in D or Db: soprano clef with three sharps or four flats respectively;
in B or Bb basso: mezzo-soprano clef with six sharps or one flat respectively;
in Bb alto: as for Bb basso, but an octave higher;
in C: baritone clef, with one sharp, an octave up.

Upward transpositions are more difficult to transcribe suitably; the following, which are just possible, create almost as many problems as they solve.

In G: alto clef, with two sharps, an octave higher;
in A and Ab: bass clef, with four sharps or three flats respectively, two octaves higher.

Those players who use the clef method of transposition, however, would probably do so only for the larger intervals. For transpositions of a third or less up or down one of the following methods is more convenient.

(c) Each note may be transposed mentally by the required interval, and the resulting note fingered. The following passage, for example, from the first movement of Brahms's second symphony,

EX.23 Allegro non troppo

146

if played on the horn in F, is transposed down a minor third note by
by note:

Though this method at first proves slow and laborious, it can
eventually be carried out without continuous effort if regularly
practised in the various intervals called for by the transpositions
commonly required. Its defect is that if performed piecemeal it
gives no guarantee that the player has a clear conception of the
tonality of the passage.

(d) A more musical proceeding, because it enables the player to
see the picture as a whole, is to transpose the passage bodily into
the required key. Thus in the preceding example the part is transposed into A major with a key signature of three sharps. The following example, from the same symphony, illustrates the process
for a part in which the horn is pitched in the relatively rare key of
B basso:

EX.24   Adagio non troppo

This would be transposed into F♯ major or its enharmonic equivalent G♭ major, though in this particular case the former would be
more suitable:

Adagio non troppo

The best method is probably to combine the following three processes: (i) imprint the new key signature firmly in the mind, (ii) decide upon the vertical interval of transposition, up or down, and (iii) read horizontally, observing the interval between each note and the preceding one.

It will be noticed that every accidental in the written part remains an accidental in the transposed part. This will not occur, of course, if the transposition is from a part in which the horn is not crooked in the key of the piece. This is shown in the following example from the first movement of Dvořák's cello concerto, which has been described as one of the most beautiful melodies ever written for the horn. The instrument is crooked in E, and the part is written in the key of B♭ major so as to sound in D major. If played as for F horn the part must be transposed down a semitone and read as if written in A major:

With a four-valve horn in B♭, it could be played without the need for transposition by converting the instrument into a horn in A (thumb lever depressed) and reading the part as if written for horn in F. In a similar way, the passage in Ex. 23, for horn in D, could well be played on the A horn by reading it as if written for horn in E♭, a very commonly required transposition in music of the classical era. With the double horn these procedures are not possible unless the instrument is fitted with an A and E valve.

The next example, from the first movement of Beethoven's seventh symphony, lies very high for the horn in F, and is much more easily performed on the B♭ horn or the B♭ section of the double horn, when it can be played almost entirely with the second valve, not using harmonics higher than the twelfth:

transposed for horns in F:

and for horns in B♭:

A part to be played on the F horn must be transposed into the key with one sharp more, or one flat less, than the key signature of the piece; on the B♭ horn the key will be that with two sharps more or two flats less. The most common transpositions required are those from parts for horn in E, E♭, D, and C. Horn parts in G and in B♭ basso are not unusual, but other transpositions are comparatively rarely met with. A list of the crook changes required during a performance of Mozart's *Magic Flute* will give an idea of the sort of transpositions a modern player must be prepared to undertake. These are E♭, C, G, E♭, B♭ alto, G, E♭, G, F, C, G, F, E, D, F, E♭, F, G and E♭. Wagner's operas would show much the same range, though his system of notation is not always easy to understand, and he was quite capable, as Forsyth says, of writing *God Save the Queen* in some such way as this:

Horn

Strauss, even as late as 1945, was writing parts for horn in E♭ (as in his symphony for wind instruments and his second horn concerto). In his tone-poems he usually pitched his horns in F except in the extreme sharp keys, when he switched them into E. Even so, he was not averse from changing perhaps one pair only into E, possibly just for a bar or two, a proceeding whose logic it is difficult to fathom since he must have known that all his parts would be played on the F horn. It is now universal practice to write solely for horns in F. Under present conditions, however, when the composer can no longer be certain whether his parts will be played on the F, B♭ or A horn, it might well simplify matters for all concerned were all parts to be written as for horn in C basso. The number of leger lines required would be greatly reduced, and the bass clef rarely needed; the score-reader, too, would be more or less satisfied, having to cope only with an octave transposition. The modern trumpet player, usually playing a B♭ instrument, has no difficulty in reading from parts in C, and with practice the horn player could do the same. With this notation, an example like the following, from the opening of the last movement of Elgar's second symphony — a good example of a melodic part in the low register:

(*By permission of Novello & Co. Ltd.*)

becomes

with no irritating changes of clef and comparatively few leger lines. But changes of this sort are difficult to effect, for who is to make the first move — the composer, to whom it matters little, the player, who is already entrenched in the present system and would have to accustom himself to a new, or the score-reader, who would benefit most?

CHAPTER 13

Aesthetic: Style

One of the most intangible elements in any artistic activity, and one of the most difficult to analyse, is the inborn quality of the artist known as style. For the musical executant it is an essential adjunct to a convincing performance, recognizable easily enough when present, but much less easy to expound in words. Stendhal's definition of style in literature — 'that which consists in adding to a given thought all the circumstances calculated to produce the whole effect that the thought ought to produce' — can be applied appropriately enough to style in musical performance, with the important addition, of course, that in this sphere it is the province of the performer to divine what is 'the whole effect' that the composer's thought ought to produce.

H. Plunket Greene,[1] dealing specifically with the art of the interpreter, regarded style as *'the treatment of the subject "in large"*, both in conception, phrasing and colour; the turning out of a work of art in which the component parts fit in in proper proportion in the right places, and are forgotten in detail . . . leaving the listener with the feeling that the reading was as *inevitable* as it was true'. This is satisfactory as far as it goes, and in his book he went on to suggest how a singer might develop a style, always emphasizing, however, that an instinct for style must be present from the beginning.

Style must, of course, be based upon an adequate technique, but though style without technique is impossible, technique without style is only too common and from an aesthetic point of view virtually valueless. When technique obtrudes itself, style vanishes; a performance in which one is continually aware of the virtuosity of the performer is unlikely to possess style, for it draws attention to the performer rather than to the music, and unless this is an empty showpiece the performance will not produce the 'whole effect that it ought to produce'. Technique must be the servant, not the

[1] *Interpretation in Song*, p. 31.

master. Upon his technique — tone quality, control, agility and so on — a player bases his style, but many other elements go to its making and it is these which will determine how fully he puts his technique to the most artistic use. They will include intelligence, imagination and taste, discrimination and sensibility, individuality and temperament; and all these are influenced by physical, psychological and intellectual factors so closely interwoven that their separate effects are almost impossible to disentangle.

Occasionally a pregnant phrase from a critic may give a clearer over-all picture of the style of a performance than pages of painstaking analysis. Dissection down to minute detail lays bare the mechanics of a performance, but it can give little idea of the spirit which informs it. For example, the comment in a review of a recording of Dvořák's cello concerto that 'Casals seems to play with a sword rather than a bow' is an admirable summing-up of the style of this particular performance. But however illuminating to the listener, such a phrase cannot, and indeed is not intended to give any clue to the exact means whereby this style is achieved, and it would in fact be difficult and somewhat tedious to try to carry out an analysis of this sort. Moreover, the results would not be worth the labour involved, for style is not a thing which can or should be imitated. The performer must seek to evolve and develop a style of his own; his task is to fill in the detail within the broad outline provided by the composer in such a way that, without forcing his own personality into the foreground and equally without allowing it to be submerged without trace, he yet contrives to give a true and inevitable reading of the composer's thoughts.

The technical means that the performer employs to achieve his end will be such subtleties as a change of tone colour here, an accent there, an almost imperceptible *tenuto* on one note, a minute lightening on another; but these nuances must be those that he feels are inherent in the music rather than carefully thought out artifices superimposed upon it. It is these minute gradations of tempo, dynamics, accentuation and colour, insusceptible of notation on paper, that give the phrases point and meaning, and the piece shape and life. The whole effect must be one of spontaneity, as if the sound were emanating directly from the composer's imagination instead of suffering the twofold translation from thought into musical notation, thence into sound through the medium of the performer. Style is a matter of feeling and instinct rather than of calculation; a stylist instinctively senses the mood of a piece, instinctively he chooses the correct tempo, instinctively he adopts the right degree of flexibility in his phrasing. This is not to say that he need give no thought to his interpretation, and trust to his style to see him through; but the true stylist is likely to arrive at the correct solution of the various problems that pose themselves as the result of his thought through his innate musical feeling rather than by any intense intellectual process.

These general observations are relevant to all instrumental performance, but their special application to the art of horn playing requires more detailed consideration. For reasons already explained, the player's primary aim in most types of music must be clarity of enunciation. There is nothing more fatal to the emergence of a true style than the 'woolliness' which blurs outlines that should be sharp and creates an impression of slovenliness where precision is required. In the absence of this continual search for clarity rhythmic impulse is lost and a general feeling of flabbiness results. The emphasis on precision, however, does not imply that every attack must be made *sforzando*, nor that staccato passages must necessarily sound with the almost explosive effect that is possible if the tongue movements are very sharp and rapid. What is required, both in fast and slow-moving parts, staccato or legato, is that when an attack is made it shall be clean and well-controlled.

The horn is one of the most treacherous of all instruments to play, because it has perhaps a smaller margin of error than any other. The slightest miscalculation, which in other instruments would pass almost unnoticed, on the horn almost always leads to disaster. It is of prime importance, therefore, that the player should instil into his hearers complete certainty that such blemishes will not occur, and he will be able to do this only if he has unbounded confidence in himself and his powers. More than any other instrumentalist the horn player will reap the reward of a bold approach. Signs of tentativeness quickly communicate themselves to the listener, and even if nothing actually goes wrong he will be left with a sense of insecurity fatal to his full enjoyment because it distracts his attention from the music and concentrates it upon the technical difficulties confronting the player. A bold approach, on the other hand, not only relieves the listener of his doubts, but makes it easier for the player himself to surmount his technical problems and gives his playing a panache and vitality never attained by the less obviously confident performer. One of the marks of a great horn player is that he achieves a sense of ease and security so powerful that the possibility of a false note never arises in the listener's mind, and this is a matter not so much of technique as of overwhelming confidence.

Closely connected with a player's style is his possession of an acute ear for dynamic values, which in the case of the horn need very careful consideration. Whether in orchestral or chamber music he must be able to judge, almost instinctively, the prominence to be given to his part. Obviously this is determined by its character and the place it occupies in the general texture, but the horn is subject to special considerations whose effect is not always fully realized. Generally speaking, players often appear to restrain themselves, or to be restrained, unduly; horn solos may fail to make their full effect because they are insufficiently audible. Although technically a member of the brass group, the horn has little of the penetrating edge of the trumpet or trombone, and its bell, partially occluded by the hand, is usually facing away from the listener. As a result, dynamic markings for the horn, if interpreted on the same scale as for the heavy brass, may easily lead to its partial or even complete obliteration in places where it should stand out from the background, unless the composer has taken special account of these facts in his markings. It would not be too much to say that a player must step up the marking in a solo passage by one degree or more at times if he is to get it over. The main criterion of correct balance is not how the player sounds to himself in relation to other instruments, but how he sounds to the listener in the audience. To some extent, it is true, the player can help to give his part more prominence by imparting to it a greater intensity of expression than he would accord to a phrase of no thematic significance. With a good player this procedure is more or less instinctive, but its efficacy is limited in scope to those situations in which the horn has to contend with, at most, a fairly lightly scored accompaniment.

Such considerations of balance, and the need for the horn to make its full effect, call for a high degree of musicianship from the player. One sometimes feels that he is kept on too tight a rein. Much depends, of course, upon the circumstances. The horn, like most other instruments, sounds most characteristically itself either when entirely unaccompanied or when separated from the accompanying instruments by a wide interval. The accompaniment of middle register solo passages poses considerable problems if the instrument is to make its presence felt as a horn rather than as an anonymous and somewhat colourless member of the ensemble. It *can* make itself heard when playing a middle register part, but not so easily as some composers imagine. It is not naturally a self-assertive instrument, except in its highest register, and its timbre is all too readily assimilated to that of the strings.

The problem is complicated, of course, by the fact that it is often impossible for the player himself to tell what effect he is producing owing to the acoustics of the hall, and in broadcasting to the presence of the balance and control experts.

Perhaps the surest test of style is whether a definite individuality emerges from the playing. *Le style c'est l'homme* is nowhere more true than of instrumentalists. A player's character expresses itself in his style; impersonal renderings, however perfect technically, are dull and uninteresting. In the playing of great artists we find personal foibles which in lesser men degenerate into empty and meaningless mannerisms, but which in the greatest enhance rather than subtract from their stature. A great player is recognized as soon as heard by virtue of the strongly marked personality that is immediately apparent. It does not force itself upon the listener's attention, however, nor come between him and the music, but he is inevitably aware, if only sub-consciously, that behind the beauty of tone, the flawless technique and the interpretative sensibility which he takes for granted a powerful and intensely musical mind is at work. There should be no eccentricities, no exaggerated contrasts or over-elaboration in the playing, but instead the listener will find delightful and felicitous touches growing naturally out of the music. Spontaneity, vitality and strength, even in the gentlest moments, are the qualities we find in the playing of a great artist, playing instinct with character, based upon supreme technique put wholly at the service of the music.

But though a player's style may be — indeed, should be — highly personal, it will normally be so within limits imposed largely by national considerations. An attempt has been made in Chapter 3 to explain differences in tone quality partly, at least, in terms of national temperament and outlook, and the same factors are found to have their effect upon a player's style. Nowhere, perhaps, does the *mystique* of the horn persist more strongly than in Germany. To the German the horn is, above all, the instrument of romance. It speaks to him of dark forests and mysterious glens; it raises its voice most characteristically in heroic fanfares and massive chorales. To him *der deutschen Waldhornklang* is the dark, rich sound which composers like Weber, Wagner, Bruckner and Strauss understood to perfection. In his general style, then, the German player places high value on a full tone and large, far-carrying sound. Typically this was, until recently, somewhat veiled though not muffled, but at the present time ideals of tone quality vary considerably in different parts of the country; in some places the traditional timbre has given way to a brighter, more open sound, and to the smooth mellowness of old a certain degree of 'friction' is imparted which for some makes the sound more interesting to listen to and prevents it from cloying. But whatever type of tone quality the German player favours, the outstanding feature of his style is the intense feeling and *Innigkeit* which he brings to his playing. At times it may be felt that this very intensity is a little overdone, and that it precludes the brilliance and verve that are sometimes necessary. Putting it very broadly, one might say that the German player is at his best in German music of the nineteenth and early twentieth centuries. Whether his style has developed in response to the type of part his own composers have given him, or conversely, they have been stimulated by the art of the German horn player, is a question to which there is certainly no simple answer.

Almost at the opposite pole stands the French horn player. He thinks more in terms of brilliance and vivacity; his approach is less intense and he has, perhaps, a lighter touch. His aim is delicacy rather than weight of tone, and in pursuit of this aim he cultivates a clear and open timbre, marred to many ears by a persistent and excessive vibrato — a comparatively recent innovation (also indulged in by Soviet players) which would surely have been deprecated by the great French hand horn virtuosi.

To a great extent the American is the inheritor of a mixed tradition, for in the early years of the century most of the great American orchestras imported foreign players whose influence is still to be detected at first or second hand. It has been suggested that when a typically American style eventually crystallizes it will prove to be the most satisfying of all, incorporating the best elements of each school. At the present time it leans, in the main, towards the German ideal, to which the American adds a superficial polish which is occasionally allowed to assume too great an importance and then causes the style to degenerate into mere slickness and mechanical efficiency.

The British, as usual, manage to find a compromise. It is only recently that they have changed from the narrow-bore to the wide-bore instrument, and with memories of the tone quality of the French horn still fresh, British players produce a tone midway between the two extremes, broader and darker than the French, but with less carrying-power than the German, though in fact German-built instruments are almost exclusively used. In other respects, too, they appear to strike a happy medium between these two sharply opposed styles of playing. British reserve is less apparent than one would expect, but one is occasionally conscious that hidden reserves are not being fully tapped. Economic considerations doubtless play an important part here. Less fortunately placed than, for example, his German counterpart, the British orchestral player is often employed on a comparatively short-term contract under which he can be dismissed at short notice. In addition, he is frequently overworked in comparison with the continental player. It is not uncommon, for example, for German orchestras to employ two complete horn sections which perform at

AESTHETIC: STYLE

alternate concerts or share a concert between them. In this country
economic necessity and, perhaps, ignorance among those who do
not play the instrument of the strain that long hours of playing
impose upon the player, sometimes lead to situations in which it is
humanly impossible for him to give of his best. Much can be done
to improve physical endurance, but the mental strain of too frequent
concert performances and, even more, of recording sessions cannot
be conducive to the maintenance of a good style. Despite such
inhibiting factors, which are only now being slowly ameliorated,
during the past fifty years or so Britain has produced her fair
share, and perhaps more, of the world's leading players. Where
once she depended largely on immigrants from the Continent
for her horn players, a native tradition of playing and teaching is
now firmly enough established to supply a steady stream of excellent players to her chief orchestras.

Part IV

THE INSTRUMENT
IN CONSORT

CHAPTER 14

The Horn
in the Orchestra

The horn has been called 'the soul of the orchestra' by one composer, and 'perhaps the most beautiful of all instruments' by another. Since neither of these composers was a player of the horn, such high praise is free from the suspicion of prejudice that might otherwise be engendered. It is certainly true that composers have given many of their most inspired ideas to this instrument as a soloist in the orchestra, and while it might be claiming too much to award the horn the palm as its most versatile member, it is capable of playing a wide variety of roles, very largely owing to its ability to blend with other groups in the orchestra.

Before considering the present position of the horn in the orchestra, it will be convenient to make a brief survey of its career since it first became a regular member. As a melodic instrument it has had a somewhat chequered career. Very soon after its introduction into the orchestra in the eighteenth century an attempt was made to give it a melodic role and it was provided with florid, mostly conjunct parts such as are to be found in Bach and Handel's writing for the instrument (Ex. 29). In order to cope with these

Ex. 29

Bach: Cantata No. 14; Aria

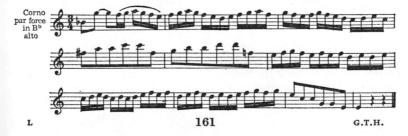

parts it was forced to explore that somewhat insecure region of its compass lying between the eighth and sixteenth harmonics, or even higher, a region where in any case the tone quality is hardly at its most characteristic. Such parts, as Carse[1] says, 'were unsuccessful attempts to force square pegs into round holes'. It was soon realised that this was not its true métier and the clarino style gave way to a less ambitious but more natural non-melodic style in which the horns were used for marking the rhythm, enriching the sustained harmonies of the woodwind, supporting and blending with the strings, and in general beginning to forge the strong links which now bind the horns with the brass, on the one hand, and the woodwind, on the other. Such solos as they were given were of the hunting-call and fanfare type (Ex. 30) which had been developed

Ex. 30

F.A. Philidor: Hunting Call from "Tom Jones"

from the available harmonics of the natural horn in its early days when it was no more than an accompaniment of the hunt. Thus, in a sense, in its new orchestral role it reverted to type, but with the important addition that its major function was now to give solidity and cohesion to the texture.

The advent of the hand horn and the development of the technique of hand stopping towards the end of the eighteenth century at first had little effect on orchestral horn parts. Haydn and Mozart used the stopped notes only rarely except in their horn concertos, and though Haydn sometimes appeared to be reintroducing the clarino style (Ex. 31), his parts became simpler,

Ex. 31

Haydn: Symphony No. 51

on the whole, in his later years. Both of these composers occasionally used four horns instead of the two which had been standard

[1] *The History of Orchestration*, p. 123.

until this time. The limitations of the instrument were made into a virtue; there was no real possibility of chromatic, harmonic or melodic progression, but Mozart and Haydn nevertheless managed to give their horn parts character and individuality. Occasional melodic passages, where these could be played on open notes, rhythmical figures, often in company with trumpets and drums, and holding notes in octaves and fifths were their staple fare in the symphonies. This may give the impression that life for the horn player was a dull affair at this time, but in fact both composers set their players plenty of technical problems, which are not always easily solved even on the modern instrument.

Beethoven used the stopped notes freely, and the scope of the instrument was thereby extended, so that once again it began to take on the function of a melodist, though a somewhat imperfect one. Further scope was given by employing two pairs of horns crooked in different keys, so that a greater selection of notes was available. Beethoven's horn parts became increasingly elaborate, and as examples of what he considered feasible there may be cited the famous solo for fourth horn in the slow movement of the ninth symphony, and the accompaniment for three horns to Leonora's aria in Act I of *Fidelio* (Ex. 32).

Ex.32

Spohr and Rossini allotted the horn even more freely chromatic passages, straining hand horn technique to its limits. Rossini, however, as a horn player himself, knew what could and what could not be done and his parts, though often difficult, were within the bounds of possibility (Ex. 33). It is obvious that by this time composers were beginning to chafe at the restraints imposed upon them by the imperfections of the hand horn, and it has been queried why Beethoven, for example, who did not normally allow himself to be checked by technical restrictions, failed to write parts for an instrument which did not yet exist, in the hope that it would eventually materialize. In fact, of course, the valve horn was within sight, but even when it did appear it was not accepted

Ex. 33

Rossini: Overture to "Semiramide"

unreservedly either by composers or players, and it was only slowly that it began to make its mark on horn parts. For the second time the horn gradually became a melodist in its own right, but this time without the necessity for climbing into its upper reaches or for producing the heterogeneous tone quality which was the best the hand horn could do when performing a melodic role.

By a lucky chance — for the horn is of all instruments the most romantic — the advent of the valve horn, imperfect though it was at the start, more or less coincided with the development of the romantic movement, and its increased potentialities in the melodic sphere were seized upon by those composers who could make best use of them. It came rather too late, perhaps, for the arch-romantic Berlioz, who was sometimes driven to use horns crooked in four different keys, with a curious effect upon the look of the score, in order that they should be able to cope with the melodic passages he wished to allot them. He could never be sure of finding valve horns in his native France, where they were viewed with a suspicion which lasted well into the second half of the century. Germany, on the other hand, adopted the valve horn with more alacrity, though at first even here composers retained the hand horn as well. Wagner, for instance, used a pair of each in his early works, as if uncertain whether the valve horn were to be used as an addition to the hand horn or as a substitute for it. As originally used the valve merely served as a quick way of changing crooks, and it was not for some time that its value as a means of providing a chromatic range of homogeneous tone quality was realized. Once this principle had been established, Wagner became the first great writer for the valve horn, not only using it as a solo instrument or in a group of up to eight to provide full harmony, but continually combining it with strings to use it as 'the most perfect of all continuo-players'.

The technique of the hand horn still left its mark on the parts written by Brahms; though he could not blind himself to the benefits conferred by the valves, he seemed still in his heart to prefer the hand horn and often crooked his two pairs of horns in different keys so as to be able to use as many open notes as possible. There still lingered a feeling that the valved notes were inferior in tone to the open, as may well have been the case before the valve had been perfected. There is no doubt, however, that the horn inspired Brahms as few other instruments did.

By virtue of its cohesive function the horn had become indispensable in the orchestra, quite apart from its value as a solo instrument of a warm and rich quality. Its importance in this role is illustrated by the fact that Bruckner, in revising the scores of his symphonies for performance, was reputed to play through the horn parts alone. Whatever the demerits of Bruckner's orchestration, there is no doubt that he understood the horn and how to use it. This is also true of Mahler, whose scores, it has been suggested, could well be regarded as a first-class school for the instrument. Besides giving it many solos in the less heavily orchestrated parts of his symphonies, he repeatedly used the unison of six, eight or even ten horns to deliver the massive chorale-like themes of which he was so fond, with an effect as majestic as anything in the history of the orchestra.

Strauss found the horn the ideal instrument for the delineation of his heroes. His horn parts, though often of a virtuoso character, ranging over an exceptionally wide compass and employing a variety of special effects, yet still bear the marks of hand horn ancestry beneath their chromatic elaboration — wide skips in the lower register giving way to closer intervals as the higher is reached. These parts, despite the formidable technique required — and in his early days they were regarded as almost unplayable — are nonetheless grateful to play, especially as the technical difficulties are now somewhat eased by the use of the double horn.

With the advent of Schoenberg and atonal music any approach to horn writing based on its hand horn ancestry became irrelevant, and a new concept of horn writing had perforce to be evolved. The problem was to counter the traditional view of the horn as an instrument inextricably bound up with the harmonic series, and to devise a language capable of coping with the angular outlines and unvocal intervals of so much of this music in an idiomatic way.

The solution to the problem is complicated, particularly in Webern's case, by the use of *Klangfarbenmelodie*, in which each instrument plays possibly only one or two notes of a theme before handing it on to another. This procedure gives the score a curiously fragmentary appearance, and usually makes quotation of a single part quite meaningless. Example 34, from Webern's symphony,

Ex. 34

(*By permission of Universal Edition (Alfred A. Kalmus Ltd.)*)

Op. 21, is by far the longest continuous passage for any instrument in the whole work, and gives a good idea of the type of horn part which must now be taken as normal. The question whether parts such as these, and even more advanced horn writing, can be considered idiomatic is one which each player must decide for himself. Schuller's[1] test is to ask whether they could be played as effectively on any other instrument. If not, then they are good horn parts.

The horn has reached its present position in the orchestra partly as the result of the demands made upon it by those composers who have written for it in a way that seemed at first to overreach its capabilities, partly owing to the enterprise of players who have shown that these difficulties can be surmounted, and partly thanks to the ingenuity and inventiveness of manufacturers who from time to time have introduced improvements and additions to the instrument with the aim of widening its scope. Whether these developments have all resulted in gain and none in loss is a debatable point, which cannot be argued here. The modern composer takes the horn as he finds it; it has had, perforce, to move with the times, and though tears may well be shed, for example, over the passing of the French horn or the indignities which, some would say, modern composers sometimes inflict on it, these must be accepted as the facts of life in the present-day horn world.

The versatility of the horn as a member of the modern orchestra has already been alluded to; its functions will now be dealt with in more detail. They can be grouped under four general heads. Of these, the most obvious, but not necessarily the most important, is its use as a solo instrument. The most effective horn solos are

[1] *Horn Technique*, p. 86.

still those in which it is allowed time to reveal its true colours; though it is capable of considerable agility it does not then have the chance to deploy the typical sonority which is its greatest asset. Its limpid tone and wide range of expression are not allowed full play in many quick-moving solos, which tend to reduce it to a more or less colourless anonymity. When given the opportunity to spread itself there is no more beautiful sound in the orchestra.

It has already been pointed out that the horn is the romantic instrument *par excellence*, and there are innumerable examples of its use in this role. Its association with the chase leads naturally to its employment in hunting scenes such as the 'Royal Hunt and Storm' in *Les Troyens* of Berlioz, where characteristic echo effects help to paint a superb picture not requiring any visual addition for its full realization. Equally romantic is Weber's sound-picture of the forest in his *Freischütz* Overture, though with modern instruments the full effect as Weber imagined it is not quite achieved, for he wrote for two horns in F, with their comparatively bright colour, answering two in C with a softer and more dreamy tone.

More recently, Delius has used the horn in very different style to express a sense of distance and solitude. One thinks especially of the echoing horns in the section of *A Mass of Life* entitled 'On the Mountains' (Ex. 35) and the intertwining pattern woven by the

Ex. 35

(*By permission of Boosey & Hawkes, Ltd.*)

arabesques of two horns against a *pianissimo* string background in *A Song of the High Hills*. His own brand of bitter-sweet nostalgia, too, is magically conveyed by the simple chords for six horns as the lovers enter the Paradise Garden in *A Village Romeo and Juliet*.

The horn sometimes shows a pastoral or rustic side to its character, as in the opening of Brahms's Serenade, Op. 11, or the

Ex. 36

(*By permission of Durand & Cie., copyright owners*)

THE INSTRUMENT IN CONSORT

Ländler of Mahler's Ninth symphony; such bucolic behaviour is at the opposite pole from the veiled mystery of the opening of D'Indy's *Istar* (Ex. 36), in which the *bouché* horn gives out, quite unaccompanied, the skeleton of the theme on which the work is based.

There can be few more dramatic openings to any symphony than that of Schubert's C major; no mighty outburst from the full orchestra, but a simple though pregnant theme delivered in unison by two unaccompanied horns (Ex. 37). No doubt Mahler had this

Ex. 37

opening in mind when he began his third symphony with the melody of an Austrian marching tune given by eight horns in unison. The use of several horns to a part is common practice with Mahler: he realised that, in the large orchestras he used, horn tone would fail to tell unless reinforced. Even in a *pianissimo* passage like the *Frère Jacques* theme in the slow movement of his first symphony he felt it wiser to allot three horns to each octave, though his aim here was probably to ensure steadiness in the low register.

Strauss also used horns in unison to bring significant themes to the fore. An example from *Don Juan* has already been quoted (Ex. 16, p. 135), and there are many similar cases in *Ein Heldenleben*. But he could also use the horn with tenderness; the closing pages of *Ein Heldenleben*, a long duet for solo violin and horn, breathe a spirit of calm and resignation in whose evocation the nobility of timbre of the horn plays a major part.

Horn calls are obviously in character. The best known and probably the most extended is that associated with Siegfried in the *Ring* (Ex. 38). This is essentially hand horn music written for the valve horn; it sounds as if it could be played on the hand horn, as indeed it could with only a few stopped notes, but it is immeasurably improved by the assistance of the valves in those few places.

The use of muted horns is now commonplace. Perhaps their greatest exponents are the modern French composers, particularly Debussy and Ravel, for whom they provide just the right air of mystery and languor in such works as *L'Après-midi d'un Faune* and the *Rapsodie Espagnole*.

Very soon after the number of horns in the orchestra had been increased to four composers began to realize how effectively they

might be employed as a group in harmony. The trio from the Scherzo of Beethoven's *Eroica* Symphony (Ex. 39) is the prototype of countless passages scored for three or four horns in harmony. From then down to Falla's *Nights in the Gardens of Spain*, Bax's *Garden of Fand*, and Stravinsky's *Le Sacre du Printemps* their sound has provided many thrilling moments. How well, too, the horn quartet, with some assistance from bassoons, is suited to give out the hymn-like Children's Prayer in the overture to Humperdinck's *Hänsel and Gretel* (Ex. 40).

Finally, to show that the simplest conception is sometimes the most inspired, there may be mentioned the three notes of Oberon's magic horn, and the highly imaginative repeated notes, tolling

Ex 39

'like a bell haunted by a human soul', in the slow movement of Schubert's C major symphony. It is impossible not to believe that

Ex. 40

Tchaikovsky was inspired by this passage when he used two horns, marked *pp*, *sons bouchés* at the start, but becoming *poco a poco più f*, to represent the clock striking twelve in his Fantasy-Overture *Hamlet*. The use of stopped horns becoming gradually more and more clangorous imparts exactly the right atmosphere of dramatic intensity.

The horn is often used to double a melodic line, especially in the tenor register. Thus the violas and cellos frequently find themselves in company with one or two horns, and horns in unison with violins on the G string provide a richer fuller sound than violins alone. Many other doublings, in unison and at the octave, will be found in almost any modern score, and the effect in practically every case is to broaden the tone or remove the 'edge', as in the unison of horn and trumpet.

A second most important function of the horn is that of filling in the middle of the texture, adding density, fullness and smoothness without making itself at all prominent. Almost any page of any symphony by Sibelius, opened at random, would provide an example of

'A shuttle of slanted bows that weaves a texture soon
Thickened with barely audible horns'

as Christopher Hassall puts it in his poem 'Symphony'. Carried to excess, the thickening becomes a blanket tending to envelop important thematic matter, a charge which has been levelled against Brahms, whose constant use of middle register horn parts has caused his orchestration to be described as thick and muddy. To some extent this is true, but Brahms's love for the horn at any rate prevents the parts from becoming uninteresting for the player. Long-held notes and internal pedal-points — and the horn can hold a note in the medium register perhaps longer than any other woodwind or brass instrument — formed a considerable part of the staple diet of the orchestral horn player, at least until comparatively recent times. In lightly scored works, such as Wagner's *Siegfried Idyll*, in which only two horns are used, the second may well have to supply the bass at some points, either with the cellos and double-basses, or even alone. At the end of Wagner's work the second horn, pitched in E, has a long-held low C, sounding E below the bass clef, for eleven bars of slow time. He may get some help here from the first player, who is not otherwise engaged, but he will not do so in an earlier passage, where he has to sustain a pedal G for some 20 to 25 seconds quite unsupported. These low register notes can have a beautiful velvety quality, but they possess no great penetrative power, and are therefore of very little use in a full *tutti*.

Since they blend so well with the woodwind, the horns are often used to complete the harmony of this group, either in block chordal progressions or in repeated chords of the same harmony, as at the opening of Mendelssohn's *Italian* symphony. In the *tutti* the horns are frequently associated with the strings or woodwind rather than with the remainder of the brass, though of course there are many cases in which the horns are used to complete brass harmony — the massive chorale-like passages in Bruckner's symphonies spring immediately to mind. They tend, however, to warm and soften the colour of trumpets and trombones, and are therefore omitted if a sharp cutting edge is required. Horns in harmony are sometimes used to accompany a melody played by another instrument; there is a mysterious passage near the end of Berg's violin concerto in which four muted horns provide almost the sole accompaniment for the chorale melody played in canon by cellos and harp (Ex. 41).

Finally, the horns may be used in a rhythmic rather than melodic or harmonic role. In this capacity they are often associated with trumpets and drums to provide accentuation or to mark a

Ex. 41

(*By permission of Universal Edition [Alfred A. Kalmus Ltd.]*)

particular rhythm. In these circumstances they should not be pitched too high, for their function here is percussive rather than colouristic. The pages of any Mozart symphony will provide examples in plenty of this sort of part.

Technically, horn parts have been becoming progressively more difficult since the instrument first joined the orchestra, apart from its first essays as a melodic instrument in the clarino register. The stimulus towards increasingly complex parts has usually been

172

provided by some physical discovery or mechanical improvement — the technique of hand stopping, the inventions of the valve and of the double horn, for example — or by the virtuosity of individual players. It is not easy to forecast what further developments in this direction are likely. To a certain degree the extensions of its capabilities that have taken place since the invention of the valve have robbed the horn of some of its individuality, and it is easy to take a conservative line and hope that this process will be carried no further. Much will depend upon the course taken by orchestral music in general; no doubt players will respond to whatever demands may be made upon them, even if some do so with a feeling of nostalgic regret for the romantic era — the golden age of the horn.

CHAPTER 15

The Horn
in Chamber Music

The term 'chamber music' has acquired a rather more extended meaning than its original use to describe music intended for performance in the home rather than in the church or in the theatre. In the seventeenth century the public concert-hall was unknown and secular music was largely in the patronage of the aristocracy, who had their own retinues of musicians to perform music written for them by a resident composer. These musicians were players of stringed and keyboard instruments, with a sprinkling of flutes, oboes and bassoons. The precursor of the horn, a crude and loud-voiced fellow, would not have been at home in such company, and was tolerated only at the hunt and on the battlefield or parade-ground. When it was used for entertainment it was allowed to be heard only at a distance, playing for the benefit of the nobility in the parks surrounding their houses, or 'on the water, or near the side of cliffs, or hanging woods', as an early English tutor for the instrument put it.

At this stage the horn was thus an almost exclusively outdoor instrument. It had been admitted to the military band, and composers now little more than names wrote works for the *Harmonie-Musik* combination of pairs of oboes, horns and bassoons which, even when played on modern instruments, have a decided tang about them. The horn was not really ready to be allowed indoors until hand horn technique had been developed and the tone refined. Haydn, and Mozart in his earlier years, both wrote many partitas, cassations, serenades and divertimenti for wind combinations which included the horn. Most of them were *pièces d'occasion* for outdoor use at such functions as weddings, but Mozart's serenades K. 375 and K. 388 for two each of oboes, clarinets, horns and bassoons, and K. 361 for thirteen wind instruments are fine works by any standard. Mozart did not hesitate to bring the horn forward to take part in some of his chamber music works, notably the quintet, K. 407, for horn, violin, two violas and cello, and the quintet, K. 452 for wind and piano, which he considered his best work up to the time of its composition.

By the beginning of the nineteenth century the horn was a fairly well-established member of chamber music groups, sometimes in combination with strings, as in Beethoven's sextet, Op. 81b, or with other wind instruments and strings, as in his septet, Op. 20, and Schubert's octet, Op. 166, but also to a growing extent with woodwind instruments alone. Thus there came into being the wind quintet, a colourful combination whose merits, though well appreciated by composers, as a glance at Appendix C will show, have been somewhat underestimated by others. The invention of valves gave further impetus to the emergence of the horn as a chamber music instrument, for it was now able to compete on more equal terms with woodwind instruments in the wind quintet, and even with the strings. Brahms's horn trio, Op. 40, ostensibly, if somewhat optimistically written for natural horn, provides a good example of a work in which the horn seems perfectly at home in the company of violin and piano.

Since the middle of last century until the present time there has been an ever-increasing output of works for a variety of combinations in which the horn is included. Many of these are admittedly lightweight in character, intended to divert rather than to edify, but there are also works of serious import among them. Schoenberg's wind quintet, Op. 26, with its technically very difficult horn part, was one of the first of his works in strict twelve-note style, and has been succeeded by a number of other important works, such as Stravinsky's septet, using serial technique.

With the compositions for larger groups of wind instruments alone we move into the borderlands of chamber music. The string quartet is, of course, the chamber music combination *par excellence*, but there has been a tendency to regard the invasion of its field by wind instruments as an unwarranted intrusion. Unrelieved wind tone, it has often been said, tends quickly to pall. The wind group, certainly, has a smaller emotional range than the string, but the increasing number of such groups in this country seems to suggest that its expressive range is not quite so limited as is often supposed, and that the striking colours it provides are more satisfying than some writers would have us believe. Tovey made a wise comment in this connection when he remarked that 'it is unreasonable to blame Mozart's glorious serenade for thirteen wind instruments for sounding like a military band; we ought rather to wish that a military band could sound like a Mozart serenade'.

THE INSTRUMENT IN CONSORT

Of all the instruments with which the horn has been allied, the piano is perhaps the least compatible, and this in spite of a comparatively large number of works written for this combination. The antipathy is based on good grounds. It has already been emphasized that the horn needs room to move and time to deploy its unique tone quality. As a solo instrument it is most at home when dealing with comparatively slow-moving material. Though capable of rapidity of execution, such as is required for contrast in an extended work of several movements, the horn does not take kindly to thematic matter of this sort unless it is carefully written with a particular eye to its special idiosyncrasies. It is significant that many of the works for the horn as solo instrument, both with piano and orchestral accompaniment, bear such titles as aria, lied, romance, poem, reverie, nocturne and the like, indicative of the singing role in which it is most effective. In concerted works, on the other hand, the agility can be provided by instruments more suited to such material, while the horn reverts to its less showy but equally important task of binding the ensemble together, emerging only when suitable melodic matter presents itself. For this reason few of the works for horn in sonata form are wholly effective — in fact it might be said that unless the composer is himself an experienced horn player, or has the good fortune to have access to the advice of such a player, he would be well-advised to think long and hard before embarking on an undertaking of this sort.

The repertoire of music for horns alone, though increasing, is still not very extensive. The sound of four or more horns in harmony is moving and impressive, as Weber, Wagner and many other composers have realized full well, but except in small doses is liable to become monotonous. The problem is to provide sufficient variety, both of tone colour and rhythmic impulse, and also to prevent the texture from becoming too thick. In fact the variety of tone colour available from a good player is wider than composers sometimes realize. Hindemith, in his sonata for four horns, utilizes an astonishingly varied range quite legitimately and exploits the full resources of the horn without ever conveying the impression that he is asking too much of it or using effect for effect's sake. The work requires a virtuoso technique, of course, but it is true horn music. The number of extended works of this calibre, however, is small, and the greater part of the repertoire is, somewhat naturally, of more interest to the player than the listener. It is interesting to note, incidentally, that in America horn ensembles of up to twenty-four instruments are becoming popular, and works have been specially written for these groups.

Appendix A

THE WAGNER TUBAS

A short note on these instruments may not be out of place since they are the closest relations of the horns and were intended to be played, the two tenors by the fifth and seventh horn players, the basses by the sixth and eighth. They were devised by Wagner to complete a fourth brass family, capable of competing with as well as contrasting with trumpets and trombones. They are more like horns than tubas, being of bore intermediate between that of the horn and the true tuba, but being properly played with a conical mouthpiece like that of the horn.

They are of two sizes, the tenor pitched in nine-foot B♭ and the bass in twelve-foot F being exactly the same length as the corresponding horns. Two of each type make up the group, with a true contrabass tuba in C sometimes supplying the bass. The compass, in actual sounds, of the tenor instrument is from E♭ to ƒ″, and of the bass from B′♭ to a′.

The instruments are built in oval tuba shape, but with the nine-to ten-inch bell pointing to the right of the player, and the valves are so arranged that they can be operated by the left hand as on the horn. Four valves are fitted, the fourth lowering by a perfect fourth but acting mainly as a sort of compensator to correct intonation in the lower valve positions.[1]

The wider bore makes these instruments freer-blowing than the horn, and hence accurate intonation becomes something of a problem, especially on the F tuba. The upper notes of this tuba are unreliable, but in practice it is rarely required to rise above middle C (actual sound).

The tone of these tubas was intended to combine something of the mellowness of the horn with the heavier quality of tuba tone. It is certainly broader than that of the horn, and has a grave majesty which makes it very effective in slow-moving elegiac music such as it is allotted in the *Ring* and in the *Adagios* of Bruckner's last symphonies.

Those who have used the Wagner tubas in their works (Wagner himself, Bruckner, Strauss, Schoenberg, Nicodé) do not appear to

---

[1] Double tubas in B♭ and F are now to be had.

have been able to make up their minds what is the most suitable notation to adopt. The following methods have been used:

(*a*) Wagner (first system, in *Das Rheingold*).
Written exactly as if for B♭ and F horns, using the old notation for the bass clef. This is the obvious method, since the instruments are to be used by horn players accustomed to this notation.

(*b*) Wagner (second system, in the prelude to *Götterdämmerung*).
As in (*a*), but an octave too high. This notation is also used by Bruckner in his seventh symphony and by Strauss in *Elektra*.

(*c*) Wagner (third system, in the remainder of *Götterdämmerung*, *Die Walküre*, and *Siegfried*).
For tenor tubas in E♭ and bass in B♭ basso. A note in the score, not in fact implemented, directs that the parts for the players should be as in (*a*).

(*d*) Bruckner (ninth symphony).
B♭ tubas as for B♭ horns; F tubas wholly in the bass clef as for horns in F, old notation.

A short passage from *Götterdämmerung* will indicate what unnecessary complications are introduced by Wagner's third method:

sounding

Appendix B

CARE AND MAINTENANCE OF THE HORN

Provided it is well looked after, the instrument should need little in the way of repair. If, however, a major fault should develop, it is advisable to have it rectified by a competent instrument repairer rather than attempt to put it right oneself. In any case, a periodic overhaul can never do any harm, and may well bring to light small defects unnoticed by the player.

A brass instrument has a better appearance if it is kept bright externally. Unless it is clear-lacquered, as many horns are nowadays, it is bound to tarnish with repeated handling, and should be cleaned at intervals with good quality metal polish. A well-polished instrument has a psychological effect on the player, giving him a sense of confidence, though it is doubtful whether a brilliant surface has any direct effect on tone quality.

Care should be taken not to drop the horn or knock it against any hard object, for the dents so caused, besides spoiling the instrument's appearance, may well have a deleterious effect on the intonation.

Perspiration should always be wiped off the instrument after playing; it has a very corrosive effect on the metal, and many players have a left-hand guard fitted, if one is not provided, and even this wears through after a few years.

The horn should be emptied of moisture before being put away in its case; a certain amount is bound to condense from the breath during playing, mainly in the first part of the tubing, and to a lesser extent in the valve slides and tuning slide. Too few horns are provided with water keys, and if the moisture is allowed to remain in the instrument it will tend to corrode the inside of the bore, leading to the formation of verdigris and detracting from the smoothness of the inner surface.

The inside of the tubing should be regularly cleaned by pouring warm soapy water through the instrument. During this process the valves should be worked up and down so that the water enters the valve chambers and slides. The initial part of the mouthpipe should be pulled through about once a month. The mouthpiece should be cleaned in a similar way, or by means of a small brush. The mouthpiece should never be left in the mouthpipe after playing, for it may become jammed, and is then difficult to remove without damaging it.

The efficiency of a piston valve action is largely dependent upon the cleanliness of the valves; if they are allowed to become dirty or corroded their speed of action is greatly impaired. The valves should therefore be cleaned regularly with a warm weak solution of soda and should then be lightly oiled with special oil sold for this purpose. The valve springs, corks and washers should be checked at the same time.

Rotary valves usually function satisfactorily so long as the instrument is regularly played. There is less chance of dust and grit entering than in piston valves since they are completely enclosed. If they stick, some makers recommend the use of warm water and soda while the valve is rotated. Others suggest the regular application of a small amount of very light oil on the axle of the rotor. If it is sluggish in action, paraffin can be used instead of the oil for a few days, and if this does not effect an improvement the rotor itself can be oiled by removing the slide of the offending valve, pouring a little oil in the 'U' of the slide, replacing it, and then inverting the whole instrument so that the oil runs up into the rotor without carrying with it any of the grease on the slide.

The cork buffers in the 'horseshoes' should be checked, for if they are not of the correct thickness the airways through the valves will not be uniform. Remove the valve cap and check the alignment of the notches on the inner valve cap and the rotor spindle. If they are not coincident, the cork must either be compressed to the correct thickness, or if it is not thick enough a new one must be fitted.

If the valve is string operated, examine the string for wear, and if necessary fit a fresh one. In any case the string should be replaced periodically, as it is inclined to stretch with use.

Finally, all slides should be cleaned regularly. They must be easily movable yet airtight, and after cleaning should therefore be lightly greased with a good lubricant of thick enough consistency to prevent the slides from moving under their own weight.

Appendix C

A LIST OF MUSIC FOR THE HORN

Sources

In addition to publishers' catalogues, the following sources have been consulted or are referred to in this list of works. Where an abbreviation has been used, it precedes the title of the source in the following list.

	Altmann, W., *Kammermusik-Katalog*. 5th ed., Leipzig, Hofmeister, 1942; 6th ed., 1945.
AMC	*MS list of works for brass instruments*. New York, American Music Centre, Inc.
AmZ	*Allgemeine musikalische Zeitung*. Leipzig, Breitkopf & Härtel, 1798–1848; Rieter-Biedermann, 1866–82.
ASCAP	*ASCAP Symphonic Catalog*. New York, ASCAP, 1959.
B	*Baker's Biographical Dictionary of Musicians*. 4th ed., New York, G. Schirmer, 1940; 5th ed., 1958.
	Catalogue of Chamber Music in the BBC Library. London, BBC, 1965.
Blom	Blom, E. *Everyman's Dictionary of Music*. London, Dent, 1946; 2nd ed., 1958.
BMI	*Pamphlets on American Composers*. New York, Broadcast Music Inc.
BQ	Rasmussen, M. ed. *Brass Quarterly*. Durham, New Hampshire, 1957–
	British Catalogue of Music. London, British National Bibliography, 1957–
Brook	Brook, Barry S. *The Symphonie concertante: an interim report*. Musical Quarterly 47, 1961.
CeBeDeM	*Catalogue des Éditions Centre Belge de Documentation Musicale*. Brussels, CeBeDeM, 1965.
CFE	*Catalog of Composers Facsimile Edition*. New York, American Composers Alliance, 1957; Supplement, 1958.
CG	*Catalogue of Members' Compositions, Vol. I.*, and *Composer*: Journal of the Composers' Guild of Great Britain. London, Composers' Guild of Great Britain, 1958–

Chapman, R. *Flute Technique.* London, Oxford
University Press, 2nd ed., 1951.

Chase   Chase, G., *America's Music.* 2nd ed., New York,
McGraw Hill Book Co., 1966.

CM Lib.   Fairfax, B. comp. *MS list of works for wind instruments.* Deposited with the Central Music Library,
Westminster, London.

Cob   Cobbett, W. W. comp. & ed. *Cobbett's Cyclopedic
Survey of Chamber Music.* London, Oxford University Press, 1929; 2nd ed., 1963.

Cowell   Cowell, H. & Cowell, S. *Charles Ives & his Music.*
New York, Oxford University Press, 1955.

MS List of works for wind instruments. Prague,
Czechoslovak Music Information Centre.

Dale   Dale, Delbert A. *Trumpet Technique.* London,
Oxford University Press, 1965.

Day, S. comp. *Classical Record Catalogue.* London,
The Gramophone.

Diapason   *Catalogue Général des Disques microsillon.* Paris,
Diapason.

DMM   Eaglefield-Hull, A. ed. *Dictionary of Modern Music &
Musicians.* London, Dent, n.d. [1924].

Donemus   *Catalogue of Instrumental Music.* Amsterdam, Donemus, 1961.

Catalogue of Vocal Music. Amsterdam, Donemus,
1961.

Catalogue of Orchestral Music. Amsterdam, Donemus,
1964.

Catalogue of Instrumental Chamber Music. Amsterdam, Donemus, 1965.

E   Eitner, R. *Biographisch-Bibliographisches Quellen-
Lexicon.* Leipzig, Breitkopf & Härtel, 1900;
Graz, Akademische Drucks und Verlagsanstalt,
1960.

Engel   Engel, H. *The Solo Concerto.* Cologne, Arno-Volk
Verlag, 1964.

Ewen   Ewen, D. *American Composers Today.* New York,
H. W. Wilson Co., 1949.

Farish, M. K. *String Music in Print.* New York,
R. M. Bowker, 1965.

F   Fétis, F. J. *Biographie Universelle des Musiciens,*
Paris, Didot, 1867–70.

Fleisher   *Catalogue of the E. A. Fleisher Library.* Philadelphia,
2 vols., privately printed, 1933–45.

A LIST OF MUSIC FOR THE HORN

Fontes artis musicae. Listes Internationales Selectives. Kassel, Bärenreiter, 1962–

FST   *Catalogue: Svensk Instrumental-Musik.* Stockholm, Föreningen Svenska Tönsattare, 1964.

G   *Grove's Dictionary of Music & Musicians.* 4th ed., London, Macmillan, 1928; Supplementary Vol., 1945; 5th ed., 1954.

Ga   Gardavský, C. ed. *Contemporary Czechoslovak Composers.* Prague, Panton, 1965.

Goldman, R. F. *The Wind Band, its Literature & Technique.* Boston, Allyn & Bacon, Inc., 1961.

Gor   Gorgerat, G. *Encyclopédie de la Musique pour Instruments à vent.* 2nd ed., Lausanne, Editions Rencontre, 1955.

Hartmann, H. ed. *Bielefelder Katalog der Schallplatten klassischer Musik.* Bielefeld, Bielefelder Verlagsanstalt.

H   Helm, S. M. *Catalog of Chamber Music for wind Instruments.* Ann Arbor, Mich., National Association of College Wind & Percussion Instrument Instructors, 1952.

Ho   Howard, J. T. *Our Contemporary Composers.* New York, Thomas Y. Crowell Co., 1941, 1948.

Ho 2   Howard, J. T. *Our American Music.* New York, Thomas Y. Crowell Co., 1965.

Husted, B. *The Brass Ensemble: Its History & Music.* Rochester, N.Y., Eastman School of Music, 1955.

IL   *The Interlochen List of Instrumental Ensembles.* 4th ed., Interlochen, Mich., National Music Camp, 1963.

Katalog der Abteilung Noten, Informationszentrum für zeitgenössische Musik. Darmstadt, Internationales Musikinstitut, 1966.

J   Jacobs, A. *A New Dictionary of Music.* Harmondsworth, Penguin, 1958, 1967.

Jensen, J. R. *A Bibliography of Chamber Music for French Horn.* Fullerton, Calif., F. E. Olds & Son, 1964.

King   King, R. *Brass Players' Guide to the Literature.* North Easton, Mass., R. King Music Company.

La   Dufourcq, N. ed. *Larousse de la Musique.* Paris, Librairie Larousse, 1957.

L. & B.   Lang, P. H. & Broder, N. ed. *Contemporary Music in Europe.* London, Dent, 1966.

Langwill, L. G. *The Bassoon & Contra-Bassoon*. London, Benn, 1965.

Machilis, J. *Introduction to Contemporary Music*. New York, W. W. Norton, 1961.

MBE   *MS list of works for brass instruments*. New York, Modern Brass Ensemble.

MGG   Blume, F. ed. *Die Musik in Geschichte und Gegenwart*. Kassel, Bärenreiter, 1949–

MT   *The Musical Times*. London, Novello, 1844–

NK   *MS list of works for wind instruments*. Oslo, Norsk Komponistforening, 1965.

Notes. Washington, Music Library Association, Inc., 1943–

Opperman, K. *Repertory of the Clarinet*. New York, Ricordi, 1960.

Pazdirek, F. *Universal-Handbuch der Musikliteratur*. Vienna [1904–10?].

Perger   Perger, L. H. *Thematisches Verzeichnis der Instrumentalwerke von Michael Haydn*. Vienna, Artaria, 1907.

R   Reis, C. R. *Composers in America*. New York, Macmillan, 1947.

Rasmussen, M. *A Teacher's Guide to the Literature of Brass Instruments*. Durham, New Hampshire, Brass Quarterly, 1964.

Rendall, F. G. *The Clarinet*. London, Williams & Norgate, 1954.

Richter, J. F. *Kammermusik-Katalog* (*1944–58*). Leipzig, Hofmeister, 1960.

Rie   Riemann, H. *Musiklexicon*. 12th ed., Schott, 1959–61.

Rothwell, E. *Oboe Technique*. London, Oxford University Press, 1953; 2nd ed., 1962.

RT   *Radio Times*. London, BBC.

Samfundet   *Catalogue: Samfundet til Udgivelse af Dansk Musik*. Copenhagen, Samfundet, 1956; Supplement, 1964.

Catalogo Generale Dischi Microsolco. Milan, Santandrea, 1953–

Schuller, G. *Horn Technique*. London, Oxford University Press, 1962.

Schwann   *Schwann Long-Playing Record Catalog*, Boston, Mass., W. Schwann, Inc.

Schweiz   *MS list of works for wind instruments*. Zürich, Schweizerisches Musik-Archiv, 1966.

Slo	Slonimsky, N. *Music of Latin America*. London, Harrap, 1946.
	Sonorum Speculum: Mirror of Dutch Musical Life. Amsterdam, Donemus, 1959–
T	Thompson, O. *International Cyclopedia of Music and Musicians.* 4th ed., London, Dent, 1956; 5th ed. 1964.
Th	Thurston, F. *Clarinet Technique.* London, Oxford University Press, 1956; 2nd ed., 1964.
Ve	Valentin, E. *Handbuch der Chormusik.* Regensburg, G. Bosse, n.d. [1953–8].
WERM	Clough, F. F. & Cuming, G. J. *World Encyclopedia of Recorded Music.* London, Sidgwick & Jackson, 1952; Supplements I–III, 1952–7.
WWM	*Who's Who in Music.* 4th ed., London, Burke's Peerage, 1962.
ZfM	Zeitschrift für Musik. Offenbach/M, Steingräber, 1920–

Abbreviations

A	Alto (or Contralto)	glock	Glockenspiel
acc	Accordion	gt	Guitar
ad lib.	ad libitum	(4) h	(4) hands
alt fl	Alto flute	harm	Harmonium
arr.	Arranged by	hn	Horn
B	Bass voice	hp	Harp
b.	Born	hpcd	Harpsichord
Bar	Baritone voice	inst.	Instrumentated
bar	Baritone (instrument)		by
		l.h.	Left hand
bc	Basso continuo	mand	Mandoline
bcl	Bass clarinet	mch	Men's chorus
bn	Bassoon	MS	Manuscript
ca	Cor anglais	MzS	Mezzo-soprano
cel	Celesta	n.d.	No date
ch	Chorus	n.p.	No place
comp.	Compiled by	ob	Oboe
cont	Continuo	ob d'am	Oboe d'amore
ct	Cornet	ondes m	Ondes martinot
cym	Cymbal	Op	Opus
d	Died	oph	Ophicleide
db	Double bass	opt	Optional
dbn	Double bassoon	orch	Orchestra
ed.	Edited by	org	Organ
elec.	Electric	perc	Percussion
fch	Women's chorus	pf	Pianoforte
fl.	Flute	picc	Piccolo
fp	First performance	rec	Recorder

APPENDIX C

rev.	Revised	trp	Trumpet
S	Soprano	v	Voice
sax	Saxaphone	vcl	Violoncello
sousa	Sousaphone	vib	Vibraphone
stg quart	String quartet (2 violins, viola, violoncello)	vla	Viola
		vla d'am	Viola d'amore
		vla da g	Viola de gamba
stgs	String orchestra	vln	Violin
T	Tenor	wind quint	Wind quintet (flute, oboe, clarinet, horn, bassoon)
tamb	Tambourine		
ten hn	Tenor horn		
timp	Timpani	ww	Woodwind
trb	Trombone	xyl	Xylophone

Notes

(a) When the instrumentation of a work is denoted by figures, these are in the order:

Flute, oboe, clarinet, bassoon — horn, trumpet, trombone, tuba — violin, viola, violoncello, double bass.

Other instruments are denoted by their names or by abbreviations.

(b) When the key of a work is given, a capital letter indicates a major key, and a small letter a minor key.

(c) A † before the title of a work indicates that a commercial long-playing recording of the work has been traced.

(d) An * after the abbreviation for a source indicates that the source refers to the location of the manuscript or of an early edition.

1. Horn & pianoforte
2. Horn with orchestra
    2.1 One or more horns with orchestra
    2.2 Horn and other instruments with orchestra
3. Horns alone

3.1 One horn	3.6 Six horns
3.2 Two horns	3.7 Seven horns
3.3 Three horns	3.8 Eight horns
3.4 Four horns	3.9 More than eight horns
3.5 Five horns	3.10 Unspecified

4. Horn(s) with other brass instruments

4.1 Two instruments	4.6 Seven instruments
4.2 Three instruments	4.7 Eight instruments
4.3 Four instruments	4.8 Nine instruments
4.4 Five instruments	4.9 Ten or more instruments
4.5 Six instruments	

A LIST OF MUSIC FOR THE HORN

1. Horn and pianoforte

Abbott, A.	Alla marcia	Arcadia, 1962
Absil, J. 1893–	Rhapsodie No. 6, Op. 120	Lemoine, 1964
Adler, S. 1925–	Sonata	King
Akimenko, F. 1876–1945	†Melody	Leeds, 1945
Aladov, N.	Sonatine, Op. 47	RS, 1954
Alexandrov, Y. 1914–	Three Pieces	RS
Alfvén, H. 1872–1960	Notturno elegiaco, Op. 5 (hn and org)	Gehrmans
Ambrosius, H. 1897–	Sonata in F	Hofmeister
Ameller, A. 1912–	Gavotte	Noël, 1953; IMC, n.d.
	Three Easy Pieces	Hinrichsen, 1960 Hinrichsen
Anderson, A. O. 1880–	Nocturne	C. Fischer
Anisimov, A.	Poema	RS, 1961
Auclert, P.	Lied	Leduc, 1952

Bach, O. 1833–93	Duet, Op. 10	Hofmeister
Bachelet, A. 1864–1944	Dans la Montagne (Rev. L. Thévet)	Leduc, 1959
Bacon, E. 1898–	Song after the Rain	Rongwen, 1959
Bakaleinikov, V. 1885–1953	†Cavatina	Belwin
	Canzona	Belwin
Baker, E. 1912–	Cantilena (1963)	MS (Composer) (37 The Warren, Carshalton Beeches, Surrey)
Balay, G. 1871–1943	Chanson du Forestier	E. & S., n.d. Leduc
Barat, J. E.	Fantaisie	Leduc
Barrows, J. R. 1913–	Sonata (1937)	MS (R)
Bassett, L. 1923–	Sonata (1952)	Morris, 1954; King, 1965
Bassett, M.	Sonata	(MT, Sept. 1965)
Beck, C. 1901–	Intermezzo	Heugel, 1948
Beethoven, L. 1770–1827	†Sonata in F, Op. 17 (1800)	Mollo, 1801; Br. & H; Bo. & H; Peters 1904; IMC; RS; Simrock
Bennett, D.	Hornascope	Southern, 1959
Benson, W. 1924–	Soliloquy	Piedmont, 1959
Bentzon, N. V. 1919–	Sonata, Op. 47	Hansen, 1950
Bernsdorf, E. 1825–1901	Sonata, Op. 18	Peters
Bernstein, L. 1918–	Elegy for Mippy I	G. Schirmer, 1950
Berthold, H. 1819–79	Three Lieder ohne Worte, Op. 2	André
Beversdorf, T. 1924–	Sonata	Andraud
Bigot, E. 1888–	Deuxième Pièce	Lemoine
	Récit, Scherzo et Finale	Lemoine, 1956
Bitsch, M. 1921–	Variations sur une Chanson française	Leduc, 1954
	Choral	Leduc, 1965
Blanc, A. 1828–85	Sonata, Op. 43	Costallat
Blažek, Z. 1905–	Sonata, Op. 75 (1964)	(Ga)
Bödecker, L. 1845–89	Serenade, Op. 20	Br. & H.
	Two Phantasiestücke	Br. & H.
Boisdeffre, R. de 1838–1906	Romance, Op. 70	Hamelle
Bonnard, G.	Sonata vergiliana	Ricordi
Boutry, R. 1932–	Chassacor	Leduc, 1956
Bowen, Y. 1884–1961	Sonata, Op. 108 (1943)	MS

Bozza, E. 1905–	En Irlande	Leduc, 1951
	Chant lointain	Leduc, 1957
	Sur les Cimes	Leduc, 1960
Bradford-Anderson, M.	†March in Canon	Bo. & H., 1952
Bréard, R.	Rhapsodie pyrenéenne	Southern
Brémond, F. 1844–1925	Première Solo	Lemoine
Brier, B.	Sonata quasi fantasia	Horn Realm
Brown, C. 1898–	Légende	Leduc, 1955
	Elégie	Leduc
Bruneau, A. 1857–1934	Fantasie	Choudens
Brusselmans, M. 1886–1960	Légende du Gapeau	Salabert, 1931
Bucchi, A.	Trois Lieder	Leduc, 1966
Burkhard, W. 1900–55	Romance	Henn; BVK, 1964
Bush, A. 1900–	Trent's broad Reaches, Op. 36	Schott, 1952
	Autumn Poem	Schott, 1955
Busser, H. 1872–	Cantecor, Op. 77	Buffet-Crampon, 1926
Butt, J. 1929–	A Horn Suite	Hinrichsen, 1961
Butterworth, N. 1934–	Prelude & Scherzo	Chappell, 1961
Campolieti, A.	Andante pastorale & Allegro	Ricordi, 1960
Canteloube, J. 1879–1957	Danse	Noël, 1953; IMC, n.d.
Capdevielle, P. 1906–	Elégie de Duino	Leduc, 1960
Carse, A. 1878–1958	Two Easy Pieces: Serenade & Scherzino	Augener
Catelinet, P. 1910–	Caprice: Ten little Indians	Hinrichsen, 1953
Cazden, N. 1914–	Sonata, Op. 33 (1941)	CFE
Cellier, A. 1883–	Ballade	Leduc, 1949
Charpentier, J. 1933–	Pour Diane	Leduc, 1962
Chaussier, H. b. 1854	Two Pieces	Millereau
	Romance sans Paroles	Millereau
	Andante & Rondo	Millereau
	Gavotte	Millereau
	Fantasie de Chasse	Millereau
Chevillard, C. 1859–1923	Allegro, Op. 18	E. & S., n.d.; Leduc
Clapisson, A. L. 1808–66	Rondo fantaisie	Richault
Clergue, J.	Prélude, Lied et Rondo (1934)	Lemoine
Clérisse, R.	†Chant sans Paroles	Leduc, 1952
	Matines	Leduc, 1956
	L'Absent	Leduc, 1957
Colomer, B. M.	Fantaisie-Légende	E. & S., n.d.
Cooke, A. 1906–	†Rondo in B♭ (1950)	Schott, 1952

189

Cooke, F. J. 1910–	Sonata	(RT, 22 Feb., 1968)
Cortese, L. 1899–	Sonata	Carisch, 1958
Coscia, S.	Romanza	Baron
Cosma, E.	Sonatina	ESPLA, 1955
Criswell, J. P.	Four Interludes	Galliard, 1965
Damase, J-M. 1928–	Pavane variée	Lemoine, 1956
	Berceuse, Op. 19	Leduc, 1951
	La Croqueuse de Diamants	Ed. Mondia
Danzi, F. 1763–1826	†Sonata in E♭, Op. 28	
	(Ed. G. Hausswald)	Hofmeister, 1958
	(Ed. J. Chambers)	IMC, 1963
	†Sonata concertante, Op. 44	Sikorski, 1957
	(Ed. J. Wojciechowski)	
Dauprat, L. F. 1781–1868	Sonata, Op. 2	Zetter
	Duo, Op. 7	Zetter
	Three Solos, Op. 11	Lemoine
	Three Solos, Op. 16	Lemoine
	Three Solos, Op. 17	Lemoine
	Three Solos, Op. 20	Lemoine
	Thème varié, Op. 24	Lemoine
Dautremer, M. 1906–	Thème varié	Leduc, 1958
Davies, H. Walford 1869–1941	Sonata in F (1891)	MS (DMM)
Delamarter, E. 1880–1953	Ballade and Poème	Witmark, 1948
Delerue, G.	Poème fantasque	Leduc, 1952
Delmas, M. 1885–1931	Enchanted Forest	
Demessieux, J. 1921–	Ballade, Op. 12	Durand, 1962
Depelsenaire, J. M.	Nocturne	Lemoine, 1958
Désenclos, A. 1912–	Cantilène et Divertissements	Leduc, 1950
Desportes, Y. 1907–	Ballade normande	Leduc, 1950
	Improvisation	Leduc, 1953
	Sicilienne et Allegro	Leduc, 1960
de Wolf, J. E.	Sonatine in oude stýl	Maurer, 1960
Diercks, J. 1927–	Phantasy in two movements	Tritone, 1960
Dobrodinský, B. 1896–	Bagatelle & Rondo	(Ga)
Domenico, O. di	Variazioni	Leduc, 1959
Donato, A. 1909–	Sonata (1950)	Remick, 1950
Douane, J.	En Forêt d'Olonne	Lemoine, 1958
Draeseke, F. 1835–1913	Adagio, Op. 31	Kistner
	Romance, Op. 32	Kistner
Dubois, P. M. 1930–	Romance sans Paroles	Leduc, 1958
Dubois, T. 1837–1924	Cavatine	Heugel

Duck, L.	The silver Huntress	Chappell, 1964
Duclos, P. 1929–	Sur la Montagne	Leduc
Dukas, P. 1865– 1935	†Villanelle (Ed. M. Jones) (Ed. J. Chambers)	Durand, 1906 G. Schirmer, 1962 IMC, 1963
Dunhill, T. F. 1877–1946	Cornucopia, Op. 95	Bo. & H., 1941
Dupuis, A. b. 1877	Variations sur un Thème populaire	Leduc, 1926
Duvernoy, F. 1771–1838	Three Sonatas, Op. 23	Costallat
Ecchevarria, V.	Intermezzo	Leduc, 1958
Eccles, H. 1670– 1742	Sonata in g (Ed. J. Eger)	IMC, 1963
Eder, H. 1916–	Sonatina, Op. 34/6	Doblinger, 1966
Eeckhaute, F.	Nacht Poema	Metropolis
Eichborn, H. L. 1847–1918	Sonata, Op. 7	Br. & H.
	Lieder, Op. 9	Br. & H.
	Lebenswogen, Op. 10	Br. & H.
	Rondo brillante, Op. 11	Br. & H.
	Erste Suite, Op. 12	Br. & H.
	Fünf Tonbilde, Op. 13	Br. & H.
	Frühling, Op. 52	Br. & H.
	Romantic Fantasy, Op. 65	Br. & H.
Eitel, E. 1913–60	Sonata in D, Op. 8 (1952)	Martin
Eschmann, J. K. 1826–82	Im Herbst, Op. 6	Br. & H.
Fattach, A.	Lyric Piece	RS
Fengler, A.	Andante appassionata, Op. 3	C. Schmidt
Ferrari, G. 1872– 1948	Sonata	MS
Finke, F. 1891–	Sonata (1946)	Br. & H. [1956]
Frackenpohl, A. 1924–	Largo & Allegro (Ed. M. Jones)	G. Schirmer, 1962
Françaix, J. 1912–	Canon à l'octave	Noël, 1953; IMC, n.d.
	Divertimento	EMT, 1959
Franz, O. 1843–89	Konzertstück, Op. 4 (2 hn)	Hofmeister; Erdmann, 1962; Southern
Frehse, A.	Andante, Op. 8	Hofmeister
	Serenade, Op. 9 (1954)	Hofmeister
	Studienkonzert für tiefes Horn	Hofmeister, 1954
Fricker, P. R. 1920–	Sonata, Op. 24	Schott, 1956
Fuchs, R. 1847–1927	Sonata, Op. 33	
Gabaye, P.	Sérénade de Printemps	Leduc, 1959
Gabelles, G.	Fantasie	Alfred
Gabler, E.	Konzertstück No. 1	Oertel
Gagnebin, H. 1886–	Aubade	Leduc, 1960
Gallay, J. F. 1795–1864	Nocturne concertante, Op. 36	Colombier

191

	Les Echos, Op. 59	Lemoine
	Trois Caprices, Op. 60	Lemoine
	9e Solo, Op. 39	Lemoine
	10e Solo, Op. 45	Lemoine
	12e Solo, Op. 55	Lemoine
	Regrets	Lemoine
Gallois-Montbrun, R. 1918–	Ballade	Leduc, 1950
	Improvisation	Leduc
Genzel, A. (Henzel, A.?)	Concertino (2 hn)	RS
Gerlach, T. 1861–1940	Romance, Op. 5/1	Kahnt
	Scherzo, Op. 5/2	Kahnt
Gethen, F.	Nocturne	Horn Realm
Gipps, R. 1921–	Sonatina, Op. 56	S. Fox, 1961
Glazunov, A. 1865–1936	†Rêverie, Op. 24	Belaieff, n.d.; Leeds, 1945
	(Ed. H. Voxman)	Rubank, 1961
	(Ed. M. Jones)	G. Schirmer, 1962
Glière, R. 1875–1956	†Four Pieces, Op. 24/6, 7, 10, 11 (1908)	Leeds, 1947; RS, 1958
Gold, E. 1921–	Sonata	MS (Horn Realm)
Goltermann, G. 1824–98	Andante, Op. 14	Br. & H.
Gottwald, H.	L'Amitié	
	Fantasie héroïque	
Grant, W. P. 1910–	Poem (hn & org)	CFE
	Essay (hn & org)	CFE
	Mirror & Ostinato (hn & org)	CFE
Grazioli, G. B.	Adagio	Southern, 1964
Gropp, H.	Sonata, Op. 5 (1922)	Br. & H.
Grudzinski, C.	Miniatures	PWM
Guilbert, R.	Puzzle	Leduc, 1947
Guillou, R.	Mon Nom est Rolande	Costallat
	Sonatine	Leduc, 1946
Guiraud, E. 1837–92	Piccolino	Durand
Gwilt, D. 1932–	Sonatina	B. & F., 1965
Gyring, E.	Andante et Cantabile	CFE
Haas, J. 1879–1960	Sonata, Op. 29	T. & J.; Schott, n.d.
Hadju, M.	Scherzino	ZV, 1955
Haller, H. 1914–	Noveletta, Op. 38	Sirius
Hamilton, I. 1922–	Aria (1951)	Schott, 1952
	†Sonata notturna	Schott, 1966
Haworth, F. 1905–	Canzona (hn, org)	Horn Realm
Hayes, J.	Recitative & Aria	Camara, 1960
Heiden, B. 1910–	†Sonata (1939)	AMP, 1955
Heise, P. 1814–79	Two Phantasiestücke	Chester
Henselt, A. 1814–89	Duet, Op. 14	Cranz

Herberigs, R. 1886–	Cyrano de Bergerac (1912)	CeBeDeM, 1961
Hermann, R.	†Concerto	EMS
Hessenberg, K. 1908–	Nocturne & Rondo, Op. 71	Leduc
Hindemith, P. 1895–1963	Sonata (1939)	Schott, 1940, 1950
	Sonata für Althorn (or hn or sax) (1943)	Schott, 1956
Hlobil, E. 1901–	Sonata, Op. 21 (1942; rev. 1948)	Artia
	Andante pastorale	HM, 1956
Høeberg, G. 1872–1950	Andante (hn & org)	Hansen
Hoffmeister, F. A. 1754–1812	Concerto (2 hn)	IMC
Holbrooke, J. 1878–1958	Ballade No. 1, Op. 94	G. & T.
Holmes, P.	Serenade	Shawnee, 1962
Horn, C. 1860–1941	Sonata in c, Op. 58	Kahnt, 1911
Houdy, P.	Lamento	Leduc, 1955
Hughes, M.	Sonata	Tritone, 1966
Hummel, F. 1855–1928	Duo, Op. 20	Schott
	Sonata, Op. 117	Protze
Hummel, J. N. 1778–1837	Notturno, Op. 99 (2 hn, pf duet)	Leuckart
Ištvan, M. 1928–	Suite (1955)	(Ga)
Ivanov, I.	Trio (2 hn)	RS
Jacqmin, F. 1793–1847	Air: 'Grenadier, que tu m'affliges', Op. 2	Schoenenberger
Jirák K. B. 1891–	Introduction & Rondo, Op. 68 (1951)	MS (MGG)
	Sonata, Op. 72 (1952)	MS (MGG, Ga)
Jones, D. R.	Allegro	Pro Art, 1963
Jongen, J. 1873–1953	Lied (1899)	CeBeDeM, 1960
Josten, W. 1885–1963	Sonata (1944)	MS (Ho)
Kalkbrenner, F. 1785–1849	Nocturne, Op. 95	Kistner, n.d.
Kaminski, H. 1886–1946	Ballade	BVK, 1943
Kaplan, D.	Serenade	Belwin, 1956
	Soliloquy	Belwin, 1956
Kauder, H. 1888–	Sonata	Bo. & H.
Kennaway, L.	Autumn Moods	NWM, 1962
Kilar, W. 1932–	Sonata (1954)	PWM, 1959
Klauss, N.	Andantino	Mills, 1961
	Cabaletta	Pro Art, 1963
Kling, H. A. L. 1842–1918	Sonata	MS (MGG)
Koechlin, C. 1867–1950	Sonata, Op. 70 (1918–25)	Eschig

	Fourteen Pieces, Op. 180 (1942)	MS (MGG)
	Pièce	Leduc
Kofroň, J. 1921–	Images: Ten Pieces	SHV, 1962
Kohout, J. 1895–1958	Seven Compositions (1926)	(Ga)
	Ballad & Pastorale (1948)	(Ga)
Korn, P. J. 1922–	Sonata, Op. 18	Simrock, 1959
Kovařovic, K. 1862–1920	Duet	MS (MGG)
Kratochvíl, J. 1924–	Suite	(Ga)
Kremenliev, B. A. 1911–	Sonata (1958)	MS (MGG)
Krol, B. 1920–	Sonata, Op. 1	Pro Musica, 1951
Krufft, N. Freiherr von, 1779–1818	Sonata	Br. & H. [ca. 1813]
	Variations sur la Cavatine de l'opéra Der Augenarzt	BAI, 1812
Krug, A. 1849–1904	Romance in A♭, Op. 105	Oertel, 1901
Kryukov, V. 1902–	Italian Rhapsody, Op. 65 (Ed. J. Chambers)	RS IMC
Labor, J. 1842–1924	Theme & Variations, Op. 10 (Ed. M. Jones)	UE G. Schirmer, 1962
Lachner, F. 1803–90	Phantasie	Gombart, 1825
	Introduction & Variations sur un thème favori suisse, Op. 12	Mechetti
Lajtha, L. 1892–1963	Intermezzo	Leduc
	Caprice	Leduc
Lebrun, G. E.	Chant du Berger	CeBeDeM
Le Flem, P. 1881–	Pièce	Eschig, 1952
Lees, B. 1924–	Sonata	MS
Leidesdorf, M. J. 1787–1840	Sonata	MS (MGG)
Leroux, X. 1863–1919	Sonata (Ed. J. Chambers)	Leduc, 1897; IMC
Lersch, E.	Sonata (1930)	C. Schmidt
Levy, E. 1895–	Sonata (1953)	(MGG)
Levy, F.	Suite	Cor, 1961
Lindpaintner, P. 1791–1856	Variations & Rondo	Br. & H.
Link, E.	Chant d'Amour	C. Schmidt
Lloyd Webber, W. S. 1914–	Summer Pastures	Ascherberg, 1960
Lonque, A. 1908–	Oktobernacht, Op. 48	Maurer, 1958
Lora, A. 1899–	Elegy	CFE
Lotzenhiser, G. W.	Autumn Dream	Belwin, 1956
Lutyens, E. 1906–	Duo, Op. 34/1 (1956)	Schott
Lyon, D.	Variations	MS
Lysenko, N. 1842–1912	Album Leaf	RS
McBride, R. 1911–	Bells (1935)	CFE

McKay, G. F. 1899–	Three pastoral Sketches	G. Schirmer
Makarov, E. 1912–	Romance	RS
Malézieux	Melodie réligieuse	Gaudet
	Romance sans Paroles	Gaudet
	Sur le Lac	Gaudet
Maniet, R.	Pièce	Maurer, 1957
	Concertino	Maurer, 1960
Marc-Carles	Choral	Leduc, 1962
Maréchal, H. C. 1842–1924	Fantaisie	Deplaix, 1899
Martelli, H. 1895–	Valse	Noël, 1953; IMC, n.d.
Mason, J.	Tenuto	CP, 1957
Matthison-Hansen, H. 1807–90	Sonata	MS (MGG)
Matys, K.	Romance, Op. 15/1	Bachmann
Maugue, J. M. L.	Motifs forestiers	UMP
Maurat, E.	Petites Inventions	Eschig, 1967
Mazellier, J. 1879–1959	Rhapsodie montagnard	Salabert
Menager, L.	Sur la Montagne, Op. 35	Junne
Meyer, J.	Cordelinette	Lemoine, 1964
Michaelis, T. 1831–87	Aus der Heimath, Op. 103	André
Mihalovici, M. 1898–	Episode	Leduc, 1959
Miroshnikov, O.	Rondo	RS, 1962
Montico, M.	Sonata villereccia	Curci, 1962
Morra, G.	Romantique	
Mortelmans, L. 1868–1952	Lyrische Pastorale	Metropolis
Moscheles, I. 1794–1870	Introduction & Rondeau, Op. 63	K. & S., 1821
Moser, R. 1892–1960	Sonata	Steingräber
Moulaert, R. 1875–1962	Eroica	Brogneaux
Mouret, J. 1682–1738	†Two Divertissements (Ed. R. Viollier & A. H. Eichmann)	Richli, 1950
Muelbe, G.	Rondino	Bo. & H.a, 1955
	Concert miniature	Bo. & H., 1955
Müller, B. E. 1825–95	Gebet (hn & org)	Zimmermann
Müller, J. P.	Nocturne	Maurer, 1956
Mulder, H. 1894–	Sonata No. 4, Op. 43	Donemus, 1944
Musgrave, T. 1928–	Music	(RT, 22 Feb., 1968)
Nelhybel, V. 1919–	Scherzo concertante	GMPC
Nelson, P.	Sonata	(Ho)
Neuling, H. 1897–	Bagatelle	Pro Musica, 1957
	Concert Cadenza	Pro Musica

Nielsen, C. A. 1865–1931	†Canto serioso	Skandinavisk, 1944
Nisle, J. F. b. 1768	Douze grands Duos, Op. 5	Werckmeister, 1805
	Deux Sonates, Op. 6	Werckmeister
	Fantasie	Br. & H., 1818
	Six Duos, Op. 51	Schlesinger
Niverd, L. 1879–	Crépuscule d'Automne	Delrieu, 1951
	Six petites Pièces de style	Andrieu, 1939
Noel-Gallon 1891–	Andante et Presto	Lemoine, 1957
Norden, H.	Passacaglia in F	Chester, 1959
Nordraak, R. 1842–66	Solo in E	Musik-Huset, 1942
Nowak, L. 1911–	Sonata	CFE
Orr, R. 1909–	Serenade	Schott, 1952
Pakhmutova, A. 1929–	Nocturne	RS
Palkovský, O. 1907–	Sonata, Op. 38 (1963)	(Ga)
Pannier, O.	Serenade, Op. 45	Grosch, 1951
Panseron, A. 1795–1859	Ecoutons les noble Sons du Cor	Lemoine
Pascal, C. 1921–	Sonata (1963)	Durand, 1963
Passani, E. B. 1905–	Vesperale	Noël, 1953; IMC, n.d.
Pelikán, M. 1922–	Suite (1955)	(Ga)
Peřina, H. 1890–1964	Sonata	(Ga)
	Impromptu	Panton, 1966
Pernoo, J. 1921–	Fantaisie brève	Leduc, 1952
Perrin, J. 1920–	Sonata	(La)
Perrini, N.	Legend	Southern, 1962
Pessard, E. L. F. 1843–1917	In the Forest, Op. 130	Southern
Peyrot, F. 1888–	Duo	Geneva, Composer, 1961
Piantoni, L. 1885–	Air de Chasse	Leduc, 1954
Pisk, P. A. 1893–	Sonata	CFE
Planel, R.	Caprice	Leduc, 1958
Poot, M. 1901–	†Sarabande	Leduc, 1953
	Légende	Leduc, 1958
Popatenko, T.	Dreams (1959)	RS
Porret, J.	Concertinos Nos. 5 & 6	Costallat
Porter, Q. 1897–1966	Sonata (1946)	Gamble, 1948
Poser, H. 1917–	Sonata, Op. 8	Sikorski, 1957
Potter, C. 1792–1871	Sonata di bravura concertante, Op. 13	Simrock, n.d.
Poulenc, F. 1899–1963	†Élégie (In Memory of Dennis Brain) (1957)	Chester, 1958
Presle, J. de la 1888–	La Rêve du jeune Faon	Leduc, 1949
	Scherzetto	de Lacour, 1935

Presser, W. 1916–	Fantasy on the Hymn Tune 'The mouldering Vine'	Tritone, 1963
Proch, H. 1809–78	Romance	Bosworth
Pugno, R.	Solo	E. & S., 1900
1852–1914	(Rev. L. Thévet)	Leduc, 1958
Pyncou, S.	Lullaby & Gavotte	Leduc, 1963
	Song & Peasant Dance	Leduc, 1963
	Dream & Syncopated Dance	Leduc, 1963
Raff, J. 1822–82	Two Romances, Op. 182	Siegel
Ramsey, H. F.	A Celtic Lament	C. Fischer, 1962
Rasmussen, A.	Mood & Nocturne, Op. 11	Hansen
Ratez, E. P.	Four Pieces	Lemoine
1851–1934		
Read, G. 1913–	Poem, Op. 31	C. Fischer
	De Profundis (hn & org)	King, 1958
Rehberg, W.	Sonata, Op. 19	MS (MGG)
1900–57		
Reiner, K. 1910–	Song from the Mountains & Dance (1948)	Orbis, 1951
Reiter, A. 1905–	Sonatine	Doblinger, 1962
Reutter, H. 1900–	Thème varié	Leduc, 1957
Reynolds, V.	Partita	Southern, 1964
Rheinberger, J. 1839–1901	Sonata in E♭, Op. 178	Kistner; Schott [1966]
Riccius, A. F. 1819–86	Introduction & Allegro, Op. 18	R. & E.
Richter, J.	Die Jagd, Op. 41 (4 hn)	André
Ries, F. 1784–1838	Sonata, Op. 34	Böhme; Richault
	Introduction & Rondeau, Op. 113/2	MS (MGG)
Rossini, G. 1792–1868	Rondo fantastique	FR
	†Prelude, Theme & Variations (1857)	
	(Ed. D. Ceccarossi)	FR, 1954
	(Ed. J. Eger)	IMC
Rueff, J. 1922–	Cantilène	Leduc, 1963
Rulst-Rema	Petit Sérénade	Maurer, 1959
Rychlík, J. 1916–64	Sonatine	SHV, 1964
Ryelandt, J. 1870–1965	Sonata, Op. 18 (1897)	CeBeDeM, 1957
Sabatini, G.	Elegia	Camara, 1960
	Puppet Waltz	Camara
Sachse, H. W. 1891–1960	Sonata, Op. 71	Hinrichsen
Sagaiv, D.	Refrain de Rhodope	RS
Saint-Saëns, C. 1835–1921	Romance in E, Op. 67 (1885)	Hamelle, 1885
	(Ed. M. Jones)	G. Schirmer, 1960
	(Ed. H. Voxman)	Rubank, 1961
Samazeuilh, G. 1877–	Evocation	Durand

Samuel-Rousseau, M. 1882–1955	Romance	Leduc, 1946
Sanders, R. L. 1906–	Sonata in B♭ (1958)	King, 1963
Schemel, W.	Andante (hn & org)	(fp Essen, 1948)
Scheurer, R.	Elégie	Belwin
Schmid, H. K. 1874–1953	Im tiefsten Walde, Op. 34/4	Schott
Schoemaker, M. 1890–1964	Variations	Brogneaux
Schouwman, H. 1902–	Two Legends, Op. 35/1 & 2	Donemus, 1944
Schreiter, H. 1915–	Sonatina, Op. 12	B. & B., 1954
Schuller, G. 1925–	Nocturne	Mills
Schumann, R. 1810–56	†Adagio & Allegro, Op. 70 (1849)	Br. & H. 1953, 1957; IMC
Scriabin, A. N. 1872–1915	†Romance (1894–7) (Ed. J. Singer)	Am-Rus, 1945
Seigle, F.	Légende	E. & S., 1927
Semler-Collery, J.	Pièce concertante	Leduc, 1954
	Pièce romantique	Decruck
Servais, T.	First Solo	Brogneaux
Setaccioli, G. 1868–1925	Sonata, Op. 31	Ricordi
Shafrannikov, C. 1898–	Melody	RS
Sinigaglia, L. 1868–1944	Two Pieces, Op. 28; Lied & Humoresque	Br. & H., 1905
Sitt, H. 1850–1922	Reverie	Bosworth
Sivic, P. 1908–	Suite	(La)
Šlik, M. 1898–	Sonata (1951)	(Ga)
Smatek, M. 1895–	Sonata	(Ga)
Souffriau, A. 1926–	Ballad	Brogneaux
Spindler, F. 1817–1905	Sonata, Op. 347	Siegel
Šťasný, V. 1885–	Three Compositions (1949)	(Ga)
Stevens, H. 1908–	Sonata (1953)	Morris, 1955
	Four short Pieces (1958)	Camara, 1960
Strauss, F. S. 1822–1905	Notturno, Op. 7	Aibl
	Romance, Op. 12	Aibl
	Theme & Variations, Op. 13	Zimmermann, 1957
	Fantasy	Belwin
Székely, E. 1912–	Sonatine (1954)	ZV, 1955
Szervánsky, E. 1911–	Little Suite	ZV, 1955
Taylor, H. S.	Sonata	MS
Taylor, P.	Sonata	(MT, March, 1967)
Tcherepnin, N. N. 1873–1945	Enchantement	Bo. & H.
	Mélodie d'Amour	Bo. & H.

A LIST OF MUSIC FOR THE HORN

Thurner, F. E. 1785–1827	Sonata, Op. 29	Peters
Tillotson, N.	Fantasy	CML, 1962
Tomasi, H. 1901–	Chant corse	Leduc, 1932
	Danse profane	Leduc, 1960
Tournemire, C. 1870–1939	Romance, Op. 6	MS (MGG)
	Fantaisie (1931)	Buffet-Crampon, n.d.
Uber, D.	Four Sketches	Musicus, 1965
Uyttenhove, Y.	Petite Pièce	Maurer, 1964
Vallier, J.	Sonatine, Op. 55	Eschig, 1964
Verrall, J. 1908–	Sonata	CFE
Vidal, P. 1863–1931	Pièce de Concert	E. & S., 1924, 1938
	Concertino	Gaudet, 1922
Vignieri, Z.	Sonata, Op. 7	RS, 1961
Vreuls	Fantasie	
Vuataz, R. 1898–	Thrène (Chant funèbre), Op. 58/7	Henn, 1960
Wagner, H. 1912–	Kleine Partita	Müller
Walker, E. 1870–1949	Adagio in E♭, Op. 11/2	Williams, 1900
Weber, A. 1930–	Improvization	Leduc, 1958
Weber, E. 1766–1826	Romance	Bosworth
Weigel, E. 1910–	Maine Sketches	Interlochen, n.d.
Werner, J. J.	Three Inventions (1961)	Billaudot, 1966
Wessel, M. 1894–	Lento : Fantasia funèbre	C. Fischer
	Scherzo	C. Fischer
Whear, P. W.	Pastorale Lament	Interlochen n.d.
White, F. H. 1884–1945	Piece	MS (T)
Wilder, A. 1907–	†Two Sonatas	(Schwann)
	†Suite	(Schwann)
Wildgans, F. 1913–65	Sonatine, Op. 5 (1927)	Doblinger, 1962
Wilm, N. 1834–1911	Romanze & Scherzo	Forberg
Windsperger, L. 1885–1935	Pieces	Schott
Woefl, J. 1772–1812	Trio (2 hn)	(Cob)
Wolff, C. 1934–	†Duet II	Peters
Wordsworth, W. 1908–	Dialogue, Op. 77 (1965)	MS (Composer) (Ard Insh, Kincraig, Kingussie, Inverness-shire, Scotland)
Young, D.	Sonata	(MT, March, 1967)
Zeller, K. 1842–92	Charakterstück in D	Br. & H.

Zenger, M. 1837–1911	Sonata, Op. 90	Rahter, 1903
Ziring, V. 1880–	Adagio & Arioso, Op. 17	RS, 1948

2. Horn with orchestra

2.1 *One or more horns with orchestra*

Addison, J. 1920–	Wellington Suite (2 hn, stgs, pf, timp, perc)	OUP, 1961
Agthe, F. W. 1794–1830	Gran Concerto in F	(Engel)
Alinovi, G. b. 1790	Divertimento	Ricordi
André, J. A. 1775–1842	Concerto	André
	Concerto (2 hn)	André
Anton, F. M. b. 1877	Musik für obbligates Horn, Op. 20 (1925) (stgs)	(Engel)
Arnold, M. 1921–	Concerto No. 1	Lengnick
	Concerto No. 2, Op. 58 (stgs)	Paterson
Atterberg, K. 1887–	Concerto, Op. 28 (1926)	Br. & H., 1928; FST
Bachelet, A. G. 1864–1944	Lamento (stgs)	Leduc [1927?]
	Dans la Montagne	Leduc, 1959
Backofen, J. G. H. 1768–1839	Concerto	(Engel)
Baeyens, A. L. 1895–	Concerto	(WWM)
Banks, D. 1923–	Concerto	Schott, 1966
Barab, S. 1921–	Concerto (stgs)	Bo. & H.
Barbier, R. A. E. 1890–	Concerto, Op. 106	CeBeDeM, 1963
Barrows, J. R. 1913–	Variations (stgs)	MS
Barsanti, F. 1690–1760	†Concerto grosso in D, Op. 33/4 (2 hn, stgs)	Eulenburg
Barth, F. P. K. 1775–1802	Concerto (2 hn)	(T)
Becker, J. J. 1886–1961	Concerto (1933)	NME
Beer, M. J. 1851–1908	Abendmusik, Op. 54 (2 hn, stgs)	Schott
Belloli, L. 1770–1817	Concertos	(T)
Bennett, R. R. 1936–	Concerto (1956)	UE
Berghmans, J.	Les Lutteurs	Leduc, 1958
Bertini, G. 1927–	Concerto	IMP
Blume, H.	Concerto	Grosch

Bonneau, P. 1918–	Souvenirs	Leduc, 1953
Børresen, H.	Serenade (1943)	Samfundet, 1943
1876–1954	(stgs, timp)	
Bowen, Y.	Concerto, Op. 150	de Wolfe
1884–1961	(stgs, timp)	
Bozza, E. 1905–	En Forêt, Op. 40	Leduc, 1941
Brandt-Buys, J.	Suite, Op. 7	Haslinger;
1868–1933	(stgs, hp)	Cranz
Braun, J. 1753–95	Concerto	(T)
Bruneau, A.	Romance	Hamelle, n.d.
1857–1934		
Bryan, G.	Concerto	MS
1895–1957		
Busser, H. 1872–	Pièce in D, Op. 39 (1910)	E. & S., n.d.
	La Chasse de St. Hubert, Op. 99	Leduc, 1937
Butt, J. 1929–	A Horn Suite	Hinrichsen, 1961
	(stgs)	
	Winsome's Folly, Suite No. 3	(WWM)
Butterworth, A.	Romanza (1952)	Hinrichsen, 1960
1923–	(stgs)	
Butterworth, N.	Concerto	(WWM)
1934–		
Chabrier, E.	†Larghetto	Costallat, 1913
1841–94		
Chavez, C. 1899–	Concerto (1930; orch. 1937)	G. Schirmer
	(4 hn)	
Cherubini, L.	Sonata No. 1	Sikorski, 1954
1760–1842	(stgs) (Ed. J. Wojciechowski)	
	†Sonata No. 2	Sikorski, 1954
	(stgs) (Ed. J. Wojciechowski)	
Cheslock, L. 1899–	Concerto (1936)	MS (Ho, R, T)
Chevreuille, R. 1901–	†Concerto, Op. 43	CeBeDeM
Clérisse, R.	Chanson à bercer	Leduc
Coar, B.	Concerto	MS
Cole, H. 1917–	Concerto	MS (CG, J)
Cooper, G. 1895–	Concerto	MS (CG)
Coscia, S.	Concertino	Baron
Crussell, B. H.	Concerto	MS
1775–1838		
Dauprat, L. F.	Concerto No. 1, Op. 1	Zetter
1781–1868		
	Concerto No. 2 in F, Op. 9	Zetter
	Concerto No. 3 in E, Op. 18	Zetter
	Concerto No. 4 in F, Op. 19	Zetter
	Concerto No. 5 in E, Op. 21	Zetter
Dietrich, A. H.	Konzertstück, Op. 27	Schweers
1829–1908		
Dimmler, A.	Concertante	Ars Viva
1753–1819	(2 hn)	
Domnich, H.	Three Concertos	Ozi
1767–1844		
	Symphonie concertante	Ozi
	(2 hn)	

Doren, T. van	Concerto	Metropolis
Dornaus, P. b. 1769	Concerto, Op. 14	André
Driessler, J. 1921–	Concerto, Op. 16	BVK, 1951
Dubois, P. M. 1930–	Concerto	Leduc, 1957
Dupuis, A. 1877–	Concerto	(DMM, T)
Duvernoy, F. 1765–1838	12 Concertos	(F)
	Concerto No. 5 in F (Ed. E. Leloir)	KaWe, 1965
Eckert, F.	Concerto in f (1913)	Jurgenson; UE
Eisner	Szene und Arie (1841)	(Engel)
	Konzert in Form einer Gesangsszene (1847)	(Engel)
Elmore, R. 1913–	Narrative	Horn Realm
Essex, K. 1915–55	Concerto	MS
Fesca, F. E. 1789–1826?	Concerto	(Engel)
Flothuis, M. 1914–	Concerto, Op. 24 (1945)	Donemus
Frankell, M. 1915–	Concerto (stgs, timp, perc)	MS (CG)
Fuchs, H.	Concerto	(Engel)
Fuchs, R. 1847–1927	Serenade, Op. 51 (2 hn, stgs)	Weinberger
Gabler, E.	Concerto in B♭ (1904)	Oertel
Gallay, J. F. 1795–1864	Concerto No. 1 in F, Op. 18	KaWe
	Concerto No. 2, Op. 28	(F)
	Rondeau	Zetter
Geiser, W. 1897–	Concertino, Op. 22	MS (G)
Gerster, O. 1897–	Concerto	Litolff
Giannini, V. 1903–66	Concerto (1945)	(Ewen)
Gillman, K.	Concerto, Op. 45	Grahl
Glazunov, A. 1865–1936	Serenade No. 2 (stgs)	Cor
Glière, R. M. 1875–1926	†Concerto in B♭, Op. 91 (Ed. J. Singer) (Ed. V. Polekh)	RS, 1952 Leeds, 1957 IMC, 1958
Goedicke, A. 1877–1957	Concerto, Op. 40	RS; IMC, 1967
Goepfert, K. A. 1768–1818	Concerto, Op. 21	André
Grant, W. P. 1910–	Concerto (1941)	MS
Graupner, C. 1683–1760	Concerto in G (2 hn)	
Handel, G. F. 1685–1759	†Concerto in F (2 hn)	Handel Gesellschaft
	Concerto in F (4 hn)	Handel Gesellschaft
Hänsel, A. fl. 1860	Concertino, Op. 80	Hofmeister
Hasquenoph, P. 1922–	Concertino (stgs)	Eschig, 1964

Haworth, F. 1905–	Pastoral Suite (stgs)	Horn Realm
Haydn, F. J.	†Concerto No. 1 in D, Hob. VII,	Br. & H., 1898;
1732–1809	d3 (1762) (Ed. J.	Bo. & H.; CB;
	Mandyczewski)	Eulenburg
	(Ed. M. Pottag)	C. Fischer
	†Concerto No. 2 in D, Hob. VII,	Br. & H., 1898;
	d 4 (Ed. J. Mandyczewski)	Bo. & H., CB;
		Eulenburg
	†Concerto in E♭, Hob. VII, d 2	KaWe
	(2 hn) (Ed. E. Leloir)	
	†Symphony No. 31 in D,	Sieber [ca. 1785];
	'Hornsignal', Hob. I, 31	Br. & H.
	(4 hn)	
	Cassatio in D	Doblinger
	(4 hn, stgs)	
Haydn, M.	†Concerto in D	
1737–1806		
Herberigs, R. 1886–	†Cyrano de Bergerac (1912)	
Hindemith, P.	†Concerto (1949)	Schott, 1950
1895–1963		
Hoddinott, A. 1929–	Aubade & Scherzo (1965)	OUP, 1966
	(stgs)	
Hoffmeister, F. A.	Concerto in E♭ (Ed. J. Chambers)	IMC, 1958
1754–1812	(2 hn)	
Hovhaness, A.	Artik, Op. 78 (1949)	Rongwen
1911–	(stgs)	
Hubler, H.	Concerto	KaWe
	(4 hn)	
Huggler, J. 1928–	Concerto	Leeds
	(stgs)	
Huguenin, C.	Three Pieces, Op. 46	Mustel
	Le Berger et le Rossignol	Mustel
Hutschenruyter, W.	Nocturne, Op. 13	Aibl
1796–1878		
Jacob, G. 1895–	Concerto	Williams, 1951
	(stgs)	
Jeppesen, K.	Concerto (1942)	MS (MGG)
1892–		
Jordan, S. 1889–	Concerto romantico, Op. 63 (1957)	NK
Kalliwoda, J. W.	Introduction & Rondo in F,	MS
1801–66	Op. 51 (1834)	
Karkoff, M. 1927–	Concerto, Op. 40	FST
Kauer, F.	Three Concertos	(MGG)
1751–1831	Concerto	(MGG)
	(2 hn)	
Kaufmann, A. 1902–	Musik, Op. 35	MS (MGG)
Kaun, B.	Sinfonia concertante	Jupiter
Kayser, L. 1919–	Concerto (1941–5)	Copenhagen,
		Composer, 1957
Keenan, G. 1906–	Andante, Interlude & Finale	(Ho 2)
	(1935) (stgs)	
Keldorfer, R.	Concerto (1928)	MS (MGG)
1901–		

Kiel, A.	Concerto, Op. 23	Oertel
1850–1907		
Kielland, O. 1901–	†Concerto grosso norvegese, Op. 18	Norsk, 1955
	(1952) (2 hn, stgs)	
Kling, H.	Concerto in F	Oertel
1842–1918		
Koechlin, C.	Poème, Op. 70b (1927)	MS (MGG)
1867–1950		
Kohout, J.	Concertino (1952)	(Ga)
1895–1958		
Komarovsky, A.	Concerto	RS
1909–		
Korn, P. J. 1922–	Concertino	Bo. & H., 1959
	(stgs)	
Koslovsky, J.	Romance	RS
b. 1757		
Krejčí, M.	Life & Time, Op. 23 (1927)	(Ga)
1891–1964	(stgs)	
Křička, J. 1882–	Concertino in F, Op. 102	SHV, 1962
Krol, B. 1920–	Concerto, Op. 29 (Study in Jazz)	Marbot, 1959
Kubín, R. 1909–	Sinfonia concertante (1937)	MS (Ga, MGG)
	(4 hn, stgs)	
Kudelski, C. M.	Concertino in E♭	Philipp
1805–77	(Ed. L. Sansone)	Sansone
Kuhlau, F. D.	Concertino, Op. 45	Peters ; C. Schmidt
1786–1832	(2 hn)	
Kurka, R.	Ballad, Op. 36	Weintraub, 1961
1921–57	(stgs)	
Lachnith, L. V.	Three Concertos	MS (MGG)
1746–1820		
Lamb, J. D.	Concerto in D	MS (Horn Realm)
Lampugnani, G. B.	Sinfonia in D (1762)	MS (MGG*)
1706–ca. 1784	(2 hn, stgs)	(Stockholm)
Lamy, F. 1881–	Cantabile et Scherzo	Leduc, 1949
Landré, G. 1905–	Romance, Op. 39	Hamelle
Larsson, L. E. 1908–	Concertino, Op. 45/5	Gehrmans, 1957
	(stgs)	
Le Boucher, M.	Astolphe	Lemoine, 1944
1882–		
	Le Cor merveilleux	Lemoine, 1944
Lebrun, J.	Concerto	
1759–1809		
Lefebvre, C. E.	Romance, Op. 30	Hamelle
1843–1917		
Leclerc, M.	Concerto	Maurer, 1959
Leschetizsky, T.	Scherzo	UE
1830–1915		
Leutwiler, T.	Concertino	Noetzel, 1960
Lewis, A. 1915–	Concerto (1958)	Lengnick, 1959
Lindpaintner, P.	Concerto	MS? (Engel, MGG)
1791–1856	Concertino in F	(Engel)
Lortzing, G. A.	Andante maestoso con	MS (MGG)
1801–51	variazioni (1820)	

Ludwig, F. 1889–	Concerto	(DMM)
Luening, O. 1900–	Serenade, Op. 18 (1927) (3 hn, stgs)	CFE
Lutyens, E. 1906–	Chamber Concerto, Op. 8/4 (1946)	Chester, 1951
Macero, T. 1925–	Polaris (stgs)	MS (Repertoire list : J. Eger)
Maniet, R.	Concertino	Maurer, 1960
Martin, E. 1915–	Concerto, Op. 12	
Massonneau, L. 1766–1848	Concerto	MS (MGG)
Maštalíř, J. 1906–	Concerto (1936)	(Ga)
	Concerto (1936) (2 hn)	(Ga)
	Nocturne (1962)	(Ga)
Matisse, K.	Concerto No. 1, Op. 12	Nagel
	Concerto No. 2, Op. 24	RS
	Concerto No. 3, Op. 39 (Ed. L. Sansone)	Sansone, n.d.
	Concerto No. 4	Schott
Maw, N. 1935–	Sonata (2 hn, stgs)	(fp, June, 1967)
Mendelssohn, A. 1910–	Divertimento (1958) (stgs)	MS? (MGG)
Mendoza-Nava, J. 1925–	Tipoi	MS (Repertoire list : J. Eger)
Mengal, J. 1796–1878	Fantasia brilliant, Op. 20	Richault
Mengal, M. J. 1784–1851	Three Concertos	MS (MGG*)
	Symphonie concertante (2 hn)	MS (MGG*)
Mengelberg, K. 1902–	Concerto (1950)	Donemus
Meulemans, A. 1884–	Concerto No. 2	CeBeDeM, 1962
Molter, J. M. 1695–1765	Concerto	MS (MGG*)
Montico, M. 1885–1959	Due Pezzi : Caccia, Elegia (stgs)	Carisch, 1950
Mozart, L. 1719–87	†Sinfonia da caccia (4 hn, stgs)	
	(Ed. M. Seiffert)	Br. & H., 1908
	(Ed. M. Langer)	UE, 1935
	†Concerto in D (stgs)	
	(Ed. E. Leloir)	Kawe
	(Ed. Lillya & Isaac)	C. Fischer
	Concerto in E♭ (2 hn, stgs)	
	(Ed. E. Leloir)	KaWe
Mozart, W. A. 1756–91	†Concerto No. 1 in D, K. 412 (1782)	Br. & H.; G. Schirmer; Eulenburg; IMC

	†Concerto No. 2 in E♭, K. 417 (1783)	André [1802]; Br. & H.; G. Schirmer; Eulenburg; IMC
	†Concerto No. 3 in E♭, K. 447 (1783)	André [1802]; Br. & H.; Eulenburg; G. Schirmer; IMC; C. Fischer
	†Concerto No. 4 in E♭, K. 495 (1786)	André [1802]; Br. & H.; Eulenburg; G. Schirmer; IMC; Bo. & H.; KaWe
	†Concert Rondo in E♭, K. 371 (1781) †Concerto in E, K. Anh. 98a (fragment)	Br. & H.; G. Schirmer, 1960
Mudge, R. 1718–63	A Medley Concerto with French Horns	(Oxford Mus., Soc. Cat., ca. 1770)
Mueller, O.	Lyrical Romance: La Chasse	Camara, 1960
Münchausen, A. Baron von, before 1756–1811	Grande symphonie concertante suivie d'un Allegro gracioso avec de cors obligés et d'un Allegro-Finale, Op. 10	Paris, Monsigny
Niemann, W. 1876–1953	Rhein Serenade (stgs)	(DMM)
Norden, H. 1909–	Passacaglia	Chester [1957]
Oates, E. H. 1891–	Introduction & Allegro (1960) (4 hn)	MS (Composer) (10 Coronation Road, Redruth, Cornwall)
Oldberg, A. 1874–1962	Concerto, Op. 20	(T)
Olsen, O. 1850–1927	Concerto, Op. 48 (1886)	MS? (MGG)
Ordoñez, C. d' 1734–86	Notturno in F (2 hn, stgs)	MS (MGG*)
Passani, E. 1905–	Concerto (stgs)	EMT, 1965
Pauer, E. 1826–1905	Concerto	Prague
Pauer, J. 1919–	†Concerto (1957)	SNKLHU, 1959
Pauwels, J. E. 1768–1804	Premier Concerto	Wiessenbruch, n.d.
Pichl, W. 1741–1805	Three Concertos	(MGG)
Piños, A. 1925–	Concerto (1953)	(Ga)
Pokorny, F. X. T. 1729–94	Concerto Three Concertos (2 hn)	MS (MGG*) MS (MGG*)

206

Pololáník, Z. 1935–	Divertimento (1960)	(Ga)
	(4 hn, stgs)	
Rayment, M.	Nocturne & Scherzo	MS (CG)
1918–		
Reger, M.	Scherzino (1899)	Br. & H., 1943
1873–1916	(stgs)	
Reicha, A.	Rondo (1820)	MS (MGG)
1770–1836		
	Solo	MS (MGG)
	Solo in G	MS (MGG)
Reinecke, C.	Notturno in E♭, Op. 112	Kistner
1824–1910		
Reiner, K. 1910–	Song from the Mountains and	Orbis, 1951
	Dance	
Reissiger, K. G.	Elégie et Rondeau, Op. 153	Klemm
1798–1859		
Riotte, P. J.	Concerto, Op. 10	MS (MGG)
1776–1856		
Ristori, E.	Concerto in a	Brogneaux
Röth, P. J.	Concerto in F (1813)	MS (MGG*)
1779–1850		
Rogers, B. 1893–	Fantasy (1952)	Presser, 1956
	(stgs, timp)	
Romberg, B.	Concertante, Op. 41	Costallat
1767–1841	(2 hn)	
Roser, F. de P.	Two Concertos	MS (MGG)
1779–1830		
Rosetti, F. A.	Three Concertos	Paris, 1784
(Rösler, F. A.)		
1750–92		
	Three Concertos, Nos. 1, 3, 4	Sieber
	Concerto No. 4 in E	Pleyel
	Concerto No. 20	Spehr
	Concerto	Paris
	(2 hn)	
	Two Sinfonias concertantes in E	Sieber
	Eleven Concertos	MS (MGG*)
		(Harburg,
		Salzburg,
		Regensburg)
	Three Concertos	MS (MGG*)
	(2 hn)	(Harburg,
		Salzburg)
Modern Editions	†Concerto in E♭ (Ed. O. Kaul)	DTB, XXV, 1925
	(Ed. S. Beck)	N.Y. Pub. Lib.
		1942
	(Ed. H. Fitzpatrick)	Sikorski, 1961
	Concerto No. 1 in E♭	
	(Ed. D. Leloir)	KaWe
	(Ed. J. Chambers)	IMC, 1960
	Concerto No. 2 in E♭	KaWe
	(Ed. E. Leloir)	

	Concerto No. 3 in E♭	KaWe
	(Ed. E. Leloir)	
	Concerto No. 4 in F	KaWe
	(Ed. E. Leloir)	
	Concerto No. 11 in E♭	KaWe
	(Ed. K. Weelink)	
	(2 hn)	
		Musica Rara
	†Concerto No. V in E♭ (2 hn)	KaWe, 1964
	(Ed. K. Weelink)	
	†Concerto in d (Ed. B. Krol)	Simrock, 1959
	Concerto in B♭	Hofmeister
	Concerto in E (Ed. J. Štephan)	Simrock, 1964
Rossini, G.	†Preludio, Tema e Variazioni	FR, 1954; IMC
1792–1868	(1857) (Ed. D. Ceccarossi)	
Rudolphe, J. J.	1er Concerto	Sieber
1730–1812	2me Concerto	Bailleux
Sabatini, G.	Classical Concerto (after Borghi)	Camara, 1963
	(stgs)	
Saint-Saëns, C.	†Romance in F, Op. 36	Hamelle, 1874
1835–1921		
	†Morceau de Concert in f, Op. 94	Durand; IMC
Schacht, T.	Concerto	MS (MGG*)
1748–1823	(2 hn)	
Schäfer, F. 1905–	Concerto	(Ga)
Schelb, J. 1894–	Concerto	MS (MGG)
Schibler, A. 1920–	Prelude, Invocation & Dance, Op. 47 (1956)	A. & S., 1956
Schlösser, L.	Concertino, Op. 16	André
1800–86		
Schmittbauer, J. A.	Two Concertos	MS (MGG)
1718–1809		
Schneider, G. A.	Concerto, Op. 86	Hofmeister
1770–1839		
Schoeck, O.	†Concerto, Op. 65	Bo. & H., 1952
1886–1957		
Schuller, G. 1925–	Concerto (1944)	MJQ
Schumann, R.	†Konzertstück, Op. 86 (1849)	Br. & H.; KaWe
1810–56	(4 hn)	
Searle, H. 1915–	Aubade, Op. 28	Schott, 1956
	(stgs)	
Seiber, M.	Notturno	Schott, 1952
1904–60	(stgs)	
Shebalin, V. I.	Concerto in C (1930)	RS, 1960
1902–		
Sikorski, K. 1895–	Concerto (1949)	PWM, 1951
Škroup, D. J.	Concerto	CHF
1765–1830		
Smatek, M. 1895–	Concertino	(Ga)
Smit, L. 1900–44	Concertino	(Re)
Spezzaferri, G.	Concerto, Op. 94	Milan, Ed.
1888–1963		Musicali

Steinmetz fl. ca. 1750	†Concerto in D (Ed. E. Leloir)	Noetzel, 1964
	Two Concertos (2 hn)	
Stich, W. (Punto, G.) 1746–1803	Fourteen Concertos	(T)
	†Concerto No. 5 in F (Ed. E. Leloir)	KaWe
	Concerto No. 7 in F (Ed. A. Gottron)	SM, 1961
Strauss, F. S. 1822–1905	†Concerto in c, Op. 8	UE; C. Fischer, n.d.
Strauss, R. 1864–1949	†Concerto No. 1 in E♭, Op. 11 (1882–3)	Aibl, 1884; UE
	†Concerto No. 2 in E♭ (1942)	Bo. & H., 1947
Sydeman, W. 1928–	Concert Piece (stgs)	(Ho)
Tayber, A. 1756–1822	Two Concertos in E♭	MS (MGG)
Telemann, G. P. 1681–1767	Concerto in E♭ (2 hn, stgs)	Br. & H., 1933 Eulenburg
	†Suite in F (Ed. H. Büttner) (2 hn, stgs)	Eulenburg; IMC
	†Concerto in D (Ed. E. Leloir) †Concerto in E (2 hn, stgs)	Pegasus, 1964
	†Concerto in D (Ed. K. Weelink) (3 hn)	KaWe
	†Concerto in E♭ (Tafelmusik III) (1733) (Ed. J. P. Hinnenthal) (2 hn, stgs)	BVK
Thatcher, H. R. 1878–	Concerto	Camara, 1961
Thiessen, K. b. 1867	Romance, Op. 38	(DMM, T)
Tischhauser, F. 1921–	Divertimento (2 hn, stgs)	(Schweiz)
Todt, J. C. 18th Cent.	Three Concertos	MS (MGG)
	Three Concertos (2 hn)	MS (MGG)
Toldi, J.	Concerto	Ars Viva
Tomasi, H. 1901–	Concerto	Leduc, 1955
	Danse profane	Leduc, 1960
Tomlinson, E. 1924–	Rhapsody & Rondo	Mills, 1962
Torelli, G. 1658–1709	Sinfonia in F (2 hn, stgs, bc)	MS (MGG)
Vandenbroeck, O. 1759–1832	Symphonie concertante in E♭ (2 hn)	Boyer [ca. 1792]; Nadermann
	Concerto No. 1	Nadermann, 1788
	Concerto No. 2	Nadermann, 1788

o

G.T.H.

Veit, W. H. 1806–64	Andante grazioso in F	MS (MGG)
Veremans, R. 1894–	Concerto	Maurer, 1965
Vignati, M. 1897–1966	Suite (1964)	(Ga)
Vinter, G. 1909–	Hunter's Moon	Bo. & H., 1942
Vivaldi, A. 1685–1745	†Concerto in F, P. 320 (Ed. G. F. Malipiero) (2 hn, stgs)	Ricordi, 1951
	†Concerto in F, P. 321 (Ed. G. F. Malipiero) (2 hn, stgs)	Ricordi, 1950
Vogel, C. 1750–94	Four Concertos	(MGG)
Weber, C. M. 1786–1826	Concertino in e, Op. 45 (1806)	Lienau; Br. & H.; KaWe
Weismann, J. 1879–1950	Concerto, Op. 118	Birnbach
Werner, J. J.	Concerto (stgs, pf, perc)	Eschig, 1965
Whettam, G. 1927–	Concerto (stgs)	de Wolfe
Whiting, A. B. 1861–1936	Suite (stgs)	(Chase)
Wilder, A. 1907–	Concerto (1955)	MS (Ho)
Woltmann, F. 1908–	Poem (1936) (stgs)	MS (Ho, R)
	Rhapsody (1935)	MS (R, T)

2.2 *Horn and other instruments with orchestra*

Absil, J. 1893–	Concerto grosso, Op. 60 (1944) (wind quint, stgs)	CeBeDeM
Addison, J. 1920–	Concertante (ob, cl, hn)	OUP
Albinoni, T. 1671–1750	†Concerto a 5 in D, Op. 5/1 (2 ob d'am, 2 hn, bn)	Hinnenthal, n.d.
Albrechtsberger, J. G. 1736–1809	Sinfonia concertante in D (Ed. O. Kapp) (hn, bn, vln, stgs)	DTÖ, 1909, 1959
Amram, D. 1930–	†Shakespearian Concerto (ob, 2 hn, stgs)	Peters, 1964
Andriessen, J. 1925–	†Movimenti (1965) (hn, trp, trb, stgs, timp)	Donemus, 1965
Arrieu, C. 1903–	Concert (wind quint, stgs)	Ricordi, 1964
Bach, J. C. 1735–82	Symphonie concertante in E♭ (2 fl, 2 hn, 2 vln)	MS? (WERM)
	Konzertante Sinfonie (wind quint)	MS? (MGG)
Bach, J. S. 1685–1750	†Brandenburg Concerto No. 1 BWV 1046 (2 ob, 2 hn, bn, stgs, bc)	Br. & H.

A LIST OF MUSIC FOR THE HORN

Baumgartner	Concerto (hn, bn)	MS (E*)
Baur, J. 1918–	Pentagramm (1966) (wind quint)	Br. & H., 1966
Bax, A. 1883–1953	Concertante (ca, cl, hn)	Chappell
Bennett, R. R. 1894–	Concerto grosso (1958) (wind quint)	Peters
Berghmans, J.	Concerto grosso (hn, trp, trb, stgs)	Leduc, 1957
Blacher, B. 1903–	Concerto, Op. 36 (cl, hn, bn, trp, hp, stgs)	B. & B., 1956
	Konzertstück (1963) (wind quint, stgs)	B. & B., 1964
Boccherini, L. 1743–1805	Serenade (2 ob, 2 hn, stgs) †Sinfonia concertante in G, Op. 8 (ob, hn, bn, stgs) Sinfonia concertante, Op. 41 (Ed. K. Haas) (ob, hn, bn, stgs)	Novello, 1964
Bochsa, N. C. 1789–1856	Symphonie concertante (hn, hp)	MS? (Engel)
Braal, A. de 1909–	Concertante Muziek (wind quint, trp, stgs, pf, perc)	Donemus, 1965
Braun, J. [1753–95?]	Concerto (cl, 2 hn, stgs)	MS (E*)
Braunfels, W. 1882–1954	Music (2 hn, vln, vla, stgs)	
Bréval, J. B. 1756–1825	Symphonie concertante, Op. 30 (ob, hn)	J. & C. [ca. 1800]
	Symphonie concertante, Op. 38 (hn, bn, hpcd)	J. & C., n.d.
Burghauser, J. 1921–	Concerto (1942) (wind quint, stgs)	CHF
Cambini, G. G. 1746–1825	Symphonie concertante (1778) (fl, ob, hn, bn)	(Brook)
Candeille, E. J. 1767–1831	Symphonie concertante (1786) (cl, hn, bn, pf)	MS? (MGG)
Cannabicth, C. 1731–98	Concerto alla Pastorale (fl, ob, hn, bn, stgs, cont)	Mannh, Musikverlag
Capuzzi, G. A. 1755–1818	Sinfonia concertante, Op. 1 (hn, 2 vln)	Venice [1790?]
Carillo, J. 1875–1965	Concertino (picc, hn, vln, vcl, hp, gt)	(Slo)
Catel, C. S. 1773–1830	Symphonie concertante (fl, cl, hn)	Ozi [ca. 1800]
	Symphonie concertante (fl, hn, bn)	Ozi [ca. 1800]
Cikker, J. 1911–	Erinnerungen, Op. 25 (1947) (wind quint, stgs)	Artia
Crussell, B. H. 1775–1838	Pièce concertante (cl, hn, bn)	

211

	Concertante in B♭, Op. 3 (cl, hn, bn) (Ed. K. Weelink)	Peters [ca. 1816] KaWe
Dalvimare, M. P. 1772–1839 (and Duvernoy, F.? 1765–1838)	Symphonie concertante (hn, hp)	Cousineau, n.d.
Danzi, F. 1763–1826	Sinfonia concertante in E♭ (1785) (fl, ob, hn, bn)	Schott [1938] Musica Rara, 1966
David, J. N. 1895–	Symphonia concertante (wind quint, stgs)	Br. & H.
David, T. C. 1925–	Concerto (1962) (wind quint, stgs)	Doblinger, 1964
Devienne, F. 1759–1803	Symphonie concertante No. 1 (1792) (hn, bn)	Imbault, 1793; J. & C.
	Symphonie concertante No. 4 (1794) (fl, ob, hn, bn)	Imbault
	2e Symphonie concertante (1800?) (= No. 5) (fl, ob, hn, bn)	Ozi [1800]; (Bibl. Nat., Paris)
Dittersdorf, K. 1739–99	†Symphonie concertante (1788) (2 ob, 2 hn, bn, stgs)	(MGG)
Dobiáš, V. 1909–	Sonata (1947; rev. 1958) (wind quint, pf, stgs, timp)	Panton, 1960
Donatoni, V. 1927–	Concertino (2 hn, 2 trp, 2 trb, stgs, timp solo)	Schott, 1953
Droste-Hülshoff, M. F. 1764–1840	Duo concertante (hn, bn)	MS? (MGG)
	Fantasie (fl, hn, vln, vcl)	MS? (MGG)
	Grand Quatuor concertant (fl, ob, hn, bn)	MS? (MGG)
Dubois, F. C. T. 1837–1924	Fantasietta (fl, hn, trp, hp, stgs, timp)	Heugel, 1914
Duncan, R. 1916–	Concerto (cl, hn, stgs)	MS (CG)
Duvernoy, F. 1765–1838	Symphonie concertante (cl, hn, bn)	(Brook)
Eben, P. 1929–	Concertino pastorale (2 ob, hn, stgs)	SHV, 1966
Eberwein, T. M. 1775–1831	Konzertante, Op. 47 (ob, hn, bn)	Br. & H. [ca. 1820]
Eler, A. F. 1764–1821	Symphonie concertante (1796) (fl, cl, hn, bn)	Nadermann, n.d.
	Symphonie concertante (fl, cl, hn)	Ozi, n.d.
Etler, A. D. 1913–	†Concerto (1960) (wind quint)	AMP
Fasch, J. F. 1688–1758	†Concerto (2 ob, 2 hn, 2 bn, stgs)	Leipzig, 1938
Filippi, A. de 1900–	Concerto (1928) (fl, ob, hn, bn, trp, stgs)	MS (Ho)

A LIST OF MUSIC FOR THE HORN

Finke, F. F. 1891–	VIII Suite (wind quint, 2 pf, stgs)	Br. & H., 1965
Fiorello, D. 1905–	Concerto (1935) (ob, hn, sousa/tuba, stgs, pf, timp)	MS (R)
Flothuis, M. 1914–	†Canti e Guiochi, Op. 66 (1964) (wind quint, stgs)	Donemus, 1965
Frédéric, D.	Symphonie concertante (cl, hn, bn)	Ozi, n.d.
Freed, I. 1900–60	Improvisation & Scherzo (ob, hn, stgs)	(Ho)
Fuchs, G. F. 1752–1821	Symphonie concertante (cl, hn)	J. & C., n.d.
Fuleihan, A. 1900–	Divertimento (1943) (ob, hn, bn, trp, stgs)	MS (R)
Gabaye, P.	Symphonie concertante (fl, ob, hn, bn, stgs)	Leduc, 1960
Gavazzeni, G. 1909–	Piccolo Concerto (1939–40) (fl, hn, stgs)	CMC
Gebauer, F. R. 1773–1844	Symphonie concertante No. 3 (hn, bn) Eight Sinfonias concertantes (fl, cl, hn, bn)	Jouve, n.d. Jouve; Sieber
Geiger, E.	Kammersymphonie, Op. 78 (wind quint, stgs, glock, timp)	Mannh. Musikverlag
Ghedini, G. F. 1892–1965	Concerto grosso in F (1927) (wind quint, stgs)	SZ
Grabner, H. 1886–	Konzert, Op. 48 (fl, cl, hn, bn, stgs)	K. & S.
Granjany, M. 1891–	Poème symphonique (hn, hp)	MS (ASCAP, G, T)
Grétry, A. E. M. 1742–1813	Concerto in C (Ed. D. Sonntag) (fl, 2 hn, stgs)	Noetzel, 1962
Gyring, E.	Divertimento (fl, cl, hn, stgs)	CFE
Gyrowetz, A. 1763–1850	Divertimento concertante (1833) (ob, cl, hn, bn)	MS? (MGG*)
Hagen, O. F. L. 1888–	Concerto grosso (2 hn, 2 trp, stgs, timp)	MS (BQ, VI, 1)
Hahn, R. 1875–1947	Concerto provencal (fl, cl, hn, bn, stgs)	(La, WERM)
Haines, E. 1914–	†Concerto (1959) (fl, cl, hn, trp, vln, vla, vcl)	AME
Henrich, H. 1891–	Kleine Suite (ob, hn, stgs)	Heinrichshofen
Herzogenberg, H. 1843–1900	Konzert (1879) (fl, ob, cl, 2 hn, 2 bn, stgs)	MS (MGG)
Hindemith, P. 1895–1963	†Concert Music, Op. 50 (1930) (4 hn, 4 trp, 3 trb, tuba, stgs)	Schott, 1931
Hoffding, F. 1899–	Sinfonia concertante, Op. 23 (wind quint, pf, stgs)	Samfundet, 1938
Hoffmeister, F. A. 1754–1812	Symphonie concertante (2 ob, 2 hn, bn)	MS (BQ, V, 2)

213

Hohensee, W. 1927–	Konzertante Ouverture	VNM, 1963
	(wind quint, stgs, perc)	
Holmboe, V.	Concerto, Op. 21	
1909–	(cl, 2 hn, 2 trp, stgs)	
	†Concerto, Op. 44	
	(2 hn, trp, stgs)	
Hovhaness, A.	Sosi	Peer
1911–	(hn, vln, stgs, pf, perc)	
Husa, K. 1921–	Serenade	Leduc, 1964
	(wind quint, stgs, xyl, hp/pf)	
Ištvan, M. 1928–	Concerto (1949)	(Ga)
	(hn, stgs, pf)	
Jadin, L. E.	Symphonie concertante	Dufaut [ca. 1820]
1768–1853	(fl, hn, bn)	
	Symphonie concertante	Sieber, n.d.;
	cl/ob, hn, bn	
	Symphonie concertante	Lelu, n.d.
	(cl/fl/ob, hn, bn)	
Kirchner, L. 1919–	Toccata (1955)	AMP
	(ob, cl, hn, bn, trp, trb, stgs, perc)	
Klebe, G. 1925–	Divertissement joyeux, Op. 5 (1949)	B. & B. 1949
	(cl, hn, bn, trp, trb, stgs, perc)	
	Espressione liriche (1956)	Schott
	(hn, trp, trb)	
Konietzny, H.	Symphonie concertante (1965)	MS (Ve)
	(wind quint, stgs, perc)	
Koutzen, B. 1901–	Concerto (1934)	EV, 1934
	(fl, cl, hn, bn, vcl, stgs)	
Kox, H. 1930–	Sinfonia concertante (1956)	Donemus, 1956
	(hn, trp, trb)	
Kremenliev, B. A.	Tune (1940)	MS? (G)
1911–	(sax, hn, stgs)	
Kreutz, A. 1906–	Concertino (1946)	MS? (Horn Realm)
	(ob, hn, stgs)	
Kreutzer, C.	Concertante	MS? (Am Z,
1780–1849	(hn, bn)	26/1824)
Krommer, F.	Concertante	MS (Am Z,
1759–1831	(fl, ob, hn, bn)	6/1803–4)
Lacroix, E. 1896–	Premières Tendresses	Costallat
	(wind quint, stgs)	
Laderman, E. 1924–	†Theme, Variations & Finale (1957)	(Schwann)
	(wind quint)	
Larsson, L. E.	Divertimento	UE, 1935
1908–	(wind quint, stgs)	
Lazar, F.	Concerto grosso	Durand
1894–1936	(2 ob, 2 hn, 2 bn, trp, stgs, timp)	
Leplin, E. 1917–	Rustic Dance (1941)	(Ho)
	(hn, stgs, 2 pf)	
Levy, F.	Concerto	Cor
	(ob, hn, bn, stgs, timp)	
Lindpaintner, P.	Symphonie concertante, Op. 36	Schott, n.d.
1791–1856	(wind quint)	

A LIST OF MUSIC FOR THE HORN

	2e Symphonie concertante, Op. 44 (wind quint)	Schott, n.d.
Mabellini, T. 1817–97	Gran Fantasia 1846 (fl, hn, trp, trb)	MS? (MGG)
Maconchy, E. 1907–	Variazioni concertante (1965) (ob, cl, hn, bn, stgs)	(MT, July, 1965)
Martelli, H. 1895–	Concertino, Op. 85 (1955) (wind quint, stgs)	Ricordi, 1956
Martin, A. 1825–56	Fantasie sur un Thème de Rossini, Op. 9 (cl, hn)	Costallat, n.d.
Martin, F. 1890–	†Concerto (1949) (wind, quint, trp, trb, stgs, timp, perc)	UE, 1950
Martin, J. J. B. 1775–1836	2e Symphonie concertante (fl, ob, hn, bn)	Paris, Composer, n.d.
Mengal, M. J. 1784–1851	Concertante (ob, hn, bn)	Gevaert, n.d.
	Concertante (2 fl, ob, cl, hn)	Gevaert, n.d.
Mercadante, S. 1797–1870	Fantasia sur il Guinamento (hn, trp)	MS? (F)
Meyer, K. H. b. 1772	Fantasie concertante, Op. 20 (fl, cl, hn, bn)	Hofmeister [ca. 1821]
Miaskowsky, N. 1881–1950	Concerto lirico, Op. 32/3 (fl, cl, hn, bn, hp, stgs)	RS, 1930
Mihály, A. 1917–	Fantasie (1955) (wind quint, stgs)	ZV, 1959
Milhaud, D. 1892–	Symphonie concertante, Op. 376 (hn, bn, trp, db)	Heugel, 1959
Möser, K. 1774–1851	Concertante (ob, 2 hn, vln, stgs)	MS (E*)
Mohler, P. 1908–	Concertino, Op. 11 (1935) (fl, cl, hn, stgs, timp, perc)	SM
Molter, J. M. 1695–1765	Sinfonia concertante (2 ob, 2 hn, bn, trp)	MS (MGG*)
Monasterio y Agüeros, J. b. 1836	Estudio de concierto (ob, cl, hn, hp, stgs)	(DMM)
Monnikendam, M. 1896–	Vision (fl, ob, hn, hp, stgs, org)	Donemus, 1962
	Concerto (hn, trp)	Donemus, 1952
Mozart, W. A. 1756–91	†Sinfonia concertante, K. 297b (1778) (ob, cl, hn, bn)	Br. & H.
Müller, F. 1786–1871	Symphonie concertante (cl, hn)	Br. & H. [1821]
	2e Symphonie concertante, Op. 31 (cl, hn)	Br. & H. [1826]
Müller, I. 1786–1854	Duo concertante (cl, hn)	(Am Z 30/1828)

215

Müller-Medek, W.	Fantasie	Grosch
	(wind quint, stgs)	
Muscaro, M.	Gde	Camara
d. 1958	(hn, bn, stgs)	
Nohr, F. 1800–75	Concertante	Kayser
	(wind quint)	
	Concertante, Op. 10	Falter, n.d.
	(wind quint)	
	Potpourri, Op. 3	Br. & H.
	(fl, cl, hn, bn)	
Paganini, N.	Concertino	MS (MGG)
1782–1840	(hn, bn)	
Perotti, G. D.	Sinfonia in D	MS (MGG*)
1750–1824	(ob, hn)	
Petrič, I.	Musique concertante	Društvo, 1962
	(wind quint, stgs, timp)	
Pfister, H. 1914–	Phantasy concertante	Heinrichshofen
	(fl, hn, hp, stgs)	
Pleyel, I.	Symphonie concertante in E,	André, n.d.
1757–1831	Op. 74	
	(fl, ob/cl, hn, bn)	
	†Symphonie concertante, No. 5	Pleyel, n.d.,
	(fl, ob, hn, bn)	Nadermann
	(Ed. F. Oubradous)	EMT, 1959
Quinet, M. 1915–	Sinfonietta	UE
	(wind quint, stgs, timp)	
Raphling, S. 1910–	Concerto No. 1	Mills
	(fl, hn, trp, stgs, pf)	
Rawsthorne, A.	Concertante pastorale	OUP, 1951
1905–	(1951)	
	(fl, hn, stgs)	
Rehberg, W.	Konzertante Musik, Op. 12 (1940)	MS? (MGG)
1900–57	(cl, hn, stgs, pf)	
Reicha, A.	Concertante	Paris, 1817
1770–1836	(wind quint)	
Rey, D. R. 1904–	Colloque instrumental (1958)	MS? (MGG)
	(fl, 2 hn, hp, stgs)	
Rieti, V. 1898–	Concerto (1923)	UE, 1924
	(wind quint)	
	Due pastorale	UE, 1925
	(fl, hn, stgs)	
Rietz, J.	Konzertstück, Op. 41 (1870)	Seitz; R. & E.,
1812–77	(wind quint)	1873
Röth, P. J.	Concertante in F (1813)	MS (MGG*)
1779–1850	(hn, bn)	
Rosetti, F. A.	Concerto	MS (MGG*)
1750–92	(2 ob, 2 hn, stgs)	
	Concerto in B♭	MS (MGG*)
	(2 fl, 2 hn, stgs)	
	Concerto	MS? (G)
	(ob, cl, hn, bn)	
	Concertino	MS? (BQV2)
	(cl/ob, hn)	

	Sinfonia concertante	(Ve)
	(fl, ob, hn, bn)	
Rosseau, N. 1907–	†Concerto à cinq, Op. 74 (1960)	
	(wind quint)	
Scaramelli	Rondo variato	Cipriani, n.d.
	(hn, vln)	
Schibler, A. 1920–	Concerto, Op. 59 (1959)	A. & S., 1959
	(hn, trp, trb, hp, double stgs, pf, perc)	
Schuller, G. 1925–	Contrasts (1961)	AMP
	(wind quint)	
Scott, T. 1912–61	Procession Canon & Jig	CFE
	(ob, hn, hp, stgs)	
Škroup, D. J. 1765–1830	Concerto	Artia
	(2 cl, hn, 2 bn, stgs)	
Smith, R. 1927–	Divertimento (1958)	(Ho)
	(2 ob, 2 hn, stgs)	
Smyth, E. 1858–1944	Concerto (1927)	Curwen
	(hn, vln)	
Stamitz, K. 1745–1801	Symphonie concertante No. 14	Sieber, n.d.
	(ob, hn, bn, vln)	
	Symphonie concertante in E♭, No. 23 (hn, bn)	Sieber, n.d.
	Three Symphonies concertantes	Leduc [ca. 1786]
	(fl, ob, 2 hn, bn)	
	Symphonie concertante No. 4 in F	UE, 1935
	(fl, ob, cl, 2 hn, vln, vcl)	
Strebotnjak, A. 1931—	Monologues (1963)	(L. & S.)
	(fl, ob, hn, stgs, timp)	
Stulicke, M. N. 18th Cent.	Concerto	MS (E*)
	(2 ob, hn, vln)	
Suter, R. 1919–	Lyrische Suite	(Ve)
	(fl, ob, cl, hn, stgs)	
Svara, D. 1902–	Konzertante Suite No. 1	(Ve)
	(fl, ob, hn, stgs)	
Swanson, H. 1909–	Night-Music	Weintraub, 1951
	(wind quint, stgs)	
Tchemberdji, N. 1903–	Suite concertante	RS, 1935
Telemann, G. P. 1681–1767	†Suite in F	Eulenburg
	(2 ob, 4 hn, stgs)	
Thalberg, S. 1812–71	Grand Divertissement, Op. 7	(MGG)
	(hn, pf)	
Titl, A. E. 1809–82	Serenade	Seeling; Gallet; C. Schmidt
	(fl, hn)	
Tulou, J. L. 1786–1865	Symphonie concertante No. 2, Op. 21	Pleyel [ca. 1814]; Lemoine, n.d.
	(fl, ob, hn, bn)	
Vandenbroeck, J. 1759–1832	Symphonie concertante	Nadermann, n.d. [1793]
	(cl, hn, bn)	
Villa-Lobos, H. 1887–1959	Fantasia	Peer
	(sax, 3 hn, stgs)	

Vinals	Symphonie concertante (hn, pf)	Pacini, n.d.
Vogel, J. C. 1756–88	Symphonie concertante (2 fl, ob, 2 hn, bn)	(T)
Vogel, L., late 18th Cent.	Concerto in G (fl, hn, vln, vcl)	MS (Cons. Brussels)
Voormolen, A. 1895–	Sinfonia concertante (1951) (cl, hn, stgs)	Donemus, 1951
Wagenseil, G. C. 1715–77	Sinfonie (4 fl, 4 hn, stgs)	Bernouilli
Wessel, M. 1894–	Symphony concertante (1929) (hn, pf)	MS (Horn Realm)
Wessely, J. 1762–1814	Zehn Variationen, Op. 15 (hn, vln)	Spehr, n.d.
Whettam, G. 1927–	Concerto grosso (wind quint, hp, stgs)	de Wolfe
Widerkehr, J. C. M. 1739–1823	Symphonie concertante No. 3 (hn, bn)	Sieber; Pleyel
	Symphonie concertante No. 5 (hn, bn)	Sieber; Schlesinger, n.d.
	Symphonie concertante No. 10 (hn, bn)	Pleyel; Ozi; Schlesinger
	Symphonie concertante No. 4 (fl, ob, cl, hn, 2 bn, vln)	J. & C.; Imbault; [ca. 1800]
	Concertante (fl, ob, cl, hn, vcl)	MS? (Am Z 6/1803–4)
Wilms [J. W. 1772–1847?]	Symphonie concertante, Op. 35 (fl, ob/cl, hn, bn)	J. Hummel
	Concertante, Op. 13 (fl, ob/cl, hn, bn)	J. Hummel, 1805
Winter, P. von 1754–1825	Sinfonie concertante, Op. 11 (cl, hn, bn, vln)	Br. & H.; Gaveaux, n.d.
Wolf-Ferrari, E. 1876–1948	Idillio-Concertino, Op. 15 (1932) (ob, 2 hn, stgs)	Ricordi, 1932
	Suite-Concertino, Op. 16 (1932) (2 hn, bn, stgs)	Ricordi, 1932
Wood, R. W. 1902–	Concertino (wind quint)	MS (CG)
Wuorinen, C. 1938–	Concertone (1960) (hn, 2 trp, trb, tuba)	CFE

3. Horns alone

3.1 *One horn*

Apostel, H. E. 1901–	Sonatine, Op. 39b	UE, 1965
Arnold, M. 1921–	Fantasy, Op. 88 (1966)	Faber, 1966
Barboteu, G.	20 Études concertantes	Choudens, 1963
Bozza, E. 1905–	18 Études en forme d'improvisation	Leduc, 1961
Brahms, J. 1833–97	10 original Études, Op. posth. (Ed. E. Leloir)	KaWe
Butt, J.	Suite	Hinrichsen
Ceccarossi, D. 1910–	10 Capricci	Ricordi

218

Dauprat, L. F.	Trois Solos, Op. 20	Lemoine
1781–1868		
Gallay, J. F.	18 Mélodies, Op. 53	Lemoine
1795–1864	(Ed. E. Leloir)	Rahter, 1961
	22 Fantaisies mélodiques, Op. 58	Lemoine
	(Ed. E. Leloir)	Rahter, 1962
Guarneri, M. C.	Étude	Rongwen, 1958
1907–		
Guillaume, E. N.	Sonata	Schott
Ketting, O. 1935–	Intrada (1958)	Donemus
Koechlin, C.	Pièce, Op. 218b (1948)	MS (MGG)
1867–1950		
Lyon, D.	Partita, Op. 6	London, IMC, 1967
Raphling, S. 1910–	Sonata (1955)	King
	Variations & Introduction (1955)	(Ho)
	Workout (1955)	(Ho)
Reinhardt, B. 1929–	Music	IMP
Reynolds, V.	48 Études	G. Schirmer, 1962
Schuller, G. 1925–	Studies for unaccompanied horn	OUP, 1962
Wellesz, E. 1885–	Fanfares, Op. 78	Rongwen, 1958

3.2 Two horns

André, J. A.	Twelve Pieces	André
1775–1842		
Bodnár, L.	21 leichte kleine Vortragsstücke	EMB, 1955
	(2–3 hn)	
Clodomir, P.	Heures musicales	Leduc, 1956
Cobb, S.	Sonatina	C. Fischer
Dauprat, L. F.	6 grands Duos, Op. 13	Zetter
1781–1868		
	20 Duets, Op. 14	Zetter; Lemoine
Degen, D. (Comp.	Fröhliche Jagd (1–2 hn)	BVK, 1939
& arr.)		
Del Mar, N. 1919–	Sonatina	MS
Flothuis, M. 1914–	Three Pieces, Op. 24a (1945)	Donemus
Gallay, J. F.	12 Duos concertantes	Pacini
1795–1864	(Ed. L. Sansone)	Sansone
	12 Nocturnes, Op. 3	Pacini
	12 petits Airs	Lemoine
	12 Duos, Op. 14	Colombier
	24 Duos, Op. 16	
	3 Grands Duos, Op. 38	Schoenenberger
Gebauer, P. P.	20 Duos	(La)
b. 1775		
Gipps, R. 1921–	A Tarradiddle, Opuscule 51	Williams, 1961
Graas, J. 1924–	Modern Duets & Trios (in	Southern
	contrapuntal style)	
Horrod, N.	Duo No. 1	KaWe
Jacqmin, F.	12 Duos, Op. 1	Schoenenberger
1793–1847		
	3 Duos concertantes, Op. 4	Schoenenberger
	3 Duos concertantes, Op. 9	Schoenenberger

Janetzky, K. (Comp. & arr.)	Waldhorn-Duette verschiedener Meister d. 18 u. 19 Jahrh. (G. P. Telemann, L. Mozart and others)	Hofmeister, 1953
Kalliwoda, J. W. 1801–66	Divertissement, Op. 59	MS (MGG)
Kenn, P. ca. 1750–1810	Mixed Duos, Op. 1	Sieber
	Short Airs, Op. 2	Ozi
Kincl, A. 1898–	Fanfare	SHV, 1966
Köhler, G. H. 1765–1833	6 Duos, Op. 160	Br. & H.
Kopprasch, W.	8 Duets	IMC, 1958; Sansone
	3 grosse Duette (Ed. A. Frehse)	Hofmeister, 1954
Lavotta, J. 1764–1820	Duette	MS (MGG)
Makovecky, J.	5 Duets (Ed. J. Štephan)	SHV, 1963
Marc-Carles	6 Duets	Leduc
Mayer, R.	12 Bicinia	Shawnee, 1965
Meifred, J. E. 1791–1867	12 easy Duos, Op. 1	Zetter
Métral, P.	Pièces en duo	Paterson, 1963
Morin, J. B. 1677–1754	Nouvelles Fanfares à 2 trompes de chasse pour sonner pendant la curée	Paris, Prault, 1734
Mozart, W. A. 1756–91	†Twelve Pieces, K. 487 (1786)	Imbault [after 1794]
	(Ed. E. Paul)	OBV, 1949
	(Ed. J. Marx)	M. & M., 1947, 1955
	(Ed. O. Stösser)	Hofmeister, 1961
	(Ed. K. Janetzky)	Hofmeister, 1953
Neuling, H. 1897–	Five Duets	Simrock
Nicolai, O. 1810–49	Six Duets for 2 horns	
	No. 1 (Ed. K. Janetzky)	Musica Rara, 1961
	No. 1	Broekmans, 1962
	Nos. 2 & 3	KaWe
	No. 2 (Ed. K. Janetzky)	Musica Rara, 1965
	No. 3 (Ed. K. Janetzky)	Musica Rara, 1966
	3 Duette (Ed. O. Stösser)	Hofmeister, n.d. [1963]
	Five Duets	Musica Rara
Pinkham, D. 1923–	Fanfare, Air & Echo (with timp)	Peters, 1963
Rasmussen, P.	Duets	Hansen
Reichardt, J. F. 1752–1814	100 leichte Übungsstücke	Leipzig, G. Fleischer, n.d.
Rimsky-Korsakov, N. 1844–1908	Two Duets (1894?)	Musica Rara, 1958; King, 1959
Rossini, G. 1792–1868	Five Duets (ca. 1805) (Ed. E. Leloir)	Simrock, 1961

A LIST OF MUSIC FOR THE HORN

Rudolphe, J. J. 1730–1812	Easy Fanfares	Sieber
Sabatini, G.	Nocturne	Cor, 1963
Schneider, W. 1907–	Klassische Spielstücke	BVK, 1956
Schubert, F. 1797–1828	Five little Duets	Br. & H.
	(Ed. E. Leloir)	Simrock, 1962
	(Ed. R. F. Goldman)	Mercury, 1946
Schuller, G. 1925–	Four Duets	OUP, 1962
Stich, J. W.	12 Duos (Ed. E. Leloir)	KaWe
(Punto, G.) 1746–1803	8 Duos (Ed. E. Leloir)	KaWe
Stieber, H. 1886–	Turmmusik Nr. 1	Hofmeister, 1953
Stösser, O.	Duette alter Meister, 2 vols	Hofmeister, n.d. [ca. 1962]
Stravinsky, I. 1882–	Canons	MS
Szervánsky, E. 1911–	Duos	ZV, 1953
Tuch, H. A. G. 1766–1821	12 Stücke, Op. 21	Dessau, 1808
	12 Duette, Op. 33 (1814)	(MGG)
Türrschmidt, C. 1753–97	50 Duos	Simrock; Janet: Menzel
	6 Duos, Opp. 1 & 2	Sieber
Valsa, J. 1752–92	2 Sets of Duets	Sieber
Vandenbroeck, O. 1759–1832	Duos, Op. 1	Nadermann, n.d.
	Duos, Op. 2	Nadermann, n.d.

3.3 Three horns

Artot, J. D. 1803–87	Twelve Trios	Schott [1875?]
Clark, F.	Seicento	Musicus, 1959
Cowell, H. 1897–1965	Hymn & Fuguing Tune No. 12	AMP, 1960
Dauprat, L. F. 1781–1868	Trois grands Trios, Op. 4	Zetter; Lemoine
	Grand Trio, Op. 46	Lemoine [ca. 1840]
Duvernoy, F. 1765–1838	4 Trios (Ed. Zimolong)	Sikorski, 1963
Frehse, A.	Twelve Trios, Op. 10 (Ed. L. Sansone)	Hofmeister, 1929 Sansone
Gallay, J. F. 1795–1864	Three grand Trios, Op. 10 (Ed. E. Leloir) St. Hubert: 6 Fanfares	Colombier KaWe Schoenenberger, n.d.
Horrod, N.	Scherzo	KaWe
Jacobson, I. D.	Three Holidays	Mills, 1961
Janetzky, K. (Comp. & arr.)	Jägerstücklein: Volks-und Jägerlieder (3–4 hn)	Hofmeister, 1956
Kenn, P. ca. 1750–1810	36 Trios	Ozi
	Collection of Airs	Ozi

221

APPENDIX C

Kling, H. A. L. 1842–1918	30 selected Pieces	BMI
Mercadante, S. 1795–1870	Terzettino	(Cob)
Reicha, A. 1770–1836	†Six Trios, Op. 48	
	24 Trios, Op. 82	Pleyel, n.d.
	†6 Trios from Op. 82	Merseburger
	(Ed. A. Frehse & F. von Glasenapp)	Hofmeister, 1953
	(Ed. J. Chambers)	IMC, 1958
	10 Trios from Op. 82	
	Nos. 15–24 (Ed. E. Leloir)	KaWe
	8 Trios from Op. 82	
	(Ed. E. Leloir)	Simrock, 1964
Rudolphe, J. J. 1730–1812	24 Fanfares	Bailleux
Schneider, G. A. 1770–1839	18 Trios, Op. 56 (Ed. A. Kranz)	Pro Musica, 1949
Stich, J. W. (Punto, G.) 1748–1803	20 Trios (Ed. E. Leloir)	KaWe
Wilhelmer, A.	Sonatine	ÖBV, 1949

3.4 Four Horns

Antoine, F.	Quartet, Op. 52	Vienna, 1929
Arnell, R. 1917	Music for horns, Op. 82	Southern, 1965
Artot, J. D. 1803–87	12 Quartets	Schott, 1875
Atterberg, K. 1887–	Sorgmarsch	FST
Bantock, G. 1868–1946	Serenade (1903)	MS (lost)
Barbier, R. A. E. 1890–	Quatuor, Op. 93	Maurer, 1957
Beck, R. I. 1881–	Quartet, Op. 1	G. & S., 1909
Becker, H. 1863–1941	Sinfonietta	Grosch
Bozza, E. 1905–	Suite	Leduc, 1952
Brandt, V.	Country Pictures (Ed. A. Ostrander)	IMC, 1958
Cadow, P. 1923–	Drei Stücke (1954)	Bläserschiff, n.d.
Castelnuovo- Tedesco, M. 1895–1968	Chorale with Variations, Op. 162	Elkan, 1956
Chavez, C. 1899–	Sonata (1930)	(Blom)
Clark, F.	St. Hubert's Hunting Song	Musicus, 1960
Cofield, F. W.	Winter Sunset	Rubank, 1961
Coscia, S.	Suite	Baron
Daniel, G.	Theme & Variations	Horn Realm
Dauprat, L. F. 1781–1868	Six Quartets, Op. 8	Zetter; Lemoine [ca. 1840]
Del Castille, L.	Divertimento	Horn Realm

Diercks, J. 1927–	Quartet	Tritone, 1962
Diewitz, A. b. 1867	Quartet	Hofmeister, 1926
Dillon, R.	Etude	Bo. & H., 1961
	Barcarolle	Bo. & H., 1962
Doran, M.	Andante & Allegro	Horn Realm
Dubensky, A. 1890–	Theme & Variations (1932)	MS (R)
	Prelude & Fugue (1933)	MS (R)
Dubois, P.M. 1930–	Quartet	Leduc, 1962
Egizi, A.	Quartetto	Horn Realm
Faulx, J. B.	Divertissement	Maurer, 1957
Flothuis, M. 1914–	Quattro Invenzioni, Op. 64 (1963)	Donemus, 1964
Freed, I. 1900–60	Divertimento	Horn Realm
Gallay, J. F. 1795–1864	Quartet, Op. 26 (Ed. E. Leloir)	KaWe
Gethen, F.	Four Part Invention (4 or 8 hn)	Horn Realm
Goepfart, K. E. 1859–1942	Serenade, Op. 18	C. Fischer
Goller, V. 1873–1953	Fanfaren	Doblinger
Graas, J. 1924–	Three Quartets	Mills, 1958
Griend, K. van der 1905–50	Quartet (1949)	Donemus
Gumbert, F. 1841–1906	Ausgewählte Quartetten (4 vols.)	Hofmeister, 1877
Harris, Arthur 1927–	Theme & Variations	Shawnee, 1963
	Diversion	Horn Realm
Herrmann, H. 1896–	Little Suite	Rahter, 1963
Hindemith, P. 1895–1963	†Sonata (1952)	Schott, 1953
Holzner, P.	Der Heide Ruf	Leipzig, Composer, 1943
Homilius, K. 19th Cent.	Quartet, Op. 38	Hofmeister, 1893
Hornoff, A.	Variationen über das Volkslied 'Ein Männlein steht im Walde'	Hiob, 1956
Ingalls, A.	Suite	Horn Realm
Janetzky, K.	Musik für 4 Waldhörner (Kauffmann, Ochs, Ortwein, Thilman)	Hofmeister, 1956
Johnson, C. W.	Mood pensive	Rubank
Kauder, H. 1888–	Kleine Festmusik	Horn Realm
Kauer, G.	Four Pieces	Horn Realm
Kauffmann, L. J. 1901–44	Allegro commodo (1930)	MS (MGG)
Kay, U. 1917–	Serenade No. 2 (1957)	Leeds, 1964
Keyes, N. 1928–	Quartet	Horn Realm
Kienzl, W. 1857–1941	Waldstimmungen : Drei Konzertstücke, Op. 108	Oertel, 1926
Kletsch, L.	Suite	Kasparek, 1951
Koechlin, C. 1867–1950	20 Sonneries pour trompes de chasse, Op. 123 (1932)	MS (MGG)
	20 Sonneries pour trompes de chasse, 2e series, Op. 142 (1935)	MS (MGG)

223

Koepke, P.	Introduction & Scherzo	Rubank, 1959
Koetsier, J. 1911–	Cinq Nouvelles, Op. 34a (1947)	Donemus, 1954
Kohn, K.	Quartet	Horn Realm
Korn, P. J. 1922–	Serenade	Horn Realm
Krause, E. 1840–1916	Am Festmorgen	Hoffmann, 1887
Krol, B. 1920–	Kleine Festmusik, Op. 16	Br. & H., 1953
Kronke, E. 1865–1938	Miniatures	Schott, 1911
Langley, J. W. 1927–	Quartet	Hinrichsen, 1963
	Sonata elegiaca (1957)	MS (Composer)
Lesur, D. 1908–	Five Interludes	Schneider; IMC, 1958
Liftl, F. J.	Suite, Op. 185	C. Schmidt, 1927
Linn, R.	Quartet	Horn Realm
Lo Presti, R. 1933–	Suite No. II	Shawnee, 1962
Luening, O. 1900–	Variations on 'Christus der ist mein Leben' (1918)	CFE
Lütgen, W. 1835–70	Quartet, Op. 19 (Ed. K. Janetzky)	Hofmeister, 1953
McKay, F. H.	Petite Suite, Op. 15	C. Fischer
	Divertimento, Op. 16	C. Fischer
	Suite, Op. 21	Barnhouse
	Two Pieces	Gamble
McKay, G. F. 1899–	Fiesta mejicana	C. Fischer
	Arctic Legend	Horn Realm
	American Panorama	C. Fischer
Maggio, A.	Quartet	Horn Realm
Malige, F. 1895–	Quartet in drei Sätzen	Br. & H., 1953
Marsick, A. 1877–1959	Quartet	CeBeDeM, 1960
Mayer, R.	Four little Pieces	Horn Realm
Mechura, E. L. 1804–70	†Fanfares de chasse	MS?
Melartin, E. 1875–1937	Quartet, Op. 185	
Mendoza, J.	Al Fresco	Horn Realm
Millar, R.	Quartet	Horn Realm
Miller, M.	Quartet	Horn Realm
Mitjushin, A. 1888–	†Concertino (1952)	RS, 1952
Moulaert, R. 1875–1962	Andante (1903)	Maurer, 1957
Müller, B. E. 1825–95	29 Quartets	Zimmermann, 1907
Mueller, F.	Introduction & Scherzo	Horn Realm
Neidhardt, A. H. 1793–1861	Quartets	(T)
Nelhybel, V. 1919–	†Quartet	GMPC, 1965
Neuling, H. 1897–	Jagd-Quartett über deutsche Jagdsignale und Jagdlieder	Pro Musica, 1957
Ochs, R. 1887–	Vergnügliche Musik	Pro Musica, 1949
Ostrander, A.	Baroque Suite	Musicus
Ostransky, A.	Aeolian Suite	Rubank

Otey, W. 1914–	Symphonic Sketches	Baron
	Prelude, Scherzo, Passacaglia	Sansone
Otto, E. J. 1804–77	Quartet, Op. 107	Hofmeister, 1897
Paepke, O.	Suite, Op. 6	Böhm, 1938
Pâque, M. J.	Trois courtes Pièces, Op. 131	MS (MGG)
1867–1939	(1936)	
Périlhou, A.	Chasse	Heugel [ca. 1902]
1846–1936		
Poldini, E.	Serenade	UE, 1954
1869–1957		
Präger, P.	Quartet, Op. 151	Rühle
	Quartet, Op. 155	Rühle
Raphling, S. 1910–	Quartet	Horn Realm
Reicha, J. 1746–95	Quartet (Ed. K. Weelink)	KaWe
Rein, W. 1893–1955	Divertimento	Schott, 1961
	Waldmusik	Schott, 1961
Reynolds, V.	Short Suite	King, 1957
Rimsky-Korsakov,	Notturno (ca. 1888) (Ed. R. King)	King, 1957;
N. 1844–1908		Musica Rara,
		1958
Rossini, G. 1784–1849	Le Rendez-vous de la chasse (1828)	FR, 1959
	(Ed. E. Leloir)	Simrock, 1963;
		M. & M.
Rummel, C.	12 Quartets, Opp. 60b, 69b	Schott
1787–1849		
Scarmolin, A. L.	Lento	C. Fischer
1890–		
	Album Leaf	Barnhouse, 1965
Schafer, M.	Chaste Fugue	Horn Realm
Schaffner, N. A. ca.	Three Quartets	Br. & H.
1790–1860		
Schelb, J. 1894–	Quartet	MS (MGG)
Schmidt, W.	Variations on a Hexachord	Horn Realm
Schmutz, A. D.	Divertimento	Belwin, 1952
Strong, G. T.	Legend	Henn, 1913
1856–1948		
Süssmuth, R.	Suite, Op. 32	Br. & H.
Suttner, J. 1881–	Four Quartets	Grosch
Tchaikovsky, P.	Adagio	MS
1840–93		
Tcherepnin, N. N.	Six Quartets	Jurgenson, 1910;
1873–1945		Belaieff;
		Forberg;
		Musicus
Thilman, J. P. 1906–	Die Vier-Hörner Musik	(MGG)
Tice. D.	Quartet	Horn Realm
Tippett. M. 1905–	†Sonata (1955)	Schott 1957
Tomasi, H. 1901–	Petite Suite	Leduc
Uber, D.	Suite	Southern, 1965
Weber, F. D.	Three Quartets (Ed. K. Janetzky)	Hofmeister, 1953
1766–1842		
Weiss, A. 1891–	Rhapsody (1957)	CFE
Wessel, M. 1894–	Sonata	Horn Realm

P

225

Wilder, A. 1907–	Four Studies	M. & M.
Windsperger, L.	Three Suites, Op. 31	Schott
1885–1935		
Winter, J.	Quartet	Horn Realm
Zbinden, J. F. 1917–	Three Pieces, Op. 20	Br. & H., 1954

3.5 *Five Horns*

Molnár, A. 1890–	La Caccia	(G)
Schuller, G. 1925–	Five Pieces (1952)	Bruzzichelli, 1965
Siklós, A. 1878–1942	Idyll & Hunting Song	

3.6 *Six Horns*

Johnson, R.	Suite	Horn Realm
Mayer, R.	Fantasia	Southern, 1963
Molnár, A. 1890–	Turmmusik	(G)
Wuensch, G.	Sextet	Horn Realm

3.7 *Seven Horns*

Ikonen, L. 1888–	Kullervo Suite	(G)
Rogers, M.	Sierra Nevada	Horn Realm
Schaffer, J.	Angel's Suite	Horn Realm

3.8 *Eight Horns*

Gwilt, D. 1932–	Sonata (1963)	MS (CG)
Harris, Albert 1927–	Theme & Variations	King, 1960
Huffman, W.	Octet	Horn Realm
Hyde, G.	†Color Contrasts	Horn Realm
Ingalls, A.	Exercise	Horn Realm
Kaun, B.	Suite	Horn Realm
Klein, B.	Suite	Horn Realm
Knight, M. 1933–	Sinfonia	Horn Realm
Kohn, K.	Motet	Horn Realm
Korn, P. J. 1922–	Passacaglia & Fugue	Horn Realm
Kramer	Lento & Allegro	MS (IL)
Lo Presti, R. 1933–	†Suite No. I	Shawnee
Maštalíř, J. 1906–	Serenade (1937)	(Ga)
Mayer, J.	Festmusik	Horn Realm
Molnár, A. 1890–	Partita e Preghiera	(G)
Oldberg, A.	Le Son du Cor	(Pottag Coll.,
1874–1962		Muncie, Ind., U.S.A.)
Russel, A.	Nebulae	Horn Realm
Schaffer, J.	Opus for 8 horns	Horn Realm
Wessel, M. 1894–	Lento & Allegro	Horn Realm
Wuensch, G.	Ricercar (8 hn, org)	Horn Realm

3.9 *More than eight Horns*

Dew, O.	Corni-copia (12 hn)	MS (IL)

Garcia, R.	†Variations on a five note Theme (10 hn)	Horn Realm
McKay, G. F. 1899–	Fanfare & Procession (12 hn)	Horn Realm
Maxwell, C.	Music for horns (10 hn)	Horn Realm
Mayer, R.	Praeludium (12 hn)	Horn Realm
	Song (12 hn)	Horn Realm
	Capriccio (12 hn)	Horn Realm
	Finale (12 hn)	Horn Realm
Schuller, G. 1925–	Lines & Contrasts (1960) (16 hn)	AMP
Schwinger	March of the Jaris (12 hn)	Horn Realm
	Suite (12 hn)	Horn Realm

3.10 Unspecified

D'Andrieu, J. F. ca., 681–1738	†Messe solenelle de St. Hubert trompes de chasse, org	
Frevert, W.	†Die deutsche Jagdsignalen und Brackenjagdsignale	Berlin, Parey, 1951
Tyndare-Gruyer	Methode complete de Trompe de chasse (duets, trios, quartets, hunting calls)	

4. Horn(s) with other brass instruments

4.1 Two instruments

Dijk, J. van 1918–	Serenade (1955)	1100	Donemus, 1956
Kahila, K.	Andante & Allegro	1010	(King)
Kazdin, A.	12 Duets	1100	King, 1964
King, R.	French Suite	1100	King, n.d.

4.2 Three instruments

Armbruster, R.	Scarlattina	1110	(Schweiz)
Bassett, L. 1923–	Trio	1110	CFE, 1957
Bentzon, N. V. 1919–	Trio, Op. 82	1110	Hansen, 1964
Bialosky, M.	Two Movements	1110	King, 1954
Butterworth, A. 1923–	Trio (1962)	1110	MS (CG)
Cabus, P. 1923–	Sonata a tre	1110	Maurer, 1962
Childs, B. 1926–	Trio	1110	CFE
	Divertimento (1959)	1110	CFE
Cowell, J.	Trio	1110	Camara, 1960
Dedrick, A.	Three to go	1110	Kendor, 1966
Flothuis, M. 1914–	Sonatine, Op. 26 (1945)	1110	Donemus, 1946
Gebhard, L. 1907–	Sonatine, Op. 3	1100-pf	Böhm, 1935
Haubiel, C. 1894–	Athenaeum Suite	1110	CP

Henry, O.	Variations	1110	Washington, Pa., Composer, 1961
Houdy, P.	Divertissement	1100-pf	Leduc, 1956
Hughes, M.	Divertimento	1110	Tritone, 1964
Jong, C. de	Suite of Wisconsin Folk Music	1110	Templeton, 1964
Karjalainen, A. 1907–	Trio, Op. 4	1110	MS?
Knight, M.	Cassation	1110	Tritone, 1962
Koepke, P.	Lonely River	1100-pf	Rubank, 1959
	Gaudy Dance	1100-pf	Rubank, 1959
Kohs, E. 1916–	Trio No. 1 (1957)	1110	CFE
Kroeger, K. 1932–	Sonata breve	1110	Tritone, 1962
Landowski, M. 1915–	Trio (1954)	1100-pf	MS (MGG)
Leclercq, E.	Suite classique	1110	Brogneaux, 1959
Lombardo, R.	Trio	1110	(MBE) (60, Main Street, Hastings on Hudson, N.Y., U.S.A.)
Louel, J. 1914–	Trio (1951)	1110	CeBeDeM, 1956, 1966
Lovelock, W. 1899–	Trio	1100-pf	Horn Realm
Lyon, D.	Little Suite (1965)	1110	Ascherberg, 1966
Maniet, R.	Trio No. 1	1110	Maurer, 1958
Marek, R.	Trio	1110	King, 1959
Meulemans, A. 1884–1966	Trio No. 1	1110	Brogneaux, 1933
	Trio No. 2	1110	CeBeDeM, 1961
Nagel, R. 1924–	Trio	1110	Mentor
Nelhybel, V. 1919–	†Trio	1110	GMPC, 1965
Ostrander, A.	Suite	1110	Musicus
Pelemans, W. 1901–	Sonata (1956)	1110	Maurer, 1956
Petersen, T.	Divertimento	1110	Kendor, 1964
Poulenc, F. 1899–1963	†Sonata (1922)	1110	Chester, 1924
Presser, W. 1916–	Prelude, Fugue & Postlude	1110	Louisville, 1966
Quinet, M. 1915–	Sonata à trois	1110	CeBeDeM, 1961
Reid, A.	November Nocturne	1110-opt vib	Kendor, 1966
Roberts, W.	Walk in the Country	1110	Cor
Ruelle, F.	Trio	1110	Maurer, 1965
Sanders, R. L. 1906–	Trio	1110	King, 1961
Scharrès, C.	Divertimento	1110	Brogneaux, 1958
Šimai, P. 1930–	Introduzione ed Allegro (1958)	1110	SHF

Thielman, R.	Two Moods	1110	Kendor, 1962
Thomson, V. 1896–	Portrait of Louise Ardent (1929, 1940)	1100-pf	C. Fischer
Werner, J. J.	Canzoni per sonar	1110	UMP
Westcott, F.	Prelude, Pavan & Galliard	1101/1110	Hinrichsen, 1962
Wright, J. 1911—	Trio (1964)	1110	MS (Composer) (45, Twickenham Road, Teddington, Middlesex)
Young, P. 1912–	Theme & Variations (1961)	1110	MS (Composer) (Technical College, Wulfrana St., Wolverhampton, Staffs.)
Zbinden, J. F. 1917–	Trio de cuivres, Op. 13	1110	Sidem, 1958

4.3 Four instruments

Addison, J. 1920–	Divertimento, Op. 9	1210	Williams, 1954
Andriessen, J. 1925–	Introduction & Allegro (1958)	1210	Donemus, 1958
Badings, H. 1907–	Drie Nederlandse Dansen (1950)	1210	Lispet
	Koperqwartet (1947)	1210	Jeanette
Baker, D. N.	Hymn & Deviations	1111	MBQ, n.d.
Barrell, B. 1919–	Suite, Op. 21 (1959)	2020/2110	MS (Composer) (37, Graham Road, Ipswich, Suffolk)
Berger, J. 1909–	Intrada	1210	King, 1961
Bernstein, L. 1918–	Fanfare for Bima	1111	G. Schirmer, 1950, 1962
Beversdorf, T. 1924–	Three Epitaphs (1955)	1210	Interlochen, n.d.
Biersack, A. 1908–	Konzertante Musik	1210	Hofmeister, 1958
Boda, J. 1922–	Prelude, Scherzo, Postlude	1210	Louisville, 1965
Boedijn, G. 1893–	Quartet No. 2, Op. 111 (1947)	1210	Donemus, 1961
	Quartet No. 3		Donemus
Borowsky, F. 1872–1956	Morning Song	1210	Bo. & H.
Bright, H.	Legende & Canon	1210	AMP, 1953
Burgon, G.	Divertimento	1210	Chappell, 1966

Butterworth, A. 1923–	Quartet (1962)	1210	MS (CG)
	Scherzo (1958)	1210	Hinrichsen, 1965
Butterworth, N. 1934–	3 16th Century Motets	2110	NWM, 1965
Catelinet, P. 1910–	Two Divertissements	1030	Hinrichsen
Chailley, J. 1910–	Suite du XVe Siècle	1210	
Chase, A.	Quartet No. 1	1210	Camara, 1960
Cohen, S. B.	Quartet	1210	Belwin
	Four Travellers	1210	G. Schirmer, 1962
Cruft, A. 1921–	Four English Keyboard Pieces	1210	Williams, 1955
Cundell, E. 1893–1961	Two Pieces	1210	Williams, 1957
Donato, A. 1909–	Suite	1210	Interlochen, 1961
Felderhof, J. 1907–	Divertimento (1950)	1210	Donemus
Fiorello, D. 1905–	Summer Music (1948)	1210	New York Educational Pub.
Gabaye, P.	Récréation	1110-pf	Leduc, 1958
Gardner, J. 1917–	Theme & Variations, Op. 7 (1951)	1210	OUP, 1953
Geraedts, J. 1924–	Kleine Kopermusik (1951)	1210	Donemus, 1953
Glazunov, A. 1865–1936	In Modo religioso, Op. 38	1111	Belaieff, 1893
		1120	Marks, 1948
	(Ed. R. King)	1111	King
		1120	IMC
Grant, W. P. 1910–	Laconic Suite No. 1	1210	CFE
	Excursions: Suite No. 2	1210	CFE
	Brevities: Suite No. 3	1210	CFE
Haddad, E.	Quartet	1210	(MBE)
Heldenberg, A.	Quartet (1954)	1210/1201	Brogneaux, 1954
Hemel, O. van 1892–	Four brass Quartets (1955)	1210	Donemus, 1955
Henry, O.	Quartet	1210	Washington, Pa., Composer
Hovhaness, A. 1911–	†Sharagan & Fugue, Op. 58	1201	King, 1950
Jacob, G. 1895–	Scherzo (1944)	1210	Williams, 1954
Kayser, L. 1919–	Variazioni sopra 'In dulci jubilo'	1111	Copenhagen, Composer [1964?]
Keller, H. 1915–	Quartet	1210	King, 1954
Kesnar, M.	Intermezzo	1210	Presser, 1957
Ketting, O. 1935–	Sonata (1955)	1210	Donemus, 1957

A LIST OF MUSIC FOR THE HORN

Knox, C.	Solo for Trumpet	solo trp, 1110	Louisville, 1966
Koepke, P.	Fanfare Prelude	1200-pf	Rubank, 1958
	Canzona	1200-pf	Rubank, 1959
Koetsier, J. 1911–	Kleine Suite, Op. 33/1a (1947)	1210	Donemus, 1954
	Quartettino, Op. 33/2 (1950)	1210	Donemus
	Koral en Fuga over 'Neem Herr, mijn beide Handen', Op. 33/3 (1947)	1210	Donemus
Kreisler, A. von	Concert Piece	1210	Southern, 1965
Landré, G. 1905–	Quartetto piccolo (1961)	1210	Donemus, 1962
Lo Presti, R. 1933–	Miniature	1210	Shawnee, 1964
Lovelock, W. 1899–	Three Pieces	1210/1201	Chappell, 1965
Lucký, S. 1919–	Quartet	1210	MS?
McKay, G. F. 1899–	Two Pieces in American folk style	1210	Presser
Maganini, Q. 1897–	Medeovale	1210	Musicus, 1940
	Lament	2200/1210	Musicus
Melartin, E. 1875–1937	Quartet, Op. 153	1210	MS?
Mitchell, L. 1923–	Folk Suite	1210	Rochester, 1955
Murphy, L.	Etude No. 1	1210	Avant, 1964
Naginski, C.	Divertimento (1939)	2110	MS (Fleisher)
Nelhybel, V. 1919–	†Piano-Brass Quartet	1110-pf	GMPC, 1964
Orrego-Salas, J. 1919–	Concertino, Op. 54	1120	MS? (Dale)
Osborne, W. 1906–	Canzone	1210	King
Ostrander, A.	Baroque Suite	1210	Musicus
Ostransky, L.	Suite	1210	Rubank
Parris, H. M.	Seven Moods	1210	EV, 1948
Petit, P. 1893–	Les quatre Vents	2101	Leduc
Phillips, B. 1907–	Prelude	1120	EV
Pisk, P. 1893–	Quartet, Op. 72 (1951)	1210	CFE
Ploner, J. E. 1894–	Kleine Blechbläsermusik	1210	Grosch, n.d.
Pozajić, M.	Skica	1210	UKBH, 1958
Praag, H. C. van 1894–	Sonata (1950)	1210	Donemus, 1950
Premru, R. E. 1934–	Quartet (1960)	1210	Premru Music
Presser, W. 1916–	Five southern Songs	1120	Purdy

Rasmussen, M. (Comp. & Ed)	Christmas Music	1201	King, 1959
Rathaus, K. 1895–1954	Invocation & Fanfare	1210	Bo. & H., 1955
Raymond, L.	Short Suite	1210	Avant, 1964
Rulst-Rema	Petite Fanfare	1210	Brogneaux, 1957
Sabatini, G.	Puppet Waltz	1210	Camara, 1961
Salzberg, M.	Inventions Nos. 1 & 2	1210	CFE
Scarmolin, A. L. 1890–	Improvviso	1210	C. Fischer
	Novelette	1210	Pro Art
	Pastel	1210	Bo. & H.
Schlag, E.	Joyful Divertissement	1210	C. Fischer
Schmutz, A. D.	Air & Scherzo	1210	C. Fischer
	Choral Prelude	1210	Ludwig, 1963
Schneider, W. 1907–	Tower Music	1210	Noetzel, 1958
Schuller, G. 1925–	Little brass Music	1111	Mentor
Schultze, G.	Quartet (1908)	1210	Seeling
Simon, A. 1850–1916	Sonatine, Op. 23/1	1210	Jurgenson, 1889; Andraud
	Quartet Op. 26 (arr. W. Sear)	1210	Cor
Smith, F.	Three Chorale Settings	1111	King, 1962
Stieber, H. 1886–	Tower Music	2200	
Stoker, R. 1938–	Five Movements (1963)	2110	MS (CG)
	Litany, Sequence & Hymn	1111	Hinrichsen
Straesser, J. 1934–	Music for brass	1210	Donemus, 1965
Strategeier, H. 1912–	Laat ons nu blij zijn	1210	Donemus
	Alleluia den blijden ton	1210	Donemus
Suter, R. 1919–	Fanfares & Pastorales	2110	(Schweiz)
Thilman, J. P. 1906–	Quartet	1210	Hofmeister, 1953
Trevarthen, R.	Sonata	1210	Louisville, 1966
Uber, D.	Two Compositions	1210	Adler, 1960
Villa-Lobos, H. 1887–1959	†Choros No. 4 (1926)	3010	Eschig, 1928
Walker, R.	Badinerie (1950)	1210	AMP, 1950
Westcott, F.	Suite	1210/1111	Hinrichsen, 1962
Whitney, M. C.	Quartet No. 1	1210	C. Fischer
Zabel, F.	Four French Pieces (Arr. A. Ostrander)	1210	IMC, 1965
Zagwijn, H. 1878–1954	Prelude & Choral	1210	Lispet, n.d.
	Entrata giocosa (1952)	1210	Donemus, 1952

A LIST OF MUSIC FOR THE HORN

4.4 *Five instruments*

Adler, S. 1925–	Five Movements	1211	King, 1965
Aliabiev, A.	Quintet	2210	RS, 1960
Andriessen, H. 1892–	Suite (1951)	1220	Donemus
	Aubade (1952)	1220	Donemus
	Pezzo festoso	0220-org	Donemus, 1962
Andriessen, J. 1925–	Quattro madrigale (1962)	1220	Donemus, 1962
Angelo, P.	Music (1962)	1211	MS (MBE)
Archer, V. 1913–	Divertimento	1211	MBQ [1963]
Arnold, M. 1921–	Quintet	1211	Paterson, 1961
Ascher, R.	Quintet (1961)	1211	Mentor
Avarmaa, O.	Suite on 'Le Roi Renaud'	1211	MBQ, 1964
Bahrct, A.	Quintet (1962)	1211	MS (MBE) (240, E. 94 St., New York, 28, N.Y., U.S.A.)
Baron, S.	Impressions of a Parade	1211	G. Schirmer, 1944, 1962
Bastien, G.	Exigence	1211	MBQ [1964]
Bazelon, I. 1922–	Quintet	1220	Bo. & H., 1965
Berman, M.	Quintet	1211	MBQ, n.d.
Billingsley, W.	Suite (1955)	1211	MS (MBE) (University of Idaho, Moscow, Idaho, U.S.A.)
Boreschansky, E.	Quintet	1211	MS (MBE)
Bozza, E. 1905–	Suite française	1211	Leduc, 1967
	Sonatina	1211	Leduc, 1951
Brant, H. 1913–	†Millennium IV	1211	(Schwann; MT, June, 1967)
Broiles, M.	Ensemble Profiles (1962)	1211	Mentor
Brott, A. 1915–	Mutual Salvation Orgy	1211	MBQ, n.d.
Brown, R.	Quintet No. 2	1211	Avant, 1963
Bubalo, R. 1927–	†Three Pieces (1959)	1211	(Schwann)
Calvert, M.	Suite from Monteregian Hills	1211	MBQ [1963]
Canning, T. 1911–	Four Christmas Pieces	1211	CFE
Cherubini, L. 1760–1842	Eight Marches (Ed. K. Haas)	3110	Mills, 1962
Childs, B. 1926–	†Variations sur une Chanson du Canotier (1963)	1211	MBQ, n.d. Ensemble, 1965
	2nd Quintet	1211	CFE
	Quintet	1111-pf	CFE

233

Cobine, A.	Trilogy (1960)	1211	MBQ [1963]
Converse, F. S. 1871–1940	Two Lyric Pieces, Op. 106	1211	Rubank, 1939
Cowell, H. 1897–1965	Action in Brass	1220/ 1200–2 bar	Musicus, 1943
Dahl, I. 1912–	†Music (1944)	1220-opt tuba	Witmark, 1949
Dela, M.	Divertissement	1211	MBQ [1963]
Dieterich, M.	Horizons	1211	Rubank, 1959
Dodgson, S. 1924–	Sonata	1211	MS (CG)
Dunnigan, P.	Quintet	1211	MS (MBE) (301, W. 20 St., New York, N.Y., U.S.A.
Easdale, B. 1909–	†Cantilena (1962)	1211	MS (CG, MBE)
Etler, A. D. 1913–	†Quintet (1963)	1211	AMP
Ewald, V. 1860–1935	†Quintet in b♭, Op. 5 (1911) (Ed. R. King)	1211	King, 1957
Farberman, H. 1929–	†Five Images (1964)	1211	(Schwann)
Fleming, R.	Three Miniatures	1211	MBQ, n.d.
	Quintet (1965)	1211	MBQ [1966]
Frackenpohl, A. 1924–	Quintet (1961)	1211	EV, 1966
Goldstein, M.	Stillpoint (1962)	1211	MS (MBE)
Grant, W. P. 1910–	Lento & Allegro	1211	CFE
Gregson, E. 1945–	Quintet	1211	(RT, Nov. 1967)
Hamilton, I. 1922–	Quintet (1964)	1211	Schott, 1966
Hammond, D.	†Quintet	1211	Mentor
Harris, Arthur 1927–	†Four Moods (1957)	1211	Mentor, 1960
Hartley, W. S. 1927–	Quintet	1211	Tritone, 1963
Haufrecht, H. 1909–	Introduction, Ceremonial & Passacaglia	1211	CFE
Henry, O.	Four Bantu Songs	1211	Washington, Pa. Composer
Holmboe, V. 1909–	Quintet, Op. 79 (1962)	1211	Hansen, 1967
Horowitz, J. 1926–	Music Hall Suite	1211	(Times, 27 Feb, 1968)
Hoskins, W. B.	Allegro ostinato	1211	CFE
	Andante	1211	CFE
Huggler, J. 1928–	Quintet	1211	CML, 1963
Jones, C.	Four Movements	1211/1220	S. Fox, 1965

Karlin, F.	Quintet	1211	MS (MBE) (315, Riverside Drive, New York, N.Y., U.S.A.)
Kiessig, G. 1885–	Intrada	1220	Parrhysius, 1938
Kvapil, J. 1892–1958	Quintet in e (1925)	1220	MS (Ga, MGG)
Lawner, M.	Chorale, Improvisation & Serenade (1963)	1211	MS (MBE)
Lebow, L.	Quintet	1211	Chicago Brass Ensemble
Leclerc, M.	Par Monts et par Vaux	1211	Maurer, 1959
Legrady, T.	Suite	1211	MBQ [1963]
Lenel, L.	Introduction & Allegro	1211	Mentor
Levy, F.	Phantasy	1211	Cor
Lubin, E.	Partita	1211	MS (MBE) (305, Riverside Drive, New York, N.Y., U.S.A.)
McCabe, J.	†Rounds	1211	Times, 27 Feb. 1968
McKay, G. F. 1899–	Sonatina expressiva	1210-bar	Southern, 1966
McLean, H.	Sonatina	1211	(AMC)
Maes, J. 1905–	Prelude & Allegro (1959)	1211	CeBeDeM, 1963
Maganini, Q. 1897–	A Flourish for a Hero	1220	
Masters, R. L.	Quintet	1220	Music Press
Maurer, L. W. 1789–1878	Scherzo & Lied (Ed. R. Nagel)	1211/2210	Mentor, 1961
	Three Pieces (Ed. R. Nagel)	1211/2210	Mentor, 1960
Mills, C. 1914–	Quintet	1220	CFE
Morel, F. 1926–	Quintette pour cuivres	1211	MBQ, n.d.
Morgan, G.	Quintet (1959)	1211	MS (MBE) (c/o Music Dept., Lycoming College, Williamsport, Penn., U.S.A.)
Moss, L. 1927–	Music for five	1220/1211	Merion, 1965
Nagel, R. 1924–	March: This old Man	1211	Mentor, 1960
	Suite	1111-pf	Mentor
Ostransky, L.	Character Variations on a modal Theme	1211	Rubank, 1959
Petyrek, F. 1892–1952	Schlussmusik zum Eintedankfest	1211	Ullmann, 1940
Pisk, P. 1893–	Introduction & Allegro (1962)	1211	MS (MBE)
Presser, W. 1916–	Folksong Fantasy	1211	Elkan, 1955
	Quintet (1965)	1211	Louisville, 1966
Prévost, A. 1934–	Mouvement	1211	MBQ [1964]
Purdy, W. 1941–	Music for brass	1211	MBQ [1963]

Raph, A.	Call & Response	1211	Musicus, 1962
Rathaus, K. 1895–1954	Tower Music	1220	AMP, 1960
Rebner, W. 1910–	Variations	1220	Modern, 1962
Reynolds, V.	Suite	1211	MS (Dale)
Roberts, W.	Three Headlines	1211	Cor, 1960
	Dixie	1211	Cor, 1961
Robinson, K.	Quintet (1963)	1211	MS (MBE)
Rolle	Quintet No. 1 (Ed. H. Voxman)	1211	Rubank
	Quintet No. 6 (Ed. H. Voxman)	1211	Rubank
Sanders, R. L. 1906–	†Quintet in B♭ (1942)	1220	Music Press, 1948
Sauguet, H. 1901–	Golden Suite (1963)	1211	In prep.
Schmidt, W.	Variations on a negro Folksong	1211	Avant, 1959
Schmutz, A. D.	Prelude & Gavotte	1211	SB
	Rondo in F	1211	SB
Schneider, W. 1907–	Kleine Feiermusik	2201	Möseler
Schule, B. 1909–	†Résonances, Op. 58	1211	MS (MBE)
Schuller, G. 1925–	†Music for brass quintet (1961)	1211	AMP, 1962
Schwartz, E.	Three Movements	1211	MS (AMC)
Sear, W.	Quintet	1211	UBS
	Three Inventions	1211	Cor
Siegner, E.	Invention in brass	1211	MBQ [1964]
Simon, A. 1850–1916	Four Quintets, Op. 26	1211	Jurgenson, 1889
	No. 1 (Ed. Wilson)		Gamble
	No. 2 (Ed. W. Sear)		UBS
Spirea, A.	Music for brass	1211	Mills, 1962
Starer, R. 1924–	†Five Miniatures	2210	Southern, 1952
Stoltz, W.	Symphony for brass	1211	UBS
Stratton, D.	Variations on an English Folk Tune	1211	Cor
	Chorale & Fugue	1211	MS (MBE) (568, Grand St., New York, N.Y., U.S.A.)
Swanson, H. 1909	Sound Piece (1952)	1211	Weintraub, 1953
Tanenbaum, E. 1924–	Structures	1211	CFE
Townsend, D. 1921–	Tower Music	1211	MS (MBE)
Tull, F.	Demonstration Piece	1211	Avant, 1964
Uber, D.	Advanced Quintet	1211	Adler, 1960
	Greensleeves	1211	Musicus, 1960

	Adventures of a Tin Horn	1211	Musicus, 1962
	A Day at Camptown Races	1211	Musicus, 1957
Ulf, O.	Augsburger Tafelmusik	1220	Möseler, 1963
Valcourt, J.	Pentaphonie	1211	MBQ [1965]
Ward-Steinman, D. 1936–	Quintet	1211	MS (MBE) (Dept. of Music, San Diego State College, Calif., U.S.A.)
Waxman, E. 1918–	†Capriccio (1962)	1211	MS (MBE) (61-46 Little Neck Pkwy, Little Neck 62, L.I., N.Y., U.S.A.)
Weille, B.	Quintet	1211	Cor
Whear, P.	Invocation & Study	1211/1220	King, 1960
White, D. H. 1921–	Serenade in brass	1211	Shawnee, 1965
Whittenberg, C. 1927–	†Triptych (1962)	1211	(Schwann; RT, Nov. 1967)
Wigglesworth, F. 1918–	Quintet (1956)	1211	CFE
Wilder, A. 1907–	†Suite (1959)	1211	Mentor, 1960
Young, P. 1912–	Music for brass	1211	MBQ, 1964
	Triptych (1962)	1211	MS (MBE) (Technical College, Wulfrana St., Wolverhampton, Staffs.)
Zaninelli, L. 1932–	Designs	1220	Templeton, 1963
Zindars, E.	Quintet	1211	King, 1958
Zverev, V.	Suite	1220	RS, 1959

4.5 Six instruments

Bartsch, C.	Fanfare, Cantilène et Danse	1410	Maurer, 1965
Becker, A.	Paean	1211-bar	Remick
	Romance	1211-bar	Remick
Bezanson, P. 1916–	Prelude & Dance	1221	Interlochen, 1961
Böhme, O.	Sextet, Op. 30 (1911)	1211-bar	Witmark, 1934
Borowsky, F. 1872–1956	Moods	1211-bar	Bo. & H., 1955
	Twilight Hymn	1211-bar	Bo. & H.
Bozza, E. 1905–	Bis	2211	Leduc, 1963
Brown, R.	Concertino	1211-hp	Avant, 1965

Cabus, P. 1923–	Intrada	1320	Maurer, 1964
Cadow, P. 1923–	Praeludium	3300	Ultraton [1952]
	Intrada	2220	Grosch, n.d. [1954]
Cazden, N. 1914–	Suite, Op. 55 (1951)	1211-bar	AMP, 1958
Chase, A.	Fugue	1221	Camara, 1960
Clapp, P. G. 1888–1954	Suite in E♭ (1937)	1211-bar	Bo. & H., 1955
Conley, L.	Chaconne	1211-bar	Kendor, 1964
	Intrada	1011-2 cts, bar	Kendor, 1963
Constant, M. 1925–	Quatre Études de Concert	2110-pf, perc	Leduc, 1957
Converse, F. S. 1871–1940	Prelude & Intermezzo, Op. 103	1211-bar	Bo. & H., 1938
Cooke, A.	Suite	2211	Cor
Cowell, H. 1897–1965	A tall Tale	1221	Mercury, 1948
Cruft, A. 1921–	A Diversion: 'If all the World were Paper'	2220	Williams, 1960
Dietz, N. C.	Modern Moods	1211-bar	AMP, 1951
Dunham, R. L.	Sextet	1211-bar	Bo. & H., 1955
Flagello, N. 1928–	†Lyra	1320	GMPC, 1964
Fox, F.	Concertpiece	1211-pf	MBQ
Franchetti, A. 1906–	†Three Italian Masques (1953)	1211-pf	(MBE)
Harding, J. and Sommer, J.	Two Dances	1211-timp	King
Haubiel, C. 1894–	Ballade	1011-2 ct, bar	CP
Haworth, F.	Gonfalon Suite	1211-bar	Horn Realm
Henry, O.	Dichotomy	2220	Washington, Pa. Composer, 1959
Hillert, R.	Three Christmas Carols	2220	Concordia, 1964
Kabalevsky, D. 1904–	Sonatine I (Ed. Barnes)	2220	Ludwig
Kelly, B. 1934–	Fanfares & Sonatina	2220	Novello, 1966
Kiessig, G. 1885–	Five Pieces, Op. 57	2211	Parrhysius, 1937
Koepke, P.	Scherzo	1211-bar	Rubank
Kraft, K. J. 1903–	Divertimento in B♭ (1934)	2220	MS (MGG)
Kroeger, K. 1932–	Canzona	2211	Tritone, 1962
Levy, F.	Fantasy	1211-timp	Cor
Löchel, A.	Weihnächtliche Turmmusik	1221	Schott
McKay, F. H.	Fantasy	1211-bar	Barnhouse, 1956
	Narrative Sketch	1011-2 ct, bar	Barnhouse, 1956

	Second Fantasy	1211-bar	Barnhouse, 1960
	Panel in oil Color	1211-bar	Barnhouse, 1966
	Concert Prelude	1211-bar	Barnhouse
	Prologue in E	1211-bar	Barnhouse
	Romantic Mural	1211-bar	Barnhouse
	Sextet in A	1211-bar	Barnhouse
McKay, G. F. 1899–	Prelude & Allegro	1211-bar	Barnhouse, 1956
	Legends	1011-2 ct, bar	Barnhouse, 1958
Malter, L. & Azarov, M.	Six Russian Folksongs	2211	Leeds
Meyers, C. D.	Rhapsodie	1211-bar	AMP, 1950
	Autumn Moods	1211-bar	CP
Miller	Suite miniature	1211-bar	Belwin
Osborne, W. 1906–	Two Ricercari	2210-bar	King, 1948
Ostransky, L.	Passacaglia & Scherzo	1211-bar	Rubank, 1959
	Suite	1211-bar	Rubank, 1959
Phillips, I. C.	Three Hunting Songs	2220	OUP, 1963
Pinto, O.	Tom Thumb's March (Arr. H. S. Hannaford)	1211-bar	G. Schirmer, 1962
Pisk, P. 1893–	Five Variations on a trumpet Tune	1230	Peer
Saucedo, V.	Toccata	2220	EV, 1963
Schmutz, A. D.	Fantasy Sketch	1211-bar	C. Fischer
Uber, D.	Saint Louis Suite	1221	Adler
Verrall, J. 1908–	Suite	1211-bar	Merion, 1956
Viecenz, H. 1893–1959	Bläser-Suite (1953)	2220	Hofmeister, 1956
Walters, D. L.	Air for brass	1211-bar	Pro Art, 1962

4.6 Seven instruments

Berezowsky, N. 1900–53	†Suite, Op. 24 (1938)	2221	Mills, 1942
Borris, S. 1906–	Fanfare, Burletta, Canzona & March	2221	Peters
Brabec, E.	Bläsermusiken (1940)	3220	Ullmann, 1940
Cohn, A. 1910–	Music for brass Instruments, Op. 9 (1933)	1330	Southern, 1950
Cowell, H. 1897–1965	Rondo	2320	Peters, 1959
Diercks, J. 1927–	Mirror of brass (1960)	2221	Tritone, 1962
Dorward, D. 1933–	Divertimento for brass	2221	Galliard, 1966
Dubois, P. M. 1930–	Septuor	2221	Leduc, 1962
Etler, A. D. 1913–	Music (1938–9)	2221	MS (Ho 2)

Gebhard, L. 1907–	Burleske aus Op. 6	2210-pf, timp	Schott, 1939
Gerschefski, E. 1909–	Septet (1938)	2221	MS (Fleisher)
Goeb, R. 1914–	Septet (1952)	2221	CFE
Griend, K. van der 1905–50	Blechbläsermusik (1931)	2221	Donemus, 1948
Hanna, J.	Song of the redwood Tree	2220-timp, speaker	King, 1964
Huber, K. 1924–	Two Movements (1957–8)	2221	Schott, 1964
Inch, H. R. 1904–	Divertimento (1934)	2221	MS (Ho, RT)
Kurz, S. 1930–	Sonatine, Op. 18	2221	Hofmeister, 1955
Muczynski, R. 1909–	Allegro deciso, Op. 4	2211-timp	Shawnee, 1962
Nelhybel, V. 1919–	†Numismata	2221	GMPC, 1965
Thilman, J. P. 1906–	Das Sieben-Bläser Stück	2221	Litolff, n. d. [1953]
Walker, D.	Hiroshima Epitaph	1211-pf, vib	MBQ [1964]
Weber, B. 1916–	Colloquy, Op. 37	2221	CFE
Whear, P.	Three Chorales	2230	
Wright, D. 1895–1967	Sonatina	1011-2 ct, bar, euph	

4.7 Eight instruments

Ahrens, J. 1904–	Konzert	2230-org	SM, 1961
Burkhard, W. 1900–55	Zwei Choralpartiten, Op. 75	2321	BVK
Falla, M. de 1876–1946	Fanfare (Homenajes)	4300-perc	Chester
Harris, R. 1898–	Chorale & Toccata	1330-org	Mills
Leschetitzky, T. 1830–1915	Zum Feierabend	3220-timp	Parrhysius
Schäfer, D. 1873–1931	Musik für Bläser	2321	(King)
Scheurer, R.	Scherzo	2221-timp	Presser, 1956
Uber, D.	Gettysburg Suite	1331	Musicus
Zillig, W. 1905–63	Serenade I	2321	BVK, 1958

4.8 Nine instruments

Adler, S. 1925–	Praeludium	2221-bar, timp	King, 1947
Clérisse, R.	Symphonie pour les Soupirs du Roy	1231-bar, perc	

240

A LIST OF MUSIC FOR THE HORN

DeLone, P.	Introduction & Capriccio	2221-timp, perc	Templeton, 1966
Glickman, E.	Divertimento (1961)	1211-timp, 3 perc	MBQ, n.d.
Görner, H. G. 1908–	Intrada & Hymnus, Op. 20	3330	Marbot, 1959
Hewitt-Jones, T. 1926–	Fanfare on a Theme of John Blow (1962)	4310-timp	MS (CG)
Hyde, G.	Ode	8001	Horn Realm
Lachner, F. 1803–90	Nonett (Ed. K. Janetzky)	4230	Hofmeister, 1955
	Andante in A♭ (1833)	4230	MS (MGG)
Loebner, R.	Musik für Blechbläser	2220-2 pf, perc	Gerig
Malipiero, G. F. 1882–	Fanfare	4400-perc	Chester
Meyerowitz, J. 1913–	Short Suite (1954)	3321	Rongwen, 1956
Nelhybel, V. 1919–	†Three Intradas	2331	GMPC, 1964
Otten, L. 1924–	Cassation (1950)	2331	Donemus, 1956
Parris, R. 1924–	Lamentations & Praises (1962)	2331	Peters
Pilati, M. 1903–38	Divertimento (1932)	4320	MS (MGG)
Riegger, W. 1885–1961	Nonet, Op. 49	2331	AMP, 1951

4.9 Ten or more instruments

Adler, S. 1925–	Concert Piece	2331-2 bar, timp	King, 1947
	Divertimento	3331-2 bar	King, 1950
Alpaerts, F. 1876–1954	Fanfares d'inauguration	4331-timp	Metropolis, 1953
Alwyn, W. 1905–	Fanfare for a joyful Occasion	4331-timp, 3 perc	OUP, 1964
Anderson, L. 1908–	Suite for Christmas Carols	4441-bar	Mills
Arnell, R. 1917–	Ceremonial & Flourish, Op. 43	4330	AMP, 1948
	The Grenadiers	4331	Hinrichsen
Baervoets, R. 1930–	Fanfare héroïque	4331-perc	Metropolis, n.d.
Beadell, R.	Introduction & Allegro	3331-bar, timp	King, 1952
Beckhelm, P.	Tragic March	4431-bar, timp, perc	King, 1947
Beckler, S.	Three Pieces	4331-bar, org	King
Bennett, R. R. 1894–	Humoresque No. 3	6661-perc	Peters
Beyer, H.	Suite	4330-timp	King

Bilik, J. H.	Sonata	4431-bar	S. French, 1962
Bliss, A. 1891–	Greetings to a City (1961) Choirs I & II each	2231 ; timp, perc	Peters
Bonneau, P. 1918–	Fanfare	3321-timp, cym ad lib	Leduc
Bottje, W. G. 1925–	Symphonic Allegro	4631-bar, timp, perc	King, 1961
Bozza, E. 1905–	Fanfare héroïque, Op. 46	4331-timp, perc	Leduc
	Ouverture pour une Cérémonie	4341-timp, perc	Leduc, 1963
Bradley, W.	Honeysuckle & Clover	4331	NME, 1948
Brant, H. 1913–	†Millennium No. 2 (1954)	8, 10, 10, 2-perc	CFE, 1954
Castérède, J.	Trois Fanfares pour des Proclamations de Napoléon	4331-timp, perc, narr	Leduc, 1954
Chou Wen-Chung 1923–	†Soliloquy of a Bhiksuni (1958)	4131-3 perc	Peters, 1961
Civil, A. 1929–	Symphony for brass & percussion	5341-2 ct, bass trp, 4 Wagner tubas, 6 perc	MS (Composer) (Downe Hall, Downe, Kent)
Cobine, A.	Vermont Suite (1953)	3441-bar	King, 1954
Copland, A. 1900–	†Fanfare for the common Man (1943)	4231-timp, perc	Bo. & H., 1943
Cowell, H. 1897–1965	Fanfare for the Forces of Latin America	4330-perc	Bo. & H., 1943
Creston, P. 1906–	Fanfare for Paratroopers	4330-perc	Bo. & H., 1943
David, J. N. 1895–	Introitus, Choral & Fuga über ein Thema Anton Bruckners, Op. 25	4230-org	Br. & H., 1940
Debussy, C. 1862–1918	†Fanfares from 'The Martyrdom of St. Sebastian' (1911)	6431-timp	Durand, 1911
De Young, L.	Divertissement	4431-bar, timp, perc	King
Diamond, D. 1915–	Ceremonial Fanfare	6431-timp, perc	Southern, 1962
Dukas, P. 1865–1935	†Fanfare pour précéder 'La Péri'	4331	Durand, 1912
Dury, M.	Three Fanfares	4330-perc	Maurer, 1956
Flagello, N. 1928–	†Chorale & Episode (1948)	4231	GMPC, 1964
	†Concertino for pianoforte, brass and timpani (1963)	2431-pf, timp	GMPC, 1964
Franken, W. 1922–	Torenmuziek 'De Geuzen'	4330-perc, carillon	Donemus, 1963
Frid, G. 1904–	Zeven Pauken en een Koperorkest, Op. 69	4331-7 timp	Donemus, 1964

Fuleihan, A. 1900–	Fanfare for the Medical Corps	4331	Bo. & H., 1943
Ganz, R. 1877–	Brassy Prelude, Op. 33/1	4331	Mills, 1946
Geraedts, J. 1924–	Choral Fanfare	4331-timp, perc	Donemus, 1957
Glazunov, A. 1865–1936	†Fanfare for the Jubilee of Rimsky-Korsakov, 1890	4332-timp, perc	Belaieff, 1891
Goldman, R. F. 1910–	Hymn for brass Choir	4432-bar, timp	NME, 1941; King, 1959
Goossens, E. 1893–1962	Fanfare for the Merchant Marine	4231-perc	Bo. & H., 1943
Grant, W. P. 1910–	Prelude & Dance	4331	CFE
Hanna, J.	Suite	2421-bar	Tritone, 1961
Hanson, H. 1896–	Festival Fanfare (1938)	4431-timp	MS (Rochester, NY)
	Fanfare for the Signal Corps	4331-timp	Bo. & H., 1943
Hartley, W. S. 1927–	Sinfonia No. 3 (1963)	4531-bar	Tritone, 1966
Hartmeyer, J.	Negev : Tone Poem	3331-bar, timp	King, 1951
Haufrecht, H. 1909–	†Symphony (1956)	4331-timp	Bo. & H.
Hindemith, P. 1895–1963	†Concert Music, Op. 49 (1930)	4321-pf, 2 hp	Schott
Hogg, M.	Concerto for brass	3331-bar, timp	King, 1957
Holmes, P.	Suite	4331-timp	Shawnee, 1960
Jenni, D.	Allegro	4431-2 bar	CFE, 1958
Jesson, R. 1929–	Variations & Allegro	3431-bar timp, perc	King, 1954
Jolivet, A. 1905–	†Fanfares pour Britannicus	6441-2 perc	Bo. & H., 1962
Kauffmann, L. J. 1901–44	Music (1941) (Ed. K. Janetzky)	4331	Hofmeister, 1957
Kay, U. 1917–	Suite for brass Choir (1943)	4431	CFE, 1952
Kelterborn, R. 1931–	Invokatio	3331	BVK
Ketting, O. 1935–	Entrata to 'Fanfares 1956'	4831-timp, perc	Donemus, 1956
	Intrada festiva	4331-perc	Donemus, 1960
	Collage No. 9	6531-bar, perc	Donemus, 1963
Kreisler, A. von	Two Chorales	4331	Southern, 1965
Langley, J. W. 1927–	Fanfare for Midland Youth	6441-timp, perc	MS (Composer) (14 Gateley Rd. Quinton, Birmingham 32)

243

APPENDIX C

Lebow, L.	Suite for brass	3331-bar, timp, perc	King
Liadov, A. 1855–1914	†Fanfare for the Jubilee of Rimsky-Korsakov, 1890	4331-timp	Belaieff, 1891
Louel, J. 1914–	†Fanfares (1948)	4331-timp, cym	CeBeDeM
McKay, G. F. 1899–	Bravura Prelude (1939)	4441-2 bar	AMP, 1943
Maganini, Q. 1897–	Shenandoah	2331-bar	Musicus, 1958
Marks, J.	Introduction & Passacaglia	3331-bar, timp	King, 1951
	Music for brass & timpani	4331-bar, timp	King, 1954
Meriläinen, U. 1930–	Partita	4431	King, 1959
Merriman, T.	Theme & four Variations	2431-bar	AMP, 1951
Miller	Sinfonietta, Op. 13	4331-bar	Belwin
Missal, J.	Fanfare, Chorale & Procession	4442-timp	S. Fox, 1962
Mohler, P. 1908–	Fanfarenruf, Op. 38	4331-timp	Schott, 1956
Nelhybel, V. 1919–	†Slavic March	3331-bar, 2 perc	GMPC, 1965
Niblock, J.	Triptych	4331-bar, timp	Interlochen, n.d.
Novy, D.	Sonatina	3330-timp	King, 1960
Otterloo, W. van 1907–	Serenade (1944)	4431-hp/pf, cel, timp, perc	Donemus, 1948
Parris, H. M.	Four Rhapsodies	4331	EV, 1948
Petrassi, G. 1904–	Musica di ottone (1963)	4431-timp	SZ, 1964
Pisk, P. 1893–	Cortege	2331-2 ct, bar	CFE
Piston, W. 1894–	Fanfare for the Fighting French (1943)	4331-timp, 3 perc	Bo. & H., 1943
Presser, W. 1916–	Passacaglia & Fugue	4331-bar, timp, perc	Tritone, 1962
Raskin, D.	†Morning revisited	12,002-4 Wagner tubas, 2 perc	Horn Realm
Rautawaara, E. 1928–	†A Requiem of our Time, Op. 3 (1954)	4431-bar, timp, perc	King, 1958
Read, G. 1913–	Sound Piece, Op. 82 (1949)	4432-bar, timp, perc	King, 1950
	Choral & Fughetta	4431-2 bar	King, 1957
	Cherry Festival & Interlochen Bowl Fanfare	4331	MS (IL)
Reed, H. O. 1910–	Fanfares Four	4432-2 bar, perc	Mills, 1962

244

Reynolds, V.	Theme & Variations	3331-bar, timp	King, 1952
	Prelude & Allegro	4331-2 bar, timp	King
Riegger, W. 1885–1961	†Music for brass Choir, Op. 45 (1948–9)	4/8, 10, 10, 2-timp, perc	Mercury, 1949
Roussel, A. 1869–1937	†Fanfare pour un Sacre païen (1921)	4430-timp	Durand
Roy, K. G. 1924–	Tripartita, Op. 5	2331-2 bar	King, 1950
Schmidt, F. 1874–1939	Fuga solemnis	3631-timp	UE [1940?]
Schmitt, F. 1870–1958	†Fanfare (Antoine et Cléopatre), Op. 69 (1920)	4331-perc	Durand, 1921
Schuller, G. 1925–	†Symphony for brass & percussion, Op. 16 (1949–50)	4632-2 bar, timp, perc	Malcolm, 1959
Scott, W.	Rondo giojoso	4341-bar, timp, perc	King, 1956
Shahan, P. 1923–	Spectrums	4441-bar, timp, perc	King, 1955
	†Leipzig Towers	4441-bar, timp, perc	King, 1961
Shulman, A. 1915–	Top brass (six minutes for twelve) (1958)	4431	Templeton, 1958
Stolte, S.	Fanfare	2331-perc	
Strauss, R. 1864–1949	†Feierliche Einzug der Ritter Johanniterodens (1909)	4, 15, 4, 2-timp	Schlesinger 1909; Bo. & H., 1960
	†Wiener Philharmoniker Fanfare (1924)	8662, 2 timp	Bo. & H., 1960
	†Fanfare zur Eröffnung der Musikwoche der Stadt Wien (1924)	8662-2 timp	Bo. & H., 1960
Taylor, C. H.	Inscriptions in brass	4331-bar, timp, perc	G. Schirmer, 1964
Tcherepnin, A. 1889–	Fanfare	4331-perc	Bo. & H., 1964
Thomson, V. 1896–	Fanfare for France	4330-perc	Bo. & H., 1943
Tippett, M. 1905–	Fanfare No. 1	4330	Schott
	Praeludium	6330-5 tub bells, perc	Schott, 1962
Tomasi, H. 1901–	Fanfares liturgiques	4341-timp, perc	Leduc, 1952
	Procession nocturne	4341-timp, perc	Leduc, 1959
Turner, G. 1913–	Fanfare, Chorale & Finale	4331	G. Schirmer
Tyra, T.	Suite	4331-bar, timp	Southern, 1962

Uldall, H. 1903–	Music for wind & percussion	4421-perc	
Viecenz, H. 1893–1959	Bläsermusik	4331	Hofmeister
Wagenaar, B. 1894–	Fanfare for Airmen (1942)	4331-timp, perc	Bo. & H., 1943
Wagner, L.	Fanfare, Scherzo & Allegro	4631-bar, perc	King, 1964
Walton, W. 1902–	Fanfare (Arr. M. Sargent)	4331-timp, perc	OUP, 1965
Ward, R. 1917–	Fantasia (1953)	4331-timp	Galaxy, 1957
Weiss, A. 1891–	Tone Poem (1957)	4431-2 bar, 2 timp, 4 perc	CFE, 1958
Woolen, R. 1923–	Triptych, Op. 34	2431	Peters, 1960
Zador, E. 1894–	†Suite for brass	4331	Eulenburg, 1961
Zindars, E.	The brass Square	4431-timp, perc	King, 1955

5. Arrangements for brass ensemble, including horn

5.1 Two instruments

Vierdanck, J. b. ca. 1610	Capricci (Arr. E. Kiwi)	2000	BVK [1950]

5.2 Three instruments

Anon. 13th Cent.	Two Mediaeval Motets (Arr. R. King)	1010-bar	King, 1956
Lully, J. B. 1632–87	Airs de Table (Arr. Muller)	1110	Maurer, 1960
Vierdanck, J. b. ca. 1610	Capricci (Arr. H. Engel)	3000	BVK [1950]

5.3 Four instruments

Bach, J. S. 1685–1750	Contrapunctus I (Art of Fugue) (Arr. L. Waldeck)	1111	Cor
	Five Fugues (Arr. S. Snieckowski)	1210	PWM, 1955
	Fugue in D (Arr. Taylor)	1210	C. Fischer
	Fugue in g (Arr. Taylor)	1210	C. Fischer
	Six four-part Chorales (Arr. Mayes)	2200	Galliard
	Organ Prelude & Fugue; Fugue from 'Well-Tempered Clavier'	1210	IMC
Banchieri, A. 1567–1634	†Two Fantasies (Venice, 1603) (Arr. R. King)	1120	King, 1964
	Three 16th-century Motets (Arr. N. Butterworth)	1210	NWM

	Sinfonia	1210	C. Fischer
	(Arr. Q. Maganini)		
Corelli, A.	Adagio & Pastorale	1210	IMC
1653–1713			
Couperin, F.	Rondo	2110	IMC
1668–1733			
Dandrieu, J. F.	Rondo	2110	IMC
ca. 1681–1738			
Frescobaldi, G.	Gagliarda (Arr. H. Aaron)	1210	G. Schirmer, 1953
1583–1643			
Gabrieli, A.	Ricercar del sesto tuono	1210	Musica Rara, 1957
1510–86	(Arr. A. Lumsden)		
	†Ricercar del duodecimo	1120	Musica Rara, 1957
	tuono (Arr. A. Lumsden)		
Gabrieli, G.	†Canzon per sonare No. 1	1200-bar	King, n.d.
1557–1612	(La Spiritata) (Venice, 1608) (Arr. R. King)		
	†Canzon per sonare No. 2	1200-bar	King, n.d.
	(Arr. R. King)		
	Canzon per sonare No. 3	1200-bar	King, n.d.
	(Arr. R. King)		
	†Canzon per sonare No. 4	1200-bar	King, 1957
	(Arr. R. King)		
Grétry, A. E. M.	Gigue	1210	IMC
1741–1813			
Hessen, M. von	Intrada	4000	Ensemble
1572–1632			
Isaac, H.	Canzona	2011	Cor
ca. 1450–1517	(Arr. L. Waldeck)		
Josquin des Prés	The King's Fanfare	1210	C. Fischer
ca. 1445–1521	(Arr. Q. Maganini)		
Lassus, O. di	Four Tudor Canzonas	1210	
1532–94			
Lully, J. B.	Gavotte	1210	IMC
1632–87			
Maschera, F.	Canzone	2110/2020	C. Fischer, 1960
ca. 1540–84	(Arr. G. W. Lotzenhiser)		
	Canzona	2011	Cor
	(Arr. L. Waldeck)		
Pachelbel, J.	Two Magnificats	1110-bar	King
1653–1706	(Arr. R. King)		
Palestrina, G. P.	Ricercar del primo tuono	1110-bar	King, n.d.
1524–94	(Arr. R. King)		
	Lauda Sion	1210	Kendor, 1962
	(Arr. H. Schultz)		
	Mass 'Iste confessor'	1210	Kendor, 1961
	(Arr. H. Schultz)		
	Christe, lux vera	4000	Kendor, 1962
	(Arr. H. Schultz)		
Purcell, H.	†Music for Queen Mary II	1110-bar	King, 1956
1658–95	(Arr. R. King)		

Reiche, J. G. 1667–1734	Vier und Zwantzig neue Quatricinia (Leipzig, 1696) (Arr. G. Müller)	1120	Merseburger, 1958
	(Arr. D. G. Miller)		Ensemble, 1962
	Separate numbers: Five Quatricinia	1101-ten hn	Gregorius 1950
	Sonata No. 1 (Arr. R. King)	1110-bar	King, n.d.
	Sonata No. 7 (Arr. R. King)	1110-bar	King
	Sonata No. 12 (Arr. A. Frome)	1110-bar	S. Fox, 1961
	†Sonata No. 15	1110-bar	Mercury
	†Sonata No. 18 (Arr. R. King)	1110-bar	King, 1960
	†Sonata No. 19 (Arr. R. King)	1111	King
	†Sonatas Nos. 21 & 22 (Arr. R. King)	1110-bar	King, 1957
	†Sonata No. 24 (Arr. R. King)	1110-bar	King, 1955
Roberday, F. ca. 1585–1651	Caprice in F	1201	Mercury, 1947
Scheidt, S. 1587–1654	Three Christmas Chorales (from Gorlitzer Tablaturbuch, 1650) (Arr. R. King)	1110-bar	King, 1958
	Da Jesus an dem Kreuze standt (Arr. R. King)	1011-bar	King
Schein, J. H. 1586–1630	Banchetto musicale No. 22 (Arr. Prufer)	4000	Br. & H.
Störl, J. G. C. 1675–1719	Sonata No. 1 (Arr. R. King)	1110-bar	King
	Six Sonatas (Arr. D. G. Miller)	1120	Ensemble, 1962
Susato, T. ca. 1500–ca. 1560	†Three Dances (Antwerp, 1551) (Arr. R. King)	1110-bar	King, 1955
Venetian Brass Music		1210	Musica Rara
Vittoria, T. ca. 1535–1611	O Sacrum convivium (Arr. H. Schultz)	4000	Kendor, 1962

5.4 *Five instruments*

Adson, J. 17th Cent.	†Two Ayres (from Courtly Masquing Ayres, 1621) (Arr. R. King)	1210-bar	King, n.d.
Anon.	†Sonata (Bänkelsänger- lieder, ca. 1684) (Arr. R. King)	1220	King, 1958
		1211	Cor

A LIST OF MUSIC FOR THE HORN

Bach, J. S. 1685–1750	Chorale & Fughetta (Arr. Fote)	1210-bar	Kendor, 1963
	Contrapunctus I (Art of Fugue) (Arr. R. King)	1210-bar	King, 1960
	Contrapunctus III (Arr. R. King)	1210-bar	King, 1955
	Contrapunctus V (Arr. R. King)	1210-bar	King, 1961
	Contrapunctus IX (Arr. J. Glasel)	1211	Mentor, 1959
	Three Chorales (Arr. J. Menken & S. Baron)	1211	Bo. & H., 1959
	Fantasie (Arr. Rosenthal)	1211	Artransa, 1965
Banchieri, A. 1567–1734	Sinfonia (Arr. H. R. Ryker)	1211	MBQ, n.d.
Brade, W. 1560–1630	†Two Pieces (1609) (Arr. R. King)	1211	King, 1961
	Four Dances (Arr. H. R. Ryker)	1211	MBQ, n.d.
East, M.	Desperavi	1211	AMP
Franck, M. ca. 1579–1639	Two Pavans (Coburgk, 1603) (Arr. R. King)	1210-bar	King, 1960
Gabrieli, A. 1510–86	Three Ricercari (Arr. L. Waldeck)	1211	Cor
Gabrieli, G. 1557–1612	†Canzona prima a 5 (Arr. A. Fromme)	1220-opt org	Mentor, 1959
	Canzona (Arr. L. Waldeck)	1211	Cor
	†16th Century Carmina (Arr. J. Glasel)	1220/1211	Mentor, 1959
Gesualdo, C. ca. 1560 –1615	Three Madrigals (Arr. Upchurch)	1220	Southern, 1965
Grcp, B. 16th Cent.	Paduana (1607) (Arr. R. King)	1210-bar	King
	Two 16th Century Flemish Songs (Arr. E. Haas)	1220	Shawnee, 1964
Haussman, V. d. ca. 1614	Paduane mit Galliarde (Arr. H. R. Ryker)	1211	MBQ, n.d.
Holborne, A. d. 1602	†Three Pieces (Arr. J. Glasel)	1211	Mentor, 1960
	†Two Pieces (Honey- suckle; Night Watch) (Arr. R. King)	1210-bar	King, n.d.
	†Five Pieces (London, 1599) (Arr. R. King)	1210-bar	King, 1961
Isaac, H. ca. 1450–1517	Canzona & Lied (Arr. H. R. Ryker)	1211	MBQ, n.d.
Kessel, J.	Sonata (1672)	1210-bar	King
Lanier, N. 1586–1666	Almand & Saraband (Arr. W. Osborne)	1220	Campion, 1961

Lassus, O. di 1530–94	Motet: Tristis est anima mea (Arr. H. R. Ryker)	1211	MBQ [1966]
Le Jeune, C.	Deba contre mes debateurs (Arr. H. R. Ryker)	1211	MBQ, n.d.
Lully, J. B. 1632–87	Overture to 'Cadmus & Hermione' (Arr. R. King)	1210-bar	King
Marenzio, L. 1553–99	La Bella (Arr. H. R. Ryker)	1211	MBQ, n.d.
	Solo e pensoso (Arr. H. R. Ryker)	1211	MBQ, n.d.
Maschera, F. ca. 1540–84	Canzona (Arr. H. R. Ryker)	1211	MBQ [1966]
Monteverdi, C. 1567–1643	Suite (Arr. S. Beck)	1211	Mercury, 1946
Orologio, A.	Intrada No. 3 (Arr. H. R. Ryker)	1211	MBQ [1966]
Pezel, J. C. 1639–94	Hora Decima (1670) 40 Sonatas (complete) Separate numbers	1220	Musica Rara, 1967
	Twelve Sonatas (Arr. D. G. Miller)	1220	Ensemble, n.d.
	†Sonata No. 2 (Arr. R. King)	1210-bar	King, 1957
	†Sonata No. 3 (Arr. R. King)	1220	King, 1958
	†Sonata No. 5 (Arr. J. Menken & S. Baron)	1211	Bo. & H., 1959
	†Sonata No. 12 (Arr. N. C. Greenberg)	1220	Mills, 1959
	†Sonata No. 14 (Arr. L. Waldeck)	1211	Cor
	†Sonata No. 22 (Arr. R. King)	1210-bar	King, 1956
	†Sonata No. 25 (Arr. R. King)	1210-bar	King, 1962
	Sonata No. 27 (Arr. L. F. Brown)	1211	Rubank, 1958
	†Sonata No. 28 (Arr. N. C. Greenberg)	1211	Mills, 1958
	Fünfstimmigte blasendes Musik (1685) (Arr. K. Schlegel)	1220	Merseburger, 1960
	Vol. I (Arr. A. Lumsden) Vol. II	1220	Musica Rara, 1960 Musica Rara
	Six Pieces (Arr. R. King)	1210-bar	King, 1955
	Three Pieces (Arr. R. King)	1210-bar	King, 1960
	Sixteen Dances (Arr. D. G. Miller)	1220	Ensemble

A LIST OF MUSIC FOR THE HORN

Purcell, H. 1659–95	Trumpet Voluntary (Arr. J. Corley)	1210-bar	King, 1955
	Voluntary on the Old 100th (Arr. J. Corley)	1210-bar	King, 1957
	Fantasia on one Note (Arr. W. Sear)	1211	Cor
Scheidt, S. 1587–1654	Suite (Arr. D. M. Green)	1211	Presser, 1964
Schein, J. H. 1586–1630	Allemande & Tripla Nos. 1 & 2 (Arr. G. Hessler)	1211	Cor
	Allemande & Tripla Nos. 6, 7, 9 (Arr. G. Hessler)	1211	Cor
	Allemande & Tripla No. 8 (Arr. G. Hessler)	1211	Cor
	Allemande & Tripla Nos. 15 & 19 (Arr. G. Hessler)	1211	Cor
	†Two Pieces (from Banchetto Musicale, 1617) (Arr. R. King)	1210-bar	King, n.d.
	Intrada (Arr. W. Sear)	1210	Cor
Simmes, W. 16th–17th Cent.	Fantasia (Arr. H. R. Ryker)	1211	MBQ, n.d.
Speer, D. 1637–1707	Two Sonatas	1220	Ensemble
Venetian Brass Music		1220	Musica Rara

5.5 *Six instruments*

Anon.	Augsburger Tafelmusik (Arr. Ulf)	1221	Möseler, 1963
Corelli, A. 1653–1713	Pastorale from Christmas Concerto (Arr. R. King)	2210-bar	King, 1955
Franck, M. ca. 1579–1639	Two Intradas (Arr. Long)	1211-bar	
Gibbons, O. 1583–1625	Three Madrigals (Arr. M. Howe)	1211-bar	EV, 1960
Byrd, W. 1543–1623			
Morley, T. 1557–1603			
Handel, G. F. 1685–1759	Three Pieces from The Water Music (Arr. R. King)	2300-bar	King, 1955
Locke, M. 1630–77	†Music for King Charles II (Arr. R. King)	1310-bar	King, 1960
Purcell, H. 1659–95	March & Fanfare (Arr. Barnes)	1211-bar	Ludwig, 1963
	Trumpet Tune & Air (Arr. L. F. Brown)	1211-bar	Rubank, 1958
	Fantasia on one Note (Arr. Q. Maganini)	1221	Musicus, 1960

APPENDIX C

5.6 *Seven instruments*

Bach, J. S. 1685–1750	Ricercar (from The Musical Offering, 1747) (Arr. R. King)		1320-bar	King, 1956
Buonamente, G. B., d. 1643	Sonata (1636) (Arr. R. King)		2211-bar	King, n.d.
Francisque, A. ca. 1520–1605	Suite: Le Trésor d'Orphée (Arr. Berger)		2220-bar	King
Lassus, O. di 1532–94	†Providebam Dominum (Arr. R. King)	Choir I 0300 Choir II 1110-bar		King
Monteverdi, C. 1567–1643	Three Sinfonias (Ed. D. Greer)		2230/2221/ 0250	Faber, 1968

5.7 *Eight instruments*

Bonelli, A. ca. 1600	Toccata 'Athalanta' (1602) (Arr. R. King)	Choir I 1110-bar Choir II 1110-bar		King
Buxtehude, D. ca. 1637–1707	Fanfare & Chorus (Arr. R. King)		2410-bar	King
Gabrieli, G. 1557–1612	†Canzon septimi toni No. 1		2220-2 bar	Mercury, 1948
	†Canzon septimi toni No. 2 (Arr. R. King)	Choir I 1200-bar Choir II 1200-bar		King, 1958
	†Canzon noni toni (Arr. R. King)	Choir I 1200-bar Choir II 1200-bar		King
	†Canzon duo-decimi toni a 8 (Arr. R. King)	Choir I 1220 Choir II 1210-bar		King, 1958
	†Sonata pian e forte (Arr. R. King)	Choir I 1210 Choir II 0030-bar		King, 1958
	(Arr. Harvey)		2031-ct	EV
	O Magnum Mysterium (Arr. G. Draper)	Choir I 0310 Choir II 3010		OUP
	Antiphony No. 2 (Arr. G. W. Anthony)	Choir I 0220 Choir II 2010		Presser, 1958

5.8 *Nine instruments*

Campra, A. 1660–1744	Rigaudon (Arr. Wetzler)	2331	Concordia, 1964
Monteverdi, C. 1567–1643	Sonata sopra Sancta Maria ora pro nobis (Arr. R. King)	1420-2 bar	King
Schein, J. H. 1586–1630	Gagliarda	4221	Hinrichsen

5.9 *Ten or more instruments*

Bach, J. S. 1685–1750	Chorales (Arr. Gillis)	4231-2 ct, bar	Southern, 1963
	O Jesu Christ, mein's Lebens Licht (Arr. R. King)	2430-bar	King
Cesti, P. A. 1618–69	Prelude to 'Il Pomo d'oro' (1667) (Arr. B. Fitzgerald)	4331-3 ct, bar	Presser, 1963
Gabrieli, G. 1557–1612	†Canzon noni toni a 12 (Arr. F. Fennell) { Choir I Choir II Choir III	1210 1210 1210	Ensemble
	†Canzon duo- { Choir I decimi toni Choir II	1210-bar 1210-bar	King, 1958
	†Sonata octavi toni (Arr. { Choir I R. King) Choir II	1220-bar 1220-bar	King
	Canzon septimi { Choir I toni No. 1 Choir II	1220 1220	Baron
Purcell, H. 1659–95	Symphony from 'The Fairy Queen', Act 4 (Arr. R. Smith)	2630-bar	King, 1957
	Trumpet Voluntary (Arr. Brown)	2431-bar	SB, 1958

6. Chamber Music

6.1 *Two instruments*

Amram, D. 1930–	Three Songs for Marlborough	hn, vcl	Peters, 1964
Barsam, Y.	Three Encores	hn, bn	IMP
Bedard, J. B. ca. 1756–ca. 1815	Duo	hn, hp	(F)
Bochsa, R. N. C. 1789–1856	Chasse précédée d'un Andante, Op. 55	hn, hp	Lemoine, n.d.
	Duo concertante, Op. 93	hn, hp	Lemoine, n.d.
	Three Fantasies, Op. 65	hn, hp	Lemoine, n.d.
	March & Introduction, Op. 54	hn, hp	Lemoine, n.d.

	Nocturne, Op. 51	hn, hp	Simrock, n.d.
	Nocturne, Op. 94	hn, hp	Lemoine, n.d.
Bohne, R.	Serenade, Op. 35	cl, hn	A. Fischer, n.d.
Cage, J. 1912–	Music for wind instruments (1937): No. 2, Duo	ob, hn	Peters
Clapisson, A. L. 1808–66	Three Duos concertantes, Op. 27	hn, bn	Hofmeister
Conrad, C. E.	Arie	ob, hn	B. & T., n.d.
Crossley-Holland, P. C. 1916–	Incidental Music to 'The Tales of the seven Sages of Rome'	hn, hp	MS? (G)
Dauprat, L. F. 1781–1868	Air écossais varié, Op. 22	hn, hp	Zetter, n.d.
	Three Nocturnes	hn, hp	Lemoine, n.d.
Dobrzynski, I. F. 1807–67	Duo (Ed. L. Kurkiewicz)	cl, hn	PWM, 1953
Feldman, M. 1926–	Two Instruments	hn, vcl	Peters
Fuchs, G. F. 1752–1821	Six Duos, Op. 5	cl, hn	Janet, n.d.
	Three Duos, Op. 6	cl, hn	Sieber, n.d.
	Duos, Op. 32	cl, hn	Nadermann, n.d.
	Six Duos, Op. 36	cl, hn	Janet, n.d.
	Six Duos, Op. 37	cl, hn	Sieber, n.d.
Gallay, J. F. 1795–1864	Duos	hn, hp	MS? (MGG)
Gatayes, G.P.A. 1774–1846	Duo, Op. 22	hn, hp	Corbaux, n.d.
Gebauer, M. J. 1763–1812	Duos, Books I & II	fl, hn	Jouve, n.d.
Henry, O.	Three serial Duets	hn, vln	Boston, Composer, 1960
Jacqmin, F. 1793–1847	Fantasies	hn, hp	A. Petit, n.d.
	Nocturne, Op. 6	hn, hp	Costallat, n.d.
Jadin, L. E. 1768–1853	Four Airs	hn, hp	
Johnsen, H. 1916–	Prelude & Fantasy	hn, vln	
	Suite, Op. 41	fl, hn	NK
Kenn, P. ca. 1750–1810	Twelve Duos, Op. 5	cl, hn	Sieber, n.d.
Koechlin, C. 1867–1951	Petites Pièces, Op. 173 (1938)	cl, hn	MS? (G)
Kurpinski, K. K. 1785–1857	Paysage musicale, Op. 18	hn, bn	Br. & H. [ca. 1825]

Labarre, T. F. J. 1805–70	Deux Livres de Duos	hn, hp	Nadermann, n.d.
	Three Nocturnes	hn, hp	Pacini
Luening, O. 1900–	Short Fantasy (1930)	hn, vln	CFE
Makoweczky, b. ca. 1760	Duo	hn, vla	Br. & H. [1802]
Massa, A. de	Prélude réligieux	hn, hp	Legouix
Melchoir frères Early 19th Cent.	Three Duos, Op. 18	hn, bn	Costallat
Mengal, M. J. 1784–1851	Three Duos	hn, hp	Janet, n.d.
Nadermann, F. J. 1773–1835	Three Nocturnes, Op. 32	hn, hp	Costallat
	Three Nocturnes, Op. 33	hn, hp	Costallat
	L'Alliance, Op. 36	hn, hp	Costallat
	Three Nocturnes, Op. 49	hn, hp	Costallat
	Three Serenades, Op. 64	hn, hp	Costallat
Neubauer, J. 18th Cent.	Duo	hn, vla	MS? (F)
Pollet, B. ca. 1753–1823	Airs variés	hn, hp	Hanry
Prumier, A. C. 1820–84	Nocturne	hn, hp	Schoenenberger, 1846
Schenk, J. 1753–1836	Konzert-Sätze	cl, hn	MS (MGG*)
Schuller, G. 1925–	Duo (1955)	ob, hn	MS
Simonet, F. fl. 1793	Six Duos	cl, hn	Paris, 1791
Simrock, H.	Thème avec six Variations	hn, hp	Simrock
Stich, J. W. (Punto, G.) 1746–1803	Three Duos	hn, bass	Leduc [ca. 1800]
	Sonata (Ed. E. Leloir)	hn, db	KaWe
Vandenbroeck, O.J. 1758–1832	Three Duos concertantes	fl/cl, hn	Hentz, n.d.; Jouve, n.d.
Vanderhagen, A. J. F. 1753–1822	Duos	fl, hn	(MGG)
Weiss, A. 1891–	Passacaglia (1942)	hn, vla	CFE
Wildgans, F. 1913–65	Three Inventions, Op. 19a	cl, hn	Doblinger, 1961

6.2 *Three instruments*

Amram, D. 1930–	Trio (1958)	hn, bn, sax	Peters, 1965

Arkwright, M. 1863–1922	Trio	ob, hn, pf	
Austin, E. 1874–1947	Trio pastorale, Op. 15	fl, hn, pf	Larway, 1908
Banks, D. 1923–	†Trio	hn, vln, pf	Schott, 1966
Barboteu, G.	Esquisse	fl, hn, pf	Choudens
Barrows, J. R. 1913–	Trio (1937)	fl, hn, bn	MS (G, R)
Baudiot, C. N. 1773–1849	Trio	hn, vcl, pf	MS (F)
Beck, R. I. 1881–	Trio No. 1 (1937)	cl, hn, pf	MS
Berkeley, L. 1903–	†Trio, Op. 44 (1952)	hn, vln, pf	Chester, 1956
Bibl, R. 1832–1902	Stimmungen, Op. 61	hn, vcl, harm	Robitschek, n.d.
Bieber, C.	Im traute Stunde (Romanze); Unter der Linde, Op. 19/1 & 2	fl, n, pf	Oertel, n.d.
Blanc, A. 1828–85	Romance, Op. 43	ob, hn, pf	Costallat, n.d.
Bochsa, R. N. C. 1789–1856	Nocturne, Op. 3	ob, hn, hp	Lemoine, n.d
	L'Oubli, Op. 63	hn, pf, hp	Lemoine, n.d
	Serenade, Op. 76	fl, hn, hp	Lemoine, n.d
	Grand Trio concertante	hn, pf, hp	Simrock [ca. 1823]
	L'Alliance, Op. 142	fl, hn, hp	Lemoine, n.d
	Nocturne, Op. 143	cl, hn, hp	Lemoine, n.d
Boeck, I. b. 1754 & Boeck, A. b. 1757	10 Stücke, Op. 6	2 hn, bass	Br. & H., 1803
Bortolotti, M. 1926–	Studi (1960)	hn, vla, hpcd	SZ, 1965
Bowen, Y. 1884–1961	Ballade	ob, hn, pf	de Wolfe
Brahms, J. 1833–97	†Trio in E♭, Op. 40 (1865)	hn, vln, pf	Simrock, 1868; RS, 1953; Br. & H., 1954 Peters, 1954; Augener; IMC; Eulenburg
Brown, E. 1926–	Music for 'Tender Buttons'	fl, hn, hp	MS (BMI)
Casanova, A. 1919–	Trio, Op. 3 (1946)	fl, hn, vla	Bomart
Castelacci	Fantaisie dialoguée	fl, hn, gt	Paris, A. Petit

A LIST OF MUSIC FOR THE HORN

Civil, A. 1929–	Trio in E♭ (1952)	hn, vln, pf	MS (Composer) (Downe Hall, Downe, Kent)
Coscio, S.	Trio	fl, hn, pf	Baron, 1955
Cowell, J.	Trio	cl, hn, pf	Camara
	Trio	cl, hn, bn	Camara
Crussell, B. H. 1775–1838	Two Trios	cl, hn, bn	MS
Czerny, C. 1791–1857	Grand Trio No. 1 in E♭, Op. 105	hn, vln, pf	Schlesinger, n.d.
Danzi, F. 1763–1826	Trio, Op. 23	hn, bn, vln	Ricordi, n.d.
	Trio in F, Op. 24 (Ed. J. Wojciechowski)	hn, bn, vln	Simrock, 1963
Dauprat, L. F. 1781–1868	Tableau musical ou Scène	hn, pf, vln, ad lib	Paris; Composer, n.d.
Devienne, F. 1759–1803	Three Trios (Ed. E. Leloir)	cl, hn, bn	KaWe
Dickhut, C. fl. 1812–	Trio, Op. 6	fl, hn, gt	Mannheim, Heckel
	Serenade, Op. 1	fl, hn, gt	Schott
	Serenade, Op. 3	fl, hn, gt	Schott
	Serenade, Op. 4	fl, hn, gt	Schott
Doppler, A. F. 1821–83	Souvenir de Rigi: Idylle, Op. 34	fl, hn, pf	Schott, n.d.; M. & M.
Dornaus, L. fl. 1800	Six petites Pièces, Op. 1	fl, 2 hn	André, n.d.
Dressel, E. 1909–	Trio miniature	cl, hn, bn	R. & E., n.d. [1955]
Dressler, R. 1784–1835	Terzet	fl, hn, gt	Artaria, 1820
Dubois, T. 1837–1924	Cantilène	hn, vln, pf	Heugel, 1903
Duvernoy, F. 1765–1838	Three Trios (Ed. E. Leloir)	cl, hn, bn	KaWe
	Trio No 2	hn, vln, pf	KaWe
Edler, R.	Varianten, Op. 51	fl, hn, hp	Tonos
Esch, L. von	Sonatas, Op. 5	fl, hn, hpcd	London, Preston
Friedrich Alexander, 1863–1945	Trio, Op. 3	cl, hn, pf	Simrock, 1897
Fröhlich, W. 1894–	Serenade, Op. 21 (1926)	fl, vla, hn	MS (Ve)
Fuchs, G. F. 1752–1821	Three Trios, Op. 1	cl, hn, bn	Decombe, 1802
	Two Sets of Trios, Op. 45	cl, hn, bn	Sieber, n.d.
	Three Trios	2 cl, hn	Jouve, n.d.
Fux, J. J. 1660–1741	Trio	fl, hn, vln	MS? (E*)

257

Gabriel Marie 1852–1928	Nocturne	cl, hn, pf	Margueritat
Gänsbacher, J. B. 1778– 1844	Introduction & Variations	cl, hn, pf	MS (MGG)
Gebauer, F. R. 1773–1845	Six Trios, Op. 2	cl, hn, bn	MS? (E*)
	Three Trios, Op. 46	fl, hn, bn	Sieber
Gipps, R. 1921–	Scherzo, Op. 27b	ob, hn, bn	MS? (G)
Graun, C. H. ca. 1704–59	Trio Sonatas Nos. 1 & 2 in D & E	ob d'am, hn, bn	M. & M.
Handel, G. F. 1685–1759	Overture (Suite) in D (Ed. K. Haas)	2 cl, hn	Schott, 1952
	Sonata in D (Ed. J. M. Coopersmith & J. LaRue)	2 cl, hn	Mercury, 1950
Hasselmans, A. 1845–1912	Duo concertant	fl, hn, pf	Choudens
Haydn, F. J. 1732–1809	†Divertimento a tre in E♭, Hob. IV, 5 (1767) (Ed. H. C. Robbins Landon)	hn, vln, vcl	Doblinger, 1957
	Divertimento Trio (Ed. J. Werner)	cl, hn, bn	Chappell, 1962
Haydn, M. 1737–1806	Divertimento in D (Ed. R. Lauschmann)	fl, hn, bn	Hofmeister
Heidrich, M. 1864–1909	Trio in c, Op. 25	cl, hn, pf	Kistner, 1894
Henrich, H. 1891–	Trio Suite, Op. 23	ob, hn, pf	Heinrichs- hofen, 1937
Herold, L. J. F. 1791–1833	Trio	hn, 2 bn	MS? (MGG)
Herzogenberg, H. 1843–1900	Trio, Op. 61	ob, hn, pf	RB, 1889
Hill, M. W. 1891–	Trio (1937)	cl, hn, pf	MS (R, T)
Hindemith, P. 1895–1963	Trio, Op. 1	cl, hn, pf	MS (G, T)
Hoffmeister, F. A. 1754– 1812	Notturno	fl, hn, vla	MS (E*)
Holbrooke, J. 1878–1958	Trio in D, Op. 28	hn, vln, pf	RC, n.d.
Horrod, N.	Trio	hn, bn, trb	KaWe
Huhn, E. J. 1894–	Trio	fl, vla, hn	Leipzig, Composer
Jacobsohn, G. 1923–48	Adagio & Allegro	ob, cl, hn	IMP, 1953
Jadin, L. E. 1768–1853	Trois grands Trios	hn, vcl, pf	Gambaro, n.d.
	18me Pot-pourri ou Mélange d'airs	hn, hp, pf	Duhan, n.d.

A LIST OF MUSIC FOR THE HORN

Javault, L. Early 19th Cent.	Trios (2 vols)	cl, hn, bn	Janet n.d.
Kahn, R. 1865–1951	Serenade in f, Op. 73	ob, hn, pf	Simrock, 1923
Kallenberg, S. G. b. 1867	Serenade (1937)	fl, hn, pf	MS
Kallstenius, E. 1881–	Trio svagante, Op. 51	cl, hn, vcl	FST
Karg-Elert, S. 1877–1933	Trio in d, Op. 49/1	ob, cl, hn	Merseburger, 1902; Hofmeister, 1952
Kauder, H. 1888–	Trio (1947)	hn, vln, pf	Bo. & H., 1954
Kaufmann, A. 1902–	Trio, Op. 49	cl, hn, hp	MS? (MGG)
Kelly, R. 1916–	Introduction & Dialogue	hn, vcl, pf	CFE
Knapp, F.	Trio I	hn, vcl, pf	Br. & H. [ca. 1816]
Koechlin, C. 1867–1951	Petites Pièces, Op. 32 (1897–1907)	hn, vln, pf	MS (G)
Kölbel	Trio	cl, hn, bass	MS (E*)
Kohs, E. 1916–	Night Watch (1944)	fl, hn, timp	Mercury, 1965
Kowalski, J. 1912–	Miniatures	cl, hn, pf	SHF
Kraft, K. J. 1903–	Divertimento No. 2 in e (ca. 1943)	ob, ca, hn	MS (MGG)
Kratochvíl, J. 1924–	Trio	cl, hn, bn	(Ga)
Kreutzer, K. 1780–1849	Trio	cl, hn, bn	Hofmeister
Kurpinski, K. K. 1785– 1857	Nocturne, Op. 16	hn, bn, vla	Br. & H. [ca. 1825]
Labarre, T. F. J. 1805–70	Trios, Op. 6	hn, bn, hp	Pacini
Lachner, F. 1803–90	Trio in B♭ (1830)	cl, hn, pf	MS (MGG)
Lange, H. 1882–	Trio, Op. 63	ob, hn, vcl	
Laquai, R. 1894–	Sonata	hn, bn, pf	
Legley, V. 1915–	Trio, Op. 11	hn, bn	CeBeDeM, 1956
Lemière de Corvey, J. F. A. 1770–1832	Trio	hn, bn, hp	Nadermann, n.d.
Lessel, F. ca. 1780–1835	Trio, Op. 4	cl, hn, pf	Eder
Levy, F.	Trio	cl, hn, bn	Cor

Lickl [J. G. 1769–1843]	Trio	cl, hn, bn	MS? (E*)
Lucas, L. 1903–	Aubade	hn, bn, pf	Chester, 1959
Lybbert, D.	Trio	cl, hn, pf	CFE
	Chamber Sonata	hn, vla, pf	MS? (N.Y. Times, Jan. 10, 1960)
	Trio	cl, hn, bn	Peters, 1962
Maes, J. 1905–	Stuk (1954)	hn, bn, trp	MS (MGG)
McCabe, J. 1939–	Dance Movements	hn, vln, pf	(Times, Dec. 4, 1967)
Marchesi, T. 1773–1852	Adagio	hn, vln, vcl	MS (MGG*)
Maxwell, C. P.	Trio	fl, hn, bn	Benjamin
Mayr, A. 1900–	Kleine Suite	fl, cl, hn	ÖBV, 1949
Mayseder, J. 1789–1863	Trio, Op. 41	hn, vln, hp	Artaria [ca. 1833]
Melchior frères Early 19th Cent.	Nocturne & Pollacca, Op. 40	hn, bn, pf	Costallat
	Trois Trios brillants, Op. 7	cl, hn, bn	Lemoine
Meredith, E.	Trio in D, Op. 28	hn, vln, pf	Modern Music, 1933
Michalsky, D. R.	Trio concertino	fl, ob, hn	Avant, 1965
Michel, J. 1745–1810	Three Trios	fl. vla, hn	Paris, Viguerie
Mikulicz, L.	Romantisches Scherzo	2 hn, hp	Fröhlich, 1940
Mills, C. 1914–	Serenade, Op. 68 (1946)	fl, hn, pf	CFE
Molbe, H. 1835–1915	Fête des Dryades, Op. 68	cl, hn, pf	Vienna, Composer
	Au Clair de la Lune, Op. 71	hn, vln, pf	Rörich [189–?]
	Air arabe, Op. 77	ob, hn, pf	Rörich [189–?]
	Ronde de Printemps, Op. 78	cl, hn, pf	Vienna, Composer
Mozart, C. T. 1784–1858	Sechs Stücke, Op. 11	fl, 2 hn	IC; Steiner
Mozin, T. 1766–1850	Trio, Op. 9	hn, pf, hp	Janet, n.d.
Müller, B. E. 1825–95	Serenade, Op. 15	fl, hn, pf	Merseburger
Müller, P. 1898–	Kleine Suite	hn, vla, hp	MS?
Nadermann, F. J. 1772–1835	Three Trios, Op. 38	hn, vln, hp	Costallat
Neumann, H.	Sérénade sur un Air favori, Op. 28	hn, 2 gt	André, n.d.
	Trio, Op. 40	cl, hn, bn	Fürstner
Nielsen, R. 1906–	Trio	ob, hn, bn	(G)

Nisle, J. F. 1782–ca.1837	Sonate	hn, vln, pf	Br. & H., [c. 1818]
	Six Trios, Op. 2	2 hn, vcl	Werckmeister [1804]
	Trio, Op. 20	fl, hn, vln	IC, n.d.
	Trio, Op. 24	hn, vln, pf	Haslinger
Otten, L. 1924–	Divertimento No. 2 (1963)	fl, hn, bn	Donemus, 1963
Pannier, O.	Trio in E♭, Op. 40	cl, hn, bn	Grosch, 1938
Pezold, C. 1677–1733	Trio	hn, vln, bass	MS (MGG*)
Pfeffinger, P. J. 1765–1821	Grand Trio	hn, vcl, pf	Paris, Carli
Platti, F. G.	Sonata	cl, hn, bn	Cor
Poessinger, F. A. ca. 1767–1827	Trio, Op. 28	fl, hn, vla	Artaria, 1806
Pollet, B. ca, 1753–1818	Trio	hn, bn, hp	Hanry
Polsterer, R. 1879–	Trio	hn, vln, pf	Brockhaus
Presser, W. 1916–	Rhapsody on a peaceful Theme	hn, vln, pf	Tritone, 1961
Raphael, G. 1903–60	Tetrachron : Sonatine, Op. 65/4 (1949)	hn, bn, vln	Br. & H., 1950
Reicha, A. 1770–1836	Twelve Trios, Op. 93	2 hn, vcl	Pleyel, n.d.
Reinecke, C. 1824–1910	Trio in a, Op. 188	ob, hn, pf	Br. & H., [1887], 1953
	Trio in B♭, Op. 274	cl, hn, pf	Senff; Br. & H., 1906
Risinger, K. 1920–	Trio (1942)	cl, hn, pf	(Ga)
Röllig, J. G. 1710–90	Nine Trios	ob, hn, bn	MS (F, MGG)
Romberg, B. 1767–1841	Fantasie, Op. 10	hn, vla, vcl	MS? (E*)
Schaffner, N. A. ca. 1790–1860	Six Trios	cl, hn, bn	Gambaro
Schmitt, N. d. ca. 1802	Divertissements	2 hn, bn	Pleyel
Schönicke, W. 1850–1917	Nocturno, Op. 27	fl, hn, pf	Zimmermann, 1900
Schroeder, H. 1904–	Trio No. 2, Op. 40	hn, vln, pf	Schott
Schuller, G. 1925–	Trio, Op. 13 (1948)	ob, hn, vla	AMP
Schwartz, E.	Divertimento	cl, hn, pf	GMPC, 1965
Schwertsik, K. 1935–	Trio	hn, vln, pf	Modern

Simonet, F. fl. 1793	Three Trios	cl, hn, bn	Paris, 1791
Sobeck, J. 1831–1914	Duo concertante, Op. 5	cl, hn, pf	B. & B.
Spell, R.	Ballade	fl, hn, pf	Whitney, 1882
Sperger, J. M. d. 1812	Sonata (Ed. Malarić)	hn, vla, db	KaWe
	Sonata (Ed. Malarić)	2 hn, db	KaWe
Stier, A. 1880–	Trio, Op. 12	cl, hn, pf	MS? (T)
Strube, G. 1867–1953	Trio (1936)	cl, hn, pf	MS (H, R, T)
Süssmayer, F. X. 1766–1803	Trio (fragments)	fl, hn, vla	MS (Br. Mus.)
Tandler, A.	Frühlingsstimmen, Op. 33	hn, vln, pf	Blaha
Tcherepnin, I. 1943–	Entourages	hn, pf, perc	(MGG)
Telemann, G. P. 1681–1767	Concerto a tre in F (Ed. F. Schroeder)	rec, hn, hpcd	Noetzel, 1962
Thurner, F. E. 1785–1827	Trio, Op. 56	ob, 2 hn	Probst [1823]; Kistner
Tillmetz, R. 1847–1915	Nocturne, Op. 31	fl, hn, pf	K. & S.
Tovey, D. 1875–1940	Trio in c, Op. 8 (Style tragique) (1905)	cl, hn, pf	Schott, 1906
Tranchell, P. 1922–	Trio (1942)	hn, vln, pf	MS? (G)
Ullrich, H. J. 1888–	Trio Phantasie, Op. 20 (1924)	hn, vln, pf	M. & H., 1947 Doblinger, 1964
Verrall, J. 1908–	Divertimento (1939)	cl, hn, bn	CFE
Viecenz, H. 1893–1959	Terzetto	2 ob, hn	Hofmeister, 1956
Volkmann, R. 1815–83	Schlummerlied, Op. 76	cl, hn, hp	Schott, 1882
Wehrli, W. 1892–1944	Trio	hn, vln, pf	(T)
Weigl, V.	New England Suite	hn, vln, pf	CFE
Weisgarber, E.	Divertimento	hn, vla, pf	Cor, 1963
Widerkehr, J. C. M. 1739–1823	Three Trios	fl, hn, bn	Paris (Brit. Mus.)
Zelenka, I. 1936–	Trio	hn, vln, pf	Modern, 1959

6.3 Four instruments

Abeltshauser fl. 1825	Six Quartets, Op. 1	2 fl, 2 hn	Schott, n.d.
	Six Quartets, Op. 2	2 fl, 2 hn	Schott, n.d.
	Six Pieces, Op. 4	fl, cl, hn, bn	Schott, n.d.

A LIST OF MUSIC FOR THE HORN

Absil, J. 1893–	Danses bulgares, Op. 102	fl, ob, hn, bn	Lemoine, 1960
Achron, J. 1886–1943	Suite from incidental music to 'Golen'	hn, trp, vcl, pf	MS (Fleisher)
Aimon, P. L. F. 1779–1866	Récréation	hn, 2 vcl, pf	Pacini, n.d.
Ambrosius, H. 1897–	Quartet, Op. 44a	fl, cl, hn, pf	MS (Ve)
Anders, D.	Three Inventions (1945)	hn, vln, vcl, pf	(Lib. of Congress)
Angerer, P. 1927–	Konzertantes Quartet	ob, hn, vla, vcl	Hug
Apostel, H. E. 1901–	Quartet, Op. 14	fl, cl, hn, bn	UE, 1952
Asioli, B. 1760–1832	Quartet	fl, hn, vln, bass	(F)
Aspelmayr, F. 1728–86	Six Serenades, Op. 1	fl, hn, vcl, bass	Lyon
Badings, H. 1907–	Drie Nederlandse Dansen	2 cl, hn, bn	Donemus, 1951
Becher, H. 1863–1941	Heiteres Quartet in B♭, (Potpourri)	ob, cl, hn, bn	L. & Z., 1933
Beckerath, A. von 1901–	Divertimento	hn, vln, vla, vcl	Noetzel, 1957
Berwald, F. A. 1796–1868	Quartet in E♭ (1819)	cl, hn, bn, pf	Gehrmans
Boatwright, H. 1918–	Serenade (1952)	cl, hn, vln, vcl	MS (NY Pub. Lib)
Bochsa, K. d. 1821	First Suite of Airs, Op. 12	fl, ob, hn, bn	Lemoine, n.d., Andraud
	Second Suite of Airs, Op. 31	fl, ob, hn, bn	Lemoine, n.d., Andraud
Bochsa, R. N. C. 1789–1856	Serenade, Op. 4	fl, hn, 2 hp	Lemoine, n.d.
	Aubade, Op. 140	fl, hn, vcl, hp	Lemoine, n.d.
Braun, C. A. P. 1788–1835	Quartet, Op. 1	2 fl, 2 hn	Peters, n.d.
	Two Quartets	fl, ob, hn, bn	Br. & H., n.d.
Brod, H. 1801–39	Airs en quatuor	ob, cl, hn, bn	Pleyel, n.d.
	Quartet	fl, hn, bn, pf	Gallet
Bruneau, E.	Quartet	fl, ob, hn, pf	Pérégally, 1902
Buch	Three Quartets, Op. 1	hn, vln, vla, bass	Paris, 1788
Butt, J. 1929–	Winsome's Folly	ob, cl, hn, bn	Bo. & H., 1957
Catel, C. S. 1773–1830	Three Quartets	fl, cl, hn, bn	Ozi, 1796
Chailley, J. 1910–	Suite du XVe Siècle	ob, hn, bn, tabor	Leduc, 1950

Chapple, B.	Quartet	cl, hn, vln, pf	(fp, Cheltenham, 1967)
Claflin, A. 1898–	Recitativo, Aria & Stretto	hn, vln, vcl, pf	CFE
Czerny, C. 1791–1857	Grande Sérénade en Quatuor, Op. 126	cl, hn, vcl, pf	Richault, n.d.
Dalberg, J. 1760–1812	Quartet, Op. 25	ob, hn, bn, pf	André, n.d.
Démar, J. S. 1763–1832	Le Ranz des Vaches, Op. 25	fl, cl, hn, hp	Dufaut
Deslandres, A. E. M. 1840–1911	3e Méditation	hn, vln, vcl, hp	Pérégally, n.d.
Dessau, P. 1894–	Concertino	fl, cl, hn, vln	Schott, 1925
Devienne, F. 1759–1803	Sonata en quatuor	fl, hn, vla, pf	Bonjour, n.d.
Dickhut, C. fl. 1812	Three Serenades, Opp. 1, 3, 4	fl, hn, vla, gt	Schott, n.d.
Dittersdorf, K. D. 1739–99	Quartet	ob, cl, hn, bn	(MGG)
Domansky, A. 1897–	Divertimento	2 cl, hn, bn	C. Schmidt, 1936
Domenica, R. di 1927–	Quartet	fl, hn, vln, pf	Leeds
Doppler, A. F. 1821–83	Nocturne, Op. 19	fl, hn, vln, pf	Schott [ca. 1866]
Düring, H.	Quartet	fl, cl, hn, bn	Hedler, 1845
Duvernoy, F. 1765–1838	2e Quatuor	fl, vln, vla, db	Costallat, n.d.
Dyson, G. 1883–1964	Quartet	cl, hn, vln, pf	MS (Th)
Ehrenberg, C. E. T. 1878–1962	Quartet, Op. 40 (1943)	ob, cl, hn, bn	Simrock, 1965
Eler, A. ca. 1764–1821	Three Quartets, Op. 6	fl, cl, hn, bn	Pleyel, n.d.
	Three Quartets, Op. 10	2 cl, hn, bn	Pleyel, n.d.
	Three Quartets, Op. 11	fl, cl, hn, bn	Pleyel, n.d.
Eröd, I. 1936–	Ricercare ed Aria	fl, ob, bcl, hn	(Ve)
Fasch, J. F. 1688–1758	Quadro	ob d'am, hn, vln, bass	MS? (MGG)
Fleury, C.	Three Quartets	fl, cl, hn, bn	Lyon, Arnaud
Fuchs, G. F. 1752–1821	Six Quartets	cl, hn, bn, bass	Paris, 1798
	Three Quartets, Op. 31	cl, hn, bn, bass	Janet, n.d.
Fux, J. J. 1660–1741	Parthia in F	fl, hn, vln, cont	MS (LB, Schwerin)
Gambaro, G. B. 1785–1828	Three Quatuors concertants, Op. 4	fl, cl, hn, bn	Br. & H.
	Three Quartets, Op. 5	fl, cl, hn, bn	Gambaro

Gebauer, F. R. 1773–1845	Three Quatuors concertants, Op. 27	fl, cl, hn, bn	Sieber, n.d.
	Three Quartets, Op. 41	fl, cl, hn, bn	Sieber
Geiser, W. 1897–	Divertimento, Op. 55	ob, cl, hn, bn	Composer [1961?]
Gevaert, F. A. 1828–1908	Quartet	cl, hn, bn, pf	MS (MGG)
Girnatis, W. 1894–	Kajütsmusik	fl, hn, bn, pf	MS? (Z.f.M., 1938)
Goepfart, K. E. b. 1859	Quartet, Op. 93	fl, ob, hn, bn	Schuberth
Gossick, B.	Petite Quartette	ob, cl, hn, bn	MS (Lib. of Congress)
Granzati, G.	Quartet, Op. 1	hn, bn, pf, hp	(E*)
Gress, R.	Variationen und Fuga über eines eigenes Thema, Op. 29 (ca. 1926)	cl, hn, bn, vla	MS? (MGG)
Gruenberg, L. 1884–1964	Divertimento, Op. 66	hn, vln, vcl, pf	
Hales, H. J. 1902–	Fantasy Sonata (1952)	fl, cl, hn, pf	(G, Ve)
Hambraeus, B. 1928–	Transit No. 2	hn, trb, elec gt, pf	FST
Hänsel, P. 1770–1831	Three Quartets	fl, cl, hn, bn	Weigl; Cappi; Haslinger
Häusler, E. c. 1760–1837	Six Notturni	2 hn, 2 bn	Br. & H., n.d.
Hanke, K. c. 1750–1803	Six Quartets	hn, vln, vcl, db	MS (MGG)
Haworth, F.	The Glory and the Dream	cl, hn, vln, vcl	Horn Realm
Haydn, F. J. 1732–1809	Divertimento No. 4 in C Hob. II, 14	2 cl, 2 hn	
	(Ed. H. Reichenbach)		Hansen, 1932
	(Ed. T. Kruntjaewci)		RS, 1957
	(Ed. H. C. Robbins Landon)		Doblinger, 1959
	Twelve Nocturnes, Hob. II, D.5 (Ed. K. Janetzky)	2 fl, 2 hn	Pro Musica, 1952
	Cassation in E♭ (Ed. H. Scherchen)	2 fl, 2 hn	Ars Viva
Haydn, M. 1737–1806	†Divertimento in D (Ed. R. Lauschmann)	fl, ob, hn, bn	Merseburger, 1931; Hofmeister, 1953
Heller fl. 1797	Quartets, Op. 6	fl, cl, hn, bass	(E)
Henneberg, A. 1901–	Petit Quatuor, Op. 36	fl, ob, hn, bn	FST
Hertel, J. W. 1727–89	†Sonata a quattro	2 hn, 2 bn	Noetzel, 1959
Hoddinott, A. 1929–	Divertimento, Op. 32	ob, cl, hn, bn	OUP, 1965

Hovhaness, A. 1911–	Divertimento, Op. 61/5	ob, cl, hn, bn	Peters, 1958
Hubeau, J. 1917–	Sonatine humoresque	fl, cl, hn, pf	Noël, 1942
Hugon, G. 1904–	Prélude à quatres Eglogues de Virgil	fl, cl, hn, hp	Sofirad
Hummel, A. 1730–88	Serenata	ob, 2 hn, bn	Artia
Hurlstone, W. Y. 1876–1906	Quartet	fl, ob, hn, pf	MS (MGG)
Jadin, L. E. 1768–1853	Three Nocturnes	fl, cl, hn, bn	J. & C.; Kneusslin
Karg-Elert, S. 1877–1933	Jugend, Op. 139a (1919)	fl, cl, hn, pf	Zimmermann, 1924
Karkoff, M. 1927–	Divertimento, Op. 29	fl, ob, hn, bn	FST
Kauder, H. 1888–	Quartet (1948)	ob, cl, hn, bn	NME, 1949
Kay, N. F. 1929–	†Miniature Quartet (1950)	fl, cl, hn, bn	OUP, 1959
Kayser, P. C. 1755–1823	Deux Sonates en symphonie	2 hn, vln, hpcd	Zürich [ca. 1784]
King, M. M.	Quartet in E♭	fl, ob, hn, bn	Meldon, 1946
Klingenberg, W.	Zwei Genrebilder, Op. 35	hn, vln, vcl, pf	B. & B.
Kohl, W. b. 1753	Six Quartets, Op. 1	hn, vln, vla, bass	Sieber
	Six Quartets, Op. 2	hn, vln, vla, bass	Sieber
	Six Quartets, Op. 3	hn, vln, vla, bass	Imbault
Korn, P. J. 1922–	Fantasy	hn, vln, vcl, pf	Bo. & H.
Kreith, K. d.ca. 1807	Three Quatuors, Op. 66	fl, cl, hn, bn	Traeg, n.d.
Kreutzer, K. 1780–1849	Divertimento in G, Op. 37	fl, hn, bn, pf	Gombart [1819]
Kruger, F.	Ein lustiges Quartett	ob, cl, hn, bn	Ehrler, 1934
Kurka, R. 1927–57	Music, Op. 14	cl, hn, trp, bass	
Laderman, E. 1924–	Woodwind Sketches	fl, ob, hn, bn	CFE
Lange, H. 1882–	Serenade, Op. 45/2	ob, cl, hn, bn	Berlin, Composer, 1942
Lauber, J. 1864–1952	Four Intermezzi	fl, cl, hn, bn	Henn, 1922
Lefebvre, C. E. 1843–1917	Suite	fl, ob, cl, hn	Hamelle, n.d.
Lickl, [J. G. 1769–1843	Cassation	ob, cl, hn, bn	Eder
Lütgen, W. A. 1835–70	Notturno	2 fl, 2 hn	Schott

Maglioni, G.	Le Désir aux Bains de Lucques, Op. 42 : No. 6, Au clair de Lune	fl, hn, vln, pf	Ricordi
Makoweczky b.ca. 1760	Quartet	hn, 2 vln, bass	Br. & H. [1802]
Manicke, D.	Quartet	cl, hn, bn, pf	Simrock, 1948
Martinů, B. 1890–1959	Quartet (1924)	cl, hn, vcl, drum	MS
Meale, R. 1932–	†Les Alboradas	fl, hn, vln, pf	Bo. & H.
Melchior, A. J. 19th Cent.	Quartet No. 1	fl, cl, hn, bn	Lemoine
	Quartet in G, Op. 6	fl, cl, hn, bn	Costallat
	Quartet, Op. 8	fl, cl, hn, bn	Lemoine
	Quartet in d, Op. 20	fl, cl, hn, bn	Costallat
	Three Quartets, Op. 14	fl, cl, hn, bn	Lemoine
	Six Quartets, Op. 30	fl, cl, hn, bn	Richault
Mellnäs, A. 1933–	Tombola (1963)	hn, trb, elec gt, pf	Tonos
Mengal, M. J. 1784–1851	Three Quartets, Op.8	hn, vln, vla, bass	Nadermann, nd.
	Three Quartets, Op. 18	fl, cl, hn, bn	Lemoine, n.d.
	Three Quartets, Op. 19	fl, cl, hn, bn	Lemoine, n.d.
	Quartet, Op. 73	fl, cl, hn, bn	Br. & H.
Mozart, W. A. 1756–91	†Cassazione Quartet in E♭ (authenticity doubtful)	ob, cl, hn, bn	Baron
	Adagio, K.580a	ca, 2 hn, bn	Hinrichsen
Müller, F. A.	Three Sonatas	2 hn, vln, pf/hp	Berlin, 1796
Neglia, F. P.	Bagatella, Op. 24	fl, hn, vln, pf	Geneva, Casa Editrice Musica, 1946
Osterc, S. 1895–1941	Konzert (1929)	ob, cl, hn, vla	MS (MGG)
Padovano, A.	Rondo	ob/fl, cl, hn, bn	Zanibon, 1966
Paquis, H.	Three Quatuors, Op. 1	fl, cl, hn, bn	Costallat
	Three Quatuors, Op. 2	fl, cl, hn, bn	Costallat
Pearson, W. 1905–	The Hunt	fl, ob, cl, hn	Chappell, 1962
Petyrek, F. 1892–1951	Gute Nacht, O Welt	ob, cl, hn, bn	Doblinger
Pichler, P. 1722–96	Intrada	fl, hn, vln, bass	MS (E*) (Univ. Upsala)
	Partia a 4	fl, hn, vln, hpcd	MS (E*) (Univ. Rostock)
	Parthie	fl, hn, vln, vcl	MS (E*) (Univ. Rostock)

Placheta, H. 1892–	Quartet, Op. 10	ob, cl, hn, bn	Doblinger, 1962
Pleyel, I. 1757–1831	Quartet	cl, 2 hn, bn	Hofmeister
Puschmann, J. 18th Cent.	Three Quartets	2 cl, 2 hn	MS (F)
Regner, H. 1928–	Serenade	ob, cl, hn, bn	Noetzel, 1959
Rieti, V. 1898–	Sonata	ob, cl, hn, pf	
Riisager, K. 1897–	Divertimento (1944)	fl, ob, hn, bn	MS? (MGG)
Ristori, G. A. 1692–1753	Sinfonia in D (1736)	hn, vln, vla, bass	MS (MGG*)
Rossini, G. 1792–1868	Tema con Variazioni in F	fl, cl, hn, bn	Bologna, 1812; FR, 1957
	Quatuor	fl, cl, hn, bn	Br. & H. 1826; Ricordi
	†Six Quartets (Ed. W. Zachert) (Nos. 1-5 arr. by F. Berr from stg quarts)	fl, cl, hn, bn	Lemoine, n.d. Schott, 1935; Ricordi
Rust, F. W. 1739–96	†Sonata in C (Ed. K. Janetzky)	2 hn, vla, vcl	Pro Musica, 1950
Sabatini, G.	Quartet	ob, cl, hn, bn	Camara
Schaffner, N. A. ca. 1790–1860	Three Quatuors concertants, Op. 5	fl, cl, hn, bn	Bo. & H. Br. & H. [1819]
	Three Quatuors, Op. 20	fl, cl, hn, bn	Gallet
Schneider, G. C. F. 1786–1853	Variations	cl, hn, bn, pf	MS? (F)
Schneider, G. L. 1766–1855	Sonata, Op. 5/3	2 hn, vln, pf	Gombart [1797]
Schneider, W. 1907–	Variations on a summer Song	ob, cl, hn, bn	Möseler, 1960
	Kleines Quartett	fl, ob, cl, hn	Möseler, 1966
Schobert, J. 1720–57	Six Sinfonias	2 hn, vln, hpcd	Bremner
Scholtz, C. G. b. 1761	Quartet	hn, vln, vla, vcl	MS (F)
Schroter, O. 1881–	Foolish Fantasy	ob, cl, hn, bn	Andraud
Schuller, G. 1925–	Curtain Raiser	fl, cl, hn, pf	MS
Schurtz	Kleine Musik in drei Sätzen	ob, cl, hn, bn	Möseler, 1965
	Divertimento	ob, cl, hn, bn	Möseler, 1964
Schwegler, J. D. 1759–1817	Four Quartets, Op. 3	2 fl, 2 hn	Br. & H., [1806]
	Quartet, Op. 3/2 (Ed. H. Schultz)	2fl, 2hn	Nagel, 1941
Simrock, H.	Three Quatuors, Op. 1	hn, vln, vla, vcl	Simrock [ca. 1802]

Sola, C. b. 1786	Quartet, Op. 21	fl, cl, hn, bn	Leduc
Sourilas, T. 1859–1907	Suite	ob, hn, vcl, hp/pf	Lemoine, 1899
Spies, E. 1899–	Eine fidele Overture, Op. 61	fl, cl, hn, bn	Oertel
Spourny, W.	Parthie	hn, 2 vln, vcl	MS? (E*)
Stamitz, K. 1746–1801	†Quartet in D, Op. 8/1	fl, hn, vln, vcl	Sieber [ca. 1780], J. Hummel
	(Ed. Upmeyer)		BVK, 1954
	†Quartet in E♭, Op. 8/2	ob, cl, hn, bn	Sieber [ca. 1780]; J. Hummel
	(Ed. H. Riemann)		Br. & H.
	(Ed. G. Weigelt)		Leuckart, 1937
	†Quartet in F, Op. 8/3	ob, hn, vln, vcl	Sieber [ca. 1780]; Musica Rara, 1958
	Quartet in E♭, Op. 8/4	ob, hn, vln, vcl	Sieber [ca. 1780]; M. & M.
	Quartet in E♭, Op. 8/5	ob, hn, vln, vcl	Sieber [ca. 1780]
	Quartet in E♭, Op. 8/6	ob, hn, vln, vcl	Sieber [ca. 1780]
	†Four Serenades, Op. 28	fl, 2 hn, bn	B. Hummel
Steinfeld, A. J. 1757–1824	Six Quartets, Op. 20	2 cl, 2 hn, perc ad lib	André, 1802
Stich, J. W. (Punto, G.) 1746–1803	Six Quartets, Op. 1	hn, vln, vla, vcl	Sieber
	Six Quartets, Op. 2	hn, vln, vla, vcl	Sieber
	†No. 1 in F (Ed. A. Gottron)		BVK, 1951
	Six Quartets, Op. 3	hn, vln, vla, vcl	Sieber
	Six Quartets, Op. 18	hn, vln, vla, vcl	Sieber
	No. 1 in F. (Ed. A. Gottron)		BVK, 1960
Stoelzel, G. H. 1690–1749	Eight Trios (sic)	ob, hn, vln, bass	MS (E*)
	Sonata in f	ob, hn, vln, pf	Br. & H.; Nagel
Stringfield, L. 1897–1959	An old Bridge (1936)	ob, cl, hn, bn	Sprague-Coleman, 1940
Struck, P. ca. 1775– ca. 1823	Quartet, Op. 5	fl, 2 hn, pf	Mollo
	Sonata, Op. 17	cl, 2 hn, pf	Br. & H., 1818
Sutherland, M. 1907–	Quartet (1943)	cl, hn, vla, pf	MS? (WERM)
Tausch, F. 1762–1817	Dreizehn Stücke en Quatuor, Op. 22	2 cl, hn, bn	Schlesinger

Tseiger, Y.	Suite on Esthonian Themes	fl, ob, cl, hn	RS, 1958
Tylňák, I. 1910–	Divertimento (1961)	fl, 2 cl, hn	(Ga)
Vandenbroeck, O. J. 1759–1832	Three Quatuors concertants, Op. 1	hn, vln, vla, vcl	Boyer, 1788; Nadermann; Leduc
Vermer, J. A. b. 1769	Quartet, Op. 33	ob, hn, pf, hp	Janet
Vogel, J. C. 1758–88	Six Quartets	hn, vln, vla, vcl	Leduc
Vogt, G. 1781–1870	Trois Nocturnes ou Potpourris d'Airs connus	fl, ob, hn, bn	Pleyel, n.d.
Volkmann, W. [1837–96?]	Légende	hn, vln, pf, harm	Mustel
Walckiers, E. 1793–1866	Three Quartets, Op. 7	fl, cl, hn, bn	Costallat, 1920
	Quartet in B♭, Op. 48	fl, cl, hn, bn	Schlesinger
	Quartet in c, Op. 73	fl, cl, hn, bn	Br. & H.
Weis-Ostborn, R. 1876–	Epilog, Op. 7	2 hn, 2 bn	R. & E., 1900
Weismann, J. 1879–1950	Divertimento, Op. 38	cl, hn, bn, pf	MS? (H, T)
Wermann, F. O. 1840–1906	Largo religioso, Op. 24	hn, vln, vcl, org	Wernthal
Wetzel, H. 1858–1928	Lustige Serenade	ob, cl, hn, bn	Oertel
Winters, G. 1928–	Aspects	fl, cl, hn, hp	
Woëts, J. B.	Le Clair de la Lune varié, Op. 33	fl, hn, bn, pf	Dufaut
Wood, J.	Incidental Music to 'Land of Fame' (1943)	vl, hn, trp, org	MS (R)
Zamboni	Quartet	fl, cl, hn, bn	Cipriani
Zingel, R. E. 1876–	Elegiac Intermezzo	ob, hn, bn, hp	C. Schmidt

6.4 Five instruments

6.4.1 Wind Quintet (fl, ob, cl, hn, bn)

Absil, J. 1893–	Quintet, Op. 16 (1934)	CeBeDeM
	Suite pastorale, Op. 37 (1939)	CeBeDeM
Agay, D.	Five easy Dances	Presser, 1956
Aliabiev, A. A. 20th Cent.	Quintet	RS, 1953
Ambrosius, H. 1897–	Quintet in b, Op. 57	Leipzig, Composer, 1925
Andriessen, H. 1892–	Quintet (1951)	Donemus, 1951
Andriessen, J. 1925–	Sciarada spagnuola: Divertimento	Donemus, 1962

Angerer, P. 1927–	Quintet (1956)	Doblinger, 1963
ApIvor, D. 1916–	Quintet, Op. 31 (1960)	MS?
Ardévol, J. 1911–	Quintet (1957)	MS (N.Y. Pub. Lib.)
Arnell, R. 1917–	Cassation, Op. 45	Hinrichsen, 1962
Arnold, M. 1921–	†Three Shanties	Paterson, 1954
Arrieu, C. 1903–	†Quintet in C	Noël, 1953
Aschenbrenner, J. 1903–	Quintet (1955) (bcl for cl)	Modern
Ashton, A. 1859–1937	Quintet	MS? (DMM)
Axman, E. 1887–1949	Quintet (1938)	HM
Baaren, K. van 1906–	†Quintetto: Sovraposizioni II	Donemus, 1963
Bacewitz, G. 1913–	Quintet	Moeck; PWM
Baden, C. 1908–	Quintet	NK
Badings, H. 1907–	Quintet No. 2 (1929)	Donemus, 1929
	Quintet No. 4 (1948)	Donemus, 1949
Baeyens, A. L. 1895–	†Quintet (1950) †Divertimento	CeBeDeM, 1962
Baines, F. 1917–	Quintet	MS? (WWM)
Bakaleinikov, V. 1885–1953	Introduction & Scherzo	Belwin, 1939
Balay, G. 1871–1943	L'Aurore sur la Forêt	Buffet-Crampon, 1931; E. & S.; Leduc
	La Vallée silencieuse: Reverie	Buffet-Crampon, 1931; E. & S; Leduc
	Petite Suite miniature dans le style du XVIIIe siècle	Leduc, 1948
Balfe, M.	Quintet, Op. 2	FST
Ballif, C. 1924–	Quintet, Op. 10	B. & B.
Barati, G. 1913–	Quintet (1953)	M. & M.
Barber, S. 1910–	†Summer Music, Op. 31 (1956)	G. Schirmer, 1957
Barboteu, G.	Caricatures	Choudens, 1966
Barraine, E. 1910–	Ouvrage de Dame: Theme & Variations	Andraud, 1944
Barrows, J. R. 1913–	†March	G. Schirmer, 1950
	†Quintet in a (1936)	MS (G, R)
Barthe, A.	Aubade	Pinatel
	†Passacaille (Ed. H. Voxman)	Leduc, 1899 Rubank
Bartoš, F. 1905–	Suite: Le bourgeois Gentilhomme (1934)	HM, 1943, 1948
Bartoš, J. 1902–	Cassation, Op. 45 (1961)	(Ga)
Bartoš, J. Z. 1908–	Quintet No. 1, Op. 42 (1945–6)	Continental
Bartovský, J. 1884–1964	Quintet	(Ga)
Bauer, M. 1887–1955	Quintet	CFE

271

APPENDIX C

Baumann, M. 1917–	Kleine Kammermusik	Sirius
Baur, J. 1918–	Quintetto sereno (1958)	Br. & H., 1959
Bayer-Vetessy, G. 1923–	Serenade	Modern
Beach, H. H. A. 1867–1945	Pastorale	CP, 1942
Beekhuis, H. 1889–	Elégie en humoresque (1939)	Donemus
Beethoven, L. van 1770–1827	†Adagio & Allegro für eine Spieluhr (Arr. F. Vester)	Mills, 1966
Behrend, F. 1889–	Divertimento, Op. 104	Composer, n.d.
Belfiore, T. 1917–	Quintet	(Ve)
Benguerel, X. 1931–	Successions	JMB, 1962
Bennett, D.	Rhapsodette	C. Fischer
Bennett, R. R. 1936–	Quintet	(fp, 17 March, 1968)
Benson, W. 1924–	†March	Shawnee, 1964
Bentzon, J. 1897–1951	Racconto No. 5, Op. 46	Skandinavisk, 1948
	Suite, Op. 11	Skandinavisk
Berezowsky, N. 1900–53	Suite No. 2, Op. 22 (1937)	Mills, 1941
Berg, G. 1909–	Quintet (1962)	Copenhagen, Composer
Berger, J. 1909–	Six short Pieces	Zimmermann [ca. 1962]
Bergmann, W.	Tanzstück	Doblinger
Bergsma, W. 1921–	Five Pieces	Galaxy, 1960
	Concerto	Galaxy, 1960
Beythien, K. 1897–	Quintet in F, Op. 7	Dresden, Composer, 1925
Birtwistle, H. 1934–	†Refrains & Choruses (1957)	UE, 1961
Bissell, K. 1912–	A Folk Song Suite	Bo. & H. [1964]
Bitsch, M. 1921–	Sonatine	Leduc, 1955
	Divertissement	Leduc
Blum, R. 1900–	†Concerto	(Schweiz)
Blumer, T. 1882–1964	Serenade und Thema mit Variationen in F, Op. 34	Simrock, 1918
	Quintet in B♭, Op. 52	Zimmermann, 1924
	Schweitzer Quintet	Sikorski, 1953
	Tanzsuite in D, Op. 53	Simrock, 1925
Boedijn, G. 1893–	Quintet concertante, Op. 150	Donemus, 1957
Bois, R. du 1934–	Chants et Contrepoints	Donemus, 1962
Boisselet, P. 1917–	†Divertimento (1964)	
Bongartz, H. 1894–	Suite, Op. 11	
Bonsel, A. 1918–	Quintet No. 1 (1949)	Donemus, 1950
	Quintet No. 2 (1953)	de Wolfe
	Oude Hollandse Dansen	Donemus
	5 Karakterstukken	Donemus
Borch, G. 1871–1926	Sunrise on the Mountains	Belwin; Mills
Borkovec, P. 1894–	Quintet (1932)	HM, 1936, 1960
Borowsky, F. 1872–1956	Madrigal to the Moon	Bo. & H., 1940, 1955

272

Borris, S. 1906–	Quintet, Op. 25/2	Sirius [1950]
Bosmans, A. 1908–	Diabelliana Suite	Elkan, 1957
Bourguignon, F. de 1890–1961	Two Pieces, Op. 71 (1941)	CeBeDeM, 1956
Bowen, Y. 1884–1961	Debutante, Frolic, Burlesque	de Wolfe
Bozay, A. 1939–	Quintet, Op. 6	ZV, 1965
Bozza, E. 1905–	†Variations sur un Thème libre, Op. 42	Leduc, 1943
	†Scherzo, Op. 48	Leduc, 1944
Brant, H. 1913–	Requiem in Summer	CFE
Brenta, G. 1902–	†Le Soldat fanfaron	CeBeDeM, 1956; Metropolis
Brescia, D.	Dithyrambic Suite	(H, T)
	Second Suite (Rhapsodic)	MS (Lib. of Congress)
Brevik, T. 1932–	Divertimento	NK
Briccialdi, G. 1818–81	Quintet in D, Op. 124	Schott, 1875
Bright, H. 1916–	†Three short Dances	Shawnee, 1961
Brod, H. 1801–39	Three Quintets, Op. 2	Pacini, n.d.; Lemoine, 1921
	No. 1 in B♭; No. 2	M. & M.
Brons, C. 1931–	Balletto (1961)	Donemus, 1962
	Mutazione (1964)	Donemus
Brown, C.	Divertimento before Shakespeare's 'Merry Wives of Windsor'	Gamut, 1965
Brubeck, H. 1916–	Quintet	Derry
Brugk, H. M. 1909–	Serenade, Op. 22 (1956)	Sikorski, 1959
Bruns, V. 1904–	Quintet, Op. 16	Hofmeister, 1954
Burian, F. 1904–59	Quintet (1933)	Orbis, 1951
Bush, G. 1920–	Quintet (1963)	Galliard
Butt, J. 1929–	Winsome's Folly, Suite No. 2	Novello, 1960
Butting, M. 1888–	Quintet, Op. 30 (1925)	MS
Cage, J. 1912–	Music for wind instruments: No. 3, Quintet (1937)	Peters, 1961
Cailliet, L. 1897–	Overture in B♭	EV, 1950
	Concertino	EV, 1956
Calabro, L. 1926–	Divertimento	EV, 1966
Cambini, G. G. 1746–1829	Quintet No. 1, Op. 4	M. & M. [1965]
	†Quintet No. 3 in F, Op. 4	M. & M., 1963
Canteloube, J. 1879–1957	Suite rustique	(Th)
Carabella, E. 1891–	Suite	Ricordi, 1935
Carion, F.	Fantaisie concertante	Brogneaux, 1951
Carlstedt, J. 1926–	Sinfonietta (1959)	FST
	Quintet, Op. 19 (1962)	FST
Carter, E. 1908–	†Quintet (1948)	AMP, 1952, 1955
Carwithen, D. 1922–	Quintet	MS (Th)
Castérède, J.	Quintet	Leduc, 1955
Cazden, N. 1914–	Three Constructions, Op. 38 (1941)	Kalmus, 1951

Cellier, A. E. 1883–	Images médiévales	EMT, 1960
Chagrin, F. 1905–	Divertimento	Augener, 1952
Chailley, J. 1910–	Barcarolle	Leduc, 1948
Chavez, C. 1899–	Soli No. 2	Mills, 1963
Chaynes, C. 1925–	Serenade (1957)	Leduc, 1958
Chemin-Petit, H. 1902–	Quintet (1947)	Lienau, 1949
Chevreuille, R. 1901–	Divertissement, Op. 21 (1942)	CeBeDeM, 1958
	†Serenade, Op. 65 (1956)	CeBeDeM, 1960
Chrétien, H. 1859–1944	Arabesque	E. & S., 1921; Andraud
	Quintet in B♭	Baxter-Northrup
Cipra, M. 1906–	Quintet (1964)	Composer
Civil, A. 1929–	Quintet (1951)	MS (Composer) (Downe Hall, Downe, Kent)
Clapp, P. G. 1888–1954	Prelude & Finale (1939)	Bo. & H., 1941, 1955
Clarke, H. L. 1907–	Sarabande for the golden Goose	CFE
Cohen, S. B. 1891–	Quintet No. 2	Belwin
	Suite	C. Fischer
Coker, W.	Quintet (1955)	SPAM, 1964
Colaco Osorio-Swaab, R. 1889–	Suite (1948)	Donemus
Colgrass, M. 1932–	Quintet (1962)	Composer
Colomer, B. M.	Minuet & Bourrée	E. & S., n.d.; Leduc, 1954
Cooke, A. 1906–	Quintet (1961)	Mills
Cowell, H. 1897–1965	†Suite (1933)	Mercury, 1949
	Ballad (1955)	AMP, 1962
Crawford-Seeger, R. 1901–53	Suite	MS
Croley, R.	Quintet	Tritone, 1963
Cruft, A. 1921–	Les Buffons (John Bull)	Williams, 1957
	Worster Brawls (Tomkins)	Williams, 1957
Dahl, I. 1912–	†Allegro & Arioso (1942)	M. & M., 1962
Dahlhoff, W.	Der Choral von Leuthen	C. Schmidt, 1925
Damase, J. M. 1928–	†Seventeen Variations, Op. 22 (1950)	Leduc, 1952
Danzi, F. 1763–1826	Three Quintets, Op. Op. 56	Schlesinger, n.d.
	†No. 1 in B♭ (Ed. G. Weigelt)	Leuckart, 1941
	†No. 2 in g (Ed. H. Riemann) (Ed. G. Weigelt)	Br. & H., 1914 Leuckart, 1937
	Three Quintets, Op. 67	André, n.d.
	†No. 2 in e (Ed. H. Schulz)	Nagel, 1941
	(Ed. F. Kneusslin)	Kneusslin, 1954
	Three Quintets, Op. 68	André, n.d.
	No. 1 in A (Ed. F. Kneusslin)	Kneusslin, 1960
	No. 2 in F (Ed. F. Kneusslin)	Kneusslin, 1965
	No. 3 in d	Musica Rara, 196

Dávid, G. 1913–	Quintet	EMB, 1955; Mills, 1960
	Serenade (1955)	EMB, 1956; Mills, 1960
	Quintet No. 3	EMB, 1965
David, T. C. 1925–	Quintet (1966)	Doblinger
Debussy, C. 1862–1918	The little Negro (Arr. E. Bozza)	Leduc
De Coursey, R. 1918–	Fugue à la Rhumba	BMI (Canada)
Defossez, R. 1905–	Quintet	MS? (G)
	Burlesque (1928)	CeBeDeM
Dehnert, M. 1893–	Festliche Musik	Litolff, 1963
Dejoncker, T. 1894–	Quintet	(Ve)
Dela, M. 1919–	Petite Suite maritime	CMC
Delaney, C.	Suite	M. & M.
Delcroix, L. 1880–1938	Partita	
Demuth, N. 1898–1968	Pastorale & Scherzo	Hinrichsen
Deshayes, P. D. d. ca. 1820	1re Quintette	Gobert, n.d.
	2e Quintette	Gobert, n.d.
Deslandres, A. E. M. 1840–1911	Trois Pièces en quintette	Paris, Composer, 1903; Andraud
Desormière, R. 1898–1963	†Six Danceries du XVIe Siècle (ca for ob)	Leduc, 1942, 1951
	Acante et Céphise (after J. P. Rameau)	Leduc
Desportes, Y. 1907–	Prelude, Variations & Finale on a Gregorian Chant	Leduc; Andraud, 1938
Deserre, G. T.	Suite dans le style ancien	NEM, 1956
Diamond, D. 1915–	Quintet (1958)	Southern, 1962
Diemer, E. L.	Quintet, No. 1	Bo. & H., 1962
Diercks, J. 1927–	Quintet	M. & M.
Dobiáš, V. 1909–	†Pastorale (1943)	Panton, 1961
Döhl, F. 1936–	Klangfiguren	(Ve)
Domenico, O. di	Quintet	Leduc, 1955
Douglas, R. 1907–	Six Dance Caricatures	Hinrichsen, 1950
Draeger, W. 1888–	Quintet	(Ve)
Dragan, R.	Time of Youth	IMP
Druce, D.	Quintet	MS? (MT, Sept., 1962)
Dubois, P. M. 1930–	Fantasia	Leduc, 1956
Dubois, T. 1837–1924	Passacaille	Heugel
	1er Suite	Heugel, 1898; Mercury
Dvořáček, J. 1928–	Quintet (1951)	(Ga)
Eben, P. 1929–	Quintet	(Ve)
Eckartz, H.	Quintet	Iris [1950]
Eckhardt-Gramatté, S. C. 1902–	Quintet	CMC
Eder, H. 1916–	Quintet, Op. 25	Doblinger, 1958
Edwards, R.	Two Quintets	(Ve)
Egge, K. 1906–	Quintet, Op. 13 (1939)	Lyche

Egidi, A. 1859–1943	Quintet in B♭, Op. 18	VMK, 1937
Eisler, H. 1898–1962	Quintet, Op. 4	UE
Eisma, W. 1929–	Fontemara (1965)	Donemus, 1966
	Quintet (1955)	Donemus
Eitler, E. 1913–	Quintet (1945)	MS (Ve)
Eklund, H. 1927–	Improvisata	FST
Elliott, W.	Two Sketches	Composer
Ellis, D.	Quintet (1956–66)	(MT, Apr. 1967)
Emborg, J. L. 1876–1957	Quintet, Op. 74	Dania, 1937
Enders, A.	Quintet	Mannh. Musikverlag
Engela, D.	Divertimento	Composer, 1962
Englert, G. G. 1927–	Rime Serie, Op. 5 (1958)	Composer
Erdlen, H. 1893–	Kleine Variationen über ein Frühlingslied, Op. 27/1	Zimmermann, 1932
Eschpay, Y. [1890–1963?]	Marische Melody	Andraun
Essex, K. 1915–55	Quintet (1941)	Hinrichsen
Etler, A. D. 1913–	†Quintet No. 1 (1955)	AMP
	Quintet No. 2 (1957)	AMP, 1960
Fairlie, M. 1925–	Quintet (1962); Quintet No. 3	Composer
Farkás, F. 1905–	Serenade (1951)	EMB, 1956
	Quintet (1957)	Kultura
	Antiche Danze Ungheresi dal Secolo XVII	EMB, 1959
Farnaby, G. 1565–1640	Variations on Elizabethan Songs & Dance Airs (Arr. A. Foster)	OUP, 1957
Feld, J. 1925–	Quintet (1949)	Leduc, 1964
Fernandez, O. L. 1897–1948	Suite in F, Op. 37 (1926)	Univ, of Rio de Janeiro, 1937; AMP [1942?]
Fernström, J. A. 1897–	Quintet, Op. 59	FST
Ferrari, C.	Pastorale	Cor
Fine, I. 1914–62	†Partita (1948)	Bo. & H., 1951
	Romanza	Mills, 1963
Finke, F. 1891–	Quintet (1955)	Br. & H., 1956
Fleming, R. 1921–	Quintet	CMC
Flosman, O. 1925–	Quintet No. 1 (1948)	(Ga)
	Quintet No. 2 (1962)	(Ga)
Foerster, J. B. 1859–1951	Quintet in D, Op. 95 (1909)	HM, 1925
Förtig, D. 1935–	Quintet (1962–3)	Freiburg, Composer
Folprecht, Z. 1909–61	Quintet, Op. 17 (1938)	CHF, 1960
Fortner, W. 1907–	Five Bagatelles	Schott, 1960
Fougstedt, N. E. 1910–	Divertimento in D, Op. 35b	MS? (Gor)

Fragale, F.	Quintet	AMP, 1948
	Angora Lake	MS (San Mateo, Cal.)
	Lipone Quintet	MS (San Mateo, Cal.)
Françaix, J. 1912–	†Quintet	Schott, 1951
Francl, J. 1906–	Quintettino (1962)	(Ga)
Franco, J. 1908–	Canticle (1958)	CFE
	Seven Epigrams	CFE
Frangkiser	Episodes from Dedications	Belwin
Freed, I. 1900–60	Quintet (1949)	(Ho)
Freedman, H. 1922–	Quintet (1962)	CMC
Freyer, J.	Divertimento	Br. & H.
Fricker, P. R. 1920–	†Quintet, Op. 5 (1947)	Schott, 1951
Fudolf, M.	Musica leggiera	EMB
Fürst, P. W. 1926–	Konzertante Musik (1957)	Doblinger, 1961
Füssl, K. H. 1924–	Kleine Kammermusik	BVK, 1943
Fussan, W. 1912–	Quintet, Op. 14	Kasparek, 1948
Futterer, C. 1873–1927	Quintet (1922)	MS (Ve)
Gabaye, P.	Quintet (1959)	Leduc, 1961
Garrido-Lecca, C. 1926–	Divertimento	PAU, 1965
Gayfer, J. M. 1916–	Suite	Bo. & H., 1950
Gebauer, F. R. 1773–1844	†Quintet No. 1 in B♭	M. & M., 1966
	†Quintet No. 2 in E♭	[Sieber?]; M. & M., 1966
	Quintet No. 3 in c	M. & M., 1966
Geissler, F. 1921–	Heitere Suite	Br. & H., 1957, 1966
Genzmer, H. 1909–	Quintet (1956–7)	Litolff, 1958
Geraedts, J. 1924–	Kleine Watermuziek: Divertimento over een bekend Hollands Kinderliedje (1951)	Donemus
Gerhard, R. 1896–	†Quintet (1928)	Mills, 1960
Gerster, O. 1897–	Heitere Musik	Schott, 1938
Ghedini, G. F. 1892–65	Quintet (1910)	MS (G, MGG)
Giannini, V. 1903–66	Quintet (1934)	MS (G, Ho, R)
Gillis, D. 1912–	Suite No. 1; Sketches (1938)	Mills, 1956
	Suite No. 2; Campus Caricatures (1939)	Mills, 1956
	Suite No. 3	Mills, 1957
Giltay, B. 1910–	Quintetto	Donemus
Goeb, R. 1914–	†Prairie Songs (1947)	Peer, 1952
	†Quintet No. 1 (1949)	M. & M.
	†Quintet No. 2 (1956)	M. & M.
Goleminov, M. 1908–	Quintet	Raznoiznos, 1954
Goodenough, F. 1918–	Quintet (1954)	M. & M.
Gottlieb, J.	Twilight Crane (Yuzuru)	G. Schirmer, 1963

Gouvy, L. T. 1819–98	Serenade	Sikorski
Gow, D. 1924–	Serenata	MS?
Grainger, P. 1882–1961	†Room-Music Tit-Bits No. 3; A Walking Tune	Schott, 1912
	Lisbon	MS? (G)
Gram, P. 1881–1956	Quintet, Op. 31 (1943)	MS (G, MGG)
Grant, W. P. 1910–	Soliloquy & Jubilation, Op. 40	M. & M.
Green, R. 1908–	Quintet (1933)	MS (R)
Grimm, C. H. 1890–	A little Serenade, Op. 36	Andraud, 1937
Groot, H. de	Variations on Dutch Melodies (1944)	Broekmans
	Burla ritmica	Broekmans, 1966
Guenther, R.	Rondo	CB
Guentzel	Tarantella	Barnhouse
	Scherzo	Barnhouse
	Pastorale: In the Meadow	Barnhouse
	Intermezzo	Pro Art
Guilmant, A. 1838–1911	Canzonetta	Remick
Gwilt, D. 1932–	Quintet	MS (Ve)
Haas, P. 1899–1944	Quintet, Op. 10 (1929)	Sadló, 1934
Hába, K. 1898–	Quintet, Op. 28 (1945)	(Ga, Ve)
Hadjiev, P. 1912–	Three Sketches	Raznoiznos
Hagerup Bull, E. 1922–	Marionettes sérieuses: Capricci	NK
Hall, P. 1890–	Suite (1944)	Lyche, 1945
Hamerik, E. 1898–1951	†Quintet (1942)	Samfundet, 1944, 1952
Hannekainen, V. 1900–	Pastorale, Op. 50	Composer
Hartley, G. 1921–	†Divertissement	AMP, 1951
Hartley, W. S. 1927–	Two Pieces	Interlochen
Hashagen, K. 1924–	Rondell (1964)	Hanover, Composer, 1964
Hasse, J. F.	Kammermusik	Simrock, 1963
Haubiel, C. 1894–	Five Pieces	CP; M. & H., 1948
Haudebert, L. b. 1877	Suite dans le Style ancien	Senart, 1931
Haufrecht, H. 1909–	A woodland Serenade (1955)	Rongwen, 1956
Haug, H. 1900–67	Quintet (1955)	MS? (MGG)
Haworth, F. 1905–	Glenrose Suite (1960)	CMC
Haydn, F. J. 1732–1809	†Sieben Stücke für die Flötenuhr (Arr. F. Vester)	Mills, 1966
Heiden, B. 1910–	†Sinfonia (1949)	AMP, 1957
Heim, M.	Quintet in E♭	C. Schmidt, 1903
Hekster, W.	Quintetto	Donemus
	Pentogram (1961)	Donemus
Helger, L.	Cassation	Munich, Dehace, 1963
Henderson, T.	Quintet	MS? (MT, June, 1960)

278

Henkemans, H. 1913–	Quintet No. 1 (1934)	Donemus
	Quintet No. 2 (1962)	Donemus, 1962
Henze, H. W. 1926–	Quintet (1952)	Schott, 1953
Herberigs, R. 1886–	Concert champetre (1958)	CeBeDeM
Herrmann, H. 1896–	Pastorale Phantasietten, Op. 51	Rahter, 1963
	Romantische Episoden, Op. 13c	MS (Ve)
Hess, W. 1906–	Divertimento in B♭, Op. 51 (1947)	Hinrichsen, 1956
Hewitt-Jones, T. 1926–	Theme & Variations (1965)	Novello, 1966
Heyl, M. 1908–	Quintet in C, Op. 26	Composer [1950]
Hillman, K. b. 1867	Capriccio, Op. 57	André, 1923; Belwin
Hindemith, P. 1895–1963	†Klcine Kammermusik, Op. 24/2 (1922)	Schott, 1922, 1949
Hipman, S. 1893–	Cáslaver Suite, Op. 11 (1919)	Artia [1939]
Hirao, K. 1907–53	Quintet	Tokyo
Hirner, T. 1910–	Quintet (1960)	SHF
Hirsch, H. L. 1937–	Quintetto sereno	Peters
Hlobil, E. 1901–	Quintet, Op. 20 (1941)	CHF, 1960
Høffding, F. 1899–	Quintet, Op. 35	Skandinavisk, 1948
	Quintet No. 2, Op. 53 (1953)	Composer
Höffer, P. 1895–1949	Variations on a Theme of Beethoven (1947)	MV, n.d. [1950]; Litolff, 1956
Höller, K. 1907–	Serenade	
Hofmann, W.	Serenade	Sirius
Hohensee, W. 1927–	Quintet in D	Br. & H., 1965
Holbrooke, J. 1878–1958	Miniature characteristic Suite, Suite, Op. 33b	RC, 1910; de Wolfe
Holmboe, V. 1909–	Notturno, Op. 19 (1940)	Viking, 1948
Holst, G. 1874–1934	Quintet, Op. 14 (1903)	MS (DMM, G, MGG)
Hosmer, J. B.	Fugue in C	Gamble
Hovhaness, A. 1911–	Quintet, Op. 159	Peters, 1967
Hovland, E. 1924–	†Quintet, Op. 50	NK
Hoyer, K. 1891–1936	Serenade in F, Op. 29	Simrock, 1924
Huber, K. 1924–	Drei Sätze in zwei Teilen (1959)	BVK, 1962
Huguenin, C. 20th Cent.	Deux Pièces	Le Loche, Composer [1931?]
Hummel, B. 1925–	Quintet (1962)	Simrock, 1964
Hunter, E.	Danse humoresque	C. Fischer
Hurník, I. 1922–	Quintet, Op. 11 (1944)	MS (Ve)
	Quintet No. 2, Op. 20 (1949)	MS (Ve)
Huybrechts, A. 1899–1938	†Quintet (1936)	CeBeDeM
Ibert, J. 1890–1962	†Trois Pièces brèves (1921)	Leduc, 1930
Ingenhoven, J. 1876–1951	Quintet in C (1911)	Wunderhorn, 1912
Israel-Meyer, P.	Quintet (1964)	Composer

Jacob, G. 1895–	Quintet	MS (Composer) (1 Audley Rd., Saffron Walden, Essex)
Jacobi, F. 1891–1952	†Scherzo (1936)	C. Fischer, 1938
Jacobson, M. 1896–	Four Pieces	Curwen [ca. 1930]
Jacoby, H. 1909–	Quintet (1946)	IMP, 1951
James, P. 1890–	Suite in four Movements (1936)	C. Fischer, 1938
Járdányi, P. 1920–	Fantasia & Variations on a Hungarian Folksong	EMB, 1958
Jersild, J. 1913–	Serenade: At spille i skoven	Hansen, 1951
Jettel, R. 1903–	Quintet	Weinberger
Jirák, K. B. 1891–	Quintet, Op. 34 (1928–9)	Andraud
Jirko, I. 1926–	Suite (1949)	Panton, 1965
Johnsen, H. 1916–	Serenade, Op. 37	NK
Johnson, E.	Legend of Erin	Belwin
Johnson, H. M.	Quintet in C	C. Fischer
Jolivet, A. 1905–	Serenade (1944)	Costallat; Heugel, 1944
Jones, K. V. 1924–	Two Quintets	MS (Th)
Jong, M. de 1891–	Aphoristisch Triptyque, Op. 82 bis (1953)	CeBeDeM
Jongen, J. 1873–1953	Concerto, Op. 124 (1942)	Brogneaux; Andraud, 1948
	Première Quintette, Op. 98	Brogneaux; Andraud, 1937
Josephs, W. 1927–	Wry Rhumba	NWM, 1967
Josten, W. 1885–1963	Canzona seria	Elkan
Jungk, K. 1916–	Chaconne	Sikorski
Juon, P. 1872–1940	Quintet in B♭, Op. 84	Birnbach, 1930
Kadosa, P. 1903–	Quintet, Op. 49a	ZV, 1956
Kalabis, V. 1923–	Divertimento (1952)	CHF, 1956
Kallstenius, E. 1881–	†Divertimento, Op. 29 (1943)	FST
Kapp, V.	Suite	RS, 1959
Kardoš, D. 1914–	Quintet, Op. 6 (1938)	MS (Ga, Ve)
Karkoff, M. 1927–	Quintet, Op. 24	FST
	Serenata piccola, Op. 34c (1958)	FST
Karren, L.	Little Tale from Brittany	E. & S.; Andraud
Kasemets, U. 1919–	†Quintet, Op. 48	CMC
Kauffmann, F. 1855–1934	Quintet in E♭, Op. 40	Heinrichshofen, 1905
Kauffmann, L. J. 1901–44	Quintet	UE, 1943
Kauffmann, W. 1907–	†Partita	Templeton, 1966
Kay, N. F. 1929–	Quintet	MS (MT, Aug, 1962)
Kayn, R. 1933–	Inerziali per 5 Esecutori	Moeck, 1964
Keith, G. D.	Quintet	Bo. & H., 1948, 1955

A LIST OF MUSIC FOR THE HORN

Composer	Work	Publisher
Kelemen, M. 1924–	Contrapuntal Etudes	Ars Viva, 1966
	Entrances	Litolff
Kelly, R. 1916–	Passacaglia & Fugue	M. & M.
Kelterborn, R. 1931–	Seven Bagatelles (1957)	Modern, 1958
Kern, F.	Quintet	Grosch, 1942
Kersters, W. 1921–	Quintet (ca for ob)	(Ve)
Kilar, W. 1932–	Quintet (1952)	PWM
King, H. C. 1895–	Quintet in E♭ (1940–9)	Donemus, 1954
Kingman, D.	Quintet	Avant, 1964
Kirby, S. T.	Elfin Dance	AMP, 1951
Klebe, G. 1925–	Quintet, Op. 3 (1948)	Composer
	Quintet No. 2	Composer
Klughardt, A. F. M. 1847–1902	†Quintet in C, Op. 79	Giessel, 1901; Hofmeister, 1960
Köhler, W.	Quintet	Zierenberg, Composer
Köper, K. H. 1927–	Quintet (1954)	Composer
Kötschau, J. 1905–	Quintet, Op. 14	Zimmermann
Koetsier, J. 1911–	Divertimento, Op. 16/1 (1937)	Donemus
	2e Divertimento, Op. 35/1 (1947)	Donemus
Kohn, K.	Little Suite (1963)	Composer
Kohout, J. 1895–1958	Miniatures, Op. 17 (1946–7)	Hofmeister, 1962
	Variationen auf ein Volkslied (1945)	Mannh. Musikverlag
Kohoutek, C. 1929–	Quintet (1958)	SNKLHU, 1965
Komma, K. M. 1913–	Divertimento (1955)	Ichthys, 1957
Kont, P. 1920–	Quintet in memoriam F. Danzi (1961)	Doblinger, 1963
Koppel, H. D. 1908–	Quintet	Skandinavisk, 1947
	Sonatina, Op. 16 (1932)	MS (Ve)
Korda, V.	Quintet	Doblinger
Korn, P. J. 1922–	Prelude & Scherzo	Mercury
Kotoński, W. 1925–	Quintet	PWM, 1966
Kraft, K. J. 1903–	Divertimento No. 4 (ca. 1943)	MS (MGG)
Krasko, J. 1893–	Quintet on a Slovak Song (Sadaj slnko)	SHF
Krause-Graumnitz, H. 1911–	Kadenzen-Quartet	Br. & H.
Kreisler, A. von	Quintet	Southern, 1965
Krejčí, 1904–	Quintet	(Ve)
Křenek, E. 1900–	†Pentagramm (1957) (Revision of Quintet, 1951)	BVK, 1957
Křička, J. 1882–	Quintet 'The Wasp'	Artia
	Divertimento, Op. 99 (1950)	(Ga, Ve)
Kubik, G. 1914–	Quintet (1937)	MS? (G, H, R, T)
Kubizek, A. 1918–	Quintet	Doblinger, 1957
Kühnel, E.	Deutsche Ostseebilder	Grosch, 1942
Kunert, K. 1911–	Divertimento No. 2, Op. 18	Hofmeister, 1956
	Quintet, Op. 14	Grosch [1952]

	Quintet No. 2, Op. 17		Hofmeister [1954]
	Quintet No. 4 (1955)		Hofmeister
Kurtág, G. 1926–	Quintet, Op. 2		EMB, 1965
Kvandal, J. 1919–	Three religious Folktunes		NK
Kvapil, J.	Quintet (1925); Quintet No. 2		(Ga)
1892–1958	(1935)		
Labate, B.	Intermezzo No. 2		Mills, 1954
Labey, M. b. 1875	Quintet		Rouart, 1923; Eschig
Lacerda, O.	Variacoes e Fuga		PAU, 1965
Lachner, F.	Quintet in F (1823)		MS (MGG)
1803–90			
	Quintet in E♭ (1829)		MS (MGG)
Laderman, E. 1924–	Quintet		CFE
Laks, S. 1901–	Quintet (1929)		MS? (G)
Landré, G. 1905–	Quintetto (1930)		Donemus
	Quintet (1960)		Donemus
Láng, I.	†Quintet		EMB, 1965
Lange, H. 1882–	Quintet, Op. 14		Berlin, Composer, 1937
	Böhmische Musikanten, Op. 40		Berlin, Composer, 1937
Laudenslager, H.	Quintet		Camara; Cor
Laurischkus, M.	Aus Litauen: Suite, Op. 23		Simrock, 1914
1876–1929			
Lazarof, H. 1932–	Concertino da camera		IMP
Leduc, J. 1932–	Quintet		Maurer, 1960
Leeuw, T. de 1926–	Antifonie (1958) (with 4 sound-tracks)		Donemus, 1960
Lefebvre, C.	†Suite, Op. 57		Hamelle, 1910; CB; Belwin
1843–1917			
Legley, V. 1915–	Quintet, Op. 58 (1961)		CeBeDeM, 1963
Lehmann, H. U.	Episoden (1963–4)		Ars Viva, 1965
1937–			
Leibowitz, R. 1913–	Quintet, Op. 11 (1944)		UE; Bomart, 1958
Lendvai, E.	Quintet in A♭, Op. 23		Composer, n.d.; Hamelle, 1910; Simrock, 1922
1882–1949			
Leplin, E. 1917–	Quintet (1961)		MS (BMI)
Lessard, J. 1920–	†Partita (1952)		M. & M.
Leukauf, R.	Quintetto, Op. 25		Doblinger, 1965
Levy, F.	Lovelette		Belwin
Lickl [J. G.	Quintetto concertante		Haslinger; Kneusslin, 1966
1769–1843?]			
Liedbeck, S.	Impromptu		FST
Lilge, H.	Variationen und Fuga über ein eignes Thema, Op. 67		K. & S., 1937
b. 1870			
Lilien, I. 1897–	Quintetto No. 2 (1952)		Donemus
	Voyage au Printemps (1952)		Donemus
Lindner, F.	Quintet in B♭, Op. 1		Hofmeister
1795–1846			
Lockwood, N. 1906–	Tune Arrangements (1950)		CFE
Lohse, F. 1908–	Quintet (1960)		Litolff, 1963

Lora, A. 1899–	Quintet	CFE
Louel, J. 1914–	Quintet (1958)	CeBeDeM, 1960
Lucký, S. 1919–	†Quintet, Op. 11 (1946)	SNKLHU, 1958
Luening, O. 1900–	Fuguing Tune (1938–9)	AMP, 1944
Lundén, L. 1914–66	Variations on 'Byssan lull'	Nordiska, 1958
Lutyens, E. 1906–	†Quintet, Op. 45 (1960)	Mills
Maasz, G. 1906–	Five Variations	
McBride, R. 1911–	Cuatro milpas (1941)	CFE
	Jam Session (1941)	CP, 1944
	Five Winds blowing (1957)	CFE
McCall, H. E.	Two Tunes from Mother Goose	Andraud
Macdonald, M. 1916–	Divertimento	MS (Th)
Macero, T. 1925–	Pieces for Children	CFE
McEwen, J. 1868–1948	Under northern Skies (1939)	MS (G, MGG) (Univ. of Glasgow)
McIntyre, P. 1931–	Fantasy on an Eskimo Song	CMC
McKay, F. H.	Bainbridge Island Sketches (1932)	Barnhouse
McKay, G. F. 1899–	Quintet, Op. 11 (1932)	MS (H, R)
	Joyful Dances	Mercury, 1949
McKinley, C. 1895–	Suite (1935)	MS (R)
McPeek, B. 1934–	Quintet	CMC
Mägi, S.	Ostinato	RS, 1965
Maganini, Q. 1897–	Fox Trot Burlesque	M. & M.
Magnani, A.	Reverie	Baron
Malipiero, G. F. 1882–	†Dialoghi IV (1956)	Ricordi, 1957
Malipiero, R. 1914–	Musica da camera (1959)	SZ, 1959
Mandic, J. 1883–	Quintet (ob/ca)	UE, 1933
Manevich, A. 1908–	Nocturne & Scherzo	RS
Maniet R.	Quintet	Maurer, 1959
Mann, L. 1923–	Quintet (ca for ob)	CMC
Maréchal, H. 1842–1924	Air du Guet	Heugel, 1920
Marez Oyens, T. de 1932–	Two Sketches	Donemus, 1963
Maric, L. 1909–	Quintet (1932)	MS (Ve)
Maros, R. 1917–	Musica leggiera (1956)	EMB, 1958
Martelli, H. 1895–	Quintet No. 1 (1948)	MS? (G)
Martino, D. 1929–	Concerto (1964)	M. & M.
Martinon, J. 1909–	Quintet (1938)	MS? (B)
Martinů, B. 1890–1959	Quintet (1930)	Chester; SNKLHU, 1965
Marvia, E. 1915–	Quintet, Op. 8	Helsinki, Fazer
Mason, D. G. 1873–1953	Divertimento, Op. 26b (1926)	Witmark, 1936
Matarazzo, J.	Quintet	Camara
Mathias, W. 1934–	Quintet, Op. 22	OUP
Matthews, D. 1919–	Partita	MS?
Matys, J. 1927–	Suite : The Children's Ballet, Op. 26 (1959)	(Ga)
Maxwell, M.	Allegro	(MT, June, 1960)
Mays, W. A.	Quintet	Cincinnati, Composer, 1965

Mederacke, K. 1910–	Böhmische Suite, Op. 43	Hofmeister, 1948 1959
	Divertimento, Op. 36	Hofmeister
Meester, L. de 1904–	†Divertimento (1946)	CeBeDeM, 1962
Mendelssohn, J. A.	Figurate Hymn	C. Fischer
Mengal, M. J. 1784–1851	Three Quintets	MS? (F)
Mengelberg, M. 1935–	Omtrent een componistenactie	Donemus, 1966
Metcalf, J. 1946–	Quintet	(Horn Realm)
Meulemans, A. 1884–1966	Quintet No. 1 (1931)	Brogneaux; CeBeDeM, 1956
	Quintet No. 2 (1932)	Brogneaux; CeBeDeM, 1956
	Quintet No. 3 (1958)	CeBeDeM
Meyerowitz, J. 1913–	Quintet (1954)	Rongwen
Meyer-Tormin, W. 1911–	Kleines Quintet (1951)	B. & B., 1964
Micheelsen, H. F. 1902–	Divertimento	(Ve)
Mielenz, H. 1898–	Scherzo (ca for ob)	
Migot, G. 1891–	Quintet (1954)	Leduc, 1955
Milhaud, D. 1892–	†La Cheminée du Roi René (1939)	Andraud, 1942
	†Two Sketches	Mercury, 1942, 1946
	†Divertissement, Op. 229b	Heugel, 1958
Mills, C. 1914–	Sonata fantasia (1941)	CFE
Milner, Anthony 1925–	Quintet (1964)	Novello, 1967
Mirandolle, L.	Deux Morceaux: No. 2	La Haye, Composer, 1952
Moeschinger, A. 1897–	Quintet	
Mohr, W. 1904–	Quintet in f♯, Op. 6 (1943)	MS (Ve)
	Variationen über das Lied vom Heuschreck	Kasparek
Molnár, A. 1890–	Quintet, Op. 16	MS (Ve)
Montaneri, N.	Cinque Invenzioni	Curci, 1965
Moore, D. 1893–	Quintet (1942)	SPAM, 1947
Moritz, E. 1891–	Quintet, Op. 41	Zimmermann [1928]
Morris, F. E. 1920–	†Five esoteric Pieces (1941, 1955)	(Schwann)
Mortari, V. 1902–	Petite Offrande musicale	Leduc
Mortensen, F. 1922–	Quintet, Op. 4	Hansen, 1957
Mortensen, O. 1907–	Quintet	Hansen, 1945
Motte, D. de la 1928–	Quintet (1954)	Composer, 1954
Moyse, L. 1911–	Quintet	M. & M., 1966
Moyzes, A. 1906–	†Quintet, Op. 17 (1933)	Simrock, 1943
Mozart, W. A. 1756–91	†Andante für eine Orgelwalze, K. 616 (Arr. F. Vester)	Mills, 1963
	†Fantasie für eine Orgelwalze, K. 608 (Arr. F. Vester)	Mills, 1963

Mueller, F.	Five Pieces	Camara
	Three Transcriptions	Cor
Müller, P. 1791–1877	Three Quintets in E♭, c & A No. 1 in E♭ (Ed. W. Waterhouse)	Rühle, 1874; Musica Rara, 1962
Müller-Rudolstadt, W.	Die Leineweber	Grosch, 1933
Mulder, H. 1894–	Quintet, Op. 119	Donemus, 1961
Naylor, P.	Quintet (1962)	MS (MT, Sept. 1962)
Necke, H.	The Mill of Sans Souci	Mills
Nelhybel, V. 1919–	Quintet No. 1 (Quintetto giocoso) (1949)	Eulenburg, 1954; Peters, 1955
Newson, G. 1932–	Quintet	MS? (MT, March, 1962)
Nielsen, C. 1865–1931	†Quintet in E, Op. 43 (1922)	Hansen, 1923
Nohr, C. F. 1800–75	Potpourri, Op. 3	Br. & H.
Normand, A.	Quintet in E, Op. 45	Vernède [1890?]; Baxter-Northrup
Novák, J. 1921–	†Concertino (1958)	CHF, 1959
Nowka, D. 1904–	Quintet (1955)	(Ve)
Nyman, U. 1879–	Arctic Suite (1934)	MS (R, T)
Olsen, S. 1903–	Quintet, Op. 35 (1945)	Lyche, 1950
Onslow, G. 1784–1853	†Quintet in F, Op. 81/3 (Ed. K. Redel)	Kistner, n.d. [1852?]; Br. & H.; M. & M. Leuckart, 1956
Oppel, R. 1878–1941	Serenade in F, Op. 30	MS (DMM)
Orlando, M. 1887–	Suite	(Gor)
	Interludio sinfonico	(Gor)
Osterc, S. 1895–1941	Quintet (1932)	MS (Ve)
Otten, L. 1924–	Quintet No. 2 (1954)	Donemus
	Movements	Donemus, 1967
Ottoson, D.	Suite	FST
Oubradous, F. 1903–	Fantaisie dialoguée	OL, 1949
	Symphonies et Danses d'après J. P. Rameau	Leduc, 1954
Paciorkiewicz, T.	Quintet (1951)	PWM
Palmer, R. 1915–	Quintet (1951)	Composer
Panufnik, A. 1914–	Quintet (1953)	PWM, 1954
Papineau-Couture, J. 1916–	†Fantaisie	CMC
Paribeni, G. C. 1881–1964	Suite in tre tempi	(Ve)
Parris, H. M.	Woodwind Miniatures	Elkan, 1956
Parris, R. 1924–	Sonatina	CFE
Parrott, I. 1916–	Quintet (1948)	MS (Ve)
Partos, O. 1907–	Nebulae	IMI, 1967
Passani, E. 1905–	Quintet	EMT

Pauer, J. 1919–	†Quintet (1960)	SHV, 1963
Pedersen, P. 1935–	Quintet	CMC
Peeters, E. 1893–	Quintet (1953)	SM
Pelemans, W. 1901–	†Quintet (1948)	Maurer, 1956
	Quintet No. 2	Metropolis
Peřina, H.	Quintet	(Ga)
1890–1964		
Perissas, M.	Scotch Suite	Andraud
Perle, G. 1915–	Quintet No. 1 (1959)	CFE
	Quintet No. 2	
Persichetti, V.	†Pastoral, Op. 21 (1945)	G. Schirmer, 1951
1915–		
Pessard, E. L. F.	Aubade in D, Op. 6	Leduc, 1880; CB
1843–1917		
	Prélude et Menuet du Capitaine	Leduc
	Fracasse	
Petríc, I.	Quintet No. 1	Društvo, 1964
Petrovics, E. 1930–	†Quintet	EMB, 1965
Petrželka, V. 1889–	Miniatury, Op. 54	MS (Ve)
Pfeiffer, G. J.	Pastorale	Andraud
1835–1908		
	Trois petites Pièces de Concert	Andraud
Picha, F.	Quintet, Op. 31 (1933–4)	MS (Ga, Ve)
1893–1964		
Pierce, E. H.	Short Quintet in B♭	Remick
b. 1868		
	Allegro piacevole & Scherzo	Remick
	In merry Mood	Gamble
	Romance	Pro Art, 1942
Pierné, G.	†Pastorale, Op. 14/1	Leduc [1887],
1863–1937		1939; CB
Pierné, P.	Suite pittoresque, Op. 14	Buffet-Crampon,
1874–1952		1936; Leduc
Pijper, W.	Quintet (1929)	Donemus, 1947
1894–1947		
Pilss, K. 1902–	Serenade	Doblinger, 1957
Pisk, P. 1893–	Quintet, Op. 96	CFE
Piston, W. 1894–	†Quintet (1956)	AMP, 1957
Placheta, H. 1892–	Divertimento, Op. 8	Doblinger, 1965
Poldini, E.	General Boom-Boom	Elkan
1869–1957		
Ponse, L. 1914–	Deux Pièces (1943)	Donemus
	Quintet, Op. 32 (1961)	Donemus, 1961
Poot, M. 1901–	Concertino (1959)	Leduc, 1965
Porsch, G.	Suite modique	Remick
Porter, Q.	Divertimento	Peters, 1962
1897–1966		
Powell, M. 1923–	†Divertimento (1956)	SPAM, 1957
Praag, H. van 1894–	Quintet No. 1 (1938)	Donemus
	Quintet No. 2 (1948)	Donemus, 1949
Quinet, M. 1915–	Eight short Pieces (1946)	CeBeDeM, 1956
	†Quintet (1949)	CeBeDeM, 1957
Rainier, P. 1903–	Six Pieces (1954)	Schott, 1963

Rajter, L. 1906–	Quintet (1946)	SHF
Randerson, H. E. 1892–	Quintet	Durand
Ránki, G. 1907–	†Pentaerophonia (1958)	ZV, 1960
Ranta, S. V. 1901–60	Quintet	MS? (Gor)
Rapoport, E. 1900–	Indian Legend	AMP, 1949
Rashanis, F.	Suite	RS, 1961
Rathaus, K. 1895–1954	Galante Serenade	Bo. & H., 1949, 1955
Read, G. 1913–	Scherzino, Op. 24 (1935)	Southern, 1953
Reicha, A. 1770–1836	Concertante (1817)	MS (MGG) (Cons, Paris)
	Six Quintets, Op. 88	J. & C.; Schott; Simrock
	†No. 1 in e	Andraud; Costallat
	†No. 2 in E♭ (Ed. G. Weigelt)	Leuckart, 1937
	†No. 3 in G (Ed. F. Kneusslin)	Kneusslin, 1956; Artia, 1965
	No. 4 in d	
	†No. 5 in B♭ (Ed. H. J. Seydel)	Leuckart, 1958
	No. 6 in F	
	Six Quintets, Op. 91	J. & C.; Schott; Simrock
	†No. 1 in C (Ed. F. Kneusslin)	Kneusslin, 1965
	No. 2 in a	
	†No. 3 in D (Ed. F. Kneusslin)	Kneusslin; Artia, 1965; Peters
	No. 4 in g	M. & M.
	†No. 5 in A	Artia, 1965; AMP; Kneusslin
	No. 6 in c	
	Six Quintets, Op. 99	J. & C.; Costallat; Simrock
	No. 1 in C	AMP
	†No. 2 in f	Musica Rara, 1966
	No. 3 in A	
	No. 4 in D	
	No. 5 in b♭	
	†No. 6 in G	
	Six Quintets, Op. 100	Paris, Composer; Costallat; Schott
	No. 1 in F	
	No. 2 in c	
	No. 3 in E	
	†No. 4 in e (Ed. F. Kneusslin)	Kneusslin, 1958; Peters; Mercury, 1947
	No. 5 in a	
	No. 6 in B♭	
	Introduction & Allegro	Mercury

Reichel, B. 1901–	Prélude, Passacaille et Postlude (1951)	MS (Ve)
Reinhold, O. 1899–	Quintet (1962)	Litolff, 1964
Reiter, A. 1905–	Musik	Doblinger, 1963
Reizenstein, F. 1911–	Quintet, Op. 5 (1934)	Bo. & H., 1937
Renzi, A.	Five Bagatelles	de Santis, 1949
Reuling, W. 1802–79	Quintets	Schott
Revueltas, S. 1899–1940	Second little serious Piece	Southern
Rey, D. R. 1904–	In 5/8 time (1934)	MS? (G, MGG)
Reynolds, R. 1934–	Gathering	Peters, 1964
Ridký, J. 1897–1956	Quintet, Op. 41 (1946)	Artia
Riegger, W. 1885–1961	Quintet, Op. 51	Ars Viva, 1952
Rieti, V. 1898–	Quintet (1957)	AMP, 1963
Rietz, J. 1812–77	Quintet	Hofmeister
Rüsager, K. 1897–	Quintet (1921)	(Ve)
	Quintet (1927)	(Ve)
Rinck, J. C. H. 1770–1846	Quintet	Cor
Ristic, M. 1908–	Quintet (1936)	(Ve)
Rötscher, K. 1910–	Quintet, Op. 41	B. & B., 1964
Rohozinsky, L. 1886–1938	Quintette pastorale	MS (Ve)
Roikjer, K. 1901–	Quintet, Op. 42	Skandinavisk, 1957
Romberg, A. J. 1767–1821	Eight Quintets	Rühle
Roos, R. de 1907–	Incontri	Donemus, 1967
Ropartz, J. G. 1864–1955	†Two Pieces	Durand, 1926
Rorich, C. 1869–1941	Quintet in e, Op. 58	Zimmermann, 1921
Rosenberg, H. 1892–	Quintet (1959)	FST
Rosenthal, L.	Commedia	Chappell, 1964
Rosetti, F. A. 1746–92	†Quintet in E♭	Kneusslin, 1961; Presser, 1962
Rosseau, N. 1907–	Quintet, Op. 54 (1955)	CeBeDeM, 1959
Rota, N. 1911–	Petite Offrande Musicale	Leduc, 1955
Rüdinger, G. 1886–1946	Divertimento, Op. 45	(Ve)
Ruyneman, D. 1886–1963	Quintet: The Nightingale	Donemus, 1949
	†Reflexions No. 4	Donemus, 1961
Rychlík, J. 1916–64	Quintet (1961)	SHV, 1964
Sabalyev, B. W.	Suite	RS, 1966
Sabatini, G.	Quintet	Camara
Sachse, H. W. 1899–	Quintet (1954)	(Ve)
Sachsse, H. 1891–1960	Bläsersuite in A, Op. 32	Böhm, 1935
Saikkola, L. 1906–	Divertimento (1952)	IGNM, 1954

A LIST OF MUSIC FOR THE HORN

Salmenhaara, E. 1941–	Quintet	Finnish Music Council
Salzedo, L. 1921–	Divertimento, Op. 40	London, Composer, 1955
Santa Cruz, D. 1899–	Quintet	Peer
Santoliquido, F. 1883–	Nocturne & Pastorale	Camara
Santoro, C. 1919–	Quintet (1942)	(Ve)
Sauter, E. 1928–	Dedicatto a Shinolo (1956)	New York, Composer
Scarmolin, A. L. 1890–	Badinage	
Schaefer, T. 1904–	Quintet, Op. 5 (1934–5)	Pazdirek, 1936
Schat, P. 1935–	†Improvizations & Symphonies	Donemus, 1960
Schatt, L.	Partita	Mannh. Musikverlag
Schelb, J. 1894–	Quintet	MS (MGG)
Schibler, A. 1920–	Kaleidoscop: Five Pieces, Op. 41	A. & S.
Schierbeck, P. 1888–1949	Capriccio, Op. 53 (1940–1)	Hansen, 1951
Schindler, G. 1921–	Divertimento notturno	Modern, 1957
Schiske, K. 1916–	Quintet, Op. 24 (1945)	Doblinger, 1959
Schlemm, G. A. 1902–	Quintet (1960)	Grosch [1963]
Schmid, H. K. 1874–1953	Quintet in B♭, Op. 28	Schott [1921]
Schmidek, K.	Sonatine, Op. 31	Doblinger, 1963
Schmitt, F. 1870–1958	Chants alizés, Op. 125 (1952–5)	Durand, 1955
Schmitt, N. fl. 1800	Three Quintets	Pleyel
Schmutz, A. D.	Scherzo poétique	CB, 1938
Schneider, H.	Quintet (1958)	(Ve)
Schoenberg, A. 1874–1951	†Quintet, Op. 26 (1924)	UE, 1925
Schönberg, S. G.	Litet Stycke	FST
Schouwman, H. 1902–	Nederlandse suite op motiven uit eeu 18e eeuwe liedboek, Op. 40b	Donemus
Schroeder, H. 1896–	Divertimento (1957)	Litolff
Schubert, H. 1908–45	Musik	Mannh. Musikverlag
Schuller, G. 1925–	†Suite (1945)	M. & M., 1957
	Quintet (1958)	AMP
Schultz, S. S. 1913–	†Une Amourette; petite Sérénade (1945)	Skandinavisk, 1954
Schwake, K. K. von 1890–	Quintet in F (1925)	MS (Ve)
Scott, A. C.	Suite: From the great smoky Mountains	Williams
Schwertsik, K. 1935–	Eichendorff Quintet (picc for fl)	UE
Search, F. P. 1889–	Chinese Dance	CFE
Sehlbach, E. 1898–	†Kortum-Serenade, Op. 30	Möseler, 1952
Seiber, M. 1904–60	†Permutazioni a cinque (1958)	Schott, 1959
Seidel, J. 1908–	Two Quintets	(Ve)

T

Serebrier, J. 1938–	Pequeña musica (1955)	Peer, 1961
Šesták, Z. 1925–	Cassation (1958)	(Ga)
	Concertino (1964)	(Ga)
Seter, M. 1916–	Diptique (ca for ob)	IMI, 1966
Shapey, R. 1921–	Movements	CFE
Shepherd, A. 1880–1958	Divertissement (1943)	MS (G, R)
Sherman, R. W. 1921–	†Quintet (1963)	(Schwann)
Shulman, A. 1915–	Folksongs (1943)	(Ewen)
Siegmeister, E. 1909–	Quintet (1932)	MS (R, T)
Skorzeny, F. 1900–65	Eine Nachtmusik	Doblinger
Slavenski, J. 1896–1955	Quintet (1930)	MS (Ve)
Smetácek, V. 1906–	Aus der Leben der Insekten (1932)	Continental, 1939
Smith Brindle, R. 1917–	Segments & Variants	Hinrichsen
Smith, L. C.	Quintet (1947–51)	MS (N.Y. Pub. Lib.)
Smith, R. 1927–	Fugue	CFE
Sobeck, J. 1831–1914	Quintet in F, Op. 9	B. & B., 1879
	Quintet in E♭, Op. 11	Bosworth [1891]; Belwin
	Quintet in g, Op. 14	Bosworth [1891]; Belwin
	Quintet in B♭, Op. 23	Lehne [1897]
Sodderland, J. 1903–	Quintet	Donemus
Sodero, C. 1886–1947	Valse Scherzo	AMP, 1933
	Morning Prayer	AMP, 1933
Sorrentino, C.	Beneath the covered Bridge	Mills, 1963
Souris, A. 1899–	Rengaines (1937)	Leduc, 1955
Sowerby, L. 1895–1968	Quintet (1916)	G. Schirmer, 1931
	†Pop goes the Weasel (1927)	Fitzsimons, 1930
Spies, L. 1899–	Sonata (1959)	(Ve)
Spisak, M. 1914–	Quintet (1948)	PWN
Sprongl, N. 1892–	Quintet, Op. 20	Doblinger
Šrámek, V. 1923–	Metra symmetrica	Composer, 1961
	Five Quintets (1951–61)	MS (Ve)
Staempfli, E. 1908–	Quintet (1934)	(Ve)
Stainer, C. fl. ca. 1900	Scherzo, Op. 27	RC, 1929; Bo. & H., 1955
	Improvisation, Op. 28	Schott
Stark, R. 1847–1922	Quintet, Op. 44	Oertel
Steel, C. 1939–	Divertimento (1964)	Novello, 1965
Steggall, R. 1867–1938	Quintet, Op. 21	MS? (DMM, T)
Stein, L. 1910–	Quintet (1937)	CFE
Stoker, R. 1938–	Quintet, Op. 6 (1963)	Hinrichsen
Stone, D. 1922–	Prelude & Scherzetto	Novello, 1956
Storp, S. H. 1914–	Chamber Music	Möseler, 1962

A LIST OF MUSIC FOR THE HORN

Stringfield, L. 1897–1959	A Moonshiner laughs (1934)	Baron, 1940
Strong, G. T. 1856–1948	Five Aquarelles	ESM, 1933
Strube, G. 1867–1953	Quintet (1930)	MS (H, Ho, R, T)
Suchoň, E. 1908–	Nocturne & Serenade, Op. 5 (1932)	SHF
Suter, H. 1870–1926	Quintet	(Ve)
Suter, R. 1919–	Four Etudes	Henn, 1962
Sweelinck, J. P. 1562–1611	†Variations on a Folksong (Arr. E. Lubin)	Bo. & H., 1965
Sydeman, W. 1928–	Quintet No. 2	M. & M., 1964
Szalowski, A. 1907–	Quintet (1954)	Omega, 1956
Székely, E. 1912–	Quintet (1952)	Mills, 1960
	Quintet No. 2 (1961)	EMB, 1965
Szelikowski, T. 1896–1963	Quintet (1950)	PWM, 1956
Szervánsky, E. 1911–	Quintet No. 1 (1951)	EMB, 1957
	Quintet No. 2 (1957)	EMB, 1960, 1966
Taffanel, P. 1844–1908	†Quintet in g	Leduc, 1878; IMC
Tahourdin, P.	Three Pieces	(Horn Realm)
Takács, J. 1902–	Eine kleine Tafelmusik, Op. 74	Doblinger, 1964
Tanenbaum, E. 1924–	Sonatina	CFE
	Quintet No. 2	CFE
Taylor, L.	Suite miniature in F	MPHC
Thierac, J. 1896–	Sonatina (ca. 1960)	(Ve)
Thatcher, H. R. 1878–	Quintet	(Horn Realm)
Thilman, J. P. 1906–	Quintet, Op. 44a	MV, 1951
Tichy, O. A. 1890–	Quintet	
Tiessen, H. 1887–	Kleine Schularbeit, Op. 43a	MS? (G)
	Divertimento, Op. 51 (1942)	Kistner, 1956
Toebosch, L. 1916–	Sarabande e Allegro, Op. 71	Donemus, 1959
Tomasi, H. 1901–	Quintet	Lemoine, 1952
	†Variations sur un Thème corse	Leduc, 1938
Trede, Y. T.	Le Chant des Oiseaux	Ugrino, 1959
Tremblay, G. 1911–	Two Quintets (1940)	CFE
Trexler, G. 1903–	Spitzweg Suite (1956)	Br. & H.
Trojan, V. 1907–	†Quintet on folksong Themes, Op. 8 (1937)	SNKLHU, 1956
	Quintet (1943)	MS (MGG)
Turechek, E.	Introduction & Scherzo	Witmark, 1933
Turner, R. 1920–	Serenade (1960)	CMC
Tuthill, B. C. 1888–	Sailor's Hornpipe, Op. 14/1 (1935)	C. Fischer, 1937
Uray, E. L. 1906–	Musik	Doblinger
Valen, F. 1887–1952	†Serenade, Op. 42 (1947)	Lyche, 1954
Van Hulse, C. 1897–	Quintet, Op. 3	Shawnee, 1963
Van Vactor, D. 1906–	†Scherzo	(Schwann)

Vaubourgoin, J. E. 1880–1952	Quintet	(Ve)
Veerhoff, C. H. 1926–	Quintet	B. & B., 1963
Velden, R. van der 1910–	Concerto No. 1 (1939)	Maurer
	†Second Concerto	Metropolis, 1957
Verrall, J. 1908–	Serenade (1944)	Music Press, 1947
	Serenade No. 2 (1954)	CFE
Villa-Lobos, H. 1887–1959	†Quintet en forme de Chôros (1928) (ca/hn)	Eschig, 1928, 1953
Vincze, I. 1926–	Divertimento	EMB, 1965
Vinter, G. 1909–	Two Miniatures	Bo. & H., 1950
Vlijmen, J. van 1935–	Quintetto (1960)	Donemus, 1960
Voss, F. 1930–	Capriccioso (1965)	Br. & H.
Vredenburg, M. 1904–	Au Pays des Vendanges: Suite brève (1951)	Donemus, 1955
Vuataz, R. 1898–	Musique, Op. 48	(Ve)
Wahlich, M.	Quintet	(Ve)
Ward, W. R. [1917–?]	Little Dance Suite	Mills, 1949
Washburn, R. 1928–	Suite	EV
Waterson, J.	Quintet in F	Lafleur, 1922
Weber, A. 1930–	Quintet	Leduc, 1956
Weber, L. 1891–1947	†Quintet (1923)	Möseler
Weigl, V.	Mood Sketches	M. & M.
Weis, F. 1898–	Serenade without serious Intentions	Hansen, 1941
Weiss, A. 1891–	Quintet (1932)	CFE
	Vade Mecum (1959) (thirty pieces in various combinations from duet to quintet)	MS (BMI)
Wellesz, E. 1885–	Suite, Op. 73	Sikorski, 1956
Weston, P. (A. de Filippi) 1900–	Arbeau Suite	Concord, 1942; Augener, 1962
Whettam, G. 1927–	Quintet, Op. 19	de Wolfe
White, D. H. 1921–	†3 for 5	Templeton, 1964
Whittenberg, C. 1927–	Quintet	MS (Ve)
Wijdeveld, W. 1910–	Quintet (1934)	Donemus
Wilder, A. 1907–	Quintet No. 1	MS? (B)
	†Quintet No. 2 (1956)	(Schwann)
	†Quintet No. 3	G. Schirmer, 1960
	†Quintet No. 4 (1958)	(Schwann)
	Quintet No. 5	
	†Quintet No. 6 (1960)	(Schwann)
	†Suite	(Schwann)
Wildschut, C. 1906–50	Kleine Serenade (1946)	Donemus

Wirth, H.	Kleine Clementiade	Sikorski, 1961
	Heiteres Spiel (1937)	H. & G., 1953
Wisse, J. 1921–	Epitaphium	Donemus, 1962
	Limitazioni No. 2 (1962)	Donemus, 1962
Woestijne, D.	Musique pour cinq instruments	CeBeDeM
van der 1915–		
Wolstenholme, W.	Quintet	(DMM)
1865–1931		
Wood, C. 1866–1926	Quintet in F	Bo. & H., 1933
Wood, T.	The Brewhouse at Bures:	Stainer, 1929
1892–1950	Scherzo	
Woollet, H.	Quintet	(Ve)
1864–1936		
Wuorinen, C. 1938–	Movement	Presser, 1963
Zafred, M. 1921–	Sinfonietta	Ricordi
Zagwijn, H.	Quintetto (1948)	Donemus
1878–1954		
Zaninelli, L. 1932–	†Dance Variations	Shawnee, 1962
Zelenka, I. 1936–	Chronologie (bcl for cl)	Composer
Zender, H. 1936–	Quintet, Op. 3 (1950)	B. & B., 1953
Zilcher, H.	Quintet, Op. 91	SM, 1894;
1881–1948		Zimmermann
Zillig, W. 1905–63	Lustspielsuite (1934)	BVK
Zipp, F. 1914–	Serenade	Möseler, 1964
Zoeller, C.	Quintet, in F, Op. 132	Cubitt [1883]
(L. Marteau)		
1840–89		

6.4.2. *Other Combinations*

Aber, G. late 18th	Eight Quintets	MS (Cons. Milan)
Cent.	(2 fl, 2 hn, bass)	
Abramsky, A.	Concertino	UE, 1929
1898–	(fl, cl, hn, bn, pf)	
Adolphus, M. 1913–	Elegy, Op. 81	CFE
	(cl, hn, vln, vla, vcl)	
Alexander Friedrich,	Quintet in C, Op. 25	Br. & H., 1939
Landgraf of	(hn, vln, vla, vcl, pf)	
Hesse 1863–1945		
Amon, J. A.	Two Quintets, Opp. 110, 118	André [1817?]
1763–1825	(fl, hn, vln, vla, vcl, db ad lib)	
	Serenade	(E*) (Deutsch.
	(fl, 2 hn, vln, hp)	St. Bib.,
		Berlin)
Arnold, M. 1921–	Quintet	Paterson, 1960
	(fl, hn, bn, vln, vla)	
Aspelmayr, F.	Partita in D	Leuckart, 1965
1728–86	(2 ob, 2 hn, bn)	
	Partita in F	Leuckart, 1965
	(2 ob, 2 hn, bn)	
Bach, C. P. E.	Two little Marches (Wq 187)	Parrhysius, 1941,
1714–88	(Ed. J. Lorenz)	1952
	(2 ob, 2 hn, bn)	

Bach, J. C. 1735–82	†Four Quintets (Ed. S. Sadie) (2 cl, 2 hn, bn)	Bo. & H., 1957
	Three Marches in E♭ (Ed. J. Wojciechowski) (2 ob, 2 hn, bn)	Sikorski, 1956
	†Sei Sinfonia (Ed. F. Stein) (2 cl, 2 hn, bn)	L. & B., n.d.; Hofmeister, 1957
Baptiste, L. A. F. 1700–ca. 1765	24 Menuettes nouveaux, Op. 1 (1750–55) (2 hn, 2 vln, bass)	MS (E*)
Barber, S. 1910–	Adventure (fl, cl, hn, hp, perc)	G. Schirmer, 1964
Barraud, H. 1900–	Concertino (fl, cl, hn, bn, pf)	SEMI, 1955
Baussnern, W. von 1866–1931	Quintet in F (cl, hn, vln, vcl, pf)	Siimrock, 1905
Beethoven, L. 1770–1827	†Quintet in E♭ (Ed. W. Hess) (ob, 2 hn, bn)	Schott, 1954
	†Quintet in E♭, Op. 16 (1797) (ob, cl, hn, bn, pf)	Mollo, 1801; Br. & H.; Litolff; RS; Eulenburg; I.M.C.; Musica Rara; Peters
Bennett, R. R. 1936–⎫ Maw, N. 1935– ⎬ & Williamson, M. 1931– ⎭	Reflections on a Theme of Benjamin Britten (Homage to Britten) (fl, hn, bn, vla, hp)	MS (MT, Oct. 1963)
Besozzi, C. b. ca. 1738	24 Sonatas (2 ob, 2 hn, bn)	MS (E*, G*)
Blanc, A. 1828–85	Quintet, Op. 37 (fl, cl, hn, bn, pf)	Costallat, n.d.
Blumenthal, P. b. 1843	Pastorale, Op. 101 (fl, hn, bln, vcl, org)	Bratfisch, n.d.
Böellman, L. 1862–97	Menuet gothique (ob, ca, cl, hn, bn)	Durand, n.d.
Böhner, J. L. 1787–1860	Variations, Op. 24 (hn, stg quart)	Schott, n.d.
Brendner, 18th Cent.	Partita No. 1 (ob, hn, vln, vla d'am, bass)	(E)
Brubeck, H. 1916–	Incidental Music to Ibsen's 'Lady from the Sea' (fl, cl, hn, trp, vcl)	Derry
Büchler	Concerto (fl, hn, 2 vln, hpcd)	MS (Univ of Rostock)
Bulling, B. 1881–	Quintet (ca. 1937) (fl, hn, vln, vla, vcl)	MS (Z.f.M., 1939)
Burgstaller, A.	Quintet (ca. 1939) (ob, cl, hn, bn, pf)	MS (Z.f.M., 1939)
Bush, A. 1900–	Five Pieces (1926) (cl, hn, vln, vla, vcl)	MS (G, MGG)

Cannabich, M. F. 1723–58	Menuetto (fl, 2 hn, 2 vln)	MS (Rie)
Carcani, G. b. ca. 1703	Quintetto ex G (2 fl, 2 hn, bass)	MS (E*) (LB, Karlsruhe)
Cherubini, L. 1760–1842	Sonata (hn, stg quart)	Sikorski
Cooke, A. 1906–	Arioso & Scherzo (1955) (hn, vln, 2 vla, vcl)	MS
Corder, P. 1879–1942	Prelude (1923) (ob, hn, vln, vcl, hp)	MS (MT, 1923)
Danzi, F. 1763–1826	Quintet in d, Op. 41 (ob, cl, hn, bn, pf)	Br. & H., n.d.; Broekmans; 1962; G. Schirmer, n.d.; Musica Rara, 1961
Dauprat, L. F. 1781–1868	Trois Quintetti, Op. 6 (hn, stg quart)	Schoenenberger, n.d.; Zetter; Lemoine
Desderi, E. 1892–	Suite (ob, cl, hn, bn, pf)	MS? (MGG)
Dijk, J. van 1918–	Chorales (1962) (fl, cl, hn, bn, trp)	Donemus
Dittersdorf, K. 1739–99	†Three Partitas in F, A, D (Nos. 2, 4, 20) (Ed. G. Rhau) (2 ob, 2 hn, bn)	Br. & H., 1948
	†Partita in D, No. 20 (Ed. K. Haas) (2 ob, 2 hn, bn)	Musica Rara, 1958
	Cassatio (Krebs 134) (2 hn, vln, vla, bass)	Paris, 1776
	Parthia (Krebs 136) (2 ob, 2 hn, bn)	MS?
	Parthia in B♭ (2 ob, 2 hn, bn)	MS? (MGG)
	Notturno (2 hn, vln, vla, bass)	MS? (E*)
Domansky, A. 1897–	Quintet No. 1 (fl, 2 cl, hn, bn)	C. Schmidt, 1927
	Quintet No. 2 (fl, 2 cl, hn, bn)	C. Schmidt, 1936
Dominique, F. X.	Serenata (2 hn, 2 vln, bass)	MS (E*)
Doppler, F. 1821–83	L'Oiseau des Bois, Op. 21 (fl, 4 hn)	Schott
Dornaus, L. fl. 1800	Six petites Pièces, Op. 2 (2 cl, 2 hn, bn)	[Andre?], n.d.
Draeseke, F. A. 1835–1913	Quintet in B♭, Op. 45 (hn, vln, vla, vcl, pf)	Kistner, n.d. [1889?]
Duncan, W. E. 1866–1920	Quintet, Op. 38 (fl, cl, hn, bn, pf)	RC, 1898, 1920
Dunhill, T. F. 1877–1946	Quintet in E♭, Op. 3 (1913) (cl, hn, vln, vcl, pf)	RC, 1914; Bo. & H.

	Quintet in f	MS? (G)
Dusek, F. X.	(hn, stgs)	
1731–99	†Parthia in F	SNKLHU, 1958
Duvernoy, F.	(2 ob, 2 hn, bn)	
1765–1838	Three Quintets	(F)
Eberwein, C.	(hn, stg quart)	
1786–1868	Concerto, Op. 15	MS? (MGG)
Ebner	(fl, hn, vln, vcl, pf)	
	Adagio	Haslinger
Eichner, E.	(fl, 2 hn, bn, vln)	
1740–77	Two Divertissements	Paris, 1780
Eisma, W.	(2 cl, 2 hn, bn)	
1929–	Sonata	Donemus
Emmert, A. J.	(cl, hn, vln, vla, vcl)	
	Harmonien	Salzburg, Duyle,
Eybler, J. L.	(2 fl, 2 hn, bn)	1804
1765–1846	Five Minuets with Trios	MS (MGG)
Fähs	(2 fl, 2 ob, hn)	
18th Cent.	Concerto à 5	MS (E*)
Feldman, M. 1926–	(hn, 2 vln, vla, cont)	
	de Kooning	Peters
Fibich, Z.	(hn, vln, vcl, pf, perc)	
1850–1900	Quintet in D, Op. 42 (1892)	Urbánek, 1894
Fiorello, D. 1905–	(cl, hn, vln, vcl, pf)	
	Quintet	(Ho)
Fiorillo, F.	(hn, stg quart)	
1755–ca. 1824	Quintet	Sieber
Frid, G. 1904–	(fl, hn, vln, vla, vcl)	
	Sérénade, Op. 4 (1928)	Donemus, 1949
Froelich, F. T.	(fl, 2 cl, hn, bn)	
1803–36	Quintet (1833)	MS (MGG)
Frugatta, G.	(2 hn, 2 vln, pf)	
1860–1933	Quintetto (1899)	MS? (MGG)
Gassmann, F.	(cl, hn, vln, vcl, pf)	
1729–74	Partita (Ed. W. Höckner)	Doblinger
Gieseking, W.	(2 cl, 2 hn, bn)	
1895–1956	Quintet in B♭ (1920)	Fürstner, 1923
Gilbert, A.	(ob, cl, hn, bn, pf)	
	Nine or ten Osannas	(Times, 22 Nov.,
	(cl, hn, vln, vcl, pf)	1967)
Glazounov, A.	Idyll	RS, 1960; Cor,
1865–1936	(hn, stg quart)	1963
Glinka, M. I.	Serenade on Themes from	Jurgenson
1803–57	Donizetti's 'Anna Bolena'	
	(1832)	
Golabek, J.	Partita	PWM
1739–89	(2 cl, 2 hn, bn)	
Grimm, C.	Potpourri	Schott, n.d.
1819–88	(hn, stg quart)	
Grund, F. W.	Quintet in E♭, Op. 8	Peters, n.d.
1791–1874	(ob, cl, hn, bn, pf)	
Gyrowetz, A.	Two Serenades, Op. 3	Imbault, n.d.
1763–1858	(2 cl, 2 hn, bn)	

Häser, A. F. 1779–1844	Ollapotrida (fl, cl, hn, bn, pf)	Peters
Hamm, J. V.	Viergesprache (fl, ob, cl, hn, pf)	Schott
Handel, G. F. 1685–1759	†Two Arias (Ed. K. Haas) (2 ob, 2 hn, bn)	Musica Rara, 1958
Harris, R. 1898–	Quintet (1932) (fl, ob, hn, bn, pf)	MS? (H, Ho, R, T)
Hauff, W. G. ca. 1755–1807	Quintet (Ed. K. Weelink) (hn, stg quart)	KaWe
Haydn, J. 1732–1809	†Divertimento = Sonata No. 4 in E♭, Hob. XIV, 1	MV, 1953
	(Ed. K. Janetzky) (2 hn, vln, vcl, hpcd) Cassation, Hob. II, D 1 (2 hn, vln, vla, bass) Cassation, Hob. II, D 2 (2 hn, vln, vla, vcl) Cassation, Hob. II, F 4 (2 hn, vln, vla, bass) Cassation, Hob. II, F 5 (2 hn, vln, vla, bass) Cassation, Hob. II, D 18 (2 hn, 2 vln, vcl) Divertimento, Hob. X, 10 (baryton, 2 hn, vla, bass)	Peters, 1963
Haydn, M. 1737–1806	Quintet in E♭ (1790) (Ed. Balassa) (cl, hn, bn, vln, vla)	EMB, 1960
	Divertimento in G (Ed. L. H. Perger) (fl, hn, bn, vln, vla)	Artaria, 1907
	(Ed. A. Strassl) Romance (hn, stg quart)	Doblinger BAI, 1802
Heiden, B. 1910–	Quintet (1952) (hn, stg quart)	AMP, 1956
Herzogenberg, H. 1843–1900	Quintet in E♭, Op. 43 (ob, cl, hn, bn, pf)	Peters [1888]
Hirschbach, H. 1812–88	Quintet in B♭, Op. 40 (cl, hn, vln, vla, vcl)	K. & S., 1856
	Quintet in E♭, Op. 48 (cl, hn, vln, vla, vcl)	K. & S., 1859
Hoffmeister, F. A. 1754–1812	Serenade, Op. 9 (fl, 2 hn, vla, bass)	J. Hummel, n.d.
	Quintet in E♭ (Ed. H. Steinbeck) (hn, stg quart) (Ed. E. Leloir)	Doblinger, 1963 Simrock, 1964 MS (E*)
	Notturno in D (ob, hn, bn, 2 vln)	
	Six Quintets (fl, hn, 2 vla, bass)	Paris, Holtzapfel

Hopkins, A. 1921–	Babar the little Elephant (reciter, hn, pf, 2 perc)	(BBC, Dec. 1966)
Huber, H. 1852–1921	Quintet, Op. 136 (fl, cl, hn, bn, pf)	Hug, 1920
Hüttel, J. 1893–	Divertimento grotesque (ob, cl, hn, bn, pf)	MS (N.Y. Lib. of Congress)
Hummel, F. 1855–1928	Nocturne, Op. 42 (hn, vln, vcl, hp, org)	Siegel, 1885
Hurlstone, W. Y. 1876–1906	Quintet (1904) (fl, ob, hn, bn, pf)	MS (G, MGG)
Hyde, G.	Quintet (hn, stg quart)	Camara
Ives, C. 1874–1954	Scherzo: All the Way around and back (1908) (cl/hn, vln, pf duet, bells)	Peer, 1953
	The Seer (1913) (cl, ct/trp, alto hn, drums, pf)	MS (Cowell)
Jachino, C. 1887–	Quintet (1956) (cl, hn, vln, vla, vcl)	MS (MGG)
Jadin, L. E. 1768–1853	Trois Quintettes concertantes (fl, ob, hn, bn, pf)	Janet, n.d.
Jongen, L. 1884–	Quintuor (1958) (fl, cl, hn, bn, pf)	CeBeDeM
Kahn, R. 1865–1951	Quintet in c, Op. 54 (cl, hn, vln, vcl, pf)	B. & B., 1910
Kalkbrenner, F. 1788–1849	Quintet in a, Op. 81 (cl, hn, vcl, db, pf)	Br. & H., n.d.
Kaminski, H. 1886–1946	Quintet in f♯ (1924) (cl, hn, vln, vla, vcl)	UE, 1924
Karg-Elert, S. 1877–1933	Quintet in c, Op. 30 (1904) (ob, 2 cl, hn, bn)	Kahnt, 1911
Klička, J. 1855–1937	Hudební žert alla Haydn (fl, hn, vln, vcl, hp)	MS? (MGG)
Knorr, B. Freiherr von, late 18th Cent.	Quintetto (fl, ca, 2 hn, bn)	MS? (E*) (Musikfr., Vienna)
Koczwara, F. ca. 1750–91	Three Serenades, Op. 1 (2 hn, vln, vla, vcl)	J. Hummel [ca. 1775]
	Sonata (2 hn, 2 vla, vcl)	Thompson [ca. 1775]
Konvalinka, K. 1885–	Divertimento, Op. 23 (1928) (fl, cl, hn, bn, trp)	(Ga)
Kosá, G. 1897–	Quintet (1938) (fl, cl, hn, bn, hp)	MS (G, MGG)
Koželuch, L. A. 1747–1818	Quintet, Op. 11 (fl, hn, vln, vla, vcl)	André, n.d.
	Serenata in E♭ (fl, hn, vln, vla, vcl/bn)	(MGG*) (Herzogl. Bib., Wolfenbüttel)
Kreuz, E. 1867–1932	Quintet in E♭, Op. 49 (hn, stg quart)	Schott, 1901
Křička, J. 1882–	Concertino in F, Op. 102 (1951) (hn, stg quart)	SHV, 1962

Küffner, J. 1777–1856	Pièces d'harmonie, Op. 40 (Two for fl, 2 cl, hn, bn, one for fl, cl, basset hn, hn, bn)	Schott
	Quintetto, Op. 66 (hn, vln, 2 vla, vcl)	Schott [ca. 1818]
	Pièce d'harmonie, Op. 92 (fl, 2 cl, hn, bn)	Schott
	Quintett (fl, cl, basset hn, hn, bn)	MS (AmZ, 1816)
Lange, H. 1882–	Serenade, Op. 69 (fl, ca, hn, vla, db)	Berlin, Composer
Lannoy, H. E. J. 1787–1853	Quintet, Op. 2 (ob, cl, hn, bn, pf)	André [184?]
Lees B. 1924–	Three Variables (ob, cl, hn, bn, pf)	Bo. & H. 1964
Leplin, E. 1917–	Meditation (1946) (hn, stg quart)	MS (BMI)
Leslie, H. 1822–96	Quintet in g (ob, cl, hn, bn, pf)	MS? (F)
Lessel, F. 1780–1835	Quintet (hn, vln, vla, vcl, db)	Simrock
Linde, B. 1933–	Musica per sylvanum (fl, hn, bn, vln, xyl)	FST
Lindpaintner, P. J. 1791–1856	Adagio & Rondo (hn, stg quart)	MS (AmZ, 18)
Malzat, I. 1757–1804	Parthia in E♭ (2 cl, 2 hn, bn)	MS (MGG)
Mansuy, F. C. 1783–1847	Grand Quintet (hn, vln, vla, vcl, pf)	Pacini, n.d.
Marescalchi, L. b. 1745	Dodici Contraddanze, Op. 11 (2 hn, 2 vln, bc)	Zatta
Masék, V. 1755–1831	Notturno (2 ob, 2 hn, bn)	Artia
	Parthien in B♭, C, c, F & C (2 cl, 2 hn, bn)	MS? (MGG)
Maštalíř, J. 1906–	Quintet (1944) (hn, stg quart)	MS (Ga)
Maw, N. 1935–	Chamber Music (1962) (ob, cl, hn, bn, pf)	Chester, 1964
Mazzinghi, J. 1765–1844	Three Sonatas, Op. 30 (fl, 2 hn, vln, hp/pf)	London, Goulding, Phipps & D'Almaine, 1800
Milner, A. 1925–	Concertino da camera (cl, hn, trp, vcl, db)	MS
Molter, J. M. ca. 1695–1765	Concertino à 5 (2 fl, 2 hn, vcl)	MS (E*) (LB, Karlsruhe)
	Sonata (2 chalumeaux, 2 hn, bn)	MS (E*, MGG*)
Mozart, W. A. 1756–91	†Quintet in E♭, K. 407 (1782) (hn, vln, 2 vla, vcl)	Schmiedt & Rau [ca. 1796] André [ca. 1802], 1855; Litolff, 1870;

†Quintet in E♭, K. 452 (1786)
(ob, cl, hn, bn, pf)

Br. & H., 1883;
Eulenburg;
Peters; I.M.C.;
DVfM; AMP;
BVK; Musica
Rara;
Hinrichsen
Gombart [1800];
Richault;
André [1855];
Litolff [1866];
Eulenburg;
Br. & H., 1956;
Musica Rara;
IMC; RS;
BVK, 1958

Newson, G. 1932–	Quintet (1963) (fl, bcl, hn, bn, trp)	UE
Nielsen, C. 1865–1931	†Serenata in vano (1914) (cl, hn, bn, vcl, db)	Skandinavisk, 1942, 1955
Niewiadomski, S. 1859–1936	Flibbertigibbet (2 cl, 2 hn, db)	PWM
Nisle, J. F. 1768–ca. 1837	Quintet, Op. 26 (fl, hn, vln, vla, vcl)	Haslinger
	Quintet (fl, 2 hn, vln, vla)	IC
Novák, J. F. 1913–	Quintet (1952) (hn, stg quart)	(Ga)
Ordoñez, C. d' 1734–86	Cassationa terza (2 hn, vln, vla, bass)	Paris, n.d.
Papineau-Couture, J. 1916–	Suite (1947) (fl, cl, hn, bn, pf)	CMC
Pauer, E. 1826–1905	Quintet in F, Op. 44 (ob, cl, hn, bn, pf)	Schott [1856]
Pechazec, F. 1793–1840	Twelve Ländler (2 cl, 2 hn, bn)	Reitmayr, 1801
Pfeiffer, G. 1697–1761	Sonata in G (fl, ob, hn, bn, hpcd) (Ed. R. Lauschmann)	Hofmeister [1939] Hofmeister, 1951
Pichl, W. 1741–1804	Harmonie (2 cl, 2 hn, bn)	MS (E*)
Piticchio, F. fl. 1760	Quintet (2 ob, 2 hn, bn)	MS (E*, MGG*)
Piticchio, P. P. fl. 1780	Fifteen Quintets (2 ob, 2 hn, bn)	MS (F)
Presser, W. 1916–	Passacaglia (cl, hn, vln, vla, vcl)	CP, 1950
Ranki, G. 1907–	Quintet (1929) (ob, cl, hn, bn, pf)	MS (MGG)
Rawsthorne, A. 1905–	Quintet (ob, cl, hn, bn, pf)	OUP, 1964
Regner, H.	Eine kleine Waldmusik (ob, cl, 2 hn, bn)	Möseler, 1960

Reicha, A.	Quintet in E, Op. 106	Paris, Composer;
1770–1836	(hn, stg quart, db ad lib)	Br. & H; Cor
	Trois Andantes	MS (MGG)
	(fl, ca, cl, hn, bn)	(Cons. Paris)
Reichardt, J. F.	Quintet, Op. 2	Sieber
1752–1814	(2 fl, 2 hn, pf)	
	Quintet	
	(ob, 2 hn, bn, pf)	
Reid, J. (General)	A second Set of six Solos	Bremner, 1778
1721–1807	(2 cl, 2 hn, bn)	
Rice, N. H.	Quintet in B♭, Op. 2	Simrock, 1898
	(ob, cl, hn, bn, pf)	
Rimsky-Korsakov,	†Quintet in B♭ (1876)	Belaieff, 1911;
N. 1844–1908)	(fl, cl, hn, bn, pf)	IMC
Ristori, G. A.	Sinfonia in F (1736)	MS (MGG*)
1692–1753	(hn, 2 vln, vla, bass)	
Röntgen, J.	Quintet	MS (Gem. Mus.,
1855–1932	(fl, ob, cl, hn, pf)	The Hague)
Rolla, A. 1757–1841	2 Monferine	MS (E)
	(picc, cl, hn, bn, vln)	
Ron, J. M. de	Quintet, Op. 1	Br. & H. [ca. 1816]
1789–1817	(fl, cl, hn, bn, pf)	
Rosetti, F. A.	Notturno in D (Ed. V.	Artia, 1957
1750–92	Belsky)	(MAB, 32)
	(fl, hn, vln, vla, vcl)	
	Quintet	Sieber
	(fl, hn, vln, vla, vcl)	
Rubinstein, A.	Quintet in F, Op. 55	Schuberth;
1829–94	(fl, cl, hn, bn, pf)	Hamelle, n.d.
		[1861]
Rummel, C.	Quintet, Op. 41	Schott
1787–1849	(ob, cl, basset hn, hn, bn)	
Ruyneman, D.	Divertimento (1927)	Chester, 1928
1886–1963	(fl, cl, hn, vla, pf)	
Sammartini, G. B.	Concertino	MS (E*)
1701–75	(2 ob, 2 hn, bn)	
Sayve, A. de	Grand Quintetto	Falter [ca. 1821]
	(fl, cl, hn, bn, pf)	
Schacht, T.	Quintet	MS (MGG*)
1748–1823	(ob, hn, vln, vla, vcl)	
Schäfer, K. H. 1899–	Quintet	(Ve)
	(fl, hn, vln, vla, vcl)	
Schuller, G. 1925–	Perpetuum mobile (1949)	MS (Horn
	(4 hn, bn/tuba)	Realm)
Schumann, R.	†Andante & Variations in	Br. & H.
1810–56	B♭, Op.46 (1843)	
	(hn, 2 vcl, 2 pf)	
Seiff, G.	Six Pièces d'harmonie	Br. & H., [ca.
	(2 cl, 2 hn, bn)	1816]
Shapey, R. 1921–	De Profundis	Leeds
	(fl, ob, cl, hn, solo db)	
Shrifrin, S. 1926–	†Serenade (1955)	Litolff, 1958
	(ob, cl, hn, vla, pf)	

Sinigaglia, L. 1868–1944	Romance, Op. 3 (hn, stg quart)	Ricordi [ca. 1903]
Sperger, J. d. 1812	Notturno (2 hn, bn, 2 vla)	MS (E*)
Spindler, F. 1817–1905	Quintet, Op. 2 (?) (ob, cl, hn, bn, pf)	Leuckart
	Quintet in F, Op. 360 (ob, cl, hn, bn, pf)	Leuckart, 1888
Spohr, L. 1784–1859	Grand Quintuor in c, Op. 52 (1820) (fl, cl, hn, bn, pf) (Ed. Schmitz)	Peters [1821] Br. & H. BVK, 1950
Staden, J. 1581–1634	Venus Kräntzlein (Ed. A. Bonsel) (fl, ob, ca, cl, hn)	de Wolfe
Stamitz, K. 1745–1801	†Quintet in E♭ (ob, hn, bn, 2 vla)	(Schwann)
	Quintet, Op. 11/1 (ob, hn, 2 vla, bass)	Heina
	Quintet, Op. 11/2 (ob, hn, 2 vla, bass)	Heina
	Quintet, Op. 11/3 (ob, hn, 2 vla, bass)	Heina
	Quintet, Op. 13/1 (ob, hn, 2 vla, bass)	MS
	Quatre Sérénades, Op. 28 (2 fl, 2 hn, bn)	B. Hummel
	Twelve Serenades, Op. 28 (2 fl, 2 hn, bn)	Sikorski
Steffani, J. ca. 1736–1819	Six Parties, Op. 1 (2 cl, 2 hn, bn)	J. Hummel
Stephen, D. 1869–1946	Quintet in d, Op. 3 (fl, cl, hn, bn, pf]	Br. & H. [1899]
Stich, J. W. (Punto, G.) 1746–1803	Quintet (fl, hn, vln, vla, vcl)	Sieber [c. 1789]
Stölzel, G. H. 1690–1749	Sonata in F (Ed. G. Hausswald) (ob, hn, vln, vcl, hpcd)	Br. & H., 1952
Strauss, R. 1864–1949	Till Eulenspiegel einmal anders (Arr. W. Hasenöhrl) (cl, hn, bn, vln, db)	Peters
Strong, G. T. 1856–1948	Quintet (hn, stg quart)	MS? (H, T)
Tadolini, G. 1793–1872	Gran Quintetto in D (fl, ob, hn, bn, pf)	(MGG)
Taubert, E. E. 1838–1934	Quintet in B♭, Op. 48 (fl, cl, hn, bn, pf)	B. & B., 1892
Telemann, G. P. 1681–1767	†Zwei Ouvertüren-Suite (1733) (Ed. J. Hinnenthal) (2 ob, 2 hn, bn)	Leuckart, 1937
	Suite in F (Ed. H. Büttner) (2 hn, 2 vln, vcl)	Eulenburg [ca. 1939]
Theuss, K. T. b. 1785	Serenade, Op. 21 (fl, cl, 2 hn, bn)	Gombart
Thieriot, F. 1838–1919	Quintet in a, Op. 80 (ob, cl, hn, bn, pf)	Senff [ca. 1903]

Thomson, V. 1896–	†Sonata da chiesa (1925) (cl, hn, trp, trb, vla)	NME, 1944
Uber, A. 1783–1824	Variations sur la Cavatine 'Mir leuchtet die Hoffnung' (hn, stg quart)	André, n.d.
Uber, C. B. 1746–1812	Quintetto : Sonate a 5 voix (2 hn, vln, bass, hpcd)	Br. & H. [ca. 1772]
	Nine Divertimenti (2 hn, vln, bass, hpcd)	(T)
Vallentin, A. 1906–	Quintet in G, Op. 30 (ob, cl, 2 hn, bn)	Duisberg, Composer, 1941
Vaňhal, J. K. 1739–1813	Three capital Quintets (2 hn, vln, vla, bass)	London, Babb [1780?]
	Cassatio in G (2 hn, vln, vla, vcl)	MS (MGG*)
	Cassatio in E (2 hn, vln, vla, vcl)	MS (MGG*)
	Cassatio in D (fl, 2 hn, vla, bass)	MS (MGG*)
Verhey, T. H. H. 1848–1929	Quintet in E♭, Op. 20 (ob, cl, hn, bn, pf)	Br. & H., 1884
Villers, H. L. M. 1780–1855	Quintet, Op. posth. (ob, hn, db, hp, pf)	Chatot, 1863
Volbach, F. 1861–1942	Quintet in E♭, Op. 20 (ob, cl, hn, bn, pf)	Br. & H., 1884
	Quintet in E♭, Op. 24 (1901) (ob, cl, hn, bn, pf)	Br. & H., 1902
Walker, E. 1870–1949	Quintet in b♭ (1900) (hn, stg quart)	MS (DMM, G. T)
Wangermann, F. L.	Pièces d'harmonie, Op. 3 (fl, ob, basset hn, hn, bn)	Schott
Widerkehr, J. C. M. 1739–1823	Six Quintets (fl, cl, hn, bn, pf)	Janet
Wilder, A. 1907–	Quintet (1960) (hn, stg quart)	(Ho)
Witt, F. 1770–1837	Quintet, Op. 6 (ob, cl, hn, bn, pf)	Br. & H.
Wolf, F. X. late 18th Cent.	Two Quintets (2 cl, 2 hn, bn)	Huläufer
Wood, H. 1932–	Quintet (cl, hn, vln, vcl, pf)	(Cheltenham, 1967)
Woollett, H. 1864–1936	Cinq Pièces (2 fl, cl, hn, pf)	MS? (H)
Zwiesel, J. D.	Quintet (fl, cl, hn, bn, pf)	Schwaab

6.5 *Six instruments*

Achron, J. 1886–1943	Sextet, Op. 73 (wind quint, trp)	NME, 1942
Addison, J. 1920–	Serenade (1957) (wind quint, hp)	OUP, 1958

Alary, G. 1850–1929	Sextet (wind quint, pf)	Durdilly
Albert, K. 1901–	Werkstuk (wind quint, vla)	(WWM)
Allers, H. G.	Suite (fl, ob, cl, 2 hn, bn)	Möseler, 1964
Alter, M. 1904–	Sextet (1933) (wind quint, trp)	MS (R)
Altman, E.	Kleine Tanz-Suite nach Tänzen einen alten Sonderhäuser Tanzbuch (ca. 1800) (fl, ob, cl, 2 hn, bn)	Hofmeister
Amy, G. 1936–	Alpha-Beth (wind quint, bcl)	Heugel
Andersen, A. J. 1845–1926	Adagio (2 hn, 3 vcl, db)	MS? (G)
Andriessen, J. 1925–	L'Incontro di Cesare e Cleopatre (1956) (wind quint, pf)	Donemus
Arrieu, C. 1903–	Concert (wind quint, pf)	Ricordi, 1964
Bach, J. C. 1735–82	†Sextet in C, Op. 3 (ob, 2 hn, vln, vcl, hpcd)	André, n.d.; Musica Rara
Bach, W. F. E. 1759–1845	†Sextet in E♭ (cl, 2 hn, vln, vla, vcl)	MV, 1951; Peters, 1954
Badings, H. 1907–	Sextet (1952) (wind quint, pf)	Donemus, 1957
Barrows, J. R. 1913–	Variations (1935) (hn, 5 stgs)	(G, R)
Bean, C.	Sextet (1956) (fl, ob, hn, trp, trb, tuba)	MS (Composer) (Univ. of Illinois, Urbana, Ill., U.S.A.)
Beethoven, L. van 1770–1827	†Sextet in E♭, Op. 71 (2 cl, 2 hn, 2 bn) †Sextet in E♭, Op. 81b (2 hn, stg quart)	Br. & H., 1810, 1956; IMC Simrock, 1810; Peters, 1956; Br. & H., 1956; Litolff; IMC; Eulenburg
	†March in B♭ (2 cl, 2 hn, 2 bn) Minuet & March (2 cl, 2 hn, 2 bn)	Br. & H., 1864, 1888 Marks, 1948
Béreau, J. S.	Sextuor (wind quint, hp)	Choudens, 1964
Berkeley, L. 1903–	Sextet, Op. 47 (cl, hn, stg quart)	Chester, 1957
Blumer, T. 1882–1964	Sextett, Original-Thema mit Veränderungen, Op. 45 (wind quint, pf)	Simrock, 1922

	Sextet (Kammersymphonie), Op. 92	R. & E.
	(wind quint, pf)	
Boccherini, L.	Sextet in E♭, Op. 42/1	Pleyel [ca. 1797]
1743–1805	(hn, 2 vln, vla, 2 vcl)	
	(Ed. P. Bormann)	Sikorski, 1954
	(Ed. K. Janetzky)	Br. & H., 1954; IMC
	†Sextet in E♭, Op. 42/2	Pleyel [ca. 1797]
	(ob, hn, bn, vln, vla, db)	
	(Ed. P. Bormann)	Sikorski, 1957
	(Ed. K. Haas)	Novello, 1961; IMC
Boeck, I. b. 1754 and Boeck, A. b. 1757	Sextet in F, Op. 7 (2 hn, stg quart)	Br. & H., n.d. [ca. 1803]
	Sextet in E, Op. 8 (2 hn, stg quart)	Br. & H., n.d. [ca. 1803]
Boisdeffre, R. de 1838–1906	Scherzo, Op. 49 (wind quint, pf, db ad lib)	Hamelle, 1894
Bolzoni, G. 1841–1919	Un Corno inopportuno (hn, stg quart, db)	Ricordi, 1907
	Sextet (ob, 2 cl, hn, 2 bn)	(DMM)
Bossi, R. 1883–1965	Tema variata, Op. 10a [wind quint, trp]	Böhm [1939]
Brandl, J. 1760–1837	Sextet, Op. 16 (hn, bn, vln, 2 vla, vcl)	Offenbach [Andre?] 1799
Brauer, M. 1855–1918	Sextet in C (wind quint, pf)	Br. & H., 1920; AMP
Brehme, H. 1904–57	Sextet (1935) (fl, cl, hn, vln, vla, vcl)	(Ve)
Brescia, D.	Suite (1928) (wind quint, pf)	MS (Copy in Lib. of Congress)
Breton, T. 1850–1923	Sextet (wind quint, pf)	UME [ca. 1900]
Bruneau, E.	Sextet in C (wind quint, pf)	Schneider, 1904
Bullerian, H. 1885–	Sextet in G♭, Op. 38 (wind quint, pf)	Simrock, 1924
Bumcke, G. b. 1876	Sextet in A, Op. 19 (ca, cl, bcl, sax, hn, bn)	E. & R., 1908; Saturn
Cadow, P. 1923–	Pastorale in alten Stil (2 ob, ca, hn, 2 bn)	Ultraton [1953]
Carrillo, J. 1875–1965	Fantasia sonido 13 (1925) (picc, hn, vln, vcl, gt, hp)	(G, Slo)
Casadesus, R. 1899–	Sextet, Op. 58 (wind quint, pf)	Durand, 1961
Choulet, C.	Sextet, Op. 18 (fl, ob, hn, vln, vla, vcl)	Costallat, 1845
Chou Wen-Chung 1923–	Suite (1951) (wind quint, hp)	Peters, 1962
Cohn, J. 1910–	Sextet (fl/picc, ob, cl, hn, bn, pf)	MS (Copy in Lib. of Congress)

Colomer, B. M.	Caprice moldave	(Ve)
	(wind quint, pf)	
Crawford-Seeger, R.	Suite (1928)	MS (R, T)
1901–53	(wind quint, pf)	
Crosse, G. 1938–	Canto, Op. 4 (1961; rev. 1963)	OUP
	(wind quint, trb)	
Cruft, A. 1921–	Dance Movement (Ballabile) from	Elkin, 1964
	Divertissement, Op. 28	
	(wind quint, pf)	
Dale-Miller, R.	Three American Dances, Op. 25	C. Fischer, 1949
	(wind quint, pf)	
Danzi, F. 1763–1826	Sextet in E♭, Op. 10	Schott, n.d.
	(2 hn, stg quart)	
	Sextet, Op. 15	Falter, n.d.
	(2 hn, stg quart)	
David, J. N. 1895–	Kume, kum, Geselle min:	Br. & H., 1940
	Divertimento, Op. 24	
	(wind quint, pf)	
Deshayes, P. D.	Première Suite d'harmonie	PIC
ca. 1760–ca. 1820	(2 cl, 2 hn, 2 bn)	
Desportes, Y. 1907–	Prelude & Pastorale	Andraud
	(wind quint, pf)	
Devasini, G.	Sextet	Ricordi, 1843
	(fl, ob, 2 cl, hn, bn)	
Dijk, J. van 1918–	Chorales	Donemus, 1965
	(fl, alt ob, cl, hn, bn, trp)	
Dionisi, R.	Divertimento	Zanibon, 1966
	(wind quint, pf)	
Dohnányi, E. von	Sextet in C, Op. 37 (1933)	Lengnick, 1948
1877–1960	(cl, hn, vln, vla, vcl, pf)	
Donovan, R. F.	Sextet (1932)	CFE
1891–	(wind quint, pf)	
Doppler, A. F.	Das Waldvöglein: Idylle,	Schott, n.d.
1821–83	Op. 21	
	(fl, 4 hn, harm/pf)	
Dresden, S.	Petite Suite in C (1913)	de Wolfe
1881–1957	(wind quint, pf)	
	Suite naar Rameau (1916–48)	de Wolfe
	(wind quint, pf)	
	Third Suite (1920)	de Wolfe
	(wind quint, pf)	
Druschetzky, G.	Sextet (Ed. L. Kalmár)	ZV, 1964
1745–1819	(2 cl, 2 hn, 2 bn)	
Dukelsky, V. 1903–	Nocturne	C. Fischer, 1947
	(wind quint, pf)	
	Three Pieces	C. Fischer
	(wind quint, pf)	
Dusek, F. X.	Partita in A	(WERM)
1731–99	(2 ob, 2 hn, 2 bn)	
Eberl, A. F. J.	Sextet in E♭, Op. 47	Haslinger, n.d.
1765–1809	(cl, hn, vln, vla, vcl, pf)	
Ebers, K. F.	12 petites Pièces	J. Hummel
1770–1836	(2 basset hn, 2 hn, 2 bn)	

Eggert, J. 1779–1813	Sextet (cl, hn, vln, vla, vcl, db)	Br. & H., n.d.
Erlanger, G. 1842–1908	Sextet in E♭, Op. 41 (cl, hn, bn, vln, vla, vcl)	Kistner, n.d. [1882]
Esch, L. von, late 18th Cent.	Airs champêtres, Op. 4 (ob. cl, 2 hn, bn, db)	MS? (E*)
Etler, A. D. 1913–	Concerto (wind quint, vln)	AMP
Farrenc, L. 1804–75	Sextet, Op. 40 (wind quint, pf)	MS? (MGG)
Fasch, J. F. 1688–1758	Piece (ob d'am, 2 hn, 2 vln, bass)	MS (E*)
Feldman, M. 1926–	Two Pieces (fl, alt fl, hn, trp, vln, vcl)	Peters
	Durations V (hn, vln, vcl, pf/cel, vib, hp)	Peters
Flament, E. 1880–1958	Poème nocturne (wind quint, pf)	E. & S.
Flothuis, M. 1914–	Divertimento, Op. 46 (1952) cl, hn, bn, vln, vla, db	Donemus, 1952
Forster, C. 1673–1745	Konzert in E♭ (hn, 2 vln, vla, bass, hpcd)	Hofmeister, 1956
Fogg, E. 1903–39	Sextet (wind quint, pf)	MS?
Franckenstein, C. 1875–1942	Sextet, Op. 3 (hn, stg quart, pf)	MS (MGG)
Frensel-Wegener, E. 1901–	Sextet (1927) (wind quint, pf)	Donemus
Frid, G. 1904–	Sextet (wind quint, pf)	Donemus, 1965
Froschauer, H.	Sextet (fl, ob, 2 cl, hn, bn)	Doblinger, 1962
Fuchs, G. F. 1752–1821	Sextet, Op. 34 (cl, hn, bn, vln, vla, db)	Imbault
Fuhrmeister, F. b. 1862	Gavotte & Tarantella, Op. 6 (wind quint, pf)	Giessel, 1902; Zimmermann
Galindo, B. 1911–	Sextet (fl, cl, hn, bn, trp, trb)	(Slo)
Gan, N. K.	Kinderbilder Suite (fl, ob, 2 cl, hn, bn)	RS, 1955
Genin, T. 19th Cent.	Sextuor (wind quint, pf)	Demets, 1906; Eschig
Gilbert, A.	Serenade (ob, hn, vln, vla, db, gt)	
Glazounov, A. 1865–1936	Serenade (hn, stg quart, db)	RS, 1961
Gleissner, F. b. 1760	Six Pieces (fl, 2 cl, 2 hn, bn)	André
Gnessin, M. F. 1883–1957	Adygeya, Op. 48 (1933) (cl, hn, vln, vla, vcl, pf)	RS, 1937
Godron, H. 1900–	Serenade (1947) (wind quint, pf)	Donemus

Goeb, R. 1914–	Declarations	CFE
	(wind quint, vcl)	
Goehr, A. 1932–	Suite, Op. 11 (1961)	Schott, 1962
	(fl, cl, hn, vln/vla, vcl, hp)	
Göpfert, C. A.	12 Pieces, Op. 26	André, n.d.
1768–1818	2 cl, 2 hn, 2 bn	
Görner, H. G. 1908–	Kammerkonzert, Op. 29	Litolff, 1964
	(wind quint, pf)	
Gossec, F. J.	Andante	Fischbacher, n.d.
1733–1820	(2 cl, 2 hn, 2 bn)	
	Six Serenades	MS? (F)
	(fl, hn, bn, vln, vla, bass)	
Grabner, H. 1886–	Wilhelm Busch-Suite, Op. 33	K. & S., 1932
	(fl, ob, cl, sax, hn, bn)	
Graun, J. G.	8 Sinfonien	MS (E*)
1698–1771	(2 fl, 2 ob, 2 hn)	
Graupner, C.	Three Sonatas	MS (E*, MGG)
1683–1760	(2 hn, 2 vln, vla, hpcd)	
Greenberg, L. 1926–	Sextet (1963)	CMC
	(wind quint, pf)	
Griefsbacher	Allegro und Romanze	MS (E*)
	(2 cl, 2 hn, 2 bn)	
Gwinner	Sechs nederdeutsche Volkstänze	Möseler
	(2 cl, 2 hn, trp, trb)	
Gyring, E.	Sextet: Fantasy	CFE
	(fl, cl, hn, vln, vla, vcl)	
Haddad, D.	Blues au vent	Templeton, 1966
	(wind quint, perc)	
Häusler, E. ca.	Grand Sextet, Op. 21	Gombart, n.d.
1760–1837	(2 hn, stg quart)	
Harris, R. 1898–	Fantasy (Sextet) (1932)	SPAM, 1938
	(wind quint, pf)	
Hartley, W. S.	Sextet	Composer, Elkins,
1927–	(wind quint, db)	W. Virginia
Haydn, F. J.	Sextet No. 14, Hob. II, 14 (Ed. K.	Musica Rara,
1732–1809	Janetzky)	1957
	(ob, hn, bn, vln, vla, bass)	
	Divertimento, Hob. II, F 1	
	(2 hn, 2 vln, vla, bass)	
	Divertimento, Hob. II, B 5	
	(2 hn, 2 vln, vla, bass)	
	Divertimento in E♭, (Eine	Vieweg
	Abendmusik) Hob. II, 21 (Ed.	
	A. Egidi)	
	(2 hn, 2 vln, vla, bass)	
	Divertimento in D, Hob. II, 22	Peters, 1958
	(Ed. E. Lassen)	
	(2 hn, 2 vln, vla, vcl)	
	Cassation, Hob. II, D 4	
	(fl, 2 hn, vln, vla, bass)	
	Cassation, Hob. II, C 4	
	(2 hn, 2 vln, vla, bass)	
	Cassation, Hob. II, Es 6	

	(2 hn, 2 vln, vla, bass)	
	†Divertimento No. 1 in F, Hob. II, 15	
	(Ed. H. C. Robbins Landon)	Doblinger, 1959
	(Ed. F. Spiegel)	OUP, 1960
	(2 ob, 2 hn, 2 bn)	
	†Divertimento No. 2 in F, Hob. II, 23	
	(Ed. H. C. Robbins Landon)	Doblinger, 1959
	(Ed. A. Lumsden)	Musica Rara, 1959
	(2 ob, 2 hn, 2 bn)	
	†Divertimento No. 3 in C, Hob. II, 7	
	(Ed. H. C. Robbins Landon)	Doblinger, 1959
	(Ed. K. Haas)	Musica Rara, 1958
	(2 ob, 2 hn, 2 bn)	
	†Divertimento No. 5 in D, Hob. II, D 18	
	(Ed. H. C. Robbins Landon)	Doblinger, 1959
	(2 ob, 2 hn, 2 bn)	
	†Divertimento No. 6 in G, Hob. II, 3	
	(Ed. H. C. Robbins Landon)	Doblinger, 1960
	(2 ob, 2 hn, 2 bn)	
	†Divertimento No. 7 in G, Hob. deest	
	(Ed. H. C. Robbins Landon)	Doblinger, 1960
	(2 ob, 2 hn, 2 bn)	
	†Divertimento No. 8 in D, Hob. deest	
	(Ed. H. C. Robbins Landon)	Doblinger, 1960
	(2 ob, 2 hn, 2 bn)	
	Parthia in B♭, Hob. II, B 7	
	(2 cl, 2 hn, 2 bn)	
	Parthia in F, Hob. II, F 12	
	(2 ob, 2 hn, 2 bn)	Musica Rara, 1960
	Suite a 6, Hob. II, Es 17	
	(2 cl, 2 hn, 2 bn)	
	March in G (1772) (Ed. A. Lumsden)	Musica Rara, 1959
	(2 ob, 2 hn, 2 bn)	
	Two Cassations	
	(2 ca, hn, trp, vla, bass)	
Haydn, M. 1737–1806	Notturno in F (Ed. A. Strassl)	Doblinger, 1963
	(2 hn, 2 vln, vla, db)	
	†Divertimento in G	(Schwann)
	(2 hn, 2 vln, vla, db)	
	Divertimento in G	MS (Perger)
	(ob, 2 hn, bn, vla, violone)	
	Divertimento in D	MS (Perger)
	(2 ob, 2 hn, 2 bn)	
Heinichen, J. D. 1683–1729	Sonata in F	MS (E*)
	(2 hn, 2 vln, vla, bass)	

Hemel, O. van 1892–	Sextet (1962) (wind quint, pf)	Donemus
Hengeveld, G. 1910–	Variations on a Theme of Paganini (wind quint, pf)	Donemus
Hewitt-Jones, T. 1926–	Prelude, three Miniatures & Fugue (1953) (fl, vl, hn, vln, vla, vcl)	MS (MT, Dec. 1966)
Heyse, A. G.	Serenade, Op. 2 (2 fl, 2 hn, bass, hp)	Böhme
Hill, E. B. 1872–1960	†Sextet in B♭, Op. 39 (1934) (wind quint, pf)	SPAM, 1938
Hoffmeister, F. A. 1754–1812	Serenade, Op. 9 (fl, 2 hn, vln, vla, vcl)	J. Hummel; Noetzel
	Notturno No. 4, Op. 61 (fl, 2 hn, bn, vln, db)	Kunze
	Nocturne (2 hn, vln, vla, vcl, db)	Peters, n.d.
	Variations (2 cl, 2 hn, 2 bn)	MS (E*, MGG)
	Notturno (fl, ob, hn, vln, vla, vcl)	MS (Nat. Mus., Prague)
Holbrooke, J. 1878–1958	3rd Sextet in f, Op. 33a (wind quint, pf)	Riorden, 1906; Chester, 1922
Holewa, H. 1905–	Concertino (1960) (cl, hn, vla, hp, pf, perc)	FST
Huber, H. 1852–1921	Sextet in B♭ (1900?) (wind quint, pf)	Hug, 1924
Hüttell, J. 1893–	Divertissement grotesque (wind quint, pf)	(T)
Hummel, F. H. 1765–1814	Grand Sextet in F, Op. 19 (2 hn, 2 vla, vcl, pf)	Böhme, n.d.
Hummel, J. N. 1778–1837	Sextet, Op. 18 (2 hn, vln, vla, vcl, pf)	
Husa, K. 1921–	Sérénade (wind quint, pf)	Leduc, 1966
Huybrechts, A. 1899–1938	Sextet (1927) (2 fl, ob, cl, hn, bn)	CeBeDeM
Indy, V. d' 1851–1931	Sarabande & Menuet, Op. 24 bis (wind quint, pf)	Hamelle, 1918; IMC
Ireland, J. 1879–1962	Sextet (cl, hn, stg quart)	Augener, 1961
Jacob, G. 1895–	Sextet (1956) (wind quint, pf)	Musica Rara, 1962
Jacobi, W. 1894–	Suite, Op. 21 (wind quint, pf)	MS (Ve)
Jadin, L. E. 1768–1853	Trois Sextuors concertantes (2 cl, 2 hn, 2 bn)	Dufaut, n.d.
Janáček, L. 1854–1928	†Suite: Mládí (1924) (fl/picc, ob, cl, bcl, hn, bn)	HM, 1925, 1947; Artia, 1949, 1958

Jaunez, A.	Sextet, Op. 4	Costallat, n.d.
	(2 hn, 2 vla, 2 vcl)	
	Grand Sextuor, Op. 5	Richault, n.d.
	(fl, 2 hn, vln, 2 vcl)	
Javault, L. Early 19th Cent.	Six Sextets	Gaveaux, n.d.
	(fl, ob, cl, hn, 2 bn)	
Jentsch, W. 1900–	Kleine Kammermusik (Thema mit Variationen), Op. 5	R. & E., 1935
	(wind quint, pf)	
Jettel, R. 1903–	Sextet	Rubato [1952?];
	(fl, ob, 2 cl, hn, bn)	Doblinger
Johnsen, H. 1916–	Sextet	NK
	(wind quint, vib)	
Jongen, J. 1873–1953	Rhapsody, Op. 70 (1922)	CeBeDeM, 1922
	(wind quint, pf)	
Juon, P. 1872–1940	Divertimento in F, Op. 51	Schlesinger, 1013;
	(wind quint, pf)	Lienau
Kabeláč, M. 1908–	Sextet, Op. 8 (1940)	HM; SNKLHU,
	(fl, ca, 2 cl, hn, bn)	1956
Kahowez, G. 1940–	Structures	Wewerka, 1965
	(wind quint, pf)	
Kalkbrenner, F. 1785–1849	Grand Sextuor, Op. 135	Kistner, n.d.
	(2 hn, vln, vcl, db, pf)	
Karren, L.	Humoristic Scenes	Andraud
	(fl, ob, cl, bcl, hn, dbn)	
Keith, G. D.	Journey of the Swagmen	Remick
	(wind quint, pf)	
Kelterborn, R. 1931–	Meditationen	Pegasus, 1965
	(2 cl, 2 hn, 2 bn)	
Kilpatrick, J. F.	Sextet	CFE
	(fl, hn, stg quart)	
Kleinsinger, G. 1914–	Design for woodwinds	AMP, 1946
	(fl, ob, 2 cl, hn, bn)	
Koehler, B. J. b. 1777	Jeu de dez d'ecossaises	Leuckart, 1803
	(2 cl, 2 hn, bn, trp)	
Köhler, G. H. 1765–1833	Three Partien	Becker, 1798
	(2 cl, 2 hn, 2 bn)	
Koetsier, J. 1911–	Introduction et Follaterie avec un Thème, Op. 31	Donemus, 1961
	(wind quint, pf l.h.)	
Kohn, K.	Serenade (1962)	Composer
	(wind quint, pf)	
Koppel, H. D. 1908–	Sextet, Op. 36 (1942)	Skandinavisk,
	(wind quint, pf)	1947
Kont, P. 1920–	Suite aus dem Ballet 'Die traurigen Jäger'	Modern
	(fl, 2 hn, vln, db, timp)	
Kox, H. 1930–	Sextuor No. 3 (1959)	Donemus
	(wind quint, pf)	
	Sextuor No. 4 (1961)	Donemus, 1961
	(wind quint, pf)	
Kreutzer, K. 1780–1849	Sextuor	Paris, Composer
	(wind quint, pf)	

Krommer, F. V.	Partita in E♭	Peters, 1817
1759–1831	(Ed. K. H. Gutte)	Hofmeister, 1957
	(2 cl, 2 hn, 2 bn)	
Kubik, G. 1914–	†Trivialities, Op. 5 (1934)	MS? (G, H, Ho,
	(fl, hn, stg quart)	R, T)
Lacroix	Sextet	MS (Curtis Inst.)
	(wind quint, pf)	
Laderman, E. 1924–	Sextet	CFE
	(wind quint, db)	
Ladmirault, P.	Choral & Variations (1935)	Lemoine, 1952
1877–1944	(wind quint, pf)	
Lakner, Y. 1924–	Sextet (1951)	IMI, 1962
	(wind quint, pf)	
Lang, J. G. 1724–94	Sinfonia pastorale	André, n.d.
	(Ed. W. Höckner)	Portius, 1940
	(2 hn, stg quart)	
Langlé, H. F. M.	Six Sinfonias, Op. 1	Paris, 1782
1741–1807	(2 cl, 2 hn, 2 bn)	
Laube, A. 1718–84	Neun Parthien	MS? (MGG)
	(2 ob, 2 hn, 2 bn)	
Lavainne, F.	Sextet, Op. 61	Girod
	(ob, cl, hn, bn, vcl, db)	
La Violette, W.	Sextet (1940)	MS? (B)
1894–	(wind quint, pf)	
Lefebvre, C. E.	Intermezzo scherzando, Op. 80	Noël
1843–1917	(fl, ob, 2 cl, hn, bn)	
	Second Suite, Op. 122	Leduc; Andraud
	(fl, ob, 2 cl, hn, bn)	
Legley, V. 1915–	Sextet, Op. 19 (1945)	CeBeDeM, 1956;
	(wind quint, pf)	Brogneaux
Lessel, F. 1780–1835	Partita in E♭	MS? (MGG)
	(2 cl, 2 hn, 2 bn)	
Leye, L. 19th Cent.	Sextet, Op. 3	Sinner, 1844
	(fl, basset hn, 2 hn, bn, pf)	
Linek, J. 1725–91	†Symphonia pastoralis	Pro Musica, 1948
	(Ed. W. Höckner)	
	(2 hn, stg quart)	
Luening, O. 1900–	Sextet, Op. 2 (1919)	CFE
	(fl, cl, hn, vln, vla, vcl)	
Macdonald, M.	La Chasse	MS?
1916–	(2 ob, 2 hn, 2 bn)	
Macero, T. 1925–	From here to there	CFE
	(fl, ob, cl, sax, hn, bn)	
Major, J. G.	Sextet, Op. 39	MS (Ve)
1858–1925	(wind quint. pf)	
Malherbe, E. H. P.	Sextet, Op. 31	MS (DMM, MGG)
b. 1870	(fl, ob, ca, cl, hn, bn)	
Malzat, I.	Parthia in E♭	MS (MGG*)
1757–1804	(2 ob, 2 hn, 2 bn)	
Manicke, D.	Sextet	Simrock, 1964
	(2 cl, 2 hn, 2 bn)	
Mapes, G.	Passacaglia	MS (H)
	(fl, ob, ca, cl, hn, bn)	

Margola, F. 1908–	Sonata a sei (wind quint, pf)	(Ve)
Martinů, B. 1890–1959	Serenade No. 1 (1932) (cl, hn, 3 vln, vla)	Melantrich, 1949; Artia, 1955
Mašek, V. 1755–1831	Todten Marsch (2 hn, 2 bn, 2 trp)	MS? (MGG)
	Sextetto in B♭ (2 hn, stg quart)	MS? (MGG)
Mattheson, J. 1681–1764	Overture avec sa Suite pour les hautbois de M. le Général de Schoulenbourg (3 ob, 2 hn, bass)	MS (MGG)
Matys, J. 1927–	Variations on Death, Op. 27 (1959) (hn, stg quartet, reciter)	(Ga)
Maxwell Davies, P. 1934–	Alma Redemptoris Mater (1957) (fl, ob, 2 cl, hn, bn)	Schott, 1965
Meulemans, A. 1844–1966	Aubade (1934) (wind quint, pf)	CeBeDeM, 1957; Maurer
Michael, D. M. 1751–1825	Parthia VI (Ed. D. M. McCorkle) (2 cl, 2 hn, 2 bn)	Bo. & H., 1966
Mignone, F. 1897–	Sextet (1935) (wind quint, pf)	ENM, 1937
Miroglio, P. J. b. ca. 1750	Sestetto (2 hn, 2 vln, vla, bass)	MS (E*)
Molter, J. M. ca. 1695–1765	Sinfonia concertante (2 ob, 2 hn, bn, trp)	MS
Moritz, D. M.	Parthia VI (Ed. D. M. McCorkle) (2 cl, 2 hn, 2 bn)	Bo. & H., 1966
Moscheles, I. 1794–1870	Sextet in E♭, Op. 35 (1815) (fl, 2 hn, vln, vcl, pf)	Richault, n.d.; Hofmeister [1825]
Moulaert, R. 1875–1962	Sextet (1925) (wind quint, pf/hp)	CeBeDeM
	Concerto (1950) (wind, quint, hp)	CeBeDeM
	†Petite Flore (1937) (wind quint, vln)	MS?
Mozart, W. A. 1756–91	†Divertimento in B♭, K. 196f (1775)	Br. & H. [1801]
	(Ed. F. Spiegel) (2 ob, 2 hn, 2 bn)	Schott, 1956
	†Divertimento No. 8 in F, K. 213 (1775) (2 ob, 2 hn, 2 bn)	André [ca. 1801]; Br. & H., 1880, 1954; Eulenberg
	(Ed. G. Weigelt) (wind quint)	Leuckart, 1954
	†Divertimento No. 9 in B♭, K. 240 (1776) (2 ob, 2 cl, 2 hn)	André [ca. 1801]; Br. & H., 1880, 1954; Eulenburg
	(Ed. G. Weigelt) (wind quint)	Leuckart, 1936

	†Divertimento No. 12 in E♭, K. 252 (1776) (2 ob, 2 hn, 2 bn)	André [ca. 1801]; Br. & H., 1880, 1954; Eulenburg
	†Divertimento No. 13 in F, K. 253 (1776) (2 ob, 2 hn, 2 bn)	André [ca. 1801]; Br. & H., 1880, 1954; Eulenburg
	(Ed. G. Weigelt) (wind quint)	Leuckart
	†Divertimento No. 14 in B♭, K. 270 (1777) (2 ob, 2 hn, 2 bn)	André [ca. 1801]; Br. & H., 1880, 1954; Eulenburg
	(Ed. G. Weigelt) (wind quint)	Leuckart
	†Divertimento No. 16 in E♭, K. 289 (1777) (2 ob, 2 hn, 2 bn)	Br. & H., 1880, 1954; Eulenburg
	†Divertimento No. 7 in D, K. 205 (1773) (2 hn, bn, vln, vla, db)	Br. & H.; Eulenburg
	†Divertimento No. 10 in F, K. 247 (1776) (2 hn, stg quart)	Artaria, 1799; Br. & H.; Eulenburg
	†Divertimento No. 15 in B♭, K. 287 (1777) (2 hn, stg quart)	André [1792]; Br. & H.; Eulenburg
	†Divertimento No. 17 in D, K. 334 (1779) (2 hn, stg quart)	André [1792]; IMC; Br. & H.; Eulenburg
	†Ein musicalische Spass, K. 522 (Dorfmusikanten-Sextett) (1787) (2 hn, stg quart)	André [1801]; Br. & H., 1956; Eulenburg; IMC
	†Serenade in E♭, K. 375 (1782) (original version)	André [1792]; Br. & H.; Eulenburg
	(Ed. K. Haas)	Musica Rara, 1955
	(Ed. F. Spiegel) (2 cl, 2 hn, 2 bn)	Schott, 1957
Müller, L. R.	Tänzerische Impressionen (wind quint, db)	Br. & H.
Mulder, E. W. 1898–1959	Sextet (1946) (wind quint, pf)	Donemus
Mysliveček, J. 1737–81	Sinf. Serenata in G (2 hn, vln, vla, bass)	MS (MGG)
Neuhauser, L. 18th Cent.	Nocturne (2 hn, vln, vla, vcl, mand)	MS? (F)
Nisle, J. F. b. 1768	Sextet (fl, hn, bn, vla, db, pf)	MS (Musikfr., Vienna)
Oliver, J. A. 18th Cent.	40 Divertimenti (2 cl, 2 hn, 2 bn)	London, 1792

A LIST OF MUSIC FOR THE HORN

Onslow, G.
1784–1853

Sextet in E♭, Op. 30
(fl, cl, hn, bn, db, pf)
Grand Sextuor, Op. 77b (from
Nonet, Op. 77)
(fl, cl, hn, bn, db, pf)

Br. & H. [ca.
1826]; AMP
Brandus [ca.
1851]; Br. & H.

Osborne, G. A.
1806–93

Sextuor in G, Op. 63
(fl, ob, hn, vcl, db, pf)

Lemoine, n.d.
[1847]

Osieck, H. 1910–

Divertimento (1950)
(wind quint, pf)

Donemus

Ozi, E. 1754–1813

Nouvelles Suites de Pièces
d'harmonie: Ouverturen,
Arietten
(2 cl, 2 hn, 2 bn)

Paris, Le Menu &
Boyer, 1783,
1789

Paër, F. 1771–1839

La douce Victoire, Fantaisie
(2 fl, 2 hn, bn, pf)

Schoenenberger

Panizza, J. 19th
Cent.

Sextet
(fl, 2 cl, 2 hn, bn)

Artaria

Paz, J. C. 1897–

Concerto No. 2, Op. 24
(1934)
(ob, 2 hn, bn, trp, pf)

MS (Dale, T)

Pepping, E. 1901–

Divertimento (1924)
(ob, cl, hn, bn, vla, vcl)

MS (MGG)

Perkowski, P. 1901–

Sextet
(cl, hn, trp, vln, vcl, pf)

MS? (MGG)

Pijper, W.
1894–1947

Phantasie (W. A. Mozart)
(1927)
(wind quint, pf)
Sextet (1923)
(wind quint, pf)

Donemus, 1948

Donemus, 1948

Pleyel, I. J.
1757–1831

Pièces d'harmonie
(2 cl, 2 hn, 2 bn)

(MGG)

Polívka, V.
1896–1948

Suite (1933)
(wind quint, vla)

MS (Ga, MGG)

Polsterer, R. b. 1879

Sextet
(fl, cl, 2 hn, bn, pf)

Brockhaus

Ponfick, F. 19th
Cent.

Sextuor, Op. 8
(2 hn, vln, vla, vcl, pf)

Ries, n.d. [ca.
1879]

Poulenc, F.
1899–1963

†Sextet (1930–32; rev. 1940)
(wind quint, pf)

Hansen, 1945

Pouwels, J. 1898–

Sextet (1958)
(wind quint, pf)

Donemus

Praag, H. van 1894–

Divertimento (1938)
(wind quint, vln)
Four Reflections (1950)
(wind quint, vln)

Donemus

Donemus

Puschmann, J. 18th
Cent.

Trois Pièces en harmonie
(2 cl, 2 hn, 2 bn)

MS (F)

Quef, C. 1873–1931

Suite, Op. 4
(wind quint, pf)

Noël, 1902

Quinet, M. 1915–

Ballade (1962)
(wind quint, vln)

CeBeDeM

Ratner, L. 1916–

†Serenade (1951)
(ob, hn, stg quart)

MS (Copy in Lib.
of Congress)

315

Read, G. 1913–	Nine by Six (1951) (wind quint, trp)	MS (Ho) (School of Music, Boston Univ.)
Rebner, W. 1910–	Sextet (wind quint, bcl)	Modern, 1962
Reed, H. O. 1910–	Symphonic Dances (wind quint, pf)	Mills, 1963
Reinecke, C. 1824–1910	Sextet, Op. 271 (fl, ob, cl, 2 hn, bn)	Zimmermann, 1904
Reuchsel, A. 1875–1931	Sextuor (wind quint, pf)	Lemoine, 1909
Rheinberger, J. 1839–1901	Sextet, Op. 191b (wind quint, pf)	Leuckart, 1900
Riegel, H. J. 1741–99	Six Symphonies (2 hn, 2 vln, vcl, pf)	MS? (T)
Riegger, W. 1885–1961	†Concerto, Op. 53 (1953) (wind quint, pf)	Merrymount, 1954
Ries, F. 1784–1838	Sextuor in g, op. 142 (cl, hn, bn, db, hp, pf)	Schott, n.d. [1879]
Rietz, J. 1812–77	Konzertstück, Op. 41 (wind quint, pf)	Seitz
Riisager, K. 1898–	Concerto, Op. 28a (wind quint, pf)	Nordiska
Righini, V. 1756–1812	Serenade (2 cl, 2 hn, 2 bn)	Br. & H.; Gombart [ca. 1800]
Ringbom, N. E. 1907–	Sextet (1951) (ob, ca, cl, bcl, hn, bn)	(Gor, La, MGG)
Röser, V. b. 1735	1re Suite des Ariettes (2 cl, 2 hn, 2 bn)	Bérault, 1771
	9e Suite des Airs (2 cl, 2 hn, 2 bn)	Bérault, 1772
	40 Divertissements militaires (2 cl, 2 hn, 2 bn)	Sieber, 1771–82
	Suite de Pièces d'harmonie (2 cl, 2 hn, 2 bn)	Sieber, 1782
	XVI Marches et Airs (2 cl, 2 hn, 2 bn)	J. Hummel
Roos, R. de 1907–	Sextuor (1935) (wind quint, pf)	Donemus
Rosetti, F. A. 1752–92	Partita (ob, 2 cl, 2 hn, bn)	Kneusslin, 1954
	Notturno in D (Ed. V. Belsky) (fl, 2 hn, vln, vla, vcl)	SNKLHU, 1957
	Parthia in d (ob, ca, 2 hn, 2 bn)	MS (MGG*)
	Sextet in E♭ (fl, 2 cl, 2 hn, bn)	Sikorski
Rossi, A. de 18th Cent.	Concerto (2 hn, 2 vln, vla, bass)	MS (E*)
Roussel, A. 1869–1937	†Divertissement, Op. 6 (1906) (wind quint, pf)	Rouart, n.d., [1906]; Salabert

Rousselot, S.	Sextet	Catelin
b. ca. 1800	(ob, cl, hn, bn, vcl, db)	
Sabatini, G.	Elegia	Camara
	(hn, stg quart, hp)	
Sammartini, G. B.	Sonatas	MS (E*)
1701–75	(2 hn, 2 vln, vla, bass)	
Schadewitz, K.	Sextet (1924)	MS (Ve)
1887–1945	(wind quint, pf)	
Scherrer, H.	Altfranzösische Tänze, Op. 11	C. Schmidt [1899]
b. 1865	(fl, ob, 2 cl, hn, bn)	
Schmitt, J. 1734–91	Divertimento in D	MS (Musikfr.
	(fl, 2 hn, vln, vla, vcl)	Vienna)
Schneider, G. A.	Six Pièces d'harmonie	Gombart
1770–1839	(2 cl, 2 hn, 2 bn)	[ca. 1800]
Schroeder, H. 1904–	Sextet, Op. 36	Schott, 1959
	(wind quint, pf)	
Schwertsik, K.	Proviant	(Ve)
1935–	(wind quint, trp)	
Seiber, M. 1904–60	Serenade (1925)	Hansen, 1957
	(2 cl, 2 hn, 2 bn)	
	Fantasy (1945)	SZ, 1956
	(fl, hn, stg quart)	
Seidel, L.	Sextet	J. Hummel [ca.
1765–1831	(fl, ob, 2 hn, bn, pf/hpcd)	1800]; M. & M.
Shanks, E.	Night Music for Six	Gamble
	(wind quint, pf)	
Smit, L. 1900–45	Sextuor (1933)	Donemus
	(wind quint, pf)	
Stabinger, M.	Sextets	Venice, 1792
ca. 1750–ca. 1815	(fl, 2 hn, 2 vln, vcl)	
Stamitz, K.	Four Divertissements	J. Hummel
1745–1801	(2 cl, 2 hn, 2 bn)	
	Parthia à 6	MS
	(2 hn, 2 vln, vla, bass)	
	Sestetto	MS
	(2 hn, vln, vla, vla da g, vcl)	
Stein, L. 1910–	Sextet	Camara
	(wind quint, sax)	
Steinmetz	Partia	MS? (E)
	(2 hn, 2 vln, vla, bass)	
	Sextuor	MS (E)
	(2 hn, 2 vln, vla, bass)	
Stepan, J. A.	Concerto in D (Ed. V. Belsky)	SNKLHU, 1959
1726–97	(fl, 2 hn, vln, bass, hpcd)	(MAB, Vol. 39)
Stich, J. W.	Sextet, Op. 34	Leduc [ca. 1801]
(Punto, G.)	(cl, hn, bn, vln, vla, db)	
1740–1803		
Stöhr, R.	Sextet in E, Op. 2	Eulenburg
b. 1874	(cl, 2 hn, vln, vla, vcl)	
Stoker, R. 1938–	Sextet, Op. 16 (1963)	MS (CG)
	(cl, hn, bn, vln, vla, vcl)	
Strategeier, H.	Sextet (1951)	Donemus
1912–	(wind quint, pf)	

Streck	Nine Pièces d'harmonie	Falter; Schott,
	(fl, 2 cl, 2 hn, bn)	1828
Striegler, K.	Sextet in E♭, Op. 58	MS (LB,
1886–1958	(wind quint, pf)	Dresden)
Stulicke, M. N.	Pastorella	MS (E*)
18th Cent.	(ob, hn, stg quart)	
Stutschewsky, J.	Sextet (1959)	Tel Aviv,
1891–	(fl, ob, cl, 2 hn, bn)	Composer
Subotnick, M. 1933–	Play! No. 1 (1964)	(Chase)
	(wind quint, pf, tape)	
Sugár, R. 1919–	Frammenti musicali	EMB, 1963
	(wind quint, pf)	
Sutermeister, H.	Serenade No. 2 (1961)	Schott, 1963
1910–	(wind quint, trp)	
Svensson, S. E.	Sextet	FST
	(wind quint, bcl)	
Tansman, A. 1897–	La Danse de la Sorcière, from	Eschig, 1924
	'Le Jardin du Paradis'	
	(wind quint, pf)	
Thomson, V. 1896–	Barcarolle (1940)	Mercury, 1948
	(fl, ca, cl, bcl, hn, bn)	
Thuille, L.	†Sextet in B♭, Op. 6	Br. & H., 1899,
1861–1907	(wind quint, pf)	1955
Toch, E. 1887–1964	†Five Pieces, Op. 83 (1961–2)	Mills
	(wind quint, perc)	
Todt, J. C.	Concertino in E	MS (MGG*)
18th Cent.	(2 hn, 2 vln, vla, db)	
Trexler, G. 1903–	Sextet (1958/9)	(Ve)
	(wind quint, pf)	
Tuthill, B. C. 1888–	Variations on 'When Johnny	Galaxy, 1934
	comes marching Home', Op. 9	
	(wind quint, pf)	
Uber, C. B.	Six Divertimenti (1783)	(MGG, T)
1746–1812	(fl, 2 hn, vln, vcl, hpcd)	
	Two Concertinos	(MGG, T)
	(fl, basset hn, 2 hn, vla, hpcd)	
Van der Velden, R.	Sextet (1948)	Metropolis
1910–	(wind quint, pf)	
Vandor, I. 1932–	Serenata (1964)	SZ, 1964
	(fl, bcl, hn, vln, vla, hp)	
Vaňhal, J. K.	Five Notturni	MS (MGG*)
1739–1831	(fl, 2 hn, vln, vla, bass)	
	Cassatio in D	MS (MGG*)
	(2 hn, 2 vln, vla, bass)	
Vellones, P.	À Versailles, Op. 60/7	Ed. Regia
1889–1939	(wind quint, pf)	(Choudens),
		1934; Baron
Villa-Lobos, H.	Chorôs No. 3 (Pica-Pao) (1925)	Eschig, 1928
1887–1959	(cl, sax, 2 hn, bn, trp, mch ad lib)	
Vranický, A.	Six hunting Marches	Artia
1761–1820	(2 cl, 2 hn, 2 bn)	
Weber, E. von	Sextuor, Op. 35	Ebner [1886]
1766–1826	(hn, stg quart, pf)	

A LIST OF MUSIC FOR THE HORN

Weiss, A. 1891–	Sextet (1947)	CFE
	(wind quint, pf)	
Wessel, M. 1894–	Sextet (1928)	MS (R, T)
	(wind quint, pf)	
Whettam, G. 1927–	Fantasy Sextet	de Wolfe
	(wind quint, pf)	
White, F. H.	Clarinda's Delight	Curwen
1884–1945	(fl, ob, cl, 2 hn, perc)	
Winnubst, J.	Kleine Serenade (1924)	Donemus
1885–1934	(wind quint, pf)	
Winter, P.	Sextet in d, Op. 9	Br. & H., 1803;
1754–1825	(2 hn, stg quart)	Nadermann
	Divertimento	MS
	(2 hn, 2 vln, vla, bass)	
	Harmonie à 6	MS
	(2 cl, 2 hn, 2 bn)	
Wolf, F. X.	Two Serenades, Op. 1	[André] 1795
Late 18th Cent.	(2 cl, 2 hn, 2 bn)	
Zagwijn, H.	Suite (1912)	Donemus
1878–1954	(wind quint, pf)	
	Scherzo (1946)	Donemus
	(wind quint, pf)	
	Nocturne (1918)	Donemus
	(fl, ca, cl, hn, hp, cel)	
Zelenka, I. 1936–	Früh-Stück	Modern
	(alto fl, bcl, hn, hp, gt, timp)	
Zimmermann, A.	Five Sextets	MS? (E*)
1741–81	(2 hn, 2 vln, vla, bass)	

6.6 Seven Instruments

Aubéry du Boulley, P. L. 1796–1870	Septet, Op. 69 (1010–1000–1101–gt)	Richault, n.d.; Costallat, n.d.
Avidom, M. 1908–	Enigma (1962) (1111–1000–0000–pf, perc)	MS (Ve)
Baaren, K. van 1906–	Sestetto (1952) (1111–1000–1001)	Donemus, 1952
Bach, C. P. E. 1714–88	Six Sonatas (1775) (Wq 184) (2021–2000–0000)	
	(Ed. J. Lorenz)	Ricordi, 1939
	(Ed. U. Leupold)	Litolff, 1937
	(Ed. K. Janetzky)	Musica Rara, 1958
	†Nos. 2, 4, 5 (Ed. F. Oberdörffer)	Lienau, 1935
	Sechs kleine Stücke oder Märsche (Wq 185) (0221–2000–0000)	
	(Ed. F. Oberdörffer)	Lienau, 1935
	(Ed. J. Lorenz)	Parrhysius, 1941
	(Ed. E. Simon)	Marks, 1948
	Sechs Polonaisen (Wq 190); Polacca (0020–2000–2001)	MS

319

Bach, J. C. F. 1732–95	†Septet in c, Op. 3 (0100–2000–1110–hpcd) Septet in E♭ (1794) (1100–2000–1100–cont)	K. & S., 1920 (WERM, Supp. III)
Beethoven, L. van 1770–1827	†Septet in E♭, Op. 20 (1800) (0011–1000–1111)	Hoffmeister, 1802 Br. & H., Peters; Litolff; Bo. & H., Eulenburg; IMC
	Eleven Viennese Dances (Wo O 17) Nos. 1, 3–8 (0020–2000–2001) Nos. 9–11 (2000–2000–2001)	Br. & H., 1907
Berry, W.	Divertimento (1111–1000–0000–pf, perc)	EV
Berwald, F. A. 1796–1868	†Septet in B♭ (1828) 0011–1000–1111	MKS, 1883; Suecia, 1946
Blanc, A. 1828–85	Septet in E, Op. 40 (0011–1000–1111) Septet in E, Op. 54 (1100–1000–0111–pf)	Costallat [ca. 1864] Richault; Costallat [ca. 1870]
Blum, C. L. 1786–1844	Three Serenades, Opp. 49, 50, 51 (1100–1000–2101)	Schott, n.d.
Boccherini, L. 1743–1805	Serenade (0200–2000–2001) (Ed. K. Haas)	Guéra, n.d.; Eulenburg, 1956
Borris, S. 1906–	Intrada serena No. 1 (1111–1110–0000)	Sirius
Bowen, Y. 1884–1961	Phantasy Septet (0010–1000–2110–pf)	MS? (DMM, Th)
Brugk, H. M. 1909–	Divertimento, Op. 29 (1111–2100–0000)	Simrock
Brunswick, M. 1902–	†Septet in seven Movements (1957) (1111–1000–0110)	CFE
Bumcke, G. b. 1876	Von Liebe und Leid, Op. 24 (1111–2000–0000–hp)	Saturn, 1912
Busch, C. 1862–1943	An Ozark Reverie (1121–2000–0000)	Fitzsimons
Converse, F. S. 1871–1940	Septet (0011–1000–1110–pf)	MS? (G)
Coscio, S.	Septet (1111–1110–0000)	Baron, 1953
Crosse, G. 1938–	Villanelles, Op. 2 (1959) (1111–1000–1010)	OUP
Degen, H. 1911–	Small Concerto No. 6 (1100–1000–0110–hpcd, timp)	Schott
Dost, R. b. 1877	Septet in G, Op. 55 (1111–1000–0000–pf, perc)	Zimmermann [1923?]
Doué, J. 1922–	Septet (1111–1110–0000)	Heugel
Driessler, J. 1921–	Aphorismen, Op. 7a (1111–ca, bcl–1000–0000)	BVK, 1954

Dubois, T. 1837–1924	Au Jardin: Petite Suite (2121–1000–0000)	Heugel, 1908
Eberl, A. F. J. 1766–1807	Septet, Op. 47 (0010–1000–2110–pf)	Haslinger, n.d.
Fasanotti, F. 1821–84	Settimino in E♭ (0112–1000–0010–pf)	Ricordi, 1842
Feldman, M. 1926–	The Straits of Magellan (1000–1100–0001–hp, gt, pf)	Peters
Feltre, Comte A. C. de 1806–50	Rondeau espagnol, Op. 2 (0000–2000–2110–pf)	(F)
Ferrari, G. G. 1759–1842	Four Septets (0000–2000–2101–pf)	MS? (E*)
Fesca, A. E. 1820–49	Grand Septuor, Op. 26 (0100–1000–1111–pf)	Litolff [ca. 1844]
	2e Grand Septuor, Op. 28 (0100–1000–1111–pf)	Richault [ca. 1844]
Flament, E. 1880– 1958	Fantasia con Fuga, Op. 28 (1112–ca–1000–0000)	E. & S., n.d.; Andraud; M. & M.
Frommel, G. 1906–	Concertino (1121–1000–ten hn/trb–0000)	Schott
Fux, J. J. 1660–1741	Partita (0100–2000–2000–bc)	MS? (MGG)
Genzmer, H. 1909–	Septet (1944) (1010–1000–1110–hp)	Schott, 1948
Ghedini, G. F. 1892–1965	Adagio & Allegro da Concerto (1936) (1100–1000–1110–hp)	Ricordi, 1937
Glinka, M. I. 1803–57	Septet in E♭ (1824) (0101–1000–2011)	RS
	Serenata (1832) (0001–1000–0111–hp)	RS
Gold, E. 1921–	Septet (1111–bcl–1000–0000–hp)	Benjamin
Grunenwald, J. J. 1911–	Le Bateau ivre (1938) (1000–1000–2110–pf)	MS (MGG)
Hába, K. 1898–	Septet, Op. 16 (1928–9) (0011–1000–1110–pf)	HM
Habert, J. E. 1833–96	Scherzo, Op. 107 (1112–2000–0000)	Br. & H.; AMP
Hawthorne-Baker, A.	Threnody (0110–1000–1110–hp)	Hinrichsen
Haydn, F. J. 1732–1809	Twelve Minuets, Hob. IX, 1 (0200–2000–2001)	
	Minuets, Hob. IX, 23 (2000–2000–2001)	
	Notturno, Hob. II, D20 (0000–2000–2210)	
	Notturno (Cassation) Hob. II, Es5 (0000–2000–2201)	
	Cassation in D, Hob. deest. (Ed. H. C. Robbins Landon) (0000–4000–1101)	Doblinger, 1960

	Serenata, Hob. II, F 11 (0000–2000–2201)	
	Cassation, Hob. II, Es 3 (0100–ca–2000–1101)	
	Cassation, Hob. II, Es 7 (0001–ca–2000–2001)	
	Cassation, Hob. II, F 2 (0101–2000–1101)	
	Cassation, Hob. II, F 3 (0000–2000–2201)	
	Cassation, Hob. II, G 2 (0000–2000–2201)	
	Concertant, Hob. II, D 14 (0100–2000–2110)	
	Divertimento in D, Hob. II, 8 (2000–2000–2001) (Ed. K. Janetzky)	Pro Musica 1953; BVK, 1953
	Divertimento, Hob. II, C 1 (1000–2000–2101)	
Heuschkel, J. P. 1773–1853	Pièces d'harmonie (1022–2000–0000)	Schott
Hindemith, P. 1895–1963	†Septet (1948) (1111–bcl–1100–0000)	Schott, 1949
Hlobil, E. 1901–	Concertino (0011–1000–2100–pf)	HM
Hoddinott, A. 1929–	Septet, Op. 10 (0011–1000–1110–pf)	OUP
Hodermann, G. C. Late 18th Cent.	Septet (0000–2000–2201)	Amsterdam
Hoffmeister, F. A. 1754–1812	Notturno (fl d'am–1000–2000–0210)	Hofdmeister, 1786
Hollander, B. 1853–1942	Septet, Op. 28 (0000–2000–2110–pf)	P. & O. [ca. 1900]; G. Schirmer
Holzmann, R. 1910–	Septuor (1011–1000–1110)	MS? (G)
Hummel, J. N. 1778–1837	†Septet in d, Op. 74 (1816) (1100–2000–0111)	Artaria, 1816; Peters, 1954; Schott
Indy, V. d' 1851–1931	Chanson et Danses in B♭, Op. 50 (1898) (1122–1000–0000)	Durand [1899]
Janáček, L. 1854–1928	†Concertino (0011–1000–2100–pf)	HM, 1926, 1949
Jones, D. 1912–	Septet (1949) (1111–bcl–1100–0000)	MS (MGG)
Juon, P. 1872–1940	Divertimento, Op. 51 (1111–1000–0001–pf)	Schlesinger, 1913
Kabalin, F.	Divertimento (1111–2100–0000)	Tritone, 1962
Kalkbrenner, F. 1785–1849	Septuor in E♭, Op. 15 (0000–2000–2200–pf)	Simrock, n.d.

A LIST OF MUSIC FOR THE HORN

	Grand Septuor in A, Op. 132 (0111–1000–0011–pf)	Br. & H. [ca. 1835]
Karjalainen, A. 1907–	Septet, Op. 22 (0111–1110–0000) (?)	MS (Gor)
Kayn, R. 1933–	Kammerkonzert (1111–1010–0000–perc)	Sikorski, n.d.
Kelterborn, L. R. E. 1891–	Hiawatha Suite (1924) (1010–1000–1110–hp)	MS (Ve)
Kittl, J. B. 1806–68	Grand Septuor in E♭, Op. 25 (1111–1000–0001–pf)	Kistner [1846]
Koechlin, C. 1867–1951	Septet, Op. 165 (1937) (1111–sax–1000–0100)	OL
Köper, K. H. 1927–	Musik (1010–sax–1110–0001)	(Modern)
Koetsier, J. 1911–	Septet, Op. 4 (1932; rev. 1957) (0011–1000–1111)	Donemus
Kozeluch, L. A. 1747–1818	Divertimento in E♭ (0002–2200–0000–pf)	MS (MGG*)
	Divertimento in B♭ (0002–2200–0000–pf)	MS (MGG*)
Kreith, K. d. ca. 1807	Partita Tono B (0221–2000–0000)	Eder
Kreutzer, K. 1780–1849	†Grand Septuor in E♭, Op. 62 (0011–1000–1111)	Pennaur [ca. 1823]; Musica Rara
Křička, J. 1882–	Concertino, Op. 76 (1940) (1111–1000–1000–pf)	MS? (G, Ga)
Krol, B. 1920–	Harfenseptett, Op. 7 (0011–1000–1110–hp)	Pro Musica, 1953
Krommer, F. V. 1759–1831	Two Concertinos, Opp. 70, 80 (1010–2000–1110)	Schlesinger
Krumpholz, J. B. 1745–90	Symphonie, Op. 11 (1000–2000–2010–hp)	Lemoine; J. & C.; Nadermann
Küffner, J. 1776–1856	Six Pièces d'harmonie, Op. 205 (1022–2000–0000)	Schott
	Pièce d'harmonie, Op. 138 (1022–2000–0000)	MS (Musikfr., Vienna)
Kummer, H.	Septet (1927) (1122–1000–0000)	MS (BQ, III, 4)
Lachner, F. 1803–90	Septett in E♭ (1824) (1010–1000–1111)	MS (MGG*)
Latilla, G. 1711–88	Sinfonia (0200–2000–2100)	MS? (MGG)
Louis Ferdinand, Prince of Prussia 1772–1806	Notturno, Op. 8 (1000–2000–1110–pf)	Br. & H. [1808]
Majo, G. di 1933–	Passacaglia (1000–sax–1000–0001–gt, vib, pf)	Ars Viva
Marescalchi, L. b. 1745	Dodici Minuetti, Op. 10 (0200–2000–2000–bc)	MS (MGG)
Mašek, V. 1755–1831	Cassatio in D (1000–2000–1001–2 violetti)	MS (MGG)

323

Maurer, L. W. 1789–1878	Variations sur un air russe, Op. 38 (1022–2000–0000)	Hofmeister
Mica, J. A. F. 1746–1811	Six Notturni (0000–2000–2201)	MS? (MGG)
Mirouze, M. 1906–57	Pièce en septuor (1111–1100–0000–pf)	Leduc, 1933
Morawetz, J.	Eight Nocturnes (ca. 1798) (fl♯d'am–1000–2000–2010)	MS (Ve)
Mortelmans, L. 1868–1952	Le Berger solitaire (1121–2000–0000)	Het Muziekfonds
Moscheles, I. 1794–1870	Grand Septuor in D, Op. 88 (1832) (0010–1000–1111–pf)	Kistner [1835]
Mouquet, J. 1867–1946	Suite (1122–1000–0000)	Lemoine, 1910; Andraud; Baron
Mozart, W. A. 1956–91	†Divertimento No. 11 in D, K. 251 (1776) (0100–2000–2110)	Br. & H., 1880, 1954; Eulenburg
Mühling, H. L. A. 1786–1847	VI Valses & XII Ecossaises, Op. 23 (1010–2000–2001)	Br. & H.
Neubauer, J. late 18th Cent.	Two Nocturnes (fl d'am–1000–2000–0210)	MS (Ve)
Neukomm, S. Ritter von 1778–1858	Septet (ca. 1832) (1111–1100–0001)	M. & M.
Niemann, W. 1876–1953	Rheinische Nachtmusik, Op. 35 (0000–2000–2111)	Wunderhorn [ca. 1914]
Nisle, J. F. b. 1768	Septetto (1011–1000–1110)	MS (MGG*) (Musikfr., Vienna)
Nono, L. 1924–	†Polifonica, Monodia, Ritmica (1010–bcl, sax, 1000–0000–pf, perc)	Ars Viva, 1954, 1965
Onslow, G. 1784–1853	†Septet in B♭, Op. 79 (1111–1000–0001–pf)	Kistner, n.d. [1852]
Pablo, L. de 1930–	Coral, Op. 2 (1111–1110–0000)	Modern, 1962
Paisello, G. 1740–1816	Six Menuette (0200–2000–2001)	(MGG)
Pannenberg, F. W. 18th Cent.	Septet (0101–basset hn–1000–0110)	MS (F)
Persichetti, V. 1915–	King Lear: Septet, Op. 35 (1948) (1111–1000–0000–pf, timp)	(Ho)
Petrini, F. 1744–1819	Sinfonie (1000–2000–2100–hp)	
Pfeiffer, F. A. 1754–87	Engloise (0200–2000–2001)	MS (MGG*)
Pichl, W. 1741–1804	Parthia (0221–2000–0000)	MS (E*)
Pierné, G. 1863–1937	Preludio e Fughetta in c, Op. 40/1 (2112–1000–0000)	Hamelle [1906]; Andraud

	Pastorale variée, Op. 30 (1112–1100–0000)	Durand
Pijper, W. 1894–1947	Septet (1920) (1111–1000–0001–pf)	Donemus, 1948
Pleyel, I. 1757–1831	Septet, Op. 8 (0000–2000–2111)	André; Sieber, n.d.
	Notturno (0000–2000–2201)	MS? (E*)
Reymann, F. G. 18th Cent.	Thirteen Concertini (1000–fl d'am–2000–0210)	Traeg
Rhené-Baton 1879–1940	Aubade, Op. 53 (1122–1000–0000)	Durand, 1940
Ries, F. 1784–1838	Grand Septuor in E♭, Op. 25 (1808) (0010–2000–1011–pf)	Simrock [1812?]; Probst
Riotte, P. J. 1776–1856	Septet, Op. 39 (0010–2000–0110–pf)	Br. & H.
Röntgen, J. 1855–1932	Serenade in A, Op. 14 (1112–2000–0000)	Br. & H. [1878]; UE
Rootham, C. B. 1875–1938	Septet (1930) (1111–1000–0100–hp)	OUP
Rosetti, F. A. 1750–92	Parthia in D (1781) (0221–2000–0000)	MS (MGG*)
	Parthia II (0221–2000–0000)	MS (MGG*)
	Partita No. 3 in D (0221–2000–0000) (Ed. F. Kneusslin)	Kneusslin, 1954
	Partita in F (0301–2000–0000–violone)	Br. & H.
	Notturno in D (1010–2000–1110)	Artia
	Four Partia in d (0102–2 ca–2000–0000)	MS
Rousselot, A. 1829–94	Septet, Op. 28 (0101–1000–1011–pf)	Richault
Sauguet, H. 1901–	Six Images pour une Vie de Jeanne d'Arc (1943) (1111–1100–0000–pf)	MS (G)
Schat, P. 1935–	Septet (1957) (1100–bcl–1000–0010–pf, perc)	Donemus, 1958
Shapey, R. 1921–	Concerto (0010–1000–1010–pf, 2 perc)	Composer, 1954
Shepherd, A. 1880–1958	Praeludium (1942) (1101–1000–1110)	MS (R)
Spohr, L. 1784–1859	Septet in A, Op. 147 (1853) (1011–1000–1010–pf)	Peters [ca. 1855]; Costallat; Musica Rara, 1966
Sprongl, N. 1892–	Septet (1111–bcl–1100–0000)	Vienna, Composer

Stalnaker, W. P.	Rondo (1949) (1011–bcl–2100–0000)	MS (Composer, Univ. of Louis- ville, Louis- ville, Ky., U.S.A.)
Steinbach, F. 1855–1916	Septet in A, Op. 7 (0110–1000–1110–pf)	Schott [1882]
Stevens, H. 1908–	Septet (1957) (0011–1000–0220)	CFE
Stieber, H. 1886–	Spielmusik No. 3 (0222–1000–0000)	Hofmeister, 1953
Stravinsky, I. 1882–	†Septet (1953) (0011–1000–1110–pf)	Bo. & H., 1953
Sylvius, C.	Septet (1111–1110–0000)	Baron, 1953
Tansman, A. 1897–	Septet (1930) (0111–1000–0111)	Eschig
Tiessen, H. 1887–	Amsel-Septett in G, Op. 20 (1914–15) (1010–1000–2110)	R. & E., 1957
Toja, G. 17th Cent.	Serenade (1121–2000–0000)	Ricordi
Travis, E.	Overture (1956) (0011–1100–0001–pf, perc)	MS (Composer, Box 436, Dallas, NC, U.S.A.)
Uber, C. B. 1746–1812	Divertimento (1000–1000–2101–hpcd)	(T)
Ulbrecht, F. J. 18th Cent.	Musica à tavola nuovamente (0021–2200–0000)	MS? (E*)
Uribe-Holguin, G. 1880–	Divertimento, Op. 89 (1000–1000–2110–hp)	MS (Ve)
Vaňhal, J. K. 1739–1813	Cassatio in F (2000–2000–1101)	MS (MGG*)
Wagenseil, G. C. 1715–77	Cinq Suites de Pièces (0022–2000–0000–pf)	MS (E*)
Weber, B. 1916–	Concerto, Op. 32 (1111–1000–0010–pf solo)	CFE
Weber, J. M. 1854–1906	Sketch from my Life (1896) (0011–2000–1110)	Aibl, 1899
Weisse, H. 1892–1940	Partita (1011–1000–1110)	MS?
Winter, P. 1755–1825	Septet in E♭, Op. 10 (0010–2000–2110)	Nadermann
Witt, F. 1770–1835	Septet (0011–1000–2110)	Schott, n.d.
Wood, C. 1866–1926	Septet (0011–1000–1111)	MS (H)
Wyner, Y. 1929–	†Serenade (1958) (1000–1110–0110–pf)	CFE
Yun, I. 1917–	†Music for seven Instruments (1111–1000–1010)	B. & B., 1960
Zach, J. 1699–1773	Concerto (Ed. W. Höckner) (0000–2000–2110–pf)	Pro Musica, 1949

Zagwijn, H. 1878–1954	Nocturne (1918) (1011–ca–1000–0000–hp, cel)	Donemus
Zwing, M.	Six Pièces d'harmonie, Op. 2 (1021–2000–0100)	Worms

6.7 *Eight Instruments*

Allen, P. H. 1883–1952	The Muses (1121–1110–0000)	Whitney
Andrico, M. 1894–	Octet, Op. 8 (0010–1000–2111) (?)	ESPLA, 1955
Angerer, P. 1927–	Quinta Ton (1111–1210–0000)	UE
Arriaga y Balzola, J. C. de 1806–26	Nada y mucho (0000–1000–2111–gt, pf)	Bilbao, 1929
Badings, H. 1907–	Octet (0011–1000–2111)	Donemus, 1952
Balakirev, M. 1837–1910	Octet, Op. 3 (1855) (1100–1000–1111–pf)	RS, 1959
Bax, A. 1883–1953	Octet (1934) (0000–1000–2211–pf)	Murdoch
Beethoven, L. van 1770–1827	†Octet in E♭, Op. 103 (0222–2000–0000)	Artaria, 1834; Br. & H., 1863, 1954; Sikorski; Broude; Peters; Eulenburg
	†Rondino in E♭, Op. 146 (0222–2000–0000)	Diabelli, 1829; Br. & H., 1863, 1954; Sikorski; Eulenburg; IMC; AMP; Mercury, 1946
	Eleven Viennese Dances No. 2 (Ed. H. Riemann) (1011–2000–2001)	Br. & H., 1907
Behrend, F. 1889–	Suite, Op. 116 (1121–bcl–2100–0000)	Composer, 1956
Berkeley, L. 1903–	Diversions (0111–1000–1110–pf)	Chester, 1964
Blacher, B. 1903–	Octet (1965) (0011–1000–2111)	B. & B., 1966
Boccherini, L. 1743–1805	Sinfonia concertante, Op. 41 (Ed. K. Haas) (0101–1000–2120)	Pleyel, n.d. Novello
Böhner, J. L. 1787–1860	Serenade, Op. 9 (1001–2000–2110)	Br. & H., n.d.
Borris, S. 1906–	Oktett, Op. 99/4 (0011–1000–2111)	Sirius
	Octet, Op. 25/3 (1111–bcl–2100–0000)	Sirius [1952]
Brun, G. b. 1878	Passacaille (2121–2000–0000)	Lemoine

Brusselmans, M. 1886–1960	Prelude & Fugue (1923) (1111–ca, bcl–1100–0000)	Salabert
Bumcke, G. b. 1876	Der Spaziergang, Op. 22 (1121–ca–1000–0000–hp)	R. & E., 1906
Burkhard, W. 1900–55	Serenade, Op. 77 (1945) (1011–1000–1101–hp)	Bo. & H., 1952
Butterley, N. 1935–	†Laudes (fl/picc/alt fl, cl/bcl–1100–1110–pf)	
Cadow, P. 1923–	Festliche Musik nach Johann Kuhnau (0200–2300–0000–timp)	Ultraton [1952]
Camilucci, G.	Duo Danzi (1110–1000–1110–pf)	Carisch, 1940
Campbell-Watson, F. 1898–	Divertimento (1121–bcl–2000–0000)	Witmark, 1948
Cartellieri, C. A. 1772–1807	Two Divertimenti (0222–2000–0000)	(E*)
Cibulka, M. A. ca. 1770	Deutsche Redouten (0101–2000–2001)	MS (E*)
Civil, A. 1929–	Octet (1951) (0222–2000–0000)	MS (Composer) (Downe Hall, Downe, Kent)
Codivilla, F. b. 1841	Octet in E♭ (1111–2010–ct–0000)	Pizzi, 1919
Cole, H. 1917–	Octet (0222–2000–0000)	MS (MT, Mar. 1962)
Dalley, O. E. 1903–	Reverie (2122–1000–0000)	Witmark, 1933
Dodd, P.	Octet (0222–2000–0000)	MS?
Dolmetsch, F.	Octet in f, Op. 27 (1010–1000–1111–pf)	Costallat, 1858
Domansky, A. 1883–	Octet (1122–2000–0000)	MS (Ve)
Downey, J.	Octet (1956–8) (1112–bcl–1100–0000)	MS (Composer, Chicago)
Dubois, T. 1837–1924	Suite No. 1 (2122–1000–0000)	Heugel, 1898
	Suite No. 2 (2122–1000–0000)	Leduc, n.d. [1898]
Dupont, J. 1906–	Octet (0011–1000–2110–pf)	Hamelle, 1934
Eberwein, T. M. 1775–1831	Musique d'harmonie (2112–2000–0000)	MS (MGG) (LB, Darmstadt)
Einem, G. von 1918–	Alpsbacher Tanz-Serenade, Op. 17 (0122–2100–0000)	Schott
El-Dabh, H. 1921–	Thumaniya (1952) (picc/fl 110–1200–0000–timp, perc)	Peters
Fellegara, V. 1927–	Octet (1953) (1111–1210–0000)	SZ, 1955
Ferguson, H. 1908–	Octet, Op. 4 (1933) (0011–1000–2111)	Bo. & H., 1934

A LIST OF MUSIC FOR THE HORN

Franzl, I.
1736–1811
Partita a 8
(0222–2000–0000)
MS (Rie)

Fricker, P. R. 1920–
Octet, Op. 30 (1958)
(1011–1000–1111)
Schott, 1959

Frommel, G. 1906–
Suite, Op. 18
(1121–dbn–2000–0000)
SM

Gál, H. 1890–
Divertimento, Op. 22 (1924)
(1121–2100–0000)
Leuckart, 1925

Gavazenni, G. 1909–
Aria
(0010–2000–2111)
Bongiovanni

Goepfert, C. A.
1768–1818
Eighteen Pieces
(0121–2100–serpent–0000)
André, n.d.

Goossens, E.
1893–1962
Octet, Op. 3 (1911)
(1010–1000–2110–hp)
MS (G)

Gouvy, L. T.
1819–98
Octet in E♭, Op. 71
(1122–2000–0000)
Kistner [1882]

Harrison, L. 1917–
Solstice
(1100–1000–0021–pf, cel)
Peer

Hartmann, E.
1836–98
Serenade, Op. 43
(1122–2000–0000)
R. & E., 1890

Hayasaka, F.
Suite in 7 parts
(1111–2000–0000–pf, xyl)
Tokyo

Haydn, F. J.
1732–1809
†Divertimento in G, Hob. X, 12
(1000–2000–2111)
Artaria, 1781;
BVK, 1952

Divertimento, Hob. II, Es 12
(0222–2000–0000)
Doblinger

Divertimento, Hob. II, Es 13
(0222–2000–0000)
Doblinger

Divertimento, Hob. II, Es 16
(0222–2000–0000)
Doblinger

Divertimento, Hob. II, F 7
(0222–2000–0000)
Kahnt, 1902;
IMC; Marks

†Parthia (Octet in F), Hob. II,
Es 14
(0222–2000–0000)
Doblinger; IMC

†Divertimento in B♭
(Ed. K. Geiringer)
(0222–2000–0000)
Schuberth, 1932

Three Feldpartiten, Hob. II, 41–3
(0222–2000–0000)
Musica Rara

Three Feldpartiten, Hob. II, 44–6
(0203–2000–serpent–0000)
Musica Rara

Hob. II, 46
(Ed. R. A. Boudreau)
(0203–2000–0000–db/dbn)
Peters, 1960

†Six Divertimenti, Hob. X, 1–5, 12
(0000–2000–2111–baryton)
Artaria, 1781

No. 1 in G, Hob. X, 12
(Ed. E. F. Schmidt)
(1000–2000–2111)
BVK, 1952

No. 5 in G, Hob. X
(Ed. E. F. Schmidt)
(1000–2000–2111)
BVK, 1952

329

†Divertimento in F, Hob. II, 16 — Hofmeister, 1954
(0002–2ca–2000–2000)
(Ed. K. Janetzky)
Concertino, Hob. II, D 15
(1000–2000–2111)
Concertino, Hob. II, D 13
(0100–2000–2111)
Three English Marches, Hob. VIII, — Musica Rara, 1960
1–3 (0202–2100–serpent–0000)

Henneberg, R.
1853–1925
Serenade — FST
(1122–2000–0000)

Henze, H. W.
1926–
†Concerto per il Marigny — Schott, 1956
(0010–bcl–1110–0110–pf)
Adagio (1963) — Schott, 1965
(0011–1000–2111)

Herrmann, G.
1808–78
Octet (1850) — MS (MGG)
(1010–1000–2111)

Herrmann, K.
1882–
Octet, Op. 35 (ca. 1926) — MS
(1100–1000–2111)

Herschel, F. W.
1738–1822
Two military Concertos — MS (G)
(0202–2200–0000)

Hindemith, P.
1895–1963
†Octet (1957–8) — Schott, 1958
(0011–1000–1211)

Hirschbach, H.
1812–88
Octet, Op. 26 — MS? (F)
(1011–1000–1111)

Hoffmann, H.
1842–1902
Octet in F, Op. 80 — Br. & H., 1880
(1011–1000–2110)

Hoffmeister, F. A.
1754–1812
Harmonie — MS? (E*)
(0222–2000–0000) (Ed. J. — (CM Lib.)
Leach)

Horowitz, J. 1927–
Phantasy on a theme of Couperin — Mills
(1122–2000–0000)

Joubert, J. 1927–
Octet, Op. 33 — Novello, 1964
(0011–1000–2111)

Juon, P.
1872–1940
Octet in B♭, Op. 27 (1904) — Schlesinger, 1905
(0111–1000–1110–pf)

Kaun, H.
1863–1932
Octet in F, Op. 34 — R. Kaun; Rühle,
(0011–1000–2111) — 1892

Kling, H. A. L.
1842–1918
Spring Poetry — Andraud
(1222–1000–0000)

Kornauth, E. 1891–
Octet, Op. 40b (1949) — MS (MGG)
(0011–1000–2111)

Kospoth, O. C. E.
1753–1817
Grosse Serenade — Berlin, Neue
(0000–2000–2211) — Musikhandlung
Grosse Serenade, Op. 11 — Speyer, 1792
(0000–2000–2211)
Grosse Serenade, Op. 12 — Speyer, 1792
(0000–2000–2211)
Grosse Serenade, Op. 13 — Darmstadt, 1793
(0000–2000–2211)

Koželuch, L. A.
1747–1818
Die wiedergebundene Töchter — MS (MGG*)
Otto desII (1794)
(0222–2000–0000)

	Cassazione	MS (MGG*)
	(1022–2000–0000–2 violetti)	
Kraft, A.	Notturno	MS (MGG)
1749–1820	(2000–2000–0220)	
Kraus, J. M.	Andante	MS (F)
1756–92	(2000–2000–2110)	
Krol, B. 1920–	Capriccio da camera, Op. 35	Simrock, 1961
	(1001–bcl–1110–0001–pf)	
Kupferman, M.	Chamber Symphony	MS (from M. & M.)
1926–	(1111–bcl–1000–0101)	
Lachner, F.	Octet in B♭, Op. 156 (1850)	Kistner [1873]
1803–90	(1122–2000–0000)	
Laurischkus, M.	Suite, Op. 23	Simrock
1876–1929	(1112–ca–2000–0000)	
La Violette, W.	Octet (1934)	MS (Ho, R, T)
1894–	(0111–1000–1111)	
Lazzari, S.	Octuor, Op. 20 (1890)	E. & S. [ca. 1920]
1857–1944	(1112–ca–2000–0000)	
Lessard, J. 1920–	†Octct (1952)	CFE
	(1011–2210–0000)	
Louis Ferdinand,	Octet in F, Op. 12	Br. & H., 1808
Prince of Prussia	(0010–2000–0220–pf)	
1772–1806		
Lutyens, E. 1906–	Suite gauloise (1944)	de Wolfe
	(0222–2000–0000)	
Mašek, V.	Nine Parthien	MS? (MGG)
1755–1831	(0222–2000–0000)	
	Three Serenades	MS? (MGG)
	(0222–2000–0000)	
Maxwell Davies, P.	Ricercar & Doubles on 'To	Schott, 1963
1934–	many a Well' (1959)	
	(1111–1000–0110–hpcd)	
Michel, J.	Three Quartetti (Divertimenti) à 8	MS?
1745–1810	(0200–2000–2110)	
Migot, G. 1891–	Sérénade	MS? (G)
	(0111–1000–2110)	
Mills, C. 1914–	Concerto sereno, Op. 77 (1948)	CFE
	(0222–2000–0000)	
Mirandolle, L.	Octet in D (1942–3)	Composer, 1944;
	(0011–1000–2111)	Baron
Molbe, H.	Octet in F, Op. 20	Rörich [1897]
1835–1915	(0011–1000–2111)	
	Octet in d, Op. 45	Hofmeister
	(0100–basset hn–1000–2111)	[1898]
	Serenata in B♭, Op. 46	Rörich [1897?]
	(0100–basset hn–1000–2111)	
Monteux, P.	Arietta & March	Mathot
1875–1964	(1111–1100–0001–perc)	
Mote, A. R.	Octet	MS? (Cob, DMM)
20th Cent.	(1011–1000–2110)	
Mozart, W. A.	†Divertimento in E♭, K. 196e	Br. & H. [1801];
1756–91	(1775) (0222–2000–0000)	Peters; Musica
		Rara, 1967

	†Divertimento in B♭, K. 196f (1775) (0222–2000–0000)	Br. & H. [1801]; Peters
	†Serenade No. 11 in E♭, K. 375 (1781) (0222–2000–0000)	André [1792]; Br. & H. [1801], 1880, 1956; Eulenburg; Peters; Broude; Musica Rara, 1961
	†Serenade No. 12 in c, K. 388 (1782) (0222–2000–0000)	André [after 1811], 1875; Br. & H.; Eulenburg; Peters; Broude; Musica Rara, 1961
	Adagio in E♭ (from K. 375) (0222–2000–0000)	Ars Viva
	Divertimenti in E♭, F, and E♭, K. Anh. 224, 225, 228 (authenticity doubtful) (0222–2000–0000)	
	†Harmonie-Musik: Die Entführung aus dem Serail (Arr. Mozart?; Giegling) (0202–2ca–2000–0000)	BVK
	Allegro, K. Anh. 96 (fragment) (0222–2000–0000)	
Müller-Zürich, P. 1898–	Marienleben, Op. 8 (1924) (1110–1000–2110)	Schott
Musgrave, T. 1928–	Chamber Concerto No. 3 (1966) (0011–1000–2111)	Chester
Mysliveček, J. 1737–81	Three Octets (0222–20000–0000)	SHV, 1962
Neuhauser, L. 18th Cent.	Nocturne (0200–2000–2101)	MS? (F)
Neukomm, S. Ritter von 1778–1858	Octetto (1111–1100–0011)	MS (Boston Pub. Lib)
Nisle, J. F. b. 1768	Otetto (1010–2000–2110)	MS (MGG*) (Musikfr., Vienna)
Nováček, R. 1866–1900	Sinfonietta, Op. 48 (1122–2000–0000)	Br. & H., 1905; M. & M.
Ordoñez, C. d' 1734–86	Notturno in F (0202–2ca–2000–0000)	MS (MGG*)
Pacini, G. 1796–1867	Octet (0101–1000–3011)	MS? (MGG)
Pascal, C. 1921–	Octuor (2112–1100–0000)	Durand, 1947
Paz, J. C. 1897–	Octeto, Op. 16 (1930) (1102–2200–0000)	MS (T)

A LIST OF MUSIC FOR THE HORN

Pentland, B. 1912–	Octet (1948) (1111–2110–0000)	CMC
Peters, G. 1866–1937	Nocturne in D (1913–4) (0111–1000–2110)	UE, 1918
Petyrek, F. 1892–1951	Divertimento in B♭ (1923) (2112–2000–0000)	UE; Andraud
Phillips, I. C.	Three hunting Songs (0222–2000–0000)	OUP
Pierné, G. 1863–1937	Petite Gavotte (1110–1000–2110)	Leduc
Pilss, K. 1902–	Octet (0011–1000–2111)	Doblinger, 1957
Piticchio, P. P. fl. 1780	Six Pieces (0402–2000–0000)	MS(F)
Pleyel, I. 1757–1831	Three Serenades (0222–dbn ad lib–2000–0000)	Simrock
Poot, M. 1901–	†Octet (0011–1000–2111)	CeBeDeM, 1948, 1965
Ranta, S. 1901–60	Suite symphonique (1926–8) (1010–1000–2110–pf)	(MGG)
Raymond, E.	Nocturne (1011–1000–1111)	MS (F)
Rebner, E. W. 1910–	Suite (0101–ca, dbn–1200–0000–perc)	MS
Reicha, A. 1770–1836	Octet in E♭, Op. 96 (0111–1000–2110)	J. & C.
	Octet (0222–2000–0000)	Musica Rara
Reinecke, C. 1824–1910	Octet in B♭, Op. 216 (1122–2000–0000)	Kistner, 1892; Zimmermann
Reuss, A. 1871–1935	Octet in B, Op. 37 (1918) (0222–2000–0000)	Halbreiter, 1920; Zimmermann
Revueltas, S. 1899–1940	Toccata (without a fugue) (1933) (picc–0030–1100–1000–timp)	Peer, 1959
Ricci-Signori, A. 1867–1965	Fantasia burlesca (1111–1000–0000–pf 4h, xyl)	Carisch, 1925
Ries, F. 1784–1838	Grand Ottetto in A♭, Op. 128 (0011–1000–1111–pf)	Probst [ca. 1831]; Kistner
Rosetti, F. A. 1746–92	Parthia in E♭ (0222–2000–0000)	MS (MGG*)
	Harmonie (0222–2000–0000)	Pleyel
Rubinstein, A. 1830–94	Otetto in D, Op. 9 (1010–1000–1111–pf)	Peters [1856?]
Saint-Saëns, C. 1835–1921	Feuillet d'album, Op. 81 (1122–2000–0000)	Leduc
Schaefer, T. 1904–	Divertimento mesto, Op. 22 (1946) (1111–1000–1110)	MS (MGG)
Schenk, J. 1753–1836	Concertante (0010–2000–1211)	MS (MGG*)
Schneider, G. A. 1770–1839	12 Harmonien (2022–2000–0000)	MS (E*)

Schubert, F. 1797–1826	†Octet in F, Op. 166 (D. 803) (0011–1000–2111)	Costallat, 1853; Schreiber [ca. 1875]; Peters, 1953; Br. & H., 1956; IMC; Bo. & H.
	†Menuet & Finale, D. 72 (0222–2000–0000)	Br. & H., 1889; AMP
Schwaen, K. 1909–	Concertino Apollineo (1101–ca, bcl–1100–0000–pf)	Litolff
Seiff, J.	Harmoniestücke (1021–2200–0000)	Falter
Sibelius, J. 1865–1957	Canzonetta, Op. 62a (0010–bcl–4000–0001–hp) (Arr. I. Stravinsky)	Br. & H.
Spohr, L. 1784–1859	†Octet in E, Op. 32 (0010–2000–1211)	Steiner, n.d.; Costallat; Eulenburg, 1888; BVK, 1958; Peters; Musica Rara, 1962
Stanford, C. V. 1852–1924	Serenade in F, Op. 95 (1011–1000–1111)	Stainer
Stieber, H. 1886–	Octet (Spielmusik No. 3) (1222–1000–0000)	Hofmeister, 1953
Stranensky, T. fl. ca. 1800	Parthia (Ed. H. Schultz) (0222–2000–0000)	Nagel, 1941
Tardos, B. 1910–	Divertimento (1936) (0222–2000–0000)	MS (G)
Tayber, A. 1756–1822	Three Octets (0200–2000–2101)	MS (E*, MGG)
Thieriot, F. 1838–1919	Octet in B♭, Op. 62 (0011–1000–2111)	RB, 1893
Thilman, J. P. 1906–	News (1111–1110–0000–pf)	n.p., Composer, 1956
Tischhauser, F. 1921–	Octet (0011–1000–2111)	(Schweiz)
Toch, E. 1887–1964	Roundelay: Cavalcade (Nos. IV & V from Five Pieces) (1111–2000–0000–2 perc)	Mills, 1963
Trost, J. K. d. 1651	Partita No. IV (0006–2000–0000)	MS (E*)
Uhl, A. 1909–	Eine vergnügliche Musik (1945) (0222–2000–0000)	UE, 1953
Varèse, E. 1883–1965	†Octandre (1923) (1111–1110–0001)	Curwen, 1924; Ricordi, 1956
Wagenaar, B. 1894–	Concerto (1942) (1111–1000–1110)	C. Fischer
Wagenseil, G. C. 1715–77	Drei Partie (0202–2 ca–2000–0000)	MS? (E*)
Wailly, P. de 1856–1933	Octet, Op. 22 (1122–1100–0000)	Rouart [ca. 1905]; Salabert

A LIST OF MUSIC FOR THE HORN

Walter, A. 1821–96	Octet in B♭, Op. 7 (0111–1000–1111)	Kistner [1850?], 1880
Walzel, L. M. 1902–	Otteto sereno (0011–1000–2111)	(WWM)
Weiland, J. J. d. 1663	Harmonie (Ed. J. J. Leach) (0222–2000–0000)	MS (CM Lib)
Weingartner, F. 1863–1942	Octet in G, Op. 73 (0011–1000–2110–pf)	Birnbach, 1925
Weisse, H. 1892–1940	Octet (0011–1000–2111)	MS?
Wellesz, E. 1885–	Octet, Op. 67 (0011–1000–2111)	Lengnick, 1950
Winter, P. von 1754–1825	Partita (0222–2000–0000)	BAI
	Ottetto (1011–2000–1110)	Br. & H. [ca. 1812]
Wuorinen, C. 1938–	Octet (0110–1010–1011–pf)	M. & M.
Zapf, J. N.	Parthia (0222–2000–0000)	MS? (E*)
Zich, O. 1879–1934	Octet (0011–1000–2111)	HM

6.8 Nine Instruments

Adaskin, M. 1906–	†Rondino (1961) (1111–1000–2110)	CMC
Altman, E.	Tanz-Suite (1122–2000–0001)	Hofmeister
Angerer, P. 1927–	Konzert (0000–2 rec–2000–2210)	Doblinger
Asioli, B. 1769–1832	Serenade (1001–2000–2101–pf)	(F)
Bach, C. P. E. 1714–88	Ten Sonatinas (Wotq. 96–105) (1762–4) (2000–2000–2110–hpcd)	MS (Cons. Brussels)
Bartoš, J. Z. 1908–	Divertimento No. 1, Op. 79 (1957) (1222–2000–0000)	Panton, 1960
Beethoven, L. van 1770–1827	Adagio & Allegro in F for a musical Clock (1799) (Arr. W. Hess) (1222–2000–0000)	Br. & H., 1957
Bertini, H. 1798–1876	Nonet in D, Op. 107 (1101–1100–0111–pf)	Lemoine
Bonvin, L. 1850–1939	Romanze, Op. 19a (1222–2000–0000)	Br. & H.
	Melodie, Op. 56b (1222–2000–0000)	Br. & H.
Bořkovec, P. 1894–	Nonet (1940–1) (1111–1000–1111)	HM, 1945
Bräutigam, H. 1914–42	Kleine Jagdmusik, Op. 11 (1938) (1222–2000–0000)	Br. & H., 1939, 1956
Bresgen, C. 1913–	Jagdkonzert (1122–1000–1001)	Schott

Brun, G. 1878–	Passacaille, Op. 25	Lemoine
	(2121–2000–0001)	
Bütow, L. 1896–	Kammersymphonie, Op. 1	MS (Ve)
	(1111–1000–1110–hp)	
Burghauser, J.	Konzert (1942)	BVK
1921–	(1111–1000–1111)	
Burian, E. F.	Nonet in D (1938)	MS? (G, Ga)
1904–59	(1111–1000–1111)	
Caturla, A. G.	†Primera Suite Cubana (1931)	NME, 1933
1906–40	(1111–ca, bcl–1100–0000–pf)	
Chavez, C. 1899–	Energia (1925)	MS (Fleisher)
	(picc–1001–1110–0111)	
Cianchi, E.	Nonetto	Paoletti, 1868
1833–90	(0222–dbn–2000–0000)	
Clementi, A. 1925–	Concertino in forma di variazioni	SZ
	(1956)	
	(1101–dbn–1000–1011–pf)	
Cole, H. 1917–	Serenade	Novello
	(1222–2000–0000)	
Czerny, C.	Nocturne, Op. 95	Kistner, n.d.
1791–1857	(1011–1000–1111–pf)	
David, T. C., 1925–	Concerto	Doblinger
	(1111–1000–1111)	
Delden, L. van	Fantasie, Op. 87	Donemus, 1965
1919–	(0222–2000–0000–hp)	
Dobiáš, V. 1909–	†Of the native Land of mine (1952)	Orbis, 1953
	(1111–1000–1111)	
Drobisch	Six Angloises neuves	MS (E*, MGG)
	(0022–2200–0000–pf)	
Druzecky, G.	Pièces d'harmonie	(F)
18th Cent.	(0222–2100–0000)	
Eisler, H.	Nonet I; Variations	Peters, 1962
1898–1962	(1011–1000–2111)	
Farrenc, L.	Nonet in E♭, Op. 38	MS (MGG)
1804–75	(1111–1000–1111)	
Feldman, M. 1926–	Numbers	Peters
	(1000–1011–1011–pf/cel, perc)	
Finzi, G. 1901–56	A Severn Rhapsody	Stainer, 1934
	(1120–2000–2110)	
Foerster, J. B.	Nonet, Op. 147 (1931)	HM, 1948
1859–1951	(1111–1000–1111)	
Folprecht, Z.	†Concertino, Op. 21 (1940)	HM, 1949
1900–61	(1111–1000–1111)	
Frankel, B. 1906–	Nonet	Mills, 1965
	(1111–1111–0000–acc)	
Froelich, F. T.	Waltzer (Ed. H. Scherchen)	Ars Viva, 1954
1803–36	(1122–2010–0000)	
Gerhard, R. 1896–	Nonet (1956)	Mills, 1957
	(1111–1111–0000–acc)	
Gilchrist, W. W.	Nonet	MS? (Chase, T)
1846–1916	(1010–1000–2111–pf)	
Gilse, J. van	Nonet (1916)	Donemus
1881–1944	(0111–1000–2111)	

Giuranna, B. 1902–	Adagio e Allegro da Concerto (1111–1000–1111)	Ricordi
Goossens, E. 1893–1962	Fantasy Nonet, Op. 40 (1924) (1122–2100–0000)	Curwen, 1926; Leduc, 1962
Gounod, C. 1818–93	†Petite Symphonie in B♭ (1222–2000–0000)	Costallat, 1904; IMC
Gouvy, L. T. 1819–98	Petite Suite gauloise, Op. 90 (1222–2000–0000)	UE, 1900
Hába, A. 1893–	†Nonet, Op. 40 (1931) (1111–1000–1111)	SHV, 1966
	Nonet, Op. 41 (1931) (1111–1000–1111)	MS? (Ga, MGG)
	†Nonet, Op. 82 (1953) (1111–1000–1111)	SNKLHU, 1960
	Nonet, Op. 95 (1963) (1111–1000–1111)	(Ga)
Hába, K. 1898–	Nonet, Op. 32 (1948) (1111–1000–1111)	MS (Ga)
Harsányi, T. 1898–1954	Nonet (1927) (1111–1000–2110)	Sirène, 1930
Hauer, M. 1883–1959	Divertimento, Op. 61 (1101–1000–2110–pf)	MS?
Haydn, F. J. 1732–1809	Eight Notturni for King Ferdinand IV of Naples (1788–90) Hob. II, 25–32 (0200–2000–0201–2 lire organizzate)	
	†No. 1 in C (Ed. E. F. Schmid) (Ed. H. C. Robbins Landon) (1100–2000–2211)	Holler, 1932 Doblinger, 1961
	†No. 2 in F	
	†No. 3 in G (Ed. A. Sandberger) (1100–2000–2211)	Sandberger, 1936
	†No. 4 in F (Ed. K. Geiringer) (1100–2000–2211)	UE, 1932
	†No. 5 in C (Ed. K. Geiringer) (1100–2000–2211)	UE, 1931
	†No. 6 in G (Ed. E. Fendler) (1100–2000–2211)	Music Press, 1946
	†No. 7 in C (Ed. E. F. Schmid) (1100–2000–2211)	MWV, 1936; BVK
	No. 8 in C (Ed. E. F. Schmid) (1100–2000–2211)	MWV, 1936; BVK
	Cassation in G, Hob. II, G 1 (Ed. H. C. Robbins Landon) (0200–2000–2210)	Doblinger, 1959
	Divertimento in C, Hob. II, 17 (Ed. R. Steppan) (0200–2000–2201)	Doblinger, 1960
	Divertimento in F, Hob. II, 20 (Ed. H. C. Robbins Landon) (0200–2000–2201)	Doblinger

Y

	Fünf Konzerte für König Ferdinand IV von Neapel: Lirenkonzerte, Hob. VIIh, 1–5 (1786) (Ed. H. C. Robbins Landon) (0000–2000–2201–2 liren/fl/ ob/rec)	Doblinger
	Six Scherzandi, Hob. II, 33–38 (Ed. H. C. Robbins Landon) (1200–2000–2001–cont)	Doblinger, 1961
Hlobil, E. 1901–	Nonet, Op. 27 (1946) (1111–1000–1111)	Orbis, 1951
Hoffmeister, F. A. 1754–1812	Serenade in B♭ (0222–dbn–2000–0000)	Simrock, n.d.
	Serenade in E♭ (Ed. E. Hess) (0222–dbn–2000–0000)	Kneusslin, 1962
Hovhaness, A. 1911–	†Tower Music, Op. 129 (1111–2111–0000)	Rongwen
Ishii, M. 1936–	Präludium and Variationen (1960) (1011–1000–1110–perc, pf)	Tokyo, Ongaku, 1962
Jaroch, J. 1920–	†Kindersuite, Op. 7 (1952) (1111–1000–1111)	SNKLHU, 1956
Jelinek, H. 1901–	Praeludium, Passacaglia & Fuga, Op. 4 (1922) (1011–1000–2111)	UE
Jeremiáš, O. 1892–1962	Overture: Fantasy on old Czech Chorales (1938) (1111–1000–1111)	Panton, 1965
Jirák, K. B. 1891–	Variations, Scherzo & Finale, Op. 45a (1942)	MS (Ve)
Jong, M. de 1891–	Nonet, Op. 33 (1939) (1111–1000–2110)	CeBeDeM
Kaffka, W. 1751–1806	Divertimento per 9 stromenti (0022–2000–0201)	MS (MGG*)
Kahn, I. 1905–56	Actus tragicus, Op. 12 (1946) (1111–1000–2110)	Bomart
	Petite Suite bretonne (1936) (1111–1000–1110–hp)	CFE
Karel, R. 1880–1945	Nonet (1945) (Instr. F. Hertl) (1111–1000–1111)	MS? (G, Ga)
Kittl, J. F. 1806–68	Nonet (1110–2000–0111–pf)	MS? (MGG)
Kornauth, E. 1891–1959	Kammermusik in f, Op. 31 (1924) (1110–1000–2111)	UE, 1925
Koschovitz, J. d. ca. 1800	Six Hongroises (1803) (0222–dbn–2000–0000)	(MGG)
	Six Hongroises (2221–2000–0000)	(MGG)
Kospoth, O. C. E. 1753–1817	Composizioni sopra il Pater noster, Op. 20 (0201–2000–2101)	André, 1794

A LIST OF MUSIC FOR THE HORN

Kozeluch, L. A. 1747–1818	Cassazione in F (1022–2000–0000–2 violetti)	MS (Herzogl. Bib. Wolfenbüttel)
Křejčí, I. 1904–	Nonet (1937) (1111–1000–1111)	MS (Ga, Ve)
Krenek, E. 1900–	Symphonic Music (Divertimento), Op. 11 (1922) (1011–1000–2111)	UE, 1923
Kretschmer, E. 1830–1908	Nonet (1111–1000–1111)	MS (MGG)
Krol, B. 1920–	Konzertante Musik, Op. 6 (0222–2000–0100)	Br. & H., 1953
Krommer, F. 1760–1831	Concertino, Op. 18 (1100–2000–2111)	Hofmeister
	Three Partitas, Op. 45 (0222–dbn–2000–0000)	BAI, 1803
	Harmonie in F, Op. 57 (0222–dbn–2000–0000)	IC, 1808; Haslinger
	Harmonie in B♭, Op. 67 (0222 dbn 2000–0000)	IC [1808?]; Haslinger
	Harmonie in E♭, Op. 69 (0222–dbn–2000–0000)	IC [1808?]; Steiner
	†Harmonie in E♭, Op. 71 (0222–dbn–2000–0000)	Haslinger [after 1826]; Schlesinger
	Harmonie in F, Op. 73 (0222–dbn–2000–0000)	Steiner [ca. 1810]; Haslinger [after 1826]
	Harmonie in C, Op. 76 (0222–dbn–2000–0000)	Steiner [ca. 1810]; Haslinger [after 1826]
	Harmonie in F, Op. 77 (0222–dbn–2000–0000)	IC [1809?]; Steiner; Haslinger [after 1826]
	Harmonie in B♭, Op. 78 (0222–dbn–2000–0000)	Steiner [ca. 1810]; Haslinger [after 1826]
	Harmonie in E♭, Op. 79 (0222–dbn–2000–0000) (Ed. K. Janetzky)	Steiner [ca. 1810] Hofmeister
	Harmonie in F, Op. 83 (0222–dbn–2000–0000)	Steiner [ca. 1810]; Haslinger [after 1826]
	Harmonie à neuf parties (0222–2000–0001)	Dufaut, n.d.
Kvapil, J. 1892–1958	Nonet (1944) (1111–1000–1111)	MS (Ga, Ve)
Lachenmann, H. 1935–	Fünf Strophen (1000–bcl–1100–0101–pf, vib, timp)	Post, n.d.
Lachner, F. 1803–90	Nonet in F (1875) (1111–1000–1111)	MS (MGG)

Lachnith, L. V. 1746–1820	Six Concerti, Opp. 9 & 10 (1100–2000–2001–pf)	Composer
Lang, J. G. 1724–ca. 1800	Concerto, Op. 4 (0200–2000–2101–hpcd)	André, n.d.
Lange, F. G. b. ca. 1861	Nonet in F (1222–2000–0000)	Seeling, 1879; Erdmann
Legley, V. 1915–	Musique de Midi, Op. 33 (1948) (1011–1000–2111)	CeBeDeM, 1956; Maurer
Leibowitz, R. 1913–	Chamber Concerto, Op. 10 (1944) (1111–1000–1111)	UE, 1947
Lekeu, G. 1870–94	Fantaisie symphonique sur deux Airs populaires angevins (0111–1000–2111)	Rouart, 1909; Salabert
Liber, J. A. 1732–1809	Divertimento (0022–2000–0201)	MS (Thurn. u. Taxis Hofbibl.)
Lutyens, E. 1906–	Chamber Concerto, Op. 8/1 (1939) (0111–1110–1110)	Chester, 1947
McPhee, C. 1901–64	†Piano Concerto (1928) (2111–1110–0000–pf)	NME, 1931
Malipiero, R. 1914–	Mosaico (1961) (1111–1000–2111)	SZ
Martín, E. 1915–	Concerto (1944) (1111–2210–0000)	MS (Composer, Municipal Con- servatory, Havana, Cuba)
Martinů, B. 1890–1959	Nonet No. 1 (1924–5) (1111–1000–1110–pf) †Nonet (1959) (1111–1000–1111)	MS (Ga) SNKLHU, 1959
Maštalíř, J. 1906–	Nonet (1935) (1111–1000–1111)	MS? (G, Ga)
Massenet, J. 1842–1912	Introduction & Variations (1111–1000–2110)	Heugel
Mayuzumi, T. 1929–	Olympics: Ballet (0000–2220–0001–pf, perc)	Peters
Merikanto, A. 1893–1958	Konzert (0010–1000–2220–vln solo)	Schott, 1925
Michl, J. W. d. 1810	Konzert (0201–2000–2101)	MS (MGG)
Molbe, H. 1835–1915	Nonet in E♭, Op. 61 (0011–ca–1000–2111) Intermezzo in g, Op. 81 (0011–ca–1000–2111) Scherzo, Op. 83 (0011–ca–1000–2111) Tanzweisen, Op. 87 (0111–1000–2111)	Hofmeister [1897] Hofmeister, 1900 Hofmeister [ca. 1900] Hofmeister [ca. 1900]
Moser, F. J. 1880–1939	Sinfonia in F, Op. 40 (1111–1000–1111)	Doblinger, 1924
Mozart, W. A. 1756–91	†Cassation in B♭, K. 99 (1769) (0200–2000–2111) †Divertimento No. 1 in E♭, K. 113 (1771) (0020–2000–2111)	Br. & H. Br. & H.; Eulenburg; BVK

	Sinfonia (Cavaliere) in B♭, K. 45b (0200–2000–2111)	Peters
Mulder, E. W. 1898–1959	Fuga IV, uit 'Ars Contrapuntica' (1940) (1110–1000–2111)	Donemus
Musgrave, T. 1928–	Chamber Concerto (1962) (0111–1110–1110)	Chester
Mysliveček, J. 1737–81	Four Overtures (0200–2000–2201)	MS (MGG)
Naumann, E. 1832–1910	Serenade in A, Op. 10 (1101–1000–2111)	Simrock [1872]; AMP
Naumann, R.	Kammermusik, Op. 31 (1110–1000–2111)	Doblinger, 1926
Neubauer, F. C. 1760–95	Parthia in B♭ (1791) (1122–2000–0001)	MS? (E*, MGG)
Nisle, J. F. b. 1768	Nonet (1000–2000–2111–pf)	MS (Musikfr., Vienna)
Novák, J. 1921–	†Baletti a nove (1955) (1111–1000–1111)	SNKLHU, 1959
Novák, J. F. 1913–	About the golden-haired Beauty (1955) (1010–1000–0000–6 hp)	(Ga)
Onslow, G. 1784–1853	Nonet in a, Op. 77 (1111–1000–1111)	Kistner, n.d.; Joubert, 1851
Osterc, S. 1895–1941	Nonet (1937) (1111–1000–1111)	MS (MGG)
Otten, L. 1924–	Divertimento No. 3 (1964) (1222–2000–0000)	Donemus
Paccagnini, A. 1930–	Musica da camera (picc–1000–bcl–1000–1011–hp, vib)	UE, 1961
Palester, R. 1907–	Divertimento (1949) (1111–1000–1111)	MS (G, MGG)
Parry, C. H. H. 1848–1918	Nonet in B♭ (ca. 1877) (1122–ca–2000–0000)	MS (G, T)
Pauer, J. 1919–	Divertimento (1961) (1111–1000–1111)	SHV, 1964
Petrželka, V. 1889–	Serenade, Op. 42 (1946) (1111–1000–1111)	MS (G, Ga, MGG)
Piston, W. 1894–	†Divertimento (1946) (2222–1000–0000)	AMP
Praag, H. van 1894–	Fantasie voor fagot en blaas-ensemble (1962) (2221–2000–0000)	Donemus
	Music for wind (2232–2000–0000)	Donemus, 1965
Rheinberger, J. 1839–1901	Nonet in E♭, Op. 139 (1111–1000–1111)	Kistner, 1885
Řídký, J. 1897–1956	†Nonet No. 1 in f, Op. 32 (1934–5) (1111–1000–1111)	HM; Sadló, 1941
	Nonet, Op. 39 (1943) (1111–1000–1111)	HM, 1950

Rochberg, G. 1918–	Chamber Symphony (1953) (1011–1110–1110)	Presser
Rosetti, F. A. 1746–92	Parthia in F (2202–2000–0001)	MS (MGG*) (Öffentl. Wiss. Bibl., Harburg)
	Divertimento (0200–2 basset hn–2000–0201)	MS (MGG*)
Roussel, A. 1864–1937	Le Marchand de sable qui passe, Op. 13 (1908) (1010–1000–2110–hp)	Demets
Rummel, C. 1787–1849	Variations sur un Thème de Méhul, Op. 40 (0222–dbn–2000–0000)	Schott
Rychlík, J. 1916–64	†African Cycle (1961) (1111–2000–0000–pf, perc)	SHV, 1963
Salieri, A. 1750–1825	Zwei Bläserserenaden (Ed. W. Höckner) (2202–2000–0001)	Doblinger
Samazeuilh, G. 1877–	Divertissement et Musette in g (1111–1000–2110)	Durand, 1902
Sammartini, G. B. 1701–75	Concertini (2200–2200–0001)	MS (E*)
Schnorrenberg, R. 1929–	Five Ensaios (1110–1100–1011–pf/hpcd)	n.p., Composer, 1956
Schoeck, O. 1886–1957	Serenade, Op. 1 (1111–1000–2110)	Hug, 1907
Schreck, G. 1849–1918	Divertimento in e. Op. 40 (2122–2000–0000) Nonet (1111–1000–2110)	Br. & H., 1905; AMP MS (Ve)
Schubert, F. 1796–1828	†Eine kleine Trauermusik in e♭ (1813) (0022–dbn–2020–0000)	Br. & H., 1889; AMP
Searle, H. 1915–	Progressions (1111–1000–1111)	(RT, March 21, 1968)
Spaetth, A.	Nonetto (0111–1000–2111)	MS
Spohr, L. 1784–1859	†Nonet in F, Op. 31 (1111–1000–1111)	Haslinger, 1876; Costallat; Litolff, 1890; Peters, 1954; BVK, 1959; M. & M.
Šrom, K. 1904–	†Fairy Tales (1952) (1111–1000–1111) Etudes (1111–1000–1111)	SHV, 1963 SNKLHU, 1965
Stanford, C. V. 1852–1924	Serenade in F, Op. 95 (ca. 1906) (1011–1000–2111)	MS (Stainer)
Stöhr, R. b. 1874	Kammersinfonie in F, Op. 32 (1912) (0111–1000–2110–hp)	Kahnt, 1920
Stürmer, B. 1892–1958	Suite, Op. 9 (2222–1000–0000)	Schott, 1923

Uber, C. B.	Divertissement (1777)	(MGG)
1746–1812	(2000–2000–2101–pf)	
Webern, A.	†Sinfonie, Op. 21 (1928)	UE, 1929
1883–1945	(0010–bcl–2000–2110–hp)	
	†Konzert, Op. 24 (1934)	UE, 1948
	(1110–1110–1010–pf)	
Williamson, M.	Concerto	(BBC, Oct. 1966)
1931–	(1111–1000–0000–2 pf, 8 h)	
Willman, A. A.	Concerto	MS
1909–	(1011–1110–1010–pf)	
Winter, P. von	Harmonia à 9	MS (Rie)
1754–1825	(0222–dbn–2000–0000)	
Wolff, C. 1934–	Nine	Peters
	(1010–1110–0020–pf, cel)	
Wolpe, S. 1902–	Concerto, Op. 22 (1933–4)	MS (Ewen)
	(1011–1110–1010 pf)	
Xenakis, I. 1922–	†Atrées (Homage à Pascal) (1962)	Ed. Franc. Mus.
	(1020–1110–1010–perc)	
Zich, O.	Chod Suite	HM
1879–1934	(1111–1000–1111)	

6.9 Ten or more Instruments

Alwyn, W. 1905–	Concerto	Lengnick
	(1100–2100–2111–perc)	
Andriessen, H.	Suite (1954)	Donemus
1892–	(1212–1220–0000)	
Andriessen, J.	Concertino voor fagot en	Donemus, 1962
1925–	blaasensemble (1962)	
	(solo bn–2222–2000–0000)	
	Respiration Suite (1962)	Donemus, 1962
	(2222–2000–0000)	
	Hommage à Milhaud (1945)	Donemus, 1948
	(1111–sax–1110–1110)	
	Rouw past Electra (1954)	Donemus, 1955
	(1212–1220–0000–timp, perc)	
Angerer, P. 1927–	Cogitatio	Doblinger
	(1111–1000–2111)	
Antoniou, T.	Concertino, Op. 21	BVK
1935–	(1122–2100–0000–pf, 4 perc)	
Arnell, R. 1917–	†Serenade, Op. 57 (1949)	Hinrichsen
	(2222–2000–0001)	
Arnold, M. 1921–	Trevelyan Suite, Op. 96	Faber, 1968
	(3220–2000–0010)	
Aubin, T. 1907–	Cressida Fanfare (1937)	Leduc, 1961
	(0002–4331–0000–timp, perc)	
	Vitrail: Fanfare	Leduc, 1964
	(2000–4331–0000–timp, perc)	
Babbitt, M. 1916–	Music for twelve instruments	Bomart
	(1948)	
	(1111–1100–1111–hp, cel)	
Badings, H. 1907–	Symphonie (1932)	Donemus
	(2222–2100–2111)	

Bardwell, W. 1915–	Antiphonie	(MT, Sept. 1966)
	(2222–2000–0000)	
Beethoven, L. van	†March No. 1 in F	Br. & H.
1770–1827	(picc–0222–dbn–2100–0000–perc)	
	†March No. 2 in C	Br. & H.
	(picc–0222–dbn–2200–0000–perc)	
	†March No. 3 in F	Br. & H.
	(picc–0222–dbn–2100–0000–perc)	
Belfiore, T. 1917–	Dimensioni (1959)	SZ
	(1122–2 sax–1110–0000–timp)	
	Paradigmi (1960)	SZ
	(2131–3220–0000–pf, xyl. 2 perc)	
Bennett, R. R.	A Jazz Calendar	Mills
1936–	(1000–3 sax–1301–0001–pf, perc)	
Bentzon, J.	†Symfonisk Trio, Op. 18 (1929)	Samfundet, 1930
1897–1951	(3 groups: I, 4 hn; II, 13 vln;	
	III, 4 vcl, 2 db)	
Benvenuti, A. 1925–	Three Studies (1960–1)	Bruzzichelli
	(1101–1110–1110–pf, xyl)	
Berg, A.	†Chamber Concerto (1925)	UE
1885–1935	(2 picc–2121–ca, bcl, dbn–2110–	
	1000–pf)	
Berger, A. 1912–	Chamber Music (1956)	CFE
	(1111–1100–2111–hp, cel)	
Berio, L. 1925–	†Serenata I	SZ, 1957
	(1121–ca–1110–1111–hp, pf)	
	Passaggio (Messa in Scena)	UE
	(2 picc–0011–bcl, dbn–1221–0111–4	
	perc, gt)	
Bernard, J. E. A.	Divertissement in F, Op. 36	Durand [ca. 1890]
1843–1902	(2222–2000–0000)	
Bialas, G. 1907–	Partita	BVK
	(1222–2000–0001)	
Birtwistle, H. 1934–	The World is discovered	UE, 1963
	(2222–2000–0000–hp, gt)	
	†Tragoedia	UE, 1967
	(1111–1000–2110–hp, claves)	
Blattner, O.	Two American Sketches	Witmark, 1942
	(2222–2000–0000)	
Blezard, W.	Polka Pantomime	MS (CG)
	(2122–2200–0000–timp, perc)	
Bloch, E.	Four Episodes (1926)	Birchard
1880–1959	(1111–1000–2111–pf)	
Boedijn, G. 1893–	Vijf concertante Epigram-	Donemus, 1959
	Schetsen, Op. 159	
	(2232–2200–0000–pf, timp, perc)	
Bois, R. du 1934–	Cercle (1964)	Donemus, 1964
	(1122–2100–0000–pf, perc)	
Bonsel, A. 1918–	Folkloristische Suite	Donemus, 1958
	(2232–2200–0000–timp, perc)	
Bortolotti, M. 1926–	Studio per Cummings No. 2	SZ, 1965
	(1964)	
	(0120–bcl–1000–0111–3 perc)	

A LIST OF MUSIC FOR THE HORN

Bozza, E. 1905–	Overture for a Ceremony (0000–3 sax–4341–0000–timp, perc)	Leduc
Brant, H. 1913–	†Galaxy II (1954) (picc–0010–2110–0000–glock. 6 timp)	CFE
Brauer, M. 1855–1918	Pan Suite (2222–2000–0001)	Br. & H., 1934
Britten, B. 1913–	†Sinfonietta, Op. 1 (1932) (1111–1000–2111)	Bo. & H., 1935
Brown, E. 1926–	Indices (1000–1100–1011–pf, gt, vib, 3 perc)	MS (BMI)
Busch, A. G. W.	Divertimento (1111–2100–2110–timp)	M. & M.
Bush, G. 1920–	Fanfare & March: The Prince of Morocco (2121–4231–0000–timp, perc)	Novello, 1965
Canino, B. 1936–	Concerto da camera No. 2 (1962) (0300–3300–0000–pf, vib, hp, 2 perc)	SZ
Caplet, A. 1878–1925	Suite persanc (1900) (2222–2000–0000)	MS (Curtis Inst)
Casadesus, F. 1870–1954	London Sketches (2222–2000–0000)	Deiss, 1916; Salabert, 1924
Caturla, A. G. 1906–40	Tres Danzas cubanas (1111–bcl–2111–0000–pf, perc)	EV
Cazden, N. 1914–	Concerto, Op. 10 (1937) (1111–2100–0110–pf)	CFE
Chandler, M.	French Suite (1962) (2232–2220–0000)	MS (CG)
Chou Wen-Chung 1923–	Two Miniatures from T'Ang (1957) (2010–1000–1110–hp, pf, perc)	CFE
Christiansen, C.	The Toy Box (2122–2110–0000)	Gehrmans
Clementi, A. 1925–	Ideogrammi Nr. 1 (1959) (2031–3210–0000–pf, xyl, 2 perc) Sette Scene (1961) (2041–4 sax–3220–0001–pf, xyl, vib, 2 perc)	SZ, 1960 SZ
Cooke, A. 1906–	Sinfonietta (1954) (1111–1100–2111)	Mills
Cossart, L. A. 1887–	Suite in F, Op. 19 (2222–2000–0000–hp)	Heinrichshofen, 1908
Crosse, G. 1938–	†Concerto da camera, Op. 6 (1962) (1111–bcl–2210–1000–2 perc)	OUP, 1966
Debussy, C. 1862–1918	Fanfare from 'Le Roi Lear' (1904) (0000–4300–0000–2 hp, perc)	Jobert, 1926
Delage, M. 1879–	Two Fables (1110–2100–2110–pf)	UMP
Delden, L. van 1919–	Sinfonia concertante (2220–bcl–2000–0002) Piccolo Concerto, Op. 67 (2222–2200–0000–pf, timp, perc)	Donemus, 1964 Donemus, 1960

345

Devienne, F. 1759–1803	Overture (2223–2210–serpent–0000–timp)	Hofmeister; M. & M.
Dijk, J. van 1918–	Serenade (3332–2200–0000–pf, timp, perc)	Donemus
Donatoni, F. 1927–	Movimento (1959) (3021–2100–0000–pf, hpcd)	SZ, 1960
Dubois, T. 1837–1924	Dixtuor in d (1111–1000–2111)	Heugel, 1909
Dvořák, A. 1841–1904	†Serenade in P, Op. 44 (1878) (0222–dbn–3000–0011)	Simrock, 1879; Artia, 1956; IMC; Musica Rara, 1961
Effinger, C. 1914–	Concerto for organ & wind, Op. 19 (1121–2200–0000–org)	Composer (Boulder, Colo.)
Egk, W. 1901–	Ein Sommertag (Ballet) (2241–2210–0002–hp, pf, cel, timp, perc)	Schott
Enesco, G. 1881–1955	†Double Quintet in D, Op. 14 (2222–2000–0000) †Sinfonia da camera, Op. 33 (1111–ca–1100–1111–pf)	Enoch (MS: Curtis Inst.) (Diapason)
Fabian, W.	Musique de concert (2222–2221–0000–timp, tamburo)	IPA, 1959
Felderhof, J. 1907–	Muziek (1930) (2222–sax–2211–0000–timp, perc)	Donemus
Feldman, M. 1926–	Ixion (3010–1110–0011–pf)	Peters
	Eleven Instruments (alto fl–1000–1111–bass trp–1010–vib, pf)	Peters
	Atlantis (1010–1110–0010–hp, xyl, vib, pf)	Peters
Flégier, A. 1846–1927	Dixtuor in f (1890) (1111–1000–2111)	Lemoine, 1903; Baron
Foerster, J. B. 1859–1951	Strakonicky Dudak (0020–2000–2111–pf, harm)	
Françaix, J. 1912–	†Serenade (1934) (1111–1110–2111)	Schott, 1959
Frankel, B. 1906–	Five Bagatelles (Cinque Pezzi notturni), Op. 35 (1111–1000–2111–hp)	Novello, 1961
	Catalogue of Incidents in Romeo & Juliet (0121–1000–1111–hp, perc)	(RT, Nov. 10, 1967)
Frid, G. 1904–	12 Metamorphosen, Op. 54a (2222–1000–0000–pf)	Donemus, 1963
Fried, O. 1871–1941	Adagio & Scherzo, Op. 2 (picc–3333–3000–0000–hp, timp)	Br. & H.
Gaillard, M. F. 1900–	Guyanes (2222–2200–0000–pf, 2 perc)	Heugel
Gerhard, R. 1896–	Sardana (1121–ca–2111–0000–perc)	MS

	Hymnody (1110–1111–0000– 2 pf, 2 perc)	OUP, 1964
Ghedini, G. F. 1892–1965	Doppio Quintetto (1921) (1111–1000–2111)	MS (MGG)
Gipps, R. 1921–	Seascape (2222–2000–0000)	S. Fox, 1961
Goeb, R. 1914–	Concertant III (3332–4331–0100 or 1111–2211–0100)	CFE
Grandis, R. de 1927–	Cadõre: Antruilles (1000–sax–2320–0001–hp, cel, pf, gt, mouth-org, perc)	BVK
Griend, K. van der 1905–50	Concertino (1932) (1121–1111–0000–pf, timp)	Donemus
Grimm, C. H. 1890–	Byzantine Suite (1111–1100–2111)	Andraud
Grossi, P. 1917–	Composizione No. 4 (1221–1210–2112)	Bruzzichelli
Gudmundsen- Holmgren, P. 1932–	Two Improvizations, Op. 9 (1100–1110–0000–pf, vib, 2 perc)	Samfundet, 1962
Hagerup-Bull, E. 1922–	Undecim Sumus (1111–1100–0011–pf, hp, perc)	NK
Hahn, R. 1875–1947	Le Bal de Beatrice d'Este (2121–2100–0000–pf, 2 hp, perc)	Heugel
Hamilton, I. 1922–	Sonatas & Variants (1111–2211–0000)	Schott
Hartmann, E. H. 1836–98	Serenade in B♭, Op. 43 (1122–2000–0011)	R. & E., 1890
Haydn, F. J. 1732–1809	Seven Marches, Hob. VIII, 1–7 (Ed. H. C. Robbins Landon) (0222–2100–serpent–0000–timp ad lib)	Doblinger, 1960
	Six Allemandes, Hob. IX, 9 (Ed. H. C. Robbins Landon) (1201–2200–2011–timp)	Doblinger
Heider, W. 1930–	Modelle (1111–sax–1100–0000–hp, pf, 4 perc)	Litolff
Hemel, O. van 1892–	Divertimento No. 2 (2222–2200–0000–pf)	Donemus, 1959
	Concerto (3333–4331–0000)	Donemus, 1960
	Three Contrasts (3333–sax–4331–0000–cel, xyl, timp, perc)	Donemus, 1963
Henkemans, H. 1913–	Primavera (1944) (1110–1000–3211)	Donemus, 1944
Henze, H. W. 1926–	Labyrinth (1951) (0100–bcl, sax–1110–0111–3 perc)	Schott
	Concerto for Pianoforte, wind & percussion (2222–2221–0000–pf, timp, perc)	Schott

APPENDIX C

	In Memoriam: Die weisse Rose (1965) (1001–ca, bcl–1110–2111)	Schott
Hewson, R.	Concert Piece for wind (1963) (2222–4231–0000)	MS (CG)
Hindemith, P. 1895–1963	Kammermusik No. 2, Op. 36/1 (1111–bcl–1110–1111–pf solo)	Schott, 1924
	Kammermusik No. 3, Op. 36/2 (1925) (1111–1110–1011–timp)	Schott
	Kammermusik No. 6, Op. 46/1 (1929) (1121–1110–0032–vla d'am)	Schott
	Kammermusik No. 7, Op. 46/2 (1929) (2122–1110–0021–org)	Schott
	Konzertsuite aus 'Der Dämon', Op. 28 (1923) (1010–1100–2111–pf)	Schott
Hovland, E. 1924–	†Music, Op. 28 (1957) (1111–1000–2111)	Lyche
Hummel, J. N. 1778–1837	Variations: Castor & Pollux (2000–2000–2111–pf)	Weinberger
Huré, J. 1877–1930	Pastorale (3122–ca–1000–0000–pf)	(Ve)
Hurník, I. 1922–	†Moments musicaux (1962) (1222–2110–0000)	SHV, 1964
	†Four Seasons (1110–1100–2111–pf)	CHF, 1956
Ibert, J. 1890–1962	Concerto for violoncello & wind (2222–1100–0010)	Heugel, 1926
Jacob, G. 1895–	Diversions (1111–1000–2111)	OUP
	Old Wine in new Bottles (2222–dbn ad lib–2200–0000)	OUP, 1960
Jadassohn, S. 1831–1912	Serenade, Op. 104c (2222–2000–0000)	Andraud
Jadin, L. E. 1768–1853	Symphony (Ed. F. von Glasenapp) (2022–2210–0000)	Hofmeister
Jolivet, A. 1905–	†Suite delphique (1942) (1110–2110–0000–ondes m, hp, timp, perc)	Pathé-Marconi, 1957
Ketting, O. 1935–	†Two Canzoni (1957) (1121–2110–0000–hp, cel, perc)	Donemus
	Variazioni (2232–2200–0000–hp, perc)	Donemus, 1960
	Interieur: Ballet Musiek (1963) (2221–2321–0000–cel, xyl, timp, perc)	Donemus
Kilar, W. 1932–	Oda (Bela Bartók in Memoriam) (vla solo–0000–4441–0000–6 perc)	PWM, 1960
Kirchner, L. 1919–	†Concerto (1960) (1111–dbn–1220–1010–cel, 3 perc)	AMP, 1962

Klingler, K. b. 1879	Variationen in A (1111–1000–2111)	Berlin, Composer, 1938
Klusák, J. 1934–	†Obrazy (Pictures) (1960) (2222–1210–0000)	Composer, 1960; SHV, 1967
Kohn, K.	Concertmusic (2222–ca, bcl–2000–0000)	M. & M.
Kosá, G. 1897–	Kammermusik (1928) (1111–1100–2222–hp)	UE
Kozeluch, L. A. 1747–1818	Harmonie (2222–2000–0000–db ad lib)	Simrock, n.d.
Křenek, E. 1900–	Capriccio (1955) (solo vcl–1111–1110–0000–timp, perc)	Schott; UE
Krommer, F. V. 1759–1831	Three Partien (0222–dbn–2100–0000)	MS (MGG*)
	Six Marches (0222–dbn–2100–0000)	BAI, 1803
	VI neue Regiments-Harmonie Märsche (0222–dbn–2100–0000)	IC; André, n.d.
Kupferman, M. 1926–	Serial Variations (1010–2000–2020–pf, timp)	MS
Lalo, E. 1823–92	Two Aubades (1871) (1111–1000–2111)	Heugel, 1872
Lampe, W. b. 1872	Serenade, Op. 7 (2222–ca, bcl, dbn–4000– 0000)	Simrock, 1904
Landré, G. 1905–	Kammersymphonie (1952) (1111–1100–2111–hp, perc)	Donemus, 1952
	Sonata festiva (1953) (1111–1100–2111–perc)	Donemus
Legley, V. 1915–	Trois Pièces, Op. 57 (1960) (1111–1000–2111)	CeBeDeM
Leleu, J. 1898–	Suite symphonique (2111–ca–1210–0000–pf, perc)	Leduc, 1926
Lendvai, E. 1882–1949	Kammersuite, Op. 32 (1111–1000–2111–hp)	Rahter, 1923
Lessard, J. 1920–	Concerto (1949) (2122–2210–0000)	Merrymount [1951?]
	Concerto (1958) (1000–2000–1111–hpcd, perc)	CFE
Lilien, I. 1897–	Sonatine apollonique (1939) (2222–2000–0000)	Donemus, 1948
Louis Ferdinand, Prince of Prussia 1772–1806	†Rondo in B♭, Op. 9 (Ed. H. Kretzschmar) (1020–2000–2111–pf)	Br. & H. [1808] Br. & H., 1910, 1926
Luening, O. 1900–	Synthesis (2222–4220–0000–perc, tape)	Peters
Luening, O, and Ussachevsky, V. 1911–	Concerted Piece (2222–4200–0000–perc, tape)	Peters
Lutyens, E. 1906–	Music for wind, Op. 60 (1965) (2222–2000–0000)	Schott

	Six Tempi for ten instruments, Op. 42 (1957) (1111–1100–1110–pf)	Mills, 1959
Macchi, E. 1928–	Composizione 3 (1111–1110–1211)	Bruzzichelli, 1960
Maderna, B. 1920–	Serenata No. 2 (1957) (1010–bcl–1100–1101–hp, pf, xyl, vib, glock)	SZ, 1957
	Serenata No. 1 (1954) (1010-bcl–1100–1101–hp, pf, xyl, vib, glock)	Ars Viva
Malipiero, G. F. 1882–	Ricercari (1925) (1111–1000–0411)	UE, 1926, 1954
	Ritrovari (1926) (1111–1000–0411)	UE, 1928, 1954
	Serenata mattutina 1112–2000–0200–cel)	UE, 1960
	Macchine (picc–0001–1100–1001–hp, pf, cel, xyl, carillon, perc)	Ricordi
Malipiero, R. 1914–	Mosaico (1961) (1111–1000–2111)	SZ, 1964
Mašek, V. 1755–1831	Concertino (2022–2000–pf, 4h)	Br. & H., n.d.
	Cassatio in E♭ (0202–2000–3102)	MS (MGG)
	Parthia in E♭ (1212–dbn–2100–0000)	MS (MGG)
Maxfield, R. V. 1927–	Structures, Op. 23 (1953) (picc–1111–ca–1120–0000)	Composer, 1954
Maxwell Davies, P. 1934–	Shakespeare Music (alto fl/picc–0111/dbn–bcl–1010–0101–gt, perc)	
	St. Michael (1957) (2222–3231–0000)	Schott, 1963
Mayer, W. 1925–	†Essay for brass & winds (1111–2211–0000–perc)	Bo. & H., 1965
Messaien, O. 1908–	†Oiseaux exotiques (1956) (2141–2100–0000–pf, glock, xyl, 2 perc)	UE
	Couleurs de la Cité celeste (1963) (0030–2440–0000–gongs, bells, xyl, xylorimba, marimba)	Leduc, 1966
	†Et exspecto Resurrectionem Mortuorum (1964) (5454–6442–0000–perc)	Leduc
Meyerowitz, J. 1913–	Ecce Homo (1957) (2222–3221–0000–hp, perc)	MS (BMI)
Milhaud, D. 1898–	†Symphony for small orchestra, No 5; Dixtuor (picc–1112–ca, bcl–2000–0000)	UE, 1922
	†La Création du Monde (1923) (2121–sax–1210–2011–pf, perc)	Salabert

	†Concertino d'Automne (1951) (1100–3000–0210–pf)	Heugel, 1952
	Concertino d'Été (1951) (solo vla–1111–1100–0021)	Heugel, 1952
Mills, C. 1914–	Chamber Concerto (1941) (1111–2000–2110)	CFE
Miroglio, F. 1924–	Espaces II (1962) (3333–4331–0000–2 hp, 8 perc)	SZ
Molbe, H. 1835–1915	Diecetto in c, Op. 21 (0011–ca–1000–3111)	Rörich, 1896
	Seven Diecetti, Opp. 91, 104, 109, 113, 118, 124, 129 (0011–ca–1000–2111–hp)	Hofmeister [1901–10]
	Hymne de Printemps, Op. 31 (0011 –ca–1000–2111–hp)	Hofmeister
	Grüne Klange (0011–ca–1000–2111–hp)	Hofmeister, 1912
	Two Intermezzi, Opp. 110, 111 (0011–ca–1000–2111–hp)	Vienna, Composer
Moór, E. 1863–1931	Double Quintet in A, Op. 101 (1111–1000–2111)	Mathot, 1913
Moreau, L. d. 1946	Nocturne (2222–2000–0000)	(Ve)
Moser, F. 1880–1939	Serenade, Op. 35 (1921) (2222–ca, bcl, dbn–4000–0000)	UE, 1922
Mouquet, J. 1867–1946	Symphonietta in C, Op. 12 (2222–2000–0000)	Lemoine
Moyse, L. 1911–	Divertimento (2222–2000–0021–timp)	M. & M.
Mozart, W. A. 1756–91	†Galimathias Musicum, K. 32 (1766) (0201–2000–2101–pf) (Ed. A. Einstein)	Den Haag, 1766; Br. & H. Peters
	†Serenade No. 1 in D, K. 100 (1769) (2200–2200–2110)	Br. & H.
	†Divertimento No. 3 in E♭, K. 166 (1773) (0222–2ca–2000–0000)	Br. & H., 1879, 1956; Eulen- burg; AMP
	†Serenade No. 3 in D, K. 185 (1773) (2000–2200–2110)	Br. & H.; Eulenburg
	†Divertimento No. 4 in B♭, K. 186 (1773) (0222–2ca–2000–0000)	Br. & H., 1879, 1956; Eulen- burg
	†Serenade No. 10 in B♭, K. 361 (1781) (0222–2 basset hn, dbn–4000– 0000)	BAI [ca. 1803]; Br. & H., 1880, Broude; AMP; Musica Rara
Musgrave, T. 1928–	Chamber Concerto No. 1 (1962) (0111–1110–1110)	Chester
Nagel, R. 1924–	Divertimento (1951) (1110–2211–0000)	CFE
Ordoñez, C. d' 1734–86	Partita per la Caccia (0202–2200–0000–timp, perc)	Traeg, 1799

351

Otterloo, W. van 1907–	†Symphonietta (1943) (picc–2222–ca, bcl, dbn–4000–0000)	Donemus, 1948
	Intrada (0001–4441–0000–timp, perc)	Donemus, 1958
Paz, J. C. 1897–	Theme & Variations (1928–9) (1122–bcl–2020–0000)	MS (Slo, T)
	Overture (1111–1110–1111)	MS (Fleisher)
Pentland, B. 1912–	†Symphony (1957) (1100–1100–1111–timp, xyl)	Toronto, BMI
Périlhou, A. 1846–1936	Divertissement (1904) (2222–4000–0000)	Heugel [ca. 1904]
Persichetti, V. 1915–	Serenade No. 1 (1929) (1111–2211–0000)	EV, 1963
Petyrek, F. 1892–1951	Arabian Suite (1924) (2122–2010–0001–hp, timp, perc)	UE
Philipott, M. 1925–	Variations (1010–1110–2111)	Heugel
Pick-Mangiagalli, R. 1882–1949	Intermezzo (2020–1000–2111–hp., pf)	Carisch
Pluister, S. 1913–	Divertimento (Muziek voor Straatmuzikanten) (1937) (2111–1110–0001–perc)	Donemus, 1953
Ponse, L. 1914–	Euterpe: Suite, Op. 37 (1964) (2232–2000–0000)	Donemus
Poot, M. 1901–	Suite (1940) (2222–2220–0000–timp)	UE
Poulenc, F. 1899–1963	Trois Mouvements perpetuelles (1918) (1111–ca–1000–2110)	Chester
Pousseur, H. 1929–	Symphonies for 15 soloists (1111–1110–2111–2 hp, pf)	UE, 1961
Praag, H. van 1894–	Dixtuor (1949) (1111–1000–2111)	Donemus
	Music for wind instruments (2222–2000–0000)	Donemus, 1965
Pratella, F. B. 1880–1955	Par un dramma orientale (1111–1000–2110–pf)	Ricordi, 1938
Prausnitz, F. 1920–	Episode (1111–1110–1100–pf)	NME, 1949
Quinet, M. 1915–	Divertimento (1958) (1111–2100–2111–timp)	CeBeDeM
Raff, J. J. 1822–82	Sinfonietta in F, Op. 188 (2222–2000–0000)	Siegel, 1874
Rajna, T. 1928–	Serenade (2111–2210–0000–pf, cymbalom)	MS
Rawsthorne, A. 1905–	Fluxion (1962–3) (1111–1110–2011–4 perc)	Tonos
Raxach, E. 1932–	Concerto (1961) (1111–1000–2111)	OUP, 1962
Rayki, G.	Burlesque (1122–3110–0000)	UE

A LIST OF MUSIC FOR THE HORN

Reger, M. 1873–1916	First Movement of Serenade (unfinished) (1904) (2222–4000–0000)	MS (MGG)
Reicha, A. 1770–1836	Double Quintet (Grand Symphonie de Salon) (1827) (1111–1000–2111)	Simrock
Reizenstein, F. 1911–	Serenade in F, Op. 29 (1951) (1222–dbn–2000–0000)	Bo. & H.
Rellstab, J. C. F. 1759–1813	Zwölf Märsche (in olla Potrida) (1790) (0222–2100–0000–timp)	(MGG)
Riegger, W. 1885–1961	Introduction & Fugue, Op. 74 (3232–4331–0010–timp)	AMP
Rieti, V. 1898–	Madrigale (1111–1100–2111–pf)	Senart; Salabert; Andraud
Rorem, N. 1923–	Sinfonia (1957) (3343–2000–0000)	Henmar, 1957
Rosetti, F. A. 1746–92	Parthia in D (1784) (2221–2000–0001)	MS (MGG*)
	Parthia für die Jagd in F (1785) (2221–3000–0001)	Mannh. Musikverlag
	Parthia in D (2212–2000–0001)	MS (MGG*)
Salieri, A. 1750–1825	Zwei Bläserserenaden (Ed. W. Höckner) (2222–2000–0001)	Doblinger
Salmhofer, F. 1900–	Kammersuite, Op. 19 (1933) (picc–1212–bcl–2000–2111– pf/hp)	UE
Salzedo, C. 1885–	Préambule et Jeux (1923) (1101–1000–2111–hp)	(Ewen)
Sauguet, H. 1901–	Bocages: trois Caprices (1949) (1222–2000–0000–hp/hpcd)	Choudens
Schmidt, F. 1874–1939	Lied, Ländler, March (1904–9) (0200–4201–0000–perc)	MS (MGG)
Schmitt, F. 1874–1951	Lied et Scherzo, Op. 54 (solo hn–picc–1122–ca–1000– 0000)	Durand, 1912
Schmittbauer, J. A. 1718–1809	Divertimenti per usirli alla tavola (picc–2202–2000–0000)	MS (LB, Karlsruhe)
Schnabel, A. 1882–1951	Duodecimet (inst. R. Leibowitz) (1121–1100–1111–perc)	from M. & M.
Schoenberg, A. 1874–1951	†Kammersinfonie, Op. 9 (1906) (1121–ca, bcl, dbn–2000–1111)	UE, 1912
	Five Orchestral Pieces, Op. 16 (Arr. A. Schoenberg & F. Griessle) (1111–1000–2111–pf, harm)	Peters, 1925
Schuller, G. 1925–	Double Quintet (ww & brass quintets)	AMP
	Twelve by Eleven (1955) (1011–sax–1110–0001–hp, pf, vib, drums)	MJQ

	†Transformations (1956) (1011–sax–1010–0001–hp, vib, drums)	Malcolm
	Atonal Jazz Study (1100–2 sax–2111–0001–pf, drums)	MJQ
	Music from 'Yesterday in Fact' (1000–bcl, sax–1100–1011–pf, drums)	MS (BMI)
	When the Saints go marchin' in (0000–5 sax–2431–0001– drums)	MS (BMI)
Schuyt, N. 1922–	Discorsi capricciosi (1965) (1222–1211–0000–perc)	Donemus, 1965
Sear, W. E.	Antiphony (1111–2211–0000)	(Ve)
Searle, H. 1915–	Variations & Finale, Op. 34 (picc–0111–1000–2111)	Schott, 1958
Sekles, B. 1872–1934	Serenade in E♭, Op. 14 (1111–1000–2111–hp)	Rahter, 1907
Skalkottas, N. 1904–49	Andante sostenuto (1111–ca, dbn–1111–0000– hp/pf, timp, perc)	UE, 1954
Smit, L. 1900–45	Concerto pour le Piano (1937) (2222–3211–0011–pf, timp)	Donemus, 1948
Sporck, G. b. 1870	Paysages normandes (2222–2000–0000)	Pfister, 1907
Stamitz, K. 1746–1801	Three Divertimenti in B♭ (2222–2000–0000)	Mannh. Musikverlag
Strauss, R. 1864–1949	†Suite in B♭, Op. 4 (1884) (2222–dbn–4000–0000)	Leuckart, 1911, 1921
	†Serenade, Op. 7 (1881) (2222–dbn–4000–0000)	Aibl, 1884; UE, 1888; IMC; M. & M.
	†Sonatina in F, Op. posth. (1943) (2232–basset hn, bcl, dbn–4000– 0000)	Bo. & H., 1964
	†Symphonie fur Bläser in E♭, Op. posth. (Sonatina No. 2) (1944–5) (2232–basset hn, bcl, dbn–4000– 0000)	Bo. & H., 1952
Stravinsky, I. 1882–	†Eight instrumental Miniatures (2222–1000–2220)	Chester, 1963
	Song of the Haulers on the Volga (picc–1111–2301–0000–perc)	Chester
	†Symphonies of wind Instruments (1920) (Rev. 1947) (3232–ca, dbn–4331–0000)	RM, 1926 Bo. & H., 1952
	†Ragtime (1918) (1010–1110–2101–cymbalom, perc)	Chester, 1920

A LIST OF MUSIC FOR THE HORN

	†Concerto: Dumbarton Oaks (1938) (1011–2000–3322)	Schott, 1938
Striegler, K. 1886–1958	Kammersinfonie, Op. 14 (1111–1000–2111)	Junne, 1912
Stringham, E. J. 1890–	Notturno (1936) (12 ww–2000–0000–hp)	(Ewen, T)
Stürmer, B. 1892–1958	Feierliche Musik (1111–1000–2111)	Tonger
Surinach, C. 1915–	David & Bathsheba (2200–2200–0002–hp, pf, 2 perc)	AMP
	Apasionada (1111–1110–0001–pf, timp, perc)	AMP
	†Doppio Concertino (1954) (1111–1100–0001–vln, pf soli– 2 perc)	Rongwen
Sutermeister, H. 1911–	Pianoforte Concerto No. 2 (1954) (2222–2220–0000–pf solo, timp, perc)	Schott
Taneiev, S. I. 1856–1915	Andante (Ed. B. Lamm) (2222–2000–0000)	RS; M. & M.
Tomasi, H. 1901–	Jeux de Geishas (1111–1000–2111–hp, perc)	Durand, 1939
Tomlinson, E. 1924–	Concertino (picc–1122–ca–2000–0000)	MS (CM Lib)
Turner, R. 1920–	†Variations & Toccata (1959) (1111–1000–2111)	CMC
Varèse, E. 1883–1965	†Hyperprism (1923) (1010–3220–0000–16 perc)	Ricordi
Verhaar, A. 1900–	Kleine Dagmuziek: Aubade (1959) (2222–2221–0001–cel, timp, perc)	Donemus, 1959
Vlad, R. 1919–	Serenata (1959) (1222–2000–0200–cel)	SZ
Vranický, A. 1761–1820	Jägermärsche (0222–dbn–2100–0000)	Artia
Wagner, R. 1813–83	†Siegfried Idyll (1870) (0122–2100–2111)	Br. & H., 1877
Warren, R. 1929–	Music for Harlequin (1122–2221–0000–timp, perc or 2222–4221–0000–timp, perc)	Novello
Welin, K. E. 1934–	Nr. 3, 1961 (1110–bcl–1110–1001–pf)	A. & S., 1962
Whettam, G. 1927–	Fantasy Concerto (2222–2000–0000)	MS
	Sinfonietta No. 2, Op. 28 (2222–2000–0000)	de Wolfe
Wijdeveld, W. 1910–	Konzertstück (1952) (1111–1000–3221)	Donemus
Wineberger, P. 1758–1821	Two Parthia (1786) (2122–4000–0000–violone)	MS (LB, Schwerin)
Woestijne, D. van der 1915–	Sérénades (1946) (1033–2111–0001–pf, perc)	CeBeDeM
Wolf-Ferrari, E. 1876–1948	Chamber Symphony in B♭, Op. 8 (1111–1000–2111–pf)	Rahter, 1903

355

Zillig, W. 1905–63   Serenade IV   BVK
                     (1111–1110–2111–hpcd, cel,
                     perc)

                     7. Horn with voices

                     7.1 *Solo voices*

Abt, F. 1819–85   Songs, Op. 79   André, n.d.
                     (2 v; cl, hn, vln)
Ander, A.   Das Alphorn   Bachmann
[1817–64?]   (v; hn, pf)
Andriessen, H.   La Vierge à Midi   Donemus
1892–   (v; fl, ob, hn, stg quart)
Antoniou, T. 1935–   Epilogue based on Homer's   BVK
                     Odyssey (1963)
                     (MzS, narrator; ob, hn, db, gt, pf,
                     perc)
ApIvor, D. 1916–   Landscapes, Op. 15   MS
                     (T; fl, cl, hn, vln, vla, vcl)
Arrigo, G. 1930–   Quarta Occasione, Op. 6 (1950)   Bruzzichelli
                     (T, 7 v; hn, vla, cel, gt, mand)
Balorre, C. de   Prelude et Salutaris   Hamelle, n.d.
                     (v; hn, vln, hp, org)
Bareux, G.   O Salutaris   Legouix, n.d.
                     (S, T; hn, vla)
Becker, J. 1811–59   Das Bächlein: 'Bächlein im   Hofmeister, n.d.
                     engen Tal'
                     (v; hn, pf)
Berlioz, H.   Le jeune Pâtre breton, Op. 13/4   Cranz; Costallat;
1803–69   (S; hn, pf)   Br. & H., n.d.
Birtwistle, H. 1934– Monody for Corpus Christi   UE, 1961
                     (S; fl, hn, vln)
Bliss, A. 1891–   A Knot of Riddles (1963)   Novello, 1965
                     (Bar; wind quint, stg quint)
Blum, C. L.   Der Ritterbube und das Kloster,   Br. & H.
1736–1844   Op. 114 (S; 2hn, vcl, pf)   [c. 1830]
Bourdeaux, L. 1929– Canciones   Heugel
                     (A; wind quint)
Brand, M. 1896–   Five Songs   UE
                     (S; fl, ob, cl, hn, vln, vcl)
Brandenburg, F.   Ein Ton voll süssem Klanges: Klemm, n.d.
                     Lied, Op. 11
                     (v; hn, pf)
Branscombe, G.   Across the blue Aegean Sea   Galaxy, 1939
1881–   (S; fl, 2 cl, hn, hp)
Britten, B. 1913–   †Serenade, Op. 31 (1943)   Bo. & H., 1944
                     (T; hn, stgs)
                     †Canticle No. 3, Op. 55: 'Still falls Bo. & H., 1956
                     the Rain' (1954)
                     (T; hn, pf)
                     †Nocturne, Op. 60   Bo. & H., 1959
                     (T; fl, ca, cl, hn, bn, hp, stgs, perc)

Bruckner, A. 1824–96	Mass in C (ca. 1842) (A; 2 hn, org)	MS (H. F. Redlich: Bruckner & Mahler)
Brunetti, A. fl. ca. 1726	Cavatina (B; ob, hn, vln, viole, bass)	MS (E*)
Cooke, A. 1906–	Five Nocturnes (1956) (S; hn, pf)	OUP, 1963
Crosse, G. 1938–	For the Unfallen, Op. 9 (1963) (T; hn, stgs) A Corpus Christi Carol (MzS; cl, hn, stg quart)	OUP OUP, 1966
Dauprat, L. F. 1781–1868	O Salutaris (T; hn, stg quart, db, hp)	MS (F)
Delage, M. 1879–	Two Fables (v; fl, ob, 2 cl, hn, bn, hp, stg quart, pf)	UMP
Denisov, E.	Chanson italiennes (S; fl, cl, hn, vln, hpcd)	(RT, Nov. 7, 1967)
Deslandres, A. E. M. 1840–1911	Panis angelicus (S, T; hn)	Pérégally, n.d.
Dickinson, P. 1935–	Five Blake Songs (1957) (T; cl, hn, bn)	MS (MT, Feb. 1965)
Diepenbrock, A. 1862–1921	Come Raggio del Sol (1917) (S; wind quint) Lied der Spinnerin (1898) (S; hn stgs) Wenn ich Ihn nur habe (1915) (S; wind quint, db)	Donemus Donemus Donemus
Dijk, J. van 1918–	Septet (1949–50) (S; fl, cl, hn, vln, vla, vcl, db)	Donemus
Dorati, A. 1906–	The two Enchantments of Li Tai Po (Bar; 3 fl, hn, hp, 2 perc)	SZ
Easdale, B. 1909–	The soft wild Fire (1966) (S, T; hn, vln, vcl, pf, org, gt)	(MT)
Eisenmann, W. 1906–	Orpheus, Eurÿdike, Hermes (speaker: fl, 2 ob, hn, bn, vln, vla, vcl, pf, timp)	Ars Viva
El Dabh, H. 1921–	Tahmeela (S; wind quint, vln)	Peters
Epstein, D. 1930–	Four Songs (v; hn, stgs)	AMP
Esser, H. 1818–82	Three Lieder, Op. 29 (v; hn, pf)	Schott, 1849
Farberman, H. 1929–	†Evolution (1954) (S; hn, 25 perc)	Broude
Farkas, F. 1905–	Kalendar (S, T; wind quint, stg quart, db, hp)	UE
Fauré, G. 1845–1924	O Salutaris (S; 2 hn, stg quart, org)	Hamelle
Feldman, M. 1926–	For Franz Kline (S; hn, vln, vcl, pf, chimes)	Peters

357

	Vertical Thoughts III (S; fl, hn, trp, tuba, vln, vcl, db, pf/cel, 2 perc)	Peters
Flothuis, M. 1914–	Lied (1943) (MzS, Bar; fl, ca, cl, bcl, hn, bn)	Donemus
Flury, R. 1896–	Nachtlieder (v; cl, hn, vln, vla, vcl, db)	Hug
Fortner, W. 1907–	Mitte des Lebens (1951) (S; fl, bcl, hn, vln, hp)	Schott, 1953
Fricker, P. R. 1920–	Three Sonnets of Cecco Angioliera da Siena, Op. 7 (1947) (T; wind quint, vcl, db)	Schott, 1949
	Cantata, Op. 37 (T; wind quint, stg quart, db)	(MT, May, 1962)
Frid, G. 1904–	Frühlingsfeier (1952) (S, A; fl, cl, hn, bn, vln, vla, vcl)	Donemus
Froidebise, P. 1914–62	Amercoeur (S; wind quint, pf)	CeBeDeM, 1956
Gallay, J. F. 1795–1864	Deux Morceaux de Concert (v; hn, pf)	Schoenenberger, 1839
	Le Bal était brillant (v; hn)	MS (MGG)
Gallico, P. 1868–1955	Septet (1924) (A; bn, stg quart, pf)	MS (R, T)
Gardner, J. 1917–	Two Songs (v; ob, hn, hp)	MS?
Ghedini, G. F. 1892–1965	Concerto spirituale (1943) (2 S; hn, 2 trp, stg quart, pf, timp)	SZ, 1946
Glanville-Hicks, P. 1912–	Thomsoniana (1949) (S; fl, hn, stg quart, pf)	AMP
Gleich, F. 1816–98	Des Bootmänners Sang, Op. 12 (T; hn, pf)	Hoffarth
Goehr, A. 1932–	The Deluge, Op. 7 (S, A; fl, hn, trp, vln, vcl, db, hp)	Schott, 1959
Gorner, J. V. 1702–62	Ausgewählte Oden und Lieder: No. 5 (Ed. M. Seiffert) (v; 2 hn, bass)	K. & S., 1930
Grabner, H. 1886–	Wilhelm Busch Suite, Op. 33 (reciter; wind quint, sax)	K. & S., 1932
Gruenberg, L. 1884–1964	The Creation, Op. 23 (1924) (Bar; fl, cl, hn, bn, vla, pf, timp, perc)	UE, 1926
Haas, P. 1899–1944	Der ausgewählte Liederzyklus, Op. 8 (T; fl, hn, vln, pf)	(Ve)
Haydn, F. J. 1732–1809	Trio: 'Pietà di me', Hob. XXIV (2 S, T; ca, hn, bn, orch)	Doblinger
	Cantilena pro Adventu: 'Ein' Magd, ein 'Dienerin', Hob. XXIII (S; 2 hn, stg quart, org)	UE; Doblinger
Heifetz, J.	Three Songs (v; hn, stgs)	MS (Repertoire list: J. Eger)

A LIST OF MUSIC FOR THE HORN

Henze, H. W. 1926–	Kammermusik (1958) (T; cl, hn, bn, stg quart, db, gt/hp)	Schott, 1959
	Apollo & Hyazinthus (1949) (A; fl, vl, hn, bn, stg quart, hpcd)	Schott, 1957
	Wiegenlied der Mutter Gottes (1948) (S; fl, cl, hn, trp, trb, vla, vcl, db, hp)	Schott
Hoffman, A. 1898–	St. Hubertus (2 v; 2 hn, pf)	Glaser
Hoven, J. 1803–83	Der Abendhimmel, Op. 32 (v; hn, pf)	Schlesinger
	Das Schifflein, Op. 18 (v; fl, hn, pf)	Schlesinger
	Einst und Jetzt, Op. 17 (v; hn [pf?])	Cranz
	Jägers Qual, Op. 37 (v; hn [pf?])	Cranz
	Schlummerlied aus 'Turandot' (v; hn, vcl [pf?])	Schott
Hovhaness, A. 1911–	Angelic Song (S; hn, stgs)	Peters
Huber, K. 1924–	Des Engels Anredung an die Seele (1957) (T; fl, cl, hn, hp)	UE, 1961
Huber-Andernach, T. 1885–	Chinesische Gesänge, Op. 25 (S, T; fl, cl, hn, pf)	T. & J.
Hybler, J. 1891–	Stars above Home (1955) (S; cl, hn, vln)	(Ga)
Ibert, J. 1890–1962	Chanson du rien (v; wind quint)	MS? (G)
Kallenberg, S. G. b. 1867	Geistliches Wiegenlied (v; fl, hn, bn, stg quart)	Böhm, 1926
Kalliwoda, J. W. 1801–66	Drei Lieder, Op. 182/1 (v; hn, pf)	Schott, n.d.
	Heimweh (v; hn, pf)	Schott
Kauffmann, L. J. 1901–44	Eine vergnügliche Hauskantate (1943) (4 v; fl, cl, bn, 2 vln, vla)	MS? (MGG)
Klein, B. O. 1858–1911	Quintet (S; hn, vln, vcl, pf)	MS? (T)
Kleinecke, W.	Zwei Lieder, Op. 5 (v; hn, pf)	Fürstner
Knight, M. 1933–	Pansies (Bar; cl, hn, vln, vcl, db)	Tritone
Kössler, H. 1853–1926	Kammergesänge (v; ob, hn, stg quart)	Simrock, 1912
Kohler, L. 1820–86	Sechs Gedichte, Op. 3 (S; hn, pf)	Litolff, 1844
Kosá, G. 1897–	Josef: Kammeroratorio (1939) (9 v; 2 hn, hp, 6 stgs)	MS (MGG)

Kossmaly, K. 1812–93	Drei Lieder (v; hn, pf)	Wunder, 1840
Krebs, K. A. 1804–80	Die Heimat, Op. 56 (v; hn, vln, vcl, pf)	Schuberth
	Seemans Liebchen, Op. 83 (v; hn, vln, vcl)	Schuberth
	Die süsse Bell, Op. 90 (v; hn, vln, vcl, pf)	Schuberth
Krejčí, I. 1904–	Nachklänge (1936) (v; wind quint)	MS (MGG)
Křenek, E.1900–	Vier Gesänge, Op. 53a (1927) (MzS; fl, 3 cl, hn, trp)	UE, 1927
Kreutzer, K. 1780–1849	Das Mühlrad, Op. 72/1 (v; hn, pf)	Cranz
Krol, B. 1920–	Horatio de vino Carmina, Op. 30 (v; hn, pf)	Marbot
Kupsch, C. G.	An ein schlafendes Mädchen, Op. 10 (T; hn, pf)	Fürstner
Lachner, F. 1803–90	Vier Gesänge, Op. 27 (v; hn, pf)	Diabelli [ca. 1833]; Cranz
	Herbstverlangen: Bewusstsein, Op. 30 (v; hn, pf)	Cranz
	Drei Lieder, Op. 34 (v; hn, pf)	Cranz
	Drei deutsche Gesänge, Op. 36 (v; hn, pf)	Cranz
	Frauenliebe und Leben, Op. 59 (v; hn, pf)	Schlesinger
Lachner, I. 1807–95	Überall du, Op. 17 (v; hn, pf)	(FP)
	Zwei Lieder, Op. 43 (v; hn, pf)	Prague, Hoff- mann, 1843
	An die Entfernte, Op. 23 (v; hn, pf)	Prague, Hoff- mann, 1843
Lagarde, P. 1717–after 1792	L'Amant malheureux (1766) (Bar; hn, bn, 2 vln, vla, bc)	(MGG)
Laznowski, J. 18th Cent.	Aria in D (S; 2 hn, 2 vln, org)	MS (G)
Lehmann, H. U. 1937–	Cantata (1963) (S; fl, hn, trp, vla)	(Ve)
Lewis, H. M. 1908–	Night Music for '43 (Bar; ob, hn, vln, vcl, pf)	MS? (R)
Ligeti, G. 1923–	Adventures for three Singers (1962) (S, A, Bar; fl, hn, vcl, db, pf, hpcd, perc)	Litolff, 1964
Lopes Graça, F. 1906–	Seven old Ballads (MzS; 2 fl, 2 cl, 2 hn, stg quart, hp, cel)	MS? (MGG)
Lord, D.	Three Songs (1965) (v; fl, hn, vcl, hp)	MS (MT, Dec. 1965)

Lutyens, E. 1906–	The Dying of Tanneguy du Bois (1937) (T; 4 hn, stgs)	MS
Malipiero, G. F. 1882–	Quattro vecchie Canzoni (1940) (S; wind quint, vla, db)	SZ, 1941
Mamangakis, N. 1929–	Kassandra (S; fl, hn, tuba, hp, 2 perc)	Modern
Méhul, E. 1763–1817	Hymne pour la Fête des Epoux (1798) (v; 2 cl, 2 hn, 2 bn)	Senart; Leduc, n.d.
Messner, J. 1893–	Zwei Marienlegenden, Op. 8 (v; hn, stg quart, hp)	Doblinger
Metzler, F. d. 1955	Bei Tag und Nacht (1949) (4 v; fl, hn, vla)	Hofmeister, 1955
Molnár, A. 1890–	Psalm LXXXIV (2 v; hn, hp)	MS?
Monod, J. L. 1927–	Passacaille (S; wind quint, trp, pf)	NME, 1952
Moscheles, I. 1794–1870	Am Bache, Op. 136 (v; hn, hp)	Kistner [1835]
Nelson, P.	Three Songs (S; 8 hn)	(Horn Realm)
Newson, G. 1932–	Three Interiors (S; wind quint, db)	MS? (MT, Oct. 1962)
Nicolai, O. 1810–49	Variations sur un Thème de 'La Somnabula', Op. 26 (S; hn, pf)	Diabelli
	Die Thräne, Op. 30 (v; hn, pf)	Cranz
	Salve Regina, Op. 39 (S; fl, ob, 2 hn, bn, stg quart, db)	Mechetti
Novák, J. 1921–	†Passer Catulli (1954) (Bar; wind quint, vln, vla, vcl, db)	SNKLHU, 1965
Orrego-Salas, J. 1919–	Canciones castellanas (1948) (v; fl, ca, cl, hn, vla, vcl, hp, perc)	Chester, 1951
Osterc, S. 1895–1941	Male pesni za Ireno (1935) (S/T; sax, hn, vla, pf)	MS (MGG)
Pablo, L. de 1930–	Glosa, Op. 10 (v; 2 hn, pf, vib)	Tonos, 1962
Paer, F. 1771–1839	Notte soave: Serenade (2 S, T, B; hn, vcl, db, pf)	(MGG)
Paisello, G. 1740–1816	Motetto (S; ob, hn, vln, bass)	MS (E*)
Perotti, G. A. 1769–1855	Gloria & Credo (Soli; ob, cl, hn, bn, vcl)	(MGG)
Pesko, Z. 1937–	Icone d'una grande Citta (1963) (S; 2 fl, 2 cl, hn, bn, 6 vln, 2 pf, 3 perc)	SZ
Petrassi, G. 1904–	Due liriche di Saffo (1941) (v; wind quint, trp, stg quart, hp)	SZ, 1942

361

Plé, S. 1897–	Ts' in Pao (v; hn, stg quart)	Lemoine
Pott, F. A. 1806–83	Posthornklänge (v; hn)	Br. & H.
Proch, H. 1809–78	Konzert-Arie, Op. 110 (S; hn, pf)	(F)
Rathgeber, J. V. 1682–1750	Requiem rurale in F (S, A; 2 hn, org)	MS (MGG*)
Rebling, G. 1821–1902	Waldsehnsucht (v; hn, pf)	Kistner
Reed, H. O. 1910–	A Psalm of Praise (S; 2 fl, ob, 2 cl, hn, bn)	MS
Reimann, I. 1820–85	Ave Maria (A; 2 hn, vln, org)	Pietsch
Reissiger, K. G. 1798–1859	Vier Gesänge, Op. 117 (S; hn, pf)	Meser
	Der wandernde Waldhornist (T; hn, pf)	Fürstner
Riegger, W. 1885–1961	La belle Dame sans Merci, Op. 4 (1924) (S, A, T; fl, ob, hn, bn, 2 vln, vcl, db)	Peer
Roberts, J. Dale	Florilegium (8 soli; ob/ca, hn, 2 vcl, hp, pf)	MS (CG)
Rogowski, M. 1881–1954	Pièsna Morza (1940) (Bar; 2 hn, pf)	MS? (G)
Roser, F. de P. 1779–1830	Tantum Ergo (4 v; 2 ob, cl, hn, bn, org)	MS (MGG*)
Salzedo, C. 1885–	Three Poems (1919) (S; ob, hn, bn, 6 hp)	(Ewen)
Samuel-Holeman, E. 1863–1942	La jeune Fille à la Fenêtre (S; ob, hn, stg quart, hp)	Br. & H., 1904
Sarti, G. 1729–1802	Two Masses (4 v; hn, stgs, org)	(MGG)
Schadewitz, K. 1887–1945	Liedsinfonie, Op. 20 (1921) (S; fl, hn, vla, pf)	Pälz, 1929
Schmid, H. K. 1874–1953	Abendfeier, Op. 43 (1923) (A; fl, cl, hn, bn, pf)	MS (Ve)
Schmidt, G. 1816–82	Postillon (v; hn, vcl, pf)	Kistner
Schenk, J. 1753–1836	Das Veilchen (1832) (v; 2 cl, 2 hn, bn, pf)	(E)
Schoeck, O. 1886–1957	Wandersprüche, Op. 42 (T/S; cl, hn, pf, perc)	Br. & H., 1930
Schouwman, H. 1902–	Drei Gedichten van P. C. Boutens, Op. 32 (1943) (S; wind quint)	Donemus
Schubert, F. 1797–1828	†Auf der Strom, D. 943 (1828) (v; hn, pf)	Leidesdorf, 1829 Br. & H., 1951; Cor
Schultz, J. P. C. 1773–1827	Zwölf Jägerlieder (v; 2 hn [pf?])	Br. & H.

Sicciardi, H. 1897–	Tres Cantos argentinos (1953) (v; picc, ob, cl, hn, bn)	MS?
Sikorski, T.	Antiphones (v; hn, pf, perc, tape)	MS
Simon, H. 1896–1948	Pans Flucht (S; wind quint)	Lienau
Skroup, F. 1801–62	An der Abendstrom, Op. 6 (v; hn, pf)	Hofmeister
	Liebes Tal, warum so stille, Op. 15 (v; hn, pf)	Hofmeister
Smalley, R. 1943–	Three Songs of D. H. Lawrence (Bar; cl, ten hn, pf)	(MT, Nov. 1965)
	Three Poems of Friedrich Hölderlin (1965) (S, T; fl, ob, bcl, hn, trp, trb, vcl, hpcd)	(MT, Feb. 1968)
Smith, R. 1927–	Palatine Songs (v; cl, hn, vcl, vib, cym)	CFE
Srebotnjak, A. 1931–	Ecstasy of Death (Bar; hn, orch)	(L. & B.)
Strömholm, F. 1941–	David's Prayer: 'Herre laer meg din vei' (S; wind quint, pf)	NK
Storch, A. 1813–88	Das Vöglein, Op. 10 (v; hn, pf)	Witzendorf
Strauss, R. 1864–1949	Das Alphorn (v; hn, pf)	MS? (G)
Studier, H. 1911–	†Liederzyklus: 'Der irre Spielmann' (T; hn, pf)	MS? (Schweitz)
Suter, R. 1919–	Musikalisches Tagebuch No. 2 (Bar; fl, cl, bcl, hn, vln, vla, vcl)	Modern
Szalonek, W. 1927–	Suita kurpiowska (A; wind quint, vln, vla, vcl, pf)	PWM, 1960
Tadolini, G. 1793–1872	Canzonet: 'Bell'eco della Scozia' (T; hn, pf)	Cranz
	La Potenza d'Amore (v; hn, pf)	Cranz
Tahourdin, P.	Space Traveller (1962) (narrator; wind quint)	MS? (MT, Sept. 1962)
Tate, P. 1911–	The Phoenix & the Turtle (1961) (T; fl, hn, 2 vcl, hpcd, pf)	OUP
	Songs of sundry Natures (1945) (Bar; fl, cl, hn, bn, pf)	OUP, 1946
	A Victorian Garland (S, A; hn, pf)	(BBC)
Taubert, C. G. W. 1811–91	Zwei Lieder, Op. 53 (v; hn, pf)	Schlesinger
Tauwitz, E. 1812–94	Trost, Op. 14 (v; hn, pf)	Leuckart
Tiehsen, O. 1817–49	Das Meer hat seinen Perlen, Op. 5 (v; hn, pf)	B. & B.

Togni, C. 1922–	Ricercar, Op. 36	Composer, 1953
	(Bar; fl, hn, vla, db, cel)	
	Gesang zur Nacht (1962)	SZ
	(S; 2 fl, ob, cl, hn, bn, vln, vla, db, hp, pf/cel, timp)	
Vivenot, R. von	Was willst du mehr, Op. 10	Haslinger
	(v; hn, pf)	[ca. 1838]
Vlijmen, J. van 1835–	Mythos (MzS; wind quint, stg quart)	Donemus, 1963
Weber, B. 1916–	†Concert Aria after Solomon, Op. 29 (1949) (S; wind quint, vln, vcl, pf)	CFE
Weigl, V.	Do not awake me	CFE
	(v; fl, cl, hn, pf)	
	Dear Earth	CFE
	(v; hn, vln, vcl, pf)	
Weill, K. 1900–50	Frauentanz, Op. 10	UE, 1924
	(S; fl, cl, hn, bn, vla)	
Wellesz, E. 1885–	Aurora, Op. 33	Curwen
	(v; fl, cl, hn, bn, stg quart, hp)	
Wirthmann, O. M. 1891–	Lieder, Op. 24 (1916) (A; fl, hn, stg quart, hp)	MS (Ve)
Wolf, H. 1860–1903	Gesang Weylas	Br. & H.
	(S; ob, hn, hp/pf)	
Wolpe, S. 1902–	Quintet	MS?
	(Bar; cl, hn, vcl, hp, pf)	
Zagwijn, H. 1878–1954	De Fluitspieler (1946) (S; wind quint, pf)	Donemus
	Suite nègre (1947)	Donemus
	(MzS; wind quint, pf)	
	Folksongs (1947)	Donemus
	(MzS, Bar; wind quint, stg quart, pf)	

7.2 *Chorus*

Allen, P. H. 1883–	Three Choruses	MS (R)
	(fch; hn, hp, pf)	
Bartoš, J. Z. 1908–	Country of Comenius, Op. 90 (1961)	(Ga)
	(Bar, fch; 2 ob, 2 hn, 2 bn)	
Bedford, H. 1867–1945	Nocturne (fch; hn, hp, timp)	MS?
Beethoven, L. van 1770–1827	Bundeslied, Op. 122 (1822–3) (S, A, ch; 2 cl, 2 hn, 2 bn)	Schott, 1825; Br. & H.
Berkeley, L. 1903–	Batter my Heart, three-person'd God (S, ch; ob, hn, vcl, db, org)	Chester
Biarent, A. 1871–1916	Nocturne (ch; hn, hp, harm, pf)	(DMM)
Boedecker, L. 1845–99	Im Nachen, auf dem Rheine, Op. 37 (ch; 2 hn, hp)	Br. & H., n.d.

Brahms, J. 1833–97	†Vier Gesänge, Op. 17 (1860) (fch; 2 hn, hp)	Simrock, 1862; Br. & H.; Peters, 1965
	Begräbnisgesang (ch; 2 ob, 2 cl, 2 bn, 2 hn, 3 trb, tuba, timp)	MF Co
Brunner, A. 1901–	Geistliches Konzert II (ch; hn, stgs)	BVK
Busser, H. 1872–	Messe de Domrémy et deux antiennes (ch; 4 hn ad lib)	Durand
Carter, E. 1908–	The Harmony of Morning (1944) (fch; fl, ob, hn, bn, stgs, pf)	AMP
Catel, C. S. 1773–1830	Ecce Panis (ch; 2 fl, 2 cl, 2 hn, 2 bn)	MF Co
Davies, H. Walford 1869–1941	Songs of Nature, Op. 24b (T, fch; fl, hn, stgs, pf)	G. & T.
Dello Joio, N. 1913–	The mystic Trumpeter (1943) (soli, ch; hn)	G. Schirmer, 1945
Dvořák, A. 1841–1904	Slavonic cradle Song (ch; 2 hn, org)	Laudy
Fanta, R. 1901–	Requiem in C (ch; 2 hn ad lib, org)	UE
Feldman, M. 1926–	Chorus and Instruments (ch; hn, tuba, vln, vcl, db, pf/cel, perc)	Peters
Freundthaler, C. fl. 1799	Masses (ch; 2 hn, org)	MS? (F)
Gál, H. 1890–	Phantasien, Op. 5 (A, fch; cl, hn, hp, stgs)	UE, 1923
Häusler, E. ca. 1761–1837	Kirchengesang (ch; 2 hn, bn)	Böhm, 1830
Haydn, M. 1737–1806	Deutsches Hochamt (ch; 2 hn, org)	Salzburg, Mayer, 1795
	Glorreiche Himmelskönigin (ch; 2 hn, org)	MS? (E*)
	Helligste Nacht (fch; 2 hn, org)	MS? (E*)
	Hymnus: Te Lucis ante terminum (ch; 2 hn)	MS
	Weihnachtslied (ch; 2 hn, org)	Grätz, Kraeer & Deyrkauf ca. [1830]
Heath, J. R. 1887–	Musique de Chambre (3 v, ch; fl, cl, hn, bn, stgs)	Chester
Henkel, M. 1780–1851	Drei deutsche Seelen Messen im Choral-Styl, Op. 32 (ch; 2 hn, org)	(E*)
Horst, A. van der 1899–1965	Twee Fragmenten, Op. 8a (1922) (fch; fl, hn)	Alsbach
Hovhaness, A. 1911–	Ave Maria, Op. 100/1 (fch/boys' ch; 2 ob, 2 hn, hp)	AMP

Jensen, A. 1837–79	Two Choruses, Op. 10: No. 1, Gesang der Nonnen (S, fch; 2 hn, hp) No. 2, Brautlied (ch; 2 hn, hp)	Schuberth, n.d.
Jochum, O. 1898–	Goldene Blütenzeit, Op. 117 (fch; fl, cl, hn) Waldkantate, Op. 124 (ch, children's ch; 2 fl, 2 hn)	Böhm, 1952 Böhm, 1952
Jungbauer, F. 1747–1823	Deutsches Stabat Mater (ch; hn, bn, org)	Niedermayr
Kaun, H. 1863–1922	Abendfeier in Venedig, Op. 17 (ch; 2 hn, stgs)	Rohlfing [1890]
Knittelmair, L. 1769–1845	Deutscher Kirchengesang zur heiligen Messe (ch; 2 hn, org)	Straubing, Schmid, 1803
Kracher, J. M. 1752–ca. 1830	Deutsche Masse in F (1817) (ch; 2 hn, org)	MS (MGG*) (Städt. Mus., Salzburg)
Krebs, J. L. 1713–80	Missa in F (ch; 2 hn, 2 vln, vla, bc) Sanctus in D (ch; 2 ob, 2 hn, 2 vln, vla, bc) Gott fahret auf mit Jauchzen (ch; 2 hn, 2 vln, vla, bc)	MS (MGG*) (Bibl. Leipzig) MS (MGG*) (Westdeutsche Bibl. Marburg) MS (MGG*) (Westdeutsche Bibl. Marburg)
Lorenz, J. b. 1862	Waldlieder, Op. 21/3: Im Wald (ch; 2 hn)	Leuckart, n.d.
Mair, F.	Jucunde (ch; 4 hn)	Cranz, n.d.
Marteau, H. 1874–1934	Gesang der Geister über den Wassern (ch; 4 hn, vln, hp, timp)	Simrock, 1927
Martinů, B. 1890–1959	Legende aus dem Rauch des Kartoffelkrautes (1957) (S, A, Bar, ch; fl, cl, hn, pf, concertina)	SNKLHU, 1960
Mašek, A. 1804–78	Drei Sing-Quartette nebst zwei Jagdstücken (ch; 4 hn)	MS? (MGG)
Mayuzumi, T. 1929–	Pratidesana (T, Bar, B, mch; 3 hn, 2 pf, timp, 3 perc)	Peters
Maxwell-Davies, P. 1934–	†O Magnum Mysterium (1960) (ch; wind quint, vla, vcl, glock, xyl, vib, perc, org)	Schott, 1962
Methfessel, A. 1785–1869	Es tönen die Hörner, Op. 22 (ch; 3 hn)	Hofmeister, n.d.
Migot, G. 1891–	La Mise au Tombeau (1949) (ch; wind quint)	MS (MGG)
Moeschinger, A. 1897–	Das Posthorn (mch; 4 hn, stgs)	MS?

Morin, J. B. 1677–1754	La Chasse du Cerf (2 soli, ch; hn, bc)	Paris, C. Ballard, 1709
Mühldorfer, W. C. b. 1837	Jagdlied (double ch; 3 hn)	Tonger, n.d.
Nuhn, F.	Abschied vom Walde (ch; 2 hn, pf ad lib)	Br. & H. [ca. 1874]
	Märzgesang (fch; 2 hn, pf duet)	Br. & H.
	Mailied (fch; 2 hn, pf)	Br. & H. [ca. 1874]
Odorich, P.	Two Ave Maria (ch; 2 hn, trb ad lib, org)	Böhm, n.d.
	Offertorium (ch; 2 hn & trb ad lib, org)	Böhm, n.d.
Othegraven, A. von 1864–1946	Die Königskinder, Op. 68 (S, mch; 3 hn, stg quart, pf)	Hainauer, 1925
Palester, R. 1907–	Cantate de la Vistule (narrator, ch; 4 hn, 2 hp, 2 pf, perc)	MS?
Pernsteiner, M.	Litania laurentata brevis, Op. 21 (ch; 2 hn, org)	(P)
Pfitzner, H. 1869–1949	Zwei Männerchöre, Op. 49: No. 2, Das Schifflein (S, mch; fl, hn)	Oertel, 1941
	Gesang der Barden (mch; 6 hn, 4 vla, 4 vcl)	Fürstner, 1906
Pijper, W. 1894–1947	Op den Weefstoel (1918) (ch; 2 fl, 2 ob, 2 cl, hn, 2 bn, pf 4 h)	Donemus, 1950
Rathaus, K. 1895–1954	Lament from 'Iphigenia in Aulis', Op. 61 (1947) (fch; hn)	AMP, 1963
Riegger, W. 1885–1961	Eternity (fch; fl, 2 hn, db)	Flammer
Ritschel, J. M. I. 1739–66	Credo concertato (ch; 2 hn, stg quart, bc)	MS (MGG*)
Ryba, J. J. 1765–1815	Ständchen (ch; 4 hn)	(AmZ 36/1834)
Schubert, F. 1797–1828	Ellens zweiter Gesang (Arr. J. Brahms) (S, fch; 4 hn, 2 bn)	MF Co.
Schumann, R. 1810–56	Das Schifflein, Op. 146/5 (1849) (S, ch; fl, hn)	Br. & H.
Sikorski, T.	Prologhi (fch; 4 fl, 4 hn, glock, marimba, vib)	PWM
Smith, R. 1927–	Set me as a Seal (fch; hn, vln, vla, vcl)	Lawson
Stockhauser	Der Allmacht Wunder (4 soli, ch; 4 hn, 6 hp)	(AmZ 26/1824)
Storch, A. M. 1815–87	Polka; Ständchen, Op. 101 (ch; 4 hn)	Cranz, n.d.

APPENDIX C

Stravinsky, I. 1882–	†Four Russian Peasant Songs (fch; 4 hn)	Chester, 1958
Thiel, C. 1862–1939	Frauenchor (fch; 2 hn, hp)	Sulzbach, n.d.
Thieriot, F. 1838–1919	Zwei Gesänge, Op. 49: No. 1, Melusine (S, ch; 2 hn)	Eulenburg, n.d.
Weber, G. 1779–1839	Aufmunterung (ch; 4 hn)	Schott, n.d.
Weigl, V.	Ode to Beauty (ch; hn, pf)	CFE
Whettam, G. 1927–	Ode to Fancy (S, A, ch; hn)	MS

7.3 Male Chorus

Beer, M. J. 1851–1908	Drei Waldlieder, Op. 35 (mch; 2 hn)	Trieste, Schmidl, n.d.
Bittner, J. 1874–1939	An die Studiosi (mch; 5 hn)	Fliegel, 1913; UE
Boeck, I. b. 1754 & Boeck, A. b. 1757	O Waldnacht grün! (mch; 2 hn)	Br. & H. [1803]
Brandt-Caspari, A. b. 1865	Drei Romanzen, Op. 6 (S, mch; hns)	Forberg, n.d.
Bruckner, A. 1824–96	Abendzauber (1878) (Bar, mch; 4 hn)	UE
Clemens, A. 1909–42	Es blies' ein Jäger wohl in sein Horn (1939) (mch; 2 hn)	Böhm
Cursch-Bühren, F. T. 1859–1908	Nachts im Walde (T, B, mch; 4 hn, pf)	Leipzig, Reinecke, n.d.
Debois, F. 1834–93	Nachtgruss (mch; 4 hn, pf)	Vienna, Wiener Musikverlagshaus, n.d.
Evers, C. 1819–75	Jagdlied und Chor (mch; 4 hn)	Schlesinger, n.d.
Göbel, J. G.	Jägerfreude, Op. 61 (mch; 4 hn)	Renner [c. 1840]
Goldmark, C. 1830–1915	Frühlingsnetz, Op. 15 (mch; 4 hn, pf)	Kistner [c. 1869]
	Meersstille und glückliches Fahrt, Op. 16	Kistner [c. 1869]
Gotthard, J. P. 1839–1919	Gesang im Freien, Op. 35 (mch; 4 hn)	Cranz, n.d.
Herbeck, J. R. von 1825–80	Die hohe Jagd (mch; 2 hn ad lib)	Gutmann, 1860
	Zum Walde, Op. 8 (mch; 4 hn)	Leuckart, 1859
Hess, E. 1912–	Im Berge (1936) (mch; 2 hn)	MS (V)
Horn, A. 1825–93	Der deutsche Männergesang, Op. 52 (mch; 4 hn, bass trb)	Schott, n.d.

A LIST OF MUSIC FOR THE HORN

	Waldlied, Op. 26	Kistner, [c. 1867]
	(mch; 4 hn)	
Hummel, F.	Waldwanderung, Op. 48	Siegel, n.d.
1855–1928	(mch; 2–4 hn)	
	Sängers Tod, Op. 121	Hochstein, 1912
	(T, B, mch; 2 hn, hp)	
	König Eriks Genesung, Op. 87	Eulenburg, 1905
	(A, T, mch; 2 hn, hp)	
Hummel, J. N.	Gesang	MS (AmZ 31/1829)
1778–1837	(mch; 4 hn)	
Hutter, H.	Morgensgruss, Op. 32	Kistner, n.d.
1848–1926	(mch; 4 hn)	
Isenmann, C.	Gesang der Mönche, Op. 21	Rühle, n.d.
1839–89	(mch; 4 hn, bass trb)	
Janotta, H.	Waldfrieden	Robitschek, n.d.
	(mch; 4 hn)	
Karow, K.	Six Chants pour la Landwehr	Bunzlau, Appun
1790–1863	(mch; hns, drums)	
Kessler, J. H. F.	Cantata	(F)
b. 1808	(mch; 4 hn)	
Kittel, J. E.	Notturno	MS?
	(mch, 4 hn, pf)	(AmZ 38/1836)
Kleinecke, W.	Chor der Spielleute	Gutmann, n.d.
	(mch; 4 hn, pf duet)	
Köhler, W.	Jägerchor, Op. 129	Kistner, n.d.
1858–1926	(mch; 4 hn)	
Kremser, E.	Dagobert Fanfare	Leuckart, n.d.
1838–1914	(mch; 2 hn)	
	Jagdlied	Leuckart, n.d.
	(mch; 4 hn)	
Krimminger, F.	Die Hirschjagd, Op. 19	Brockhaus, n.d.
	(mch; 3–4 hn)	
Krug, A.	Zwei Chöre, Op. 53: No. 1, Sylva	Br. & H., 1895
1849–1904	(mch; 4 hn)	
Liszt, F.	Uber allen Gipfeln ist Ruh' (1849)	Schuberth
1811–86	(mch; 2 hn)	[1860?]
Meindl, G.	Alpenklänge	Cranz, n.d.
	(mch; 4 hn)	
Meyerowitz, J.	Two Choruses (1953)	Rongwen, 1957
1913–	(mch; hn)	
Mendelssohn, F.	Der Jägers Abschied, Op. 50/2	Kistner
1809–47	(mch; 4 hn, bass trb)	[ca. 1840]
Milde, L.	Jägerleben, Op. 31	Siegel, n.d.
	(mch; 4 hn ad lib, pf)	
Moldenhauer, W.	Altdeutsches Hochzeitslied, Op. 10	Hochstein, 1927
	(mch; hns, timp)	
Neithardt, A. H.	Jägerlied	(AmZ 37/1835)
1793–1861	(mch; 4 hn)	
Neukäufler, F.	Gesang für das Johannisfest	Schott, n.d.
19th Cent.	(mch; 4 hn)	
Ortner, A.	Jagdchor, Op. 69	Aibl, n.d.
	(mch; 4 hn)	

2A

369

Othegraven, A. von 1864–1946	Ritter rat dem Knappen dies, Op. 29 (mch; 4 hn, pf)	Leuckart, 1907
	Abendlied (mch; 4 hn, pf)	T. & J.
Otto, E. J. 1804–77	Sechs Lieder, Op. 107/2 (mch; 4 hn)	Merseburger, n.d.
Podbertsky, T. b. 1846	Ein Lied des Volkes (4 soli, mch; 4 hn)	Kahnt, n.d.
Podhorsky, F.	Jagdlied, Op. 5 (mch; 4 hn)	Pabst, n.d.
Reinecke, C. 1824–1910	Auf der Wacht! Op. 41/3 (mch; 4 hn, bass trb ad lib)	Schuberth [ca. 1871]
	Der Jäger Heimkehr, Op. 90 (mch; 4 hn, bass trb)	Siegel, n.d.
	Requiem für die gefallene Krieger, Op. 103/2 (mch; 4 hn, db, timp)	Kistner, n.d.
Rein, W. 1893–1955	Mörike-Zyklus (1952) (mch; 3 hn)	Schott, 1953
Reiter, J. 1862–1939	Todestrost, Op. 29 (mch; 4 hn)	Leuckart, n.d.
	Winzerlied (mch; 4 hn)	T. & J.
Remy, A. W. 1831–98	Zwei Männerchöre, Op. 18 (mch; 4 hn)	Kahnt, n.d.
Schauseil, W.	Kriegslied (T, mch; 4 hn)	Berlin, Eisoldt, n.d.
Schlemm, G. 1902–	Drei Männerchöre (mch; 4 hn)	Tonos
Schmid, A. 1901–	Der Tag (mch; 2 hn)	Scholing
Schmidt-Duisberg, M.	Jagd vorbei (mch; 3 hn ad lib)	Hofmeister
	Jägerlatein (mch; 3 hn)	Hofmeister
Schreck, G. 1849–1918	Begrüssung des Meeres (mch; 2 hn, pf duet)	Kistner, n.d.
Schubert, F. 1797–1828	†Nachtgesang im Walde, Op. 139b (1827) (mch; 4 hn)	Haslinger, 1846
Schumann, R. 1810–56	Fünf Jagdlieder, Op. 137 (1849) (mch; 4 hn)	Br. & H.
Schwarz, H.	Der Jäger Heimkehr (mch; 4 hn)	Eulenburg, n.d.
Schweida, R.	Acht Lieder, Op. 11: No. 8, Bundeslied (mch; 8 hn)	Br. & H., n.d.
Siegl, O. 1896–	Volksliedsätze (mch; 3 hn)	Hochstein
Stade, F. 1817–1902	Durch schwankende Wipfel (mch; 4 hn)	Siegel
Steinhauer, K. 1852–1934	Waldeinsamkeit, Op. 32 (mch; 4 hn ad lib)	Kistner, n.d.

Stern, J. 1820–83	Der Jäger Abschied, Op. 12/1 (mch; 4 hn ad lib)	Schlesinger, n.d.
Storch, A. M. 1815–87	Grün, Op. 19 (mch; 4 hn)	Haslinger, n.d.
	Die Karthause, Op. 15 (mch; 4 hn ad lib)	Mechetti, n.d.
	Chant de Bohémiens (mch; 4 hn)	Vienna, Müller, n.d.
Stürmer, B. 1892–1958	Drei Lieder, Op. 62 (mch; 2 hn)	Schott
	Von Dämmerung zu Dämmerung (mch; 2 hn, vla)	Tonger
Stürmer, W.	Mariandel, Op. 52 (mch; 4 hn)	Schuberth, n.d.
Sturm, W. 19th Cent.	Frühlingsblick, Op. 5 (mch; 4 hn, pf)	Kistner, n.d.
Tittel, E. 1910–	Lebensmut (mch; 4 hn)	Doblinger, 1957
Walter, A. 1821–96	Lustige Musikanten, Op. 18 (mch; 4 hn ad lib)	RB [ca. 1866]
Washburn, R. 1928–	Three Shakespearian Love Songs (mch; hn, pf)	OUP, 1963
Weber, B. 1912–	Die Jägerei weiss mancherlei (mch; 4 hn)	SM, 1960
Weinberger, K. F. 1853–1908	Des Liedes Geburt, Op. 28 (mch; 4 hn ad lib, pf)	Siegel, n.d.
Weinwurm, R. 1835–1911	O zage nicht! Op. 35 (mch; hns)	Forberg, n.d.
Weinzierl, M. von 1841–98	Kampf, Op. 120 (Bar, mch; 4 hn)	Leuckart, n.d.
	Zwei Männerchöre, Op. 74 (mch; 4 hn)	Siegel, n.d.
Widmann, B. b. 1820	Das Wirtshaus, Op. 20 (mch; 4 hn)	Germann, n.d.
Witt, L. F.	Weidmannslust, Op. 57 (mch; 4 hn ad lib)	Rühle, n.d.
Zelanski, L. b. 1837	Jagdlied, Op. 33 (mch; 4 hn)	Leuckart, n.d.

7.4 Chorus with brass instruments, including horn(s)

Amory, A. H.	Orangelied (ch; 4231–timp)	Arnheim, Mastrigt
Balazs, F. 1919–	Casualty & Christmas (ch; 4231–timp, perc)	CFE
Bender, J. 1909–	Psalm 130 (ch; 2210)	Concordia
	Psalm 150 (ch; 2210)	Concordia, 1957
Boulanger, L. 1893–1918	Psalm XXIV (Bar, ch; 4341, hp, org, timp)	Durand, 1924
Braal, A. de 1909–	Profetie: Jesaja 25, 26 (1951) (Bar, ch; 2220–pf)	Donemus

Bruckner, A. 1824–96	Cantate in D: 'Auf, Brüder, auf zur hohen Festen' (1852) (4 soli, ch; 3210)	MS (H. F. Redlich: Bruckner & Mahler)
Brugk, H. M. 1909–	An die Musik (ch; 2221–timp)	Böhm
Cohen, K. H. 1851–1938	Fünf Fronleichnamshymnen, Op. 11 (ch; 2231)	Schwann
Cousins, M. T.	Hymn to the Sublime (ch; 4331–timp, perc)	MS (ASCAP)
Cruft, A. 1921–	Benedictus (ch; 4301)	Bo. & H.
Dello Joio, N. 1913–	†To St. Cecilia (ch; 3331)	C. Fischer, 1958
Doppelbauer, J. F. 1918–	Tantum ergo, Op. 15 (1949) (ch; 2221-org)	MS (V)
Fiebig, K. 1908–	Halleluja, Lob, Preis und Ehr (ch; 1210–org)	Merseburger, 1949
Filke, M. 1855–1911	Ostermotett, Op. 60/2 (ch; 2220–org, timp)	Böhm
Führer, R. 1807–61	Ecce sacerdos magnus (ch; 2010–org, timp)	Hoffmann
Greith, J.	Ecce sacerdos magnus, Op. 47 (ch; 2231)	Schwann
Groh, J. jun.	Vokalmesse (ch; 2020)	Hoffmann
Hemel, O. van 1892–	Herdenkings-Hymne (1955) (children's ch, ch; 4332–2 ct, ten hn, timp, perc)	Donemus, 1956
Hindemith, P. 1895–1963	†Apparebit repentina Dies (1947) (ch; 4231)	Schott, 1947
Hovhaness, A. 1911–	Glory to God, Op. 124 (S, A, ch; sax–4440–org, timp, perc)	Peters, 1958
Kempter, K. 1819–71	Feierklänge, Op. 69/2: Osterlied (ch; 2200–org, timp)	Böhm
	Grablied, Op. 93 (ch; 2010)	Böhm
	Pange lingua, Op. 94 (ch; 3100–org, timp)	Böhm
	Pange lingua, Op. 112 (ch; 2200–org, timp)	Böhm
Koerppen, A. 1926–	Zwei Hymnen (1952) (ch; 2331)	MS (V)
Lang, H. 1897–	Der Sonnengang des heiligen Franziskus, Op. 52 (children's ch, ch; 3331–timp, perc)	Schott, 1957
Langstroth, I. 1887–	Three American Indian Songs (fch; 2200–timp)	Gray

Layton, B. J. 1926–	Three Dylan Thomas Poems, Op. 3 (1954–6) (ch; 2220)	G. Schirmer, 1964
Liszt, F. 1811–86	Te Deum laudamus I (ch; 2220–org, timp)	Br. & H., 1936
McKay, G. F. 1899–	Choral Rhapsody, Op. 39 (ch; 4330–timp)	Chicago, Western Music Library
Mellers, W. 1914–	Two Motets (1946) (ch; 4230)	OUP
Meyerowitz, J. 1913–	How Godly is the House of God (ch; 2220–org, timp)	Rongwen, 1959
Micheelsen, H. 1902–	O Christenheit, sei hoch erfreut (ch; 1550)	BVK, 1950
Missal, J.	Gloria in excelsis Deo (ch; 4342–bar, timp)	SB, 1962
Müller, O. [b. 1870?]	Hymnus: Pange lingua gloriosi, Op. 3 (ch; 2210–db, org, timp)	Böhm
Niblock, J.	Vanity of Vanities (ch; 2220–org, timp)	Interlochen, n.d.
Philipp, F. 1890–	Ecce sacerdos, Op. 55 (ch; 2231–org)	Schwann
Pinkham, D. 1923–	Festival Magnificat & Nunc Dimittis (ch; 1210–org)	Peters, 1963
	Easter Cantata (ch; 243(1)–cel, timp, perc)	Peters, 1962
	Requiem (A, T, ch; 2220–db/org/pf)	Peters, 1963
Polzer, O.	Missa festiva (ch; 2220)	Weinberger
Raubuch, E. 1909–	Tu es Petrus: Hymnus (ch; 1110–org)	Schwann
Rubbra, E. 1901–	Veni, Creator spiritus, Op. 130 (ch; 4231)	Lengnick, 1966
Schaefers, A. 1908–	Zwei Hymnen nach Texten der Apokalypse (1954) (ch; 3231)	B. & B.
Scherr, J.	Deutsches Requiem (ch; 2010–org)	Aibl
Schmid, A. b. 1772	Dies Irae (ch; 2210)	Böhm
	Requiem & Libera (ch; 2200–db, org)	Böhm
Schroeder, H. 1904–	Fünf Hymnen zur Fronleichnamprozession (ch; 2231–2 ten hn/org)	Schwann
Schumann, G. A. 1866–1952	Drei Choral-Motetten, Op. 75: No. 3 (S, ch; 3031–org, timp)	Lienau
Schwarz-Schilling, R. 1904–	Signum magnum (1958) (ch, cong; 4440)	MS (MGG)
Stier, A. 1880–	Ich habe nun den Grund gefunden (ch; 1210–vln, timp ad lib)	BVK

Stuntz, J. H. 1793–1859	Grabgesang (ch; 4030)	Aibl
	Heldengesang in Walhalla (ch; 5210)	Falter
Täglichsbeck, T. 1799–1867	Fünf Chorgesänge, Op. 29 (ch; 2230–oph)	Falter
Tagg, L. E.	Hodie Christus natus est (ch; 2220)	SB, 1962
Tittel, E. 1910–	Missa magnus et potens, Op. 15 (ch; 2220–org)	Schwann, 1939
Tomasi, H. 1901–	Procession nocturne (S, ch; 4341–timp, perc)	Leduc, 1959
Tremmel, M. 1902–	Der 150 Psalm, Op. 20 (ch; 2220–org, timp)	Coppenrath
Walter, K. 1862–1929	Festmesse (ch; 2220–org)	Doblinger, 1958
Ward, W. R. [1917?–]	Father, we praise Thee (ch; 2331–bar)	Marks, 1957
Wedig, H. J. 1898–	Das ewige Allelujah (1953) (ch; 1220)	Stuttgart, Wildt
Willan, H. 1880–	Sing to the Lord of Harvest (arr. M. E. Hogg) (ch; 1211–bar)	Concordia, 1960
Wöss, J. von 1863–1943	Te Deum, Op. 3a (1888) (ch; 2230–org, timp)	Böhm
Wood, J. H. [b. 1915?]	Only-begotten Word of God eternal (ch; 1220–org)	Concordia

7.5 *Men's chorus with brass instruments, including horn(s)*

Attenhofer, C. 1837–1914	Waldfahrt, Op. 54 (mch; 4210)	Hug
Barber, S. 1910–	†A Stopwatch & an Ordnance Map, Op. 15 (1940) (mch; 4031–timp)	G. Schirmer, 1954
Baussnern, W. 1866–1931	Wer weiss wo (Bar, mch; 2200–timp)	Essen, Rheinischer Musikverlag
Börner, A.	Hohenzollernlied, Op. 38 (mch; 3010)	Heinrichshofen
Brambach, K. J. 1833–1902	Nänie, Op. 67 (mch; 4031–timp)	Kistner
Breu, S.	Bundesfeier, Op. 50 (mch; 4231–2 E♭ trp, bar, timp)	Kistner, 1897
Bruch, M. 1838–1920	Männerchöre, Op. 19 (mch; 2230–timp)	Siegel
Bruckner, A. 1824–96	Das deutsche Lied (1892) (mch; 4331)	UE
	Germanenzug (1863) (mch; 4431–2 ct, ten hn)	Robitschek, 1892
Burkhart, F. 1902–	Das grosse Licht (1952) (mch; 4431–timp)	Doblinger

Canning, T. 1911–	The Temptation of Jesus (narrator, mch; 2231–perc)	CFE
Frackenpohl, A. 1924–	Shepherds, rejoice (T/Bar, mch; 3031–bar)	King, 1958
Frid, G. 1904–	Das Sklavenschiff, Op. 51 (T, Bar, mch; 4331–pf, timp, xyl, perc)	Donemus, 1956
Grabner, H. 1886–	Sonnengesang (1949) (mch; 2211–timp)	Schwann
Graener, P. 1872–1944	Der Retter ist nicht weit (mch; 4330–dbn, pf/org, timp)	Eulenburg
Herzogenberg, H. 1843–1900	Begräbnis-Gesang, Op. 88 (T, mch; 403 (1))	RB [1896]
Horn, A. 1825–93	Marschlied, Op. 25 (mch; 221 (1))	R. & E.
	Des Sängers Welt, Op. 44 (mch; 3011)	Br. & H.
Huber, W. S. 1898–	Kantate nach Gedichte von C. F. Meyer (mch; 2220–org, timp)	Hug
Isenmann, C. 1839–89	Lobgesang, Op. 107 (mch; 3311–timp)	Forberg
Jadassohn, S. 1831–1902	Hymnus: Gott ist gross und allmächtig, Op. 45 (mch; 2020)	Siegel
Kaminski, H. 1886–1946	Drei Gedichte von Eichendorff: No. 3, Der Soldat (mch; 3300–perc)	UE, 1925
Köllner, E.	Hohenzollernlied, Op. 144 (mch; 2221–2 ten hn, timp)	Kahnt
	Zwei Waldlieder, Op. 75 (mach; 2210)	Pabst
Kreutzer, C. 1780–1849	Siegesbotschaft (mch; 2210–timp)	Eulenburg
Kubik, G. 1914–	Litany & Prayer (1943–5) (mch; 4331–perc)	Southern, 1953
Lang, H. 1897–	Bundeslied (mch; 4331)	Schott
Lindpaintner, P. J. 1791–1856	Chant funèbre (mch; 5030)	Zumsteeg
Lissman, K. 1902–	Beherzigung (mch; 1110)	Tonger
Liszt, F. 1811–86	Psalm XVIII (1860) (mch; 4231–timp)	Schuberth, 1871
Marx, J. 1882–1964	Morgengesang (1910) (mch; 4340–org, timp)	UE
Mendelssohn, F. 1809–47	Festgesang an die Künstler, Op. 68 (1845–6) (2 T, 2 B, mch; 2221)	Simrock
	(ed. T. Sokol) (2 T, 2 B, mch; 4431–bar)	King, 1960

	Festgesang: Begeht mit heil'gem Lobgesang (mch; 6660–oph)	Br. & H.
Meyerowitz, J. 1913–	Ave Maria stella (1954) (mch; 3331)	Rongwen
Monnikendam, M. 1896–	Ballade des Pendus (1949) (mch; 2220—pf, timp, perc)	Donemus, 1952
	Veni Creator (S, mch; 1010–org)	Donemus, 1960
Müller von Kulm, W. 1899–	Lied eines Landemanns (1948) (mch; 2200)	Hug
Othegraven, A. von 1864–1946	Drei Gesänge, Op. 10 (mch; 4231–timp, perc)	Siegel
Petrassi, G. 1904–	†Coro di Morti (1940–1) (mch; 4431–dbs, 3 pf, timp, 4 perc)	SZ, 1953
Philipp, F. 1890–	Eichendorff-Zyklus, Op. 16 (1924) (No. 1, mch; 1031, timp) (No. 2, mch; 1031, 2 pf, timp)	Schultheiss
Piston, W. 1894–	Carnival Song (1938) (mch; 4331)	Arrow, 1941
Ploner, E. 1894–	Deutsches Weihelied, Op. 11 (1924) (mch; 2221–timp)	MS (V)
Radermacher, F. 1924–	Von den Wolken (Wolkenlieder) (mch; 1110)	Volk
Röder, E.	Hymnus, Op. 14 (mch; 4030)	Hanover, Fritzsche
Roussel, A. 1869–1937	Le Bardit des Francs (1926) (mch; 4231–timp)	Durand
Rudnick, W.	Rheinsage, Op. 55 (mch; 4231–timp)	Siegel
Schneider, J. C. F. 1786–1853	Hymne: Jehova, Dir frohlockt der König, Op. 94 (mch; 4230–db, timp)	Trautwein [1834]
Schroeder, H. 1904–	Hymnen zur Fronleichnams-prozession (mch; 2241)	Schott
Seifhardt, W.	Bundeslied, Op. 2 (mch; 2231)	Kahnt
Siegl, O. 1896–	Bauernhymne (mch; 2221)	Hochstein
	Liederehrung (mch; 2220)	Hochstein
Speidel, W. 1826–99	Kaiserlied, Op. 57 (mch; 4431–oph)	Schweers
Strohbach, S. 1929–	Lob der Musik (1953) (children's ch, mch; 2230)	Br. & H.
	Das Wort und die Musik (1960) (children's ch, mch; 2330–timp)	Br. & H.
	Proprium Missae im Festo Sti. Bartholomaei Apostoli (mch; 2221–timp ad lib)	Br. & H.

Stürmer, B. 1892–1958	Choralkantate: Nun danket alle Gott (mch; 3330–timp)	Merseburger
	Herrlich der Tag (mch; 2330–perc)	Tonger
	Das Ludwigsburger Te Deum (mch; 3330–timp)	Tonger
	O Tag, O Sonne (mch; 2330–perc)	Tonger
Stuntz, J. H. 1793–1859	Bankett-Lied zu dem Maskenzug der Künstler (mch; 4510–oph, timp)	Falter [1840]
	Bardengesang (mch; 4511–oph)	Aibl
	Den bayerischen Schützenmarsch (mch; 4310)	Aibl
	Die Burgfrau (mch; 5010–oph)	Aibl
	Schützenruf (mch; 2511–oph)	Aibl
Unger, H. 1886–1958	Heimatgefühl (mch; 4230)	Tonger
	Sonnenaufgang (1952) (mch; 4230)	Tonger
Verhulst, J. J. H. 1816–91	Missa pro defunctis, Op. 51 (mch; 2231–org, perc)	Den Haag, G. H. van Eck, 1854
Weber, B. 1912–	Kling auf, mein Lied (mch; 2331)	Schott
Weegenhuise, J. 1910–	Domine salvum fac (1950–9) (mch; 4311)	Bank, 1959
Zöllner, H. 1854–1941	Nachtlied (mch; 2030–harm/pf)	Hug; Kistner
Zoll, P. 1907–	Freude (mch; 2220)	Braun-Peretti
	Gelöbnis (mch; 3330–timp)	Schwann
	Spruch (mch; 2220)	Braun-Peretti

List of Publishers

The following list of publishers includes those (marked with an *) who are no longer operative. Where possible their successors, or the firms with which they amalgamated, have been detailed. Where foreign publishers have agents in this country, these are listed.

Agent in U.K.

Adler	Henry Adler, Inc., 136 W. 46th St., New York, 36, N.Y.
Aibl	*Josef Aibl-Verlag, Munich. (Now UE)
Afas	Afas Musikverlag (Hans Dünnebeil) (See B. & B.)

APPENDIX C

Agent in U.K.

Alfred	Alfred Music Co., Inc., 145 W. 45th St., New York, 36, N.Y.	
Alsbach	G. Alsbach & Co., Voetboogstraat 19, Amsterdam.	Hinrichsen (sale) Novello (hire)
AME	American Music Edition, 250 W. 57th St., New York 19, N.Y.	
AMP	Associated Music Publishers, Inc. 1 W. 47th St., New York 36, N.Y.	Schott
Amphion	Amphion Edition, Rue Jean Ferrandini, Paris, 6.	
Am-Rus	Am-Rus Edition (See Leeds).	
Andraud	Albert J. Andraud, 2871 Erie Ave., Cincinnati, Ohio. (Now Southern.)	
André	Musikverlag Johann André, Frankfurterstr. 28, Offenbach a. M.	
Andrieu	Andrieu, Nice.	
Arcadia	Arcadia Music Publishing Co., 10 Sherlock Mews, Baker St., London, W.1.	
Arrow	Arrow Music Press Inc., 17 E. 42nd St., New York, N.Y.	
Ars-Viva	Ars-Viva-Verlag GmbH, Mainz (Now Schott)	Schott
Artaria	*Artaria & Co., Vienna.	
Artia	Artia Verlag, Ve Smečkách 30, Prague, 2.	Bo. & H.
Artransa	Artransa Music, Los Angeles, Calif.	
A. & S.	Ahn & Simrock Musikverlag, Meinekestr. 10, Berlin 15; Schützenhofster. 4, Wiesbaden.	
Ascherberg	Ascherberg, Hopwood & Crew, Ltd., 16 Mortimer St., London, W.1.	
Augener	Augener Ltd., London (See Galliard).	
Avant	Avant Music, Los Angeles, Calif.	
BAI	*Bureau d'Arts et d'Industries, Vienna.	
Bachmann	*C. Bachmann, Hannover.	
Bailleux	*A. Bailleux, Paris.	
Barnhouse	C. L. Barnhouse Pub. Co., 110 B. Ave. East, Oskaloosa, Iowa.	
B. & B.	Bote & Bock KG, Hardenbergstr. 9a, Berlin-Charlottenburg.	Schott
Bank	Annie Bank, Anna Vondelstr. Amsterdam.	Chester
Baron	M. Baron, Box 149, Oyster Bay, New York.	
Baxter-Northrup	See Keynote.	
Becker	*F. Becker, Leipzig.	
Belaieff	Ed. Belaieff, 10 Sq. Desnouettes, Paris, 15; Kronprinzstr. 26, Bonn.	Bo. & H.
Belwin	Belwin, Inc., 250 Maple Ave., Rockville Centre, Long Island, N.Y.	Leeds

A LIST OF MUSIC FOR THE HORN

Benjamin	Anton J. Benjamin, 239/241 Shaftesbury Ave., London, W.C.2.	
Bernouilli	*Bernouilli Edition, Berlin.	
B. & F.	Bayley & Ferguson, Ltd., 54 Queen St., Glasgow, C.1.	
Birchard	C. C. Birchard & Co., 221 Columbus Ave., Boston, Mass. (See SB).	
Birnbach	Musikverlag Richard Birnbach KG, Dürerstr. 28a, Berlin-Lichterfelde-West.	
Bläserschiff	Das Bläserschiff, Osthoven (See Grosch)	
Blaha	*Blaha, Prague.	
BMI (USA)	Broadcast Music, Inc., 589 5th Ave., New York, 17.	
BMI (Can)	BMI Canada Ltd., 16 Gould St., Toronto, 2, Ont.	
Böhm	Musikverlag Anton Böhm, Ludwigstr. 3, Augsburg D.	Hinrichsen
Böhme	*J. A. Böhme, Hamburg. (Successor, Aug. Cranz.)	
Bomart	Bomart Music Publications, 40–03 Broadway, Long Island City, N.Y.	
Bo. & H.	Boosey & Hawkes, Ltd., 295 Regent St., London, W. 1.; 30 W. 57th St., New York, 19; 4 Rue Drouot, Paris, 1; Kronprinzstr. 26, Bonn.	
Bongiovanni	Editore F. Bongiovanni & Figlio, Via Rizzoli 28e, Bologna.	Hinrichsen
Bonjour	*Bonjour, Paris.	
Bosworth	Bosworth & Co., 14-18 Heddon St., London, W.1.; Hohestr. 133, Köln.	
Brandus	*Brandus & Cie, Paris (See Joubert).	UMP
Bratfisch	Musikverlag Georg Bratfisch, 865 Kulmbach.	
Braun-Peretti	Braun-Peretti, Bonn.	
Bremner	*R. Bremner, Edinburgh; London.	
Br. & H.	Breitkopf & Härtel, Burgstr. 6, Wiesbaden; Breitkopf & Härtel VEB, Karlstrasse 10, Leipzig, C 1.	British & Continental
Brockhaus	Max Brockhaus, Mühlestr. 14, 785 Lörrach, Baden.	
Broekmans	Broekmans & van Poppel, Van Baerlestr. 92, Amsterdam	Hinrichsen
Brogneaux	Editions Musicales Brogneaux, 73 Paul Jansonlaan, Brussels.	
Broude	Broude Brothers Music Publishers, 56 W. 45th St., New York 36.	Schott
Bruzzichelli	Edizioni Aldo Bruzzichelli, Borgo Sanfrediano 8, Florence.	Hinrichsen
B. & T.	*Bellman & Thürner, Potschappel.	
Buffet-Crampon	*Editions Buffet-Crampon, Paris (Now Leduc).	

APPENDIX C

Agent in U.K.

BVK	Bärenreiter-Verlag KG, Heinrich Schütz Allee 29, Kassel Wilhelmshöhe; 32 Great Titchfield St., London, W. 1.; PO Box 115, New York 34; Basle; Paris.	
Camara	Camara Music Publishers, 229 W. 52nd St., New York 19.	
Campion	Campion Press, Philadelphia, Pa.	
Cappi	*J. Cappi, Vienna (Now Leuckart).	
Carisch	Carisch S. P. A., Via General Fara 39, Milan.	Hinrichsen
Catelin	*Catelin, Paris.	
CB	Cundy-Beetoney Co., Inc., 96 Bradley St., Hyde Park, Boston 36, Mass.	
CeBeDeM	Centre Belge de Documentation Musicale, 3 Rue de Commerce, Brussels.	Lengnick
CFE	Composers Facsimile Edition, American Composers Alliance, 2121 Broadway, New York 23.	
Chappell	Chappell & Co. Ltd., 50 New Bond St., London, W.1.; 609 5th Ave., New York; Schwanthalerstr. 51, Munich; 86 Bd. Haussmann, Paris.	
Chatot	*E. Chatot, Paris.	
Chester	J. & W. Chester Ltd., Eagle Court, London, E. C.1.	
CHF	Český hudební fond, Pařížská 13, Prague 1.	
Choudens	Editions Choudens, 138 Rue Jean Mermoz, Paris 8.	UMP
Cipriani	*Cipriani & Co., Bologna; Florence.	
CMC	Canadian Music Centre, 599 Ave. Rd., Toronto 7, Ont.	
CMG	Casa Musicale Giuliana, Trieste.	
CML	Chamber Music Library, New York. (See S. Fox.)	
Colombier	*J. F. Colombier, Paris.	
Colombo	Franco Colombo Inc., 16 W. 61st St., New York 23.	
Concord	Concord Music Publishing Co. (See Elkan.)	
Concordia	Concordia Publishing House, 3558 South Jefferson Ave., St. Louis, 18, Miss.	
Continental	*Edition Continental, Prague.	
Coppenrath	Musikverlag Alfred Coppenrath, 8262 Altötting.	
Cor	Cor Publishing Co., 67 Bell Place, Massapequa, New York.	

Agent in U.K.

Costallat	Editions Costallat, 60 Rue de la Chaussée D'Antan, Paris 9.	UMP
CP	Composers Press (See Elkan).	
Cranz	Musikverlag August Cranz KG, Elise-Kirchner-Str. 15, Wiesbaden.	
Cubitt	*W. D. Cubitt & Son, London.	
Curci	Edizioni Curci S.R.L., 4 Galleria del Corso, Milan.	
Curwen	J. Curwen & Sons Ltd., 29 Maiden Lane, London, W.C.2.	
Dania	Edition Dania, Kronprinsessegade 26, Copenhagen.	
Decombe	*Decombe, Paris.	
Decruck	Maurice Decruck, Paris.	
Dehace	Dehace Musikverlag, Dahlienstr. 8, Munich 45.	
Deiss	*Editions R. Deiss, Paris. (Now Salabert.)	
de Lacour	*de Lacour, Paris. (Now Leduc.)	
Delrieu	Delrieu & Cie., 41 Ave. de la Victoire, Nice.	Galliard
Demets	*E. Demets, Paris. (Now Eschig.)	
Deplaix	*Deplaix, Paris.	
Derry	Derry Music Co., 240 Stockton St., San Francisco, Calif.	
De Santis	Alberto De Santis, Via Cassia 13, Rome.	Hinrichsen
de Wolfe	de Wolfe, 80–82 Wardour St., London, W.1.	
Diabelli	*A. Diabelli, Vienna.	
Doblinger	Ludwig Doblinger KG, Dorotheengasse 10, Vienna 1.	A. Kalmus, London
Donemus	Donemus — Stichting voor Documentatie van Nederlandse Muziek, Jacob Obrechtstr. 51, Amsterdam.	Lengnick
Društvo	Društvo Slavenskih Skladateljev, Ljubljana.	
DTÖ	Denkmaler der Tonkunst in Österreich. (Agent: Akademische Druck- und Verlagsanstalt, Graz.)	
Dufaut	*Dufaut & Dubois, Paris.	
Durand	Editeurs Durand & Cie, 4 Place de la Madeleine, Paris 8.	UMP
Durdilly	*V. Durdilly, Paris.	
DVM	Deutsche Verlag für Musik, Karlstr. 10, Leipzig, C 1.	
Ebner	*Ebner, Stuttgart.	
Eder	*J. Eder, Vienna.	
Ehrler	*W. Ehrler, Leipzig.	
Elkan	H. Elkan, 1316 Walnut St., Philadelphia, Penn.	

APPENDIX C

Agent in U.K.

Elkin	Elkin & Co. Ltd., Borough Green, Sevenoaks, Kent.	
EMB	Editio Musica, 5 PF 322, Budapest.	Bo. & H.
EMS	Edition Music Service	
EMT	Editions Musicales Transatlantiques, 14 Ave. Hoche, Paris 8.	UMP
ENM	Escola Nacional de Musica, Rio de Janeiro.	
Enoch	Editeurs Enoch & Cie., 27 Bd. des Italiens, Paris 2.	UMP
Ensemble	Ensemble Publications, Box 98, Bidwell Station, Buffalo, N.Y.	
Erdmann	Rudolf Erdmann KG, Adolfsallee 34, Wiesbaden.	
E. & S.	*Evette & Schaefer, Paris. (Now Leduc.)	
Eschig	Editions Max Eschig, 48 Rue de Rome, Paris 8.	Schott
ESM	Editions du Siècle Musical, Geneva. (See Richli.)	
ESPLA	Editura de Stat pentrů Literatura si Arta, Bucharest.	
Eulenburg	Eulenburg & Co., Cobbs Wood Estate, Brunswick Rd., Ashford, Kent.	
EV	Elkan-Vogel Co., Inc., 1712–1716 Sansom St., Philadelphia 3, Penn.	UMP
Faber	Faber Music Ltd., 24 Russell Square, London, W.C.1.	
Falter	*M. Falter, Munich.	
Fischbacher	*Fischbacher, Paris.	
A. Fischer	A. E. Fischer AG, Bremen.	
C. Fischer	Carl Fischer, Inc., 62 Cooper Square, New York 3.	Hinrichsen
Fitzsimons	H. T. Fitzsimons Co., 615 N. Lasalle St., Chicago 10, Ill.	
Flammer	H. Flammer, Inc., New York.	
Fliegel	Jungdeutscher Verlag Kurt Fliegel & Co., Berlin.	
Forberg	Robert Forberg Musikverlag, Sedanstr. 18, 532 Bad Godesberg.	Hinrichsen
S. Fox	Sam Fox Publishing Co., 11 W. 60th St., New York 20.	
FR	Fondazioni Rossini, Pesaro.	
Fröhlich	*F. W. Fröhlich, Berlin.	
FST	Föreningen Svenska Tonsättare, Tegnérlunden 3, Stockholm.	
Fürstner	Adolph Fürstner, Ltd., 55 Iverna Court, London, W.8.	Bo. & H.
Galaxy	Galaxy Music Corp., 2121 Broadway, New York, 23.	
Gallet	E. Ballet & Fils, 6 Rue Vivienne, Paris.	

A LIST OF MUSIC FOR THE HORN

Galliard	Galliard, Ltd., 148 Charing Cross Rd., London, W.1.	
Gambaro	*V. Gambaro, Paris.	
Gamble	Gamble Hinged Music Corp., 312 S. Wabash, Chicago 4, Ill.	
Gamut	Gamut Publishing Co., All Saints' Passage, Cambridge.	
Gaudet	Editions E. Gaudet, Paris. (Now Salabert.)	
Gaveaux	*G. Gaveaux Frères, Paris.	
Gehrmans	A. B. Carl Gehrmans Musikvorlag, Vasagatan 46, Stockholm 1.	Bo. & H.
Gerig	Musikverlage Hans Gerig, Drususgasse 7–11, Köln 1.	
Germann	*E. Germann, Regensburg.	
Gervan	Gervan, Brussels.	
Gevaert	*Gevaert, Ghent.	
Giessel	Carl Giessel, Bayreuth.	
Girod	*E. Girod, Paris.	
Glaser	*K. Glaser, Leipzig.	
GMPC	General Music Publishing Co., New York.	Novello
Gobert	E. Gobert, Paris.	
Gombart	*G. Gombart, Augsburg.	
Grahl	H. L. Grahl Musikverlag, Günthersburger Allee 46, Frankfurt a.M.	Hinrichsen
Gray	H. W. Gray Co., Inc., 159 E. 48th St., New York, 17.	Novello
Gregorius	Gregorius-Verlag, Munster.	
Grosch	P. Grosch, Lisztstr. 18, Munich.	
G. & S.	Gries & Schornagel.	
G. & T.	Goodwin & Tabb, Ltd., 36 Dean St., London, W.1.	
Guera	*Guera, Lyon.	
Gutmann	*A. J. Gutmann, Vienna. (Now UE.)	
Hainauer	J. Hainauer, Ltd., 29 Cranbourne Gardens, London, N.W.11.	
Halbreiter	*Verlag Otto Halbreiter, Munich. (Successors, Zimmermann.)	
Hamelle	J. Hamelle, 22 Bd. Malesherbes, Paris 8.	UMP
Hanry	*Hanry, Paris	
Hansen	Wilhelm Hansen Musik-Forlag, Gothersgade 9–11, Copenhagen.	Chester
Haslinger	*T. Haslinger, Vienna. (Now Lienau.)	
Hedler	*Hedler, Frankfurt a.M.	
Heina	*F. Heina, Paris.	
Heinrichshofen	Heinrichshofens Verlag, Bremenstr. 52–58, Wilhelmshaven; Amsterdam; Locarno.	Hinrichsen

APPENDIX C

Henmar	Henmar Press, Inc., New York	Hinrichsen
Henn	Edition Henn, 8 Rue de Hesse, Geneva.	
Het Musiekfonds	Het Musiekfonds, Anvers.	
Heugel	Heugel & Cie., 2 bis Rue Vivienne, Paris, 2.	UMP
Heuwekemeijer	A. J. Heuwekemeijer, Bredeweg 21, Amsterdam.	
H. & G.	Hullenhagen & Griehl Verlage, Hamburg.	
Hinnenthal	J. P. Hinnenthal, Konigsbrucke 22, Bielefeld.	Musica Rara
Hinrichsen	Hinrichsen Edition, Ltd., 10–12 Baches St., London, N.1.	
Hiob	H. Hiob, Berlin.	
HM	*Hudební Matice, Prague. (Now SHV.)	
Hochstein	Musikverlag Hochstein & Co., Heidelberg.	
Hoffarth	*L. Hoffarth, Dresden.	
Hoffmeister	*F. A. Hoffmeister, Vienna.	
Hofmeister	Musikverlag F. Hofmeister, Eppsteinerstr. 43, Frankfurt a.M.; Karlstr. 10, Leipzig.	Novello
Holler	Holler Verlag, Leipzig.	
Horn Realm	The Horn Realm, Box 542, Far Hills, N.J. 07931.	
Hug	Hug & Co., Limmatquai 26–28, Zürich.	Hinrichsen
Huläufer	*Huläufer, Breslau.	
B. Hummel	*B. Hummel & Fils, The Hague.	
J. Hummel	*J. J. Hummel, Amsterdam.	
IC	*Imprimerie Chimique, Vienna.	
Ichthys	Ichthys-Verlag GmbH, Moserstr. 6, Stuttgart.	
IGNM	Internationale Gesellschaft für die neue Musik, Vienna.	
Imbault	*J. J. Imbault, Paris.	
IMC	International Music Company, 509 5th Ave., New York 17.	
IMI	Israeli Music Institute, 6 Ghen Blvd, Tel-Aviv.	
IMP	Israeli Music Publications, Ltd., P. O. Box 6011, Tel-Aviv.	Chester
IPA	Israeli Publishers Agency, Tel-Aviv.	
Interlochen	Interlochen Press, National Music Camp, Interlochen, Mich.	
Iris	Iris-Verlag, Hernerstr. 5, Recklinghausen.	
J. & C.	*Janet & Cotelle, Paris (Formerly Janet, Successors Costallat).	
Jeanette	Edition Jeanette, Bilthoven.	
Jobert	Société des Éditions Jobert, 44 Rue de Colisée, Paris 8.	UMP

Agent in U.K.

Joubert	Joubert & Cie., 25 Rue D'Hautville, Paris 10.	UMP
Jouve	*Jouve, Paris.	
Junne	Otto Junne GmbH, Mittererstr. 1, Munich; Nerotal 16, Wiesbaden.	
Jupiter	Jupiter Music Publishing Co., 1313 N. Highland Ave., Hollywood, Calif.	
Jurgenson	*P. Jurgenson, Moscow. (Now RS.)	
Kahnt	C. F. Kahnt, An der Hofstatt 8, Lindau Bodensee.	
Kalmus	Edwin F. Kalmus, 1345 North York Ave., Huntington Station, N.Y.	Alfred A. Kalmus, London
Kasparek	Ed. Kasparek KG, Munich.	
Kaun	*R. Kaun, Berlin.	
KaWe	Edition KaWe, Brederode Str. 90, Amsterdam 13.	
Kayser	*Kayser, Leipzig.	
Kendor	Kendor Music Inc., Delevan, N.Y.	
Keynote	Keynote Music Service, 873 S. Olive, Los Angeles, Calif.	
King	Robert King Music Co., 7 Canton St., N. Easton, Mass.	
Kistner	*F. Kistner, Leipzig. (Now K. & S.)	
Klemm	C. A. Klemm, Leipzig; Dresden; Karl Marx Stadt.	
Kneusslin	F. Kneusslin Verlag, Amselstr. 43, Basel 24.	Hinrichsen
K. & S.	Musikverlag Fr. Kistner & C. F. W. Siegel & Co., Luisenstr. 8, Lippstadt.	Novello, Hinrichsen
Kultura	Kultura: Ungarisches Aussernhandel- sunternehmen für Bücher und Zeitungen, P.O.B. 149, Budapest.	Bo. & H.
Kunze	*A. Kunze, Amsterdam.	
Lafleur	*J. R. Lafleur & Son, London. (Now Bo. & H.)	
Larway	J. H. Larway, 19 Hanover Sq., London, W.1.	
Laudy	Laudy & Co., London. (See Bosworth.)	
Lawson	Lawson-Gould Music Publishers Inc., 609 5th Ave., New York 17.	Curwen
L. & B.	*Longman & Broderip, London.	
Leduc	Alphonse Leduc & Cie., 175 Rue St. Honoré, Paris 1.	UMP
Leeds	Leeds Music Corporation, 322 W. 48th St., New York 36; Leeds Music Ltd., 25 Denmark St., London, W.C.2.	
Legouix	N. Legouix, Paris.	
Lehne	*Lehne & Co., Hannover.	
Leidesdorf	*M. J. Leidesdorf, Vienna.	

APPENDIX C

Lelu		
Lemoine	Éditeurs Henri Lemoine & Cie., 17 Rue Pigalle, Paris 9.	UMP
Lengnick	Alfred Lengnick & Co., Ltd., Purley Oaks Studios, 421a Brighton Rd., S. Croydon, Surrey.	
Leuckart	Musikverlag F.E.C. Leuckart KG, Prinzenstr. 7, Munich 19.	
Lienau	Musikverlag Robert Lienau, Lankwitzerstr. 9, Berlin-Lichterfelde-Ost.	Hinrichsen
Lispet	J. J. Lispet, Hilversum.	
Litolff	Henry Litolff's Verlag, Forsthausstr. 101, Frankfurt a.M.	Hinrichsen
Lopés	Lopés Edition, 430 Strand, London, W.C.2.	
Louisville	Louisville House, Louisville, Ky.	
Ludwig	Ludwig Music Publishing Co., 557 E. 140th St., Cleveland 10, Ohio.	
Lyche	Harald Lyche & Co.'s Musikkvorlag, Kongensgaten 2, Drammen, Oslo.	
L. & Z.	Lausch & Zweigle, Stuttgart.	
Malcolm	Malcolm Music Ltd., 157 W. 57th St., New York, 19.	
Mannh. Musikverlag	Mannheimer Musikverlag, Richard Wagnerstr. 6, Mannheim 1.	
Marbot	Marbot, Bornstr. 12, Hamburg.	
Margueritat	Éditions Margueritat, 7 Cours des petites Ecuries, Paris 10.	
Marks	Edward B. Marks Music Corp., 136 W. 52nd St., New York, 19.	
Martin	*W. Martin, Paris.	
Mathot	*Collection A. Z. Mathot, Paris. (Now Salabert.)	
Maurer	Editions Maurer, 7 Ave. du Verseau, Brussels.	
MBQ	Montreal Brass Quintet, Montreal, Quebec.	
Mechetti	*C. Mechetti, Vienna.	
Melantrich	*Vydalo hudební nakladateství Melantrich, Prague.	
Meldon	Meldon Music Publishers, Tulsa.	
Mentor	Mentor Music Inc., Rm. 141, Carnegie Hall, New York.	
Mercury	Mercury Music Corporation, 47 W. 63rd St., New York 23.	Schott
Merion	Merion Music Inc., Presser Place, Bryn Mawr, Pa.	
Merrymount	Merrymount Music, 47 W. 63rd St., New York 23.	
Merseburger	Merseburger Verlag GmbH, Alemann-str. 20, Berlin-Nikolassee.	Hinrichsen

A LIST OF MUSIC FOR THE HORN

Agent in U.K.

Metropolis	Metropolis, S.P.R.L., Ave. de France 24, Antwerp.	
MF. Co.	MF. Co., Box 351, Evanston, Ill.	
M. & H.	M. & H. Publications, Middlebury, Vt.	
Mills	Mills Music Inc., 1619, Broadway, New York 19; 20 Denmark St., London, W.C.2.	
MKS	Musikaliska Kunstförening, Stockholm.	
MJQ	MJQ Music Inc., New York (c/o AMP).	
M. & M.	McGinnis & Marx, 408 2nd Ave., New York 10.	Hinrichsen
Modern	Edition Modern, Walhallastr. 7, Munich. (Now Hans Wewerka.)	
Moeck	Herman Moeck Verlag, Hannoverschestr. 43a, Celle.	Schott
Möseler	Karl Heinrich Möseler Verlag, Gr. Zimmerhof 20, Wolfenbüttel.	Novello
Mollo	*T. Mollo, Vienna.	
Mondia	Edition Mondia, Paris.	
Morris	E. H. Morris & Co., 35 W. 54th St., New York, 19.	
MPHC	Music Publishers Holding Corp., 619 W. 54th St., New York, 19.	
Murdoch	*Murdoch & Co., London. (Now Chappell.)	
Musica Rara	Musica Rara, 2 Great Marlborough St., London, W.1.	
Music Press	Music Press Inc., New York. (See Mercury.)	
Musicus	Edition Musicus, 333 W. 52nd St., New York, 19.	
Musikk-Huset	Musikk-Huset A/S, Karl Johan Gt. 45, Oslo.	
Mustel	*Mustel & Cie., Paris.	
MV	Mitteldeutscher Verlag GmbH, Robert Blumstr. 37, Saale, Halle.	
Nadermann	*J. H. Nadermann, Paris.	
Nagel	Nagels Verlag, Kassel. (See BVK.)	
NEM	Les Nouvelles Editions Meridian, Paris.	
Niedermayr	*Niedermayr, Regensburg.	
NK	Norsk Komponistforening, Klingenberggate 5, Oslo.	
NME	New Music Editions, Presser Place, Bryn Mawr, Pa.	
Noël	Pierre Noël, Éditeur, 24 Blvd. Poissonnière, Paris 9.	UMP
Noetzel	Otto Heinrich Noetzel Verlag, Wilhelmshaven.	Hinrichsen
Nordiska	A/B Nordiska Musikförlaget, Pipersgatan 29, Stockholm, 10.	Chester

387

Agent in U.K.

Norsk	Norsk Musikforlag A/S, Karl Johansgt. 39, Oslo.	Chester
NWM	New Wind Music Co., 23 Ivor Place, London, N. W. 1.	
ÖBV	Österreichischer Bundesverlag, Schwarzenbergstr. 5, Vienna 1.	
Oertel	Musikverlag Johannes Oertel, Kärntner Platz 2, Hannover-Waldhausen.	
OL	Editions Oiseau Lyre, Les Ramparts, Monaco; 122 Rue de Grenelle, Paris 9.	UMP
Omega	Omega Music Edition, 170 W. 44th St., New York, 36.	
Orbis	Vydalo Národní hudební vydatelství Orbis, Vinohradská 46, Prague.	
OUP	Oxford University Press, 44 Conduit St., London, W.1.; 417 5th Ave., New York 16.	
Ozi	*Ozi, Paris.	
Pabst	*Verlag P. Pabst, Leipzig. (Successor, Musikverlag W. Gebauer, Wiesbaden.)	
Pacini	*A. F. G. Pacini, Paris.	
Pälz	*Pälz, Wurzburg.	
Panton	Panton, Besední 3, Prague 1; Sládkovičova 11, Bratislava.	Faber
Paoletti	*Antonio Paoletti, Florence.	
Parrhysius	Arthur Parrhysius, Berlin.	
Paterson	Paterson's Publications Ltd., 36–40 Wigmore St., London, W.1.	
PAU	Pan-American Union, Washington, D.C. (See Southern.)	
Pazdírek	O. Pazdírek, 32 Ceska Ul. Brno.	
Pegasus	Edizioni Pegasus, Locarno.	
Peer	Peer International Corp., 1619 Broadway, New York 19; Klärchenstr. 11, Hamburg 39.	
Pennaur	*A. Pennaur, Vienna.	
Pérégally	*Pérégally et Parvy Fils, Paris. (Successor, Heugel.)	
Peters	C. F. Peters Musikverlag, Forsthausstr. 101, Frankfurt a.M.; 373 Park Ave. Sth., New York 16.	Hinrichsen
Philippo	Philippo Edition, 24 Blvd. Poisonnière, Paris, 9.	
PIC	*Imprimerie du Conservatoire, Paris.	
Piedmont	Piedmont Music Co., New York.	
Pietsch	*Pietsch, Ziegenhals.	
Pinatel	*A. Pinatel, Paris.	
Pizzi	*Umberto Pizzi e Co., Bologna. (Now Bongiovanni.)	

Agent in U.K.

Pleyel	*Pleyel & Cie., Paris.	
P. &. O.	*Phillips & Oliver, London.	
Portius	Musikverlag Fr. Portius, Kreuz-nacherstr. 15, Stuttgart.	
Premru	Premru Music, 33 Springfield Gardens, London, N.W. 19.	
Presser	Theodore Presser Co., Presser Place, Bryn Mawr, Pa.	Alfred A. Kalmus, London
Pro Art	Pro Art Publications, 469 Union Ave., Westbury, N.Y.	
Probst	*Probst, Leipzig.	
Pro Musica	Pro Musica Verlag, Karl Liebknechtstr. 12, Leipzig, C 1.	
PWM	Polskie Wydawnictwo Muzycne, Foksal 18, Warsaw.	Alfred A. Kalmus, London
Rahter	D. Rahter Musikverlag, Werderstr. 44, Hamburg.	
Raznoiznos	Raznoiznos: Bulgarian State Enterprise, Sofia.	
RB	*Verlag J. Rieter-Biedermann, Leipzig. (Now Peters.)	
RC	*Rudall, Carte & Co., London. (Now Bo. & H.)	
R. & E.	Musikverlag Ries & Ehrler, Charlottenbrunnerstr. 42, Berlin-Grünewald.	Hinrichsen
Reitmayr	*Reitmayr, Straubing.	
Remick	Remick Music Corp., 488 Madison Ave., New York 22.	
Renner	*G. N. Renner, Nuremburg.	
Richault	*C. S. Richault, Paris. (Successor, Costallat.)	
Richli	Edouard Richli, Geneva.	
Ricordi	Edizioni G. Ricordi & C.s.p.a., Via Berchet 2, Milan; The Bury, Church St., Chesham, Bucks; 16 W. 61st St., New York 23; 3 Rue Requepine, Paris.	
Ries	*F. Ries, Dresden.	
Riorden	*S. Riorden, London.	
RM	Édition Russe de Musique, 22 Rue d'Anjou, Paris.	Bo. & H.
Robitschek	Musikverlag Adolf Robitschek, Vienna; Wiesbaden.	
Rochester	Rochester Music Publications, Fairport, N.Y.	
Rorich	*Rorich, Vienna.	
Rohlfing	Rohlfing Sons Music Co., Milwaukee, Wis.	

APPENDIX C

		Agent in U.K.
Rongwen	Rongwen Music Inc., 56 W. 45th St., New York 36. (See Broude.)	Schott
Rouart	Rouart, Lerolle & Cie, 29 Rue D'Astorg, Paris 8.	
RS	Russian State Publication Co. (Music), Moscow 200.	
Rubank	Rubank Inc., 5544 West Armstrong Ave., Chicago 30, Ill.	
Rubato	Rubato-Musikverlag, Vienna.	
Rühle	R. Rühle, Gutersloh.	
Rühle & W.	Rühle & Wendl, Heinrichstr. 11, Leipzig C 1.	
Sadló	Edition Sadló, 233 Kosire, Prague.	
Salabert	Éditions Salabert, 22 Rue Chauchet, Paris 9.	UMP
Samfundet	Samfundet til Udgivelse af Dansk Musik, Kronprinsessegade 26, Copenhagen.	
Sandberger	A. Sandberger, Munich.	
Sansone	L. Sansone, 234 W. 56th St., New York.	
Saturn	Saturn-Verlag, Berlin.	
SB	Summy-Birchard Publishing Co., 1834 Ridge Ave., Evanston, Ill.	Musica Rara
G. Schirmer	G. Schirmer, Inc., 609 5th Ave., New York 10017.	Chappell
Schlesinger	*Schlesinger Buch- und Musik-Handlung, Berlin. (Successor, Lienau.)	
C. Schmidt	C. F. Schmidt, Cäcilienstr. 62, Heilbronn.	Hinrichsen
Schneider	Éditions du Magasin Musical Pierre Schneider, 61 Ave. Raymond Poincaré, Paris 16.	
Schoenenberger	*G. Schoenenberger, Paris.	
Scholing	E. Scholing, Stuttgart.	
Schott	B. Schotts Söhne, Weihergarten 5, Mainz; 48 Great Marlborough St., London, W.1.; 30 Rue St. Jean, Brussels.	
Schreiber	*F. Schreiber, Vienna. (Now Cranz.)	
Schuberth	J. Schuberth & Co., Moritzstr. 39, Wiesbaden.	
Schultheiss	Musikverlag Carl L. Schultheiss KG, Denzenbergstr. 35, 74 Tübingen.	Hinrichsen
Schwaab	*F. C. Schwaab, Speyer.	
Schwann	Verlag L. Schwann, Charlottenstr. 80–86, Düsseldorf.	Hinrichsen
Schweers	Schweers & Haake, Mittelstr. 3, Bremen 1.	
Seeling	J. G. Seeling, Dresden.	

A LIST OF MUSIC FOR THE HORN

Agent in U.K.

SEMI	*Societé d'Éditions Musicales Internationales, Paris. (Successor, Eschig.)	
Senart	Éditions Maurice Senart & Cie., 20 Rue du Dragon, Paris 6.	
Senff	Bartholf Senff, Leipzig. (See Simrock.)	
Shawnee	Shawnee Press Inc., Delaware Water Gap, Pa.	
SHF	Slovenský Hudobný Fond, Gorkého 19, Bratislava.	
SHV	Statní Hudební Vydavatelství, Palackého 1, Prague 1.	
Sidem	Editions Sidem, Geneva.	
Sieber	*G. Sieber, Paris.	
Siegel	*C. F. W. Siegel, Leipzig. (See K. & S.)	
Sikorski	Musikverlag Hans Sikorski, Johnsallee 23, Hamburg 13.	Keith Prowse Music Pub., London
Simrock	Musikverlag N. Simrock, Dorotheenstr. 176, Hamburg 39; 239–241 Shaftesbury Ave., London, W.C.2.	
Sinner	*Sinner, Coburg.	
Sirène	*La Sirène Musicale, Paris. (Successor, Eschig.)	
Sirius	Sirius-Verlag, Wiclefstr. 67, Berlin, N.W. 21.	
Skandinavisk	Skandinavisk og Borups Musikforlag, Borgergade 2, Copenhagen.	Chester
SM	Süddeutscher Musikverlag (Willy Müller), Märzgasse 5, Heidelberg.	
SNKLHU	Státní nakla datelství krásná literatura, hubda a umění, Prague. (Now SHV.)	
Sofirad		
Southern	Southern Music Publishing Co., Inc., 1619 Broadway, New York 19; PO Box 329, San Antonio 6, Texas.	
SPAM	Society for the Publication of American Music. (See C. Fischer, Presser, G. Schirmer.)	
Spehr	*Spehr, Brunswick.	
Sprague-Coleman	Sprague-Coleman Co. (See Leeds.)	
Stainer	Stainer & Bell, Ltd., Lesbourne Rd., Reigate, Surrey.	
Steiner	*S. A. Steiner, Vienna.	
Steingräber	Steingräber-Verlag, Auf der Reiswiese 9, Offenbach a.M.	Bosworth
Suecia	Edition Suecia, Stockholm. (See Gehrmans.)	
SZ	Edizioni Suvini Zerboni, Galleria del Corso 4, Milan.	Hinrichsen

391

APPENDIX C

Templeton	A. Templeton Publishing Co., 10 E. 43rd St., New York 17.	
T. & J.	Musikverlag Tischer & Jagenberg, Prinzenweg 3, 813 Starnberg.	
Tonger	P. J. Tonger Musikverlag, Bergstr. 10, Rodenkirchen.	
Tonos	Tonos-Musikverlag, Aha Str. 7, Darmstadt.	British & Continental Music Agencies, London
Traeg	*J. Traeg, Vienna.	
Trautwein	Trautwein, Berlin.	
Tritone	Tritone Press, Hattiesburg, Miss.	
UBS	University Brass Series. (See Cor.)	
UE	Universal Edition AG, Karlsplatz 6, Vienna; 2–3 Fareham St., London, W.1.	Alfred A. Kalmus, London
Ugrino	Ugrino Verlag, Elbchaussee 499a, Hamburg-Blankensee.	
UKBH	Udruzenje kompozitora Bi. H., Sarajevo.	
Ullmann	E. Ullmann, Reichenberg.	
Ultraton	Ultraton-Verlag, Osthoven.	
UME	Unión Musical Española, Carrera San Jeronimo 26 Y Arenal 18, Madrid.	UMP
UMP	United Music Publishers Ltd., 1 Montague St., London, W.C.1.	
Urbánek	*Fr. A. Urbánek a synové, Prague, and Mojmir Urbánek, Prague. (See Artia.)	
Vernède	*Vernède, Versailles.	
Vieweg	Musikverlag Chr. Friedrich Vieweg, Ringstr. 47a, Berlin-Lichterfelde-West.	Musica Rara
Viking	Viking Musikforlag, Norrebrogade 34, Copenhagen N.	
VMK	Verlag für Musikalische Kultur und Wissenschaft, Wolfenbüttel.	
VNM	Vereniging voor Nederlandse Muziekgeschiednis.	
Volk	Arno-Volk Verlag, Köln.	
Weigl	*T. Weigl, Vienna.	
Weinberger	Musikverlag Josef Weinberger GmbH, Steinweg 7, Frankfurt a.M.; 33 Crawford St., London, W.1.; Mahlerstr. 11, Vienna.	
Weintraub	Weintraub Music Co., 240 W. 55th St., New York 19.	
Werckmeister	*R. Werckmeister, Berlin.	
Wernthal	O. Wernthal, Berlin.	
Wewerka	Hans Wewerka, Franz Josephstr. 2, 8 Munich 13.	

A LIST OF MUSIC FOR THE HORN

Whitney	Whitney Blake, New York.	
Wiessenbruch	*Wiessenbruch, Brussels.	
Williams	Joseph Williams, Ltd., London. (See Galliard.)	
Witmark	M. Witmark & Sons, 488 Madison Ave., New York 22.	
Witzendorf	*Witzendorf, Vienna. (Now Leuckart.)	
Wunder	*J. Wunder, Leipzig.	
Wunderhorn	*Wunderhorn-Verlag, Munich. (Now T. & J.)	
Zanibon	Edizioni Gugliemo Zanibon, Piazza del Signori 24, Padua.	Hinrichsen
Zatta	*Zatta, Venice.	
Zetter	*Zetter, Paris.	
Zimmermann	Musikverlag Wilhelm Zimmermann, Wöhlerstr. 10, Frankfurt a.M.; Querstr. 28, Leipzig C 1.	Novello
Zumsteeg	Musikverlag G. A. Zumsteeg, Hamburg.	
ZV	Zenemükiadó Vállalat, Budapest. (See Kultura.)	

Appendix D

A LIST OF MODERN MAKERS OF HORNS

Alexander	Mainz
Benicchio	Milan
Besson	London
Bohland & Fuchs	Graslitz
Boosey & Hawkes	London
Börner	Karl Marx Stadt
Conn	Elkhart
Couesnon	Paris
Courtois	Paris
Desidera	Verona
Geyer	Chicago
Holton	Elkhorn
Hüller	Diespeck
Hüttl	Baiersdorf
King	Cleveland
Klein	Coblenz
Knopf	Markneukirchen
Kruspe	Erfurt
Kujer	Hamburg
Lehmann	Hamburg
Lidl	Brno
Melchior	Kaiserslautern
Monke	Cologne
Olds	Fullerton
Orsi	Milan
Paxman	London
Pfeiffer	Rijswijk
Prinz	Berlin
Rampone & Cazzani	Milan
Reynolds	Cleveland
Sansone	New York
Scherzer	Augsburg
Schmidt	Berlin
Schöpf	Munich
Selmer	Paris

GLOSSARY OF TERMS

Thibouville-Lamy	Paris
Uhlmann	Vienna
Wunderlich	Chicago
York	Grand Rapids

GLOSSARY OF TERMS USED IN CONNECTION WITH THE HORN

Abbreviations: Fr. French; Ger. German; It. Italian.

Ansatz. (Ger.) (i) Mouthpiece. (ii) Embouchure. (iii) Tuning slide.

Aperto. (It.) Open. Cancels the instruction *chiuso.*

Attack. The stroke of the tongue by which a note or phrase is begun.

Ansetzt. (Ger.) A type of embouchure in which the mouthpiece is placed on rather than in the red part of the lower lip.

Aufsatzbogen. (Ger.) Crook inserted at the mouthpiece end of the instrument.

A-valve. An accessory valve on the B♭ horn, or on the B♭ section of a double horn, which lowers its pitch to A.

B. (Ger.) B♭.

Barillet. (Fr.) Rotary valve.

Bayreuth tubas. See *Wagner tubas.*

Bell. The end of the instrument farthest from the mouthpiece, beginning at the point where a marked flare is apparent.

Bell up. An instruction to the player to raise the bell of his instrument so as to increase the prominence of its tone.

Blechern. (Ger.) Brassy.

Bouché. (Fr.) Stopped, closed.

Campana. (It.) Bell.

   Campana in aria. Bell up.

Chiuso. (It.) Stopped, closed.

Closed. Stopped; more or less completely closing the bell with the hand.

Compensating horn. See *double horn.*

Cor. (Fr.) Horn.

   Cor à cylindres. Horn with rotary valves.

   Cor à pistons. Horn with piston valves.

   Cor chromatique. Valve horn.

   Cor de chasse. Hunting horn.

   Cor d'harmonie. Orchestral horn, with or without valves, as opposed to the *cor de chasse.*

   Cor simple. Horn without valves, hand horn, natural horn.

Corno. (It.) Horn.

   Corno a cylindro. Horn with rotary valves.

   Corno a macchina. Valve horn.

Corno a mano. Hand horn.

Corno a pistoni. Horn with piston valves.

Corno cromatico. Valve horn.

Corno di caccia. Hunting horn.

Corno ventile. Valve horn.

Corps de rechange. (Fr.) Crook.

Coulisse d'accord. (Fr.) Tuning slide.

Coup de langue. (Fr.) Stroke of the tongue, attack.

Crook. Length of tubing, usually coiled, added to the horn to lower its pitch; normally fitted into the mouthpiece end, but occasionally into the middle of the instrument.

Cuivré. (Fr.) Brassy tone obtained by using a high wind pressure. Can also be produced by stopping and increasing the wind pressure.

Cuivrer. (Fr.) Play with brassy tone.

Cuivrez les sons. The same.

Cylinder. Cylindre. (Fr.) *Cylindro.* (It.) Rotary valve.

Dämpfer(n). (Ger.) Mute(s).

Dämpfer ab. Dämpfer fort. Dämpfer weg. Take out mute.

Mit Dämpfer. Dämpfer auf. Put in the mute.

Ohne Dämpfer. Without mute.

Daumenventil. (Ger.) Valve operated by the thumb.

Descant horn. Horn pitched in a high key, e.g. in high F or G.

Diskanthorn. (Ger.) Descant horn.

Doigtez un ½ ton au dessus. (Fr.) Finger a semitone above the written note in a stopped passage. Not the normal procedure, except in France; elsewhere stopped passages are fingered a semitone below, or a stopping valve is used.

Doppelhorn. (Ger.) Double horn.

Doppelzunge. (Ger.) Double tonguing.

Double horn. A duplex horn, usually pitched in F and B♭ alto, provided with a valve for switching instantaneously from one division to the other. In some double horns the valve tubes are independent of each other in the two divisions, but in other types known as compensating horns the F section valve tubes incorporate those of the B♭ section.

Double tonguing. Rapid repetition of notes accomplished by tongue movements represented by the consonants T-K-T-K, etc.

Drehventil. (Ger.) Rotary valve.

Druckerplatte. (Ger.) Finger-plate of a rotary valve.

Écho. (Fr.) *Pianissimo* tone often obtained by stopping.

Echoton. (Ger.) The same.

Applied to a phrase played with this tone which has already been given at a higher dynamic level.

Einsatzbogen. (Ger.) Crook inserted in the middle of the horn, as in the *Inventionshorn.*

Einsetzt. (Ger.) Embouchure in which the mouthpiece is placed so that the rim rests in rather than on the red part of the lower lip.

Embouchure. Position of the lips, jaws, teeth and facial muscles adopted in playing the horn.

Embouchure. (Fr.) (i) As above. (ii) Mouthpiece.

E-valve. Accessory valve on the F horn, or on the F section of the double horn (when it is usually combined with an A-valve) which lowers its pitch to E.

Extension. Length of valve tubing inserted, usually in the A-valve of a B♭ horn, so as to give low notes not otherwise available.

Factitious notes. Notes lying below the second harmonic, not theoretically forming part of the compass of the natural horn, which can be produced by employing a very loose embouchure. Not now often used, since the same notes can be obtained more easily and certainly by using the valves.

Flatterzunge. (Ger.) Flutter-tonguing.

Flutter-tonguing. A type of tonguing, used by Strauss and other composers, in which by rolling an R with the tongue a *tremolo* effect is obtained.

French Horn. Name by which the ordinary orchestral horn was, and still is, known in England and U.S.A. Strictly speaking, the term should now be used only to distinguish the narrow-bore instrument sometimes favoured in France from the wide-bore type in general use elsewhere.

Frullato. (It.) Flutter-tonguing.

Fundamental. The generator of an harmonic series. Not easily obtainable except on the high-pitched horns and even then rarely used.

Gedämpft. (Ger.) Muted.

Gelenkventil. (Ger.) Rotary valve operated by mechanical, as opposed to string, action.

Générateur. (Fr.) Fundamental.

German horn. The wide-bore horn now almost universally used.

Gestopft. (Ger.) Closed, stopped. Often indicated by a +.

Gewöhnlich. (Ger.) In the normal manner. Used to cancel the indications *gestopft, gedämpft,* or *Schalltrichter auf.*

Griffstabelle. (Ger.) Fingering chart.

Grundton. (Ger.) Fundamental.

H. (Ger.) B♮.

Handhorn. (Ger.) Hand horn.

Hand horn. Horn without valves, on which the player, by more or less completely closing the bell with the hand, was able to sound certain notes in addition to the natural notes belonging to the instrument's harmonic series.

Harmonics. The overtones or partials produced by the column of air inside the horn when it vibrates in aliquot parts of its complete length. Together they form an harmonic series, upon which the playing of the horn is based. For convenience the fundamental is usually numbered as the first harmonic. Harmonics are present in any note sounded by the horn, and give the instrument its characteristic timbre.

Hifthorn. (Ger.) Hunting horn.

Hilfsventil. (Ger.) Accessory valve.

Hochhornist. (Ger.) Player of the horn who takes one of the higher parts, i.e. the first or third player.

Horn. (Ger.) Horn. Pl. *Hörner.*

Horntuben. (Ger.) See *Wagner tubas.*

Imboccatura. (It.) (i) Embouchure. (ii) Mouthpiece.

Inventionshorn. (Ger.) Hand horn with tuning slide which could be replaced by crooks serving to alter the pitch of the instrument.

Jagdhorn. (Ger.) Hunting horn.

Krummbogen. (Ger.) Crook. Now generally abbreviated to *Bogen.*

Mechanical action. A mechanism by which the rotor of a rotary valve is turned, using a system of levers.

Mouthpiece. A funnel-shaped or slightly cup-shaped hollow metal tube inserted in the mouthpipe. The vibration of the player's lips in contact with the mouthpiece sets the air column in vibration.

Mouthpipe. The first portion of the tubing of the horn, in which the mouthpiece is inserted. On horns without separate crooks the mouthpipe is fixed.

Mundrohr. (Ger.) Mouthpipe.

Mundstück. (Ger.) Mouthpiece.

Mute. A conical or pear-shaped stopper of wood, fibre, cardboard or metal placed in the bell so as to attenuate the tone and produce a different and characteristic tone colour. A transposing mute alters the pitch of the note as well; a non-transposing mute does not. Tunable mutes are also manufactured.

Naturale. (It.) In the normal manner, i.e. not stopped or muted.

Natural horn. Horn without valves.

Natural notes. The notes of the harmonic series; notes played without valves.

Naturhorn. (Ger.) Natural horn.

Natürlich. (Ger.) Normal; the same as *gewöhnlich.*

Naturtöne. (Ger.) Natural notes.

GLOSSARY OF TERMS

Offen. (Ger.) Open, i.e. not stopped or muted. Also used in the sense of natural, unvalved notes.

Open notes. (i) Notes obtained without the use of the valves, i.e. notes of the harmonic series.
(ii) Notes that are not stopped or muted.

Ouvert. (Fr.) Cancels the instruction *bouché.*

Partials. Notes of the harmonic series.

Pavillon. (Fr.) Bell.
Pavillon en l'air. Bell up.

Pedal note. Fundamental note.

Pedalton. (Ger.) Pedal note.

Piston. A type of valve by means of which the length of tubing is instantaneously altered by the movement of a piston in a cylinder.

Pistonventil. (Ger.) Piston valve.

Quartventil. (Ger.) Valve lowering the pitch by a perfect fourth.

Rotary valve. A type of valve which alters the length of tubing by the motion of a rotor inside a cylinder.

Schallbecher. (Ger.) *Schalltrichter.* (Ger.) Bell. *Schalltrichter auf, Schalltrichter in die Höhe, Mit aufgehobenem Schalltrichter.* Bell up.

Schmetternd. (Ger.) Brassy, *cuivré.*

Schnurenmechanik. (Ger.) String action in a rotary valve.

Slide. An adjustable, normally U-shaped, piece of tubing.
Tuning slide. Slide by which the instrument is tuned.
Valve slide. Slide by which a valve is tuned.

Sons. (Fr.) Notes.
Sons bouchés. Stopped notes.
Sons cuivrés. Brassy notes.
Sons d'écho. Sounds resembling an echo, often, but not necessarily, obtained by stopping.
Sons naturels, sons ordinaires. Normal notes, i.e. not stopped, muted or *cuivré.*
Sons ouverts. Open notes, not stopped.
Sons voilés. Veiled notes, i.e. with the tone partially attenuated with the hand.

Sordino. (It.) Mute. Pl. *sordini.*
Con sordino. Muted.
Senza sordino. Without the mute.

Sourdine. (Fr.) Mute.
Avec sourdine, mettez la sourdine. Put in the mute.
Ôtez la sourdine, sans sourdine. Take out the mute.

Stark anblasen. (Ger.) Blow strongly.

Stellventil. (Ger.) Accessory A- or E-valve.

Stimmbogen. (Ger.) Crook.

Stimmzug. (Ger.) Tuning slide.

Stopfhorn. (Ger.) Hand horn.

Stopfventil. (Ger.) Stopping valve.

Stopped notes. Notes obtained by closing the bell with the hand.

Stopping valve. An accessory valve tuned so as to nullify, when depressed, the rise in pitch produced by the closure of the bell when stopped passages are played.

String action. A mechanism in which the rotor of a rotary valve is turned by a loop of cord attached to a prolongation of the finger-plate.

Stürze. (Ger.) Bell. *Stürze in die Hohe.* Bell up.

Ton de rechange. (Fr.) Crook.

Tonguing. The action of the tongue in setting the air column in vibration; more accurately, its movement in releasing the air stream.

Trichter. (Ger.) Bell; abbr. of *Schalltrichter.*

Tripelzunge. (Ger.) Triple tonguing.

Triple tonguing. Rapid repetition of notes in groups of three, made by tongue movements represented by the consonants T-T-K, T-T-K, etc. or T-K-T, T-K-T, etc.

Trompe de chasse. (Fr.) Hunting horn.

Umschaltventil. (Ger.) Valve making the change from one section of a double horn to the other.

Valve. A device by means of which the length of the tubing of the instrument is altered by diverting the air stream through a supplementary tube whose length corresponds to a change of pitch of a tone, a semitone, and a tone and a half respectively, or more rarely other intervals.

 Ascending valve. A valve whose tube forms part of the main tubing, so that its operation gives a rise in pitch.

 Descending valve. A valve giving a fall in pitch.

Ventil. (Ger.) Valve.

 Ventilhorn. Valve horn.

 Ventilzug. Valve slide.

Voilé. (Fr.) Veiled.

Wagner tubas. Instruments devised by Wagner, the tenor pitched in B♭ and the bass in F. Though of wider bore than the horn, they are played with horn mouthpieces by horn players. See Appendix A.

Waldhorn. (Ger.) Strictly the orchestral natural horn without valves, as opposed to the *Jagdhorn.* Still used, however, as synonym for horn, even with valves.

SELECT BIBLIOGRAPHY

Zug. (Ger.) Slide.
Zunge. (Ger.) Tongue.
Zungenschlag. Stroke of the tongue.
Zungenstosz. Attack made by the tongue.
Zylinderventil. (Ger.) Rotary valve.

SELECT BIBLIOGRAPHY

Bach, V., *Embouchure and Mouthpiece Manual*, V. Bach Corporation, 1954.

Berlioz, H., *Instrumentationslehre*, ergänzt u. revidiert von Richard Strauss, Leipzig, 1905.

Blaikley, D. J., *The French Horn*, Proc. Mus. Assn., Vol. XXXV, 1909.

Borland, J. E., *The Brass Wind Instruments*, W. Scott, 1911.

Bouasse, H., en collaboration avec M. Fouché, *Instruments à Vent*, 2 vols, Paris, 1929.

Carse, A., *Musical Wind Instruments*, Macmillan, 1939.
　The History of Orchestration, Kegan Paul, 1925.
　The Orchestra in the XVIIIth Century, Heffer, 1940.
　The Orchestra from Beethoven to Berlioz, Heffer, 1948.

Casella, A. and Mortari, V., *La Technica dell'Orchestra Contemporanea*, Ricordi, 1948.

Ceccarossi, D., *Il Corno*, Ricordi, 1957.

Coar, B., *The French Horn*, De Kalb, Illinois, 1947.
　A Critical Study of the Nineteenth-Century Horn Virtuosi in France, De Kalb, Illinois, 1952.

Culver, C. A., *Musical Acoustics*, McGraw Hill Book Co., 1956.

Daubeny, U., *Orchestral Wind Instruments*, Reeves, 1920.

Donington, R., *The Instruments of Music*, Methuen, 1949.

Douglas, A., *The Electrical Production of Music*, Macdonald, 1957.

Draper, F. C., *The Boosey and Hawkes Compensating System Fully Explained*, Boosey and Hawkes, 1953.

Eichborn, H., *Die Dämpfung beim Horn*, Breitkopf and Härtel, 1897.

Farkas, P., *The Art of French Horn Playing*, Summy Birchard, 1956.
　The Art of Brass Playing, Brass Publications, 1962.

Forsyth, C., *Orchestration*, Macmillan, 1914, rev., 1935.

Freiberg, G. Ritter von, *Das Waldhorn*, Potsdam, 1938.

Geiringer, K., *Musical Instruments* (translated by Bernard Miall), Allen and Unwin, 1943.

Gevaert, F. A., *Nouveau Traité d'Instrumentation*, Lemoine, 1885.

SELECT BIBLIOGRAPHY

Gorgerat, G., *Encyclopédie de la Musique pour Instruments à Vent*, Editions Rencontre, 1955.

Greene, Plunket H., *Interpretation of Song*, Macmillan, 1956.

Hague, B., *The Tonal Spectra of Wind Instruments*, Proc. Roy. Mus. Assn., Vol. LXXIII, 1947.

Harrison, F. and Rimmer, J., *European Musical Instruments*, Studio Vista, 1964.

Husted, B. F., *The Brass Ensemble; Its History and Literature*, University of Rochester Press, 1961.

Jeans, J., *Science and Music*, Cambridge University Press, 1937.

Karstädt, G., *Lasst lustig die Hörner erschallen! Eine kleine Kulturgeschichte der Jagdmusik*, Paul Parey, 1964.

Kent, E. L., *The Inside Story of Brass Instruments*, C. G. Conn, 1956.

Koechlin, C., *Traité de l'Orchestration*, Eschig, 1949.
Les Instruments à Vent, Paris, 1948.

Kunitz, H., *Die Instrumentation: Teil VI, Horn*, Breitkopf and Härtel, 1957.

Kurka, M. J., *A Study of the Acoustical Effects of Mutes on Wind Instruments*, F. E. Olds and Sons, 1961.

Langwill, L. G., *An Index of Musical Wind-Instrument Makers*, 2nd Ed., Edinburgh, The Author, 1962.

Lloyd, Ll.S., *Music and Sound*, Oxford University Press, 1951.
The Musical Ear, Oxford University Press, 1940.

Mahillon, V., *Les Instruments à Vent: II, Le Cor*, Mahillon, 1907.

Miller, D. C., *The Science of Musical Sounds*, Macmillan, 1922.
Sound Waves, their Shape and Speed, Macmillan, 1937.

Morley-Pegge, R., *The Evolution of the French Horn from 1750 to the Present Day*, Proc. Roy. Mus. Assn., Vol. LXIX, 1943.
The Orchestral French Horn, its Origin and Evolution, Hinrichsen, 1952.
The French Horn, Benn, 1960.

Paul, E., *Das Horn und seine Entwicklung vom Natur- zum Ventilinstrumente*, Vienna, 1932.

Piersig, F., *Die Einführung des Hornes in die Kunstmusik und seine Verwendung bis zum Tode J. S. Bachs*, Niemeyer, 1927.

Piston, W., *Orchestration*, Gollancz, 1955.

Porter, M. M., *The Embouchure*, Boosey and Hawkes, 1967.

Read, G., *Thesaurus of Orchestral Devices*, Pitman, 1954.

Richardson, E. G., *The Acoustics of Orchestral Instruments*, Arnold, 1929.

Sachs, C., *Die Modernen Musikinstrumenten*, Berlin, 1923.
Handbuch der Musikinstrumentenkunde, Breitkopf and Härtel, 1930.

SELECT BIBLIOGRAPHY

Seashore, C., *The Psychology of Music*, McGraw Hill Book Co., 1938.

Scherchen: *Handbook of Conducting*, O.U.P., London, 1933.

Schneider, W., *Handbuch der Blasmusik*, Schott, 1954.

Schuller, G., *Horn Technique*, Oxford University Press, 1962.

Terry, C. S., *Bach's Orchestra*, Oxford University Press, 1932, 2nd Ed. 1961.

Thévet, L., *Méthode Complète de Cor*, Leduc, 1960.

Wellesz, E., *Die Neue Instrumentation*, Max Hesse, 1928.

Widor, C. M., *The Technique of the Modern Orchestra* (translated by E. Suddard), J. Williams, 1906.

Wood, A., *Acoustics*, Blackie, 1940.

The Physics of Music, Methuen, 1944.

Wotton, T. S., *A Dictionary of Foreign Musical Terms and Handbook of Orchestral Instruments*, Breitkopf and Härtel, 1907.

Young, T. C., *The Making of Musical Instruments*, Oxford University Press, 1939.

ARTICLES

Blandford, W. F. H., Studies on the Horn.

    (i) The French Horn in England, *Musical Times*, Aug., 1922.

    (ii) Wagner and the Horn Parts of Lohengrin, *Musical Times*, Sept., Oct., 1922.

    (iii) The Fourth Horn in the 'Choral' Symphony, *Musical Times*, Jan., Feb., Mar., 1925.

    Some Observations on 'Horn Chords: An Acoustical Problem', *Musical Times*, Feb., 1926.

    Bach's Horn Parts, *Musical Times*, Aug., 1936.

    Handel's Horn and Trombone Parts, *Musical Times*, Oct., Nov., Dec., 1939.

Brain, Aubrey, The German Horn: A Comparison, *Monthly Musical Record*, July, 1931.

Brain, Dennis, About the French Horn, *Brass Today*, Besson, 1957.

    The French Horn, *Record News*, Apr., 1958.

Bryant, R., The Wagner Tubas, *Monthly Musical Record*, Sept., 1937.

Carse, A., The French Horn in England, *Hallé*, June, 1950.

Cousins, F., The Degenerate Horn, *Music and Letters*, Oct., 1951.

Fitzpatrick, H., Notes on the Vienna Horn, *Galpin Society Journal*, March, 1961.

    Some Historical Notes on the Horn in Germany and Austria, *Galpin Society Journal*, May, 1965.

SELECT BIBLIOGRAPHY

Gregory, R., The Horn in Beethoven's Symphonies, *Music and Letters*, Oct., 1952.

Janetzky, K., Das Waldhorn-Quartett, *Musica VIII*, 1954.

Karstädt, G., Horninstrumente, *Die Musik in Geschichte und Gegenwart, Vol. VI*, 1949–
Das Horn und seine Aufgaben in heutigen Orchester, *Allgemeine musikalische Zeitung, 66*, 1939.

Kingdon-Ward, M., Mozart and the Horn, *Music and Letters*, Oct., 1950.

Kirby, P. R., Horn Chords: An Acoustical Problem, *Musical Times*, Sept., 1925.

Knott, H., The Horn, *Music and Letters*, Jan., 1951.

Leuba, C., The Viennese 'Pumpenhorn', *The Instrumentalist, 16*, 1961.

Marx, J., Introduction to 'Twelve Duos for two French Horns' by W. A. Mozart, McGinnis and Marx, 1947.

Morley-Pegge, R., The Degenerate Horn, *Music and Letters*, Jan., 1951.

Nixon, G. S., Dental Problems of the Brass Instrumentalist, *British Dental Journal*, Aug., 1963.

Payne, I. W., Observations on the Stopped Notes of the French Horn, *Music & Letters*, Apr. 1968.

Porter, M. M., Problems of the Embouchure, *Brass Today*, Besson, 1957.
Dental Aspects of Wind Instrument Playing with Special Reference to the Embouchure, *British Dental Journal*, Aug., 1952.

Schlesinger, K., Horn, *Encyclopaedia Britannica*, 11th Ed., 1910.

Schmoll, J., Middle and Low Registers on a French Horn: Using the B♭ Side of a Double Horn, *The Instrumentalist, 12*, Dec., 1967.

Vogel, M., Das Problem der Ventilkombinationen in Metall-blasinstrumentenbau, *Das Orchester, 10*, 1962.

Which Horn do You Prefer — F or B♭? A Symposium, *The Instrumentalist, 5*, Jan., Feb., 1951.

THESES

Hamilton, E. C., The Pedagogy of the French Horn. M.A., Eastman School of Music, 1945.

Martin, P. H., The French Horn: Its History, Technique and Literature. M.A., University of Southern California, 1942.

Mattoon, H., The Development and Pedagogy of the Double French Horn. M.Mus., Illinois Wesleyan University, 1951.

SELECT BIBLIOGRAPHY

Shelton, W. E., A History of the French Horn. M.Mus., University of Illinois, 1947.

Short, L. W., The History and Development of the French Horn. M. Mus. Ed., Illinois Wesleyan University, 1952.

Svitavsky, L. E., An Acoustical Study of the French Horn. M. Mus., Eastman School of Music, 1947.

Index

INDEX

DATE DUE